DANGEROUS PEOPLE

Policy, Prediction, and Practice

EDITED BY Bernadette McSherry and Patrick Keyzer

Routledge
Taylor & Francis Group
New York   London

Routledge
Taylor & Francis Group
711 Third Avenue
New York, NY 10017

Routledge
Taylor & Francis Group
27 Church Road
Hove, East Sussex BN3 2FA

© 2011 by Taylor & Francis Group, LLC
Routledge is an imprint of Taylor & Francis Group, an Informa business

Printed in the United States of America on acid-free paper
Version Date: 20110531

International Standard Book Number: 978-0-415-88495-2 (Hardback)

Library of Congress Cataloging-in-Publication Data

Dangerous people : policy, prediction, and practice / edited by Bernadette McSherry, Patrick Keyzer.
   p. cm.
  Includes bibliographical references and index.
  ISBN 978-0-415-88495-2 (hbk : alk. paper)
   1. Detention of persons--Congresses. 2. Sex offenders--Congresses. 3. Terrorists--Congresses.
4. Mentally ill offenders--Congresses. 5. Violent offenders--Congresses. I. McSherry, Bernadette. II. Keyzer, Patrick, 1966-

K5105.A6D36 2011
345'.03--dc22
                                           2011005376

Visit the Taylor & Francis Web site at
http://www.taylorandfrancis.com

and the Routledge Web site at
http://www.routledgementalhealth.com

Contents

Acknowledgments

Bernadette McSherry and Patrick Keyzer acknowledge the contribution of the Australian Research Council for funding the workshop that gave rise to this edited collection. They also thank Tali Budlender, Sandra Pyke, Sarah Lenthall, Christopher Goff-Gray, and Kathleen Patterson for their invaluable assistance in editing and formatting this book.

Eric S. Janus thanks his research assistants Joe Phelps, Emily Polachek, Leah Dudderar, and Greger Calhan for their excellent assistance in preparing his chapter.

Caroline Logan thanks Dr. James Higgins, Ms. Teresa Mallebone, and Mr. Nick Benefield for their comments on an early version of her chapter.

Ian Freckelton acknowledges the assistance provided to him by Janet Ruffles of Thomas Embling Hospital in compiling relevant Victorian figures of persons subject to and revoked from supervisory status, and also the very helpful research assistance of Sarah Lenthall in relation to his chapter.

Alex Quinn and John Crichton remain indebted to the assistance of Vivienne Gration and Sharon Bruce of the Forensic Network and Rosemary Toal of Scottish Government in assisting with and providing information for their chapter.

The Editors

Bernadette McSherry, LLB (Hons), BA (Hons), LLM (Melbourne), PhD (York University, Canada), Grad Dip (Psychology) (Monash), FASSA, FAAL, is an Australian Research Council Federation Fellow and Professor of Law at Monash University. She is the Director of the Centre for the Advancement of Law and Mental Health, and is a legal member of the Mental Health Review Board of Victoria. She has acted as a consultant to government on criminal law, sentencing, and mental health law issues, and is currently coordinating a team of 16 researchers examining mental health laws in common law countries.

Patrick Keyzer, BA (Hons), LLB (Hons), LLM, PhD (Sydney), is the Director of the Centre for Law, Governance and Public Policy, and Professor of Law at Bond University. He is a barrister who specializes in constitutional law, and has represented governments and non-government clients in the superior courts of Australia and Vanuatu, and in communications to the United Nations Human Rights Committee. His research focuses on access to justice and human rights.

List of Contributors

David J. Cooke
Professor of Forensic Clinical Psychology
Glasgow Caledonian University
Glasgow, Scotland

John Crichton
Consultant Forensic Psychiatrist
Royal Edinburgh Hospital
Edinburgh, Scotland

Rajan Darjee
Consultant Forensic Psychiatrist
Royal Edinburgh Hospital
Edinburgh, Scotland

Ian Freckelton
Professor, Faculty of Law
Department of Psychological Medicine
Department of Forensic Medicine
Monash University
Victoria, Australia

Innes Fyfe
Practice Development Manager
Risk Management Authority
Paisley, Scotland

Yvonne Gailey
Chief Executive
Risk Management Authority
Paisley, Scotland

Eric S. Janus
President and Dean
William Mitchell College of Law
St. Paul, Minnesota

Lorraine Johnstone
Lead Consultant, Clinical Forensic
    Psychologist
Glasgow Caledonian University
Glasgow, Scotland

Patrick Keyzer
Professor of Law
Director of the Centre for Law,
    Governance, and Policy
Bond University
Robina, Queensland, Australia

John Q. La Fond
Professor and Edward A. Smith/Missouri
    Chair Emeritus in Law, the Constitution,
    and Society
University of Missouri-Kansas City
Kansas City, Missouri

Caroline Logan
Consultant Forensic Clinical
    Psychologist
Greater Manchester West
    Mental Health NHS
    Foundation Trust
University of Manchester
Manchester, England

Bernadette McSherry
Australian Research Council
    Federation Fellow
Professor of Law
Monash University
Victoria, Australia

Christine Michie
Statistician and Mathematician
Glasgow Caledonian University
Glasgow, Scotland

Jillian Peterson
PhD Candidate (Psychology
    Doctoral Student)
University of California at Irvine
Irvine, California

John Petrila
Professor, Department of Mental Health
  Law and Policy
College of Behavioral and Community
  Sciences
University of South Florida
Tampa, Florida

Alex Quinn
Specialist Registrar, Orchard Clinic
Royal Edinburgh Hospital
Edinburgh, Scotland

Katharine Russell
Consultant Clinical Psychologist
Royal Edinburgh Hospital
Edinburgh, Scotland

Ronli Sifris
PhD Candidate (Faculty of Law)
Monash University
Victoria, Australia

Eric Silver
Professor of Sociology and Crime,
  Law, and Justice
Pennsylvania State University
University Park, Pennsylvania

Jennifer Skeem
Professor of Psychology and Social
  Behavior
University of California at Irvine
Irvine, California

Christopher Slobogin
Milton Underwood Professor of Law
Vanderbilt University
Nashville, Tennessee

Lindsay Thomson
Professor of Forensic Psychiatry
The University of Edinburgh
Edinburgh, Scotland

I
Parameters

1
"Dangerous" People
An Overview

BERNADETTE McSHERRY and PATRICK KEYZER

Introduction

There will always be groups of individuals deemed to be "dangerous" by society. Just which groups will be targeted may vary according to culture, place, and time. How best to punish, manage, supervise, or treat those considered dangerous has occupied the minds of many policymakers and commentators across the years. The issue of preventive detention has similarly arisen in a wide variety of public policy contexts in regimes such as those for

- the mandatory detention of asylum seekers pending determination of their refugee status;
- the quarantine of those with infectious diseases;
- the involuntary commitment of those with severe mental illnesses in psychiatric institutions;
- the detention of people under investigation for or suspected of involvement in terrorist activities; and
- the civil commitment of sex offenders.

To explore current approaches to "dangerousness" and preventive detention, in 2009, pursuant to an Australian Research Council funded project, we invited a number of legal academics and mental health professionals to write a paper in answer to one or more of the following questions:

- What are some of the practical issues that have arisen following the implementation of preventive detention/supervision schemes for high-risk offenders?
- What are some of the issues relating to assessing the risk of future harm in the management of high-risk individuals?
- What diversionary programs/sentencing options should there be for high-risk offenders with mental illnesses?
- Should hospital orders and other diversion programs be used in preference to imprisonment for offenders with mental illnesses?

The resulting papers were intensively workshopped in May 2010 at Monash University's Centre in Prato, Italy, and subsequently revised prior to publication. What emerged were different explorations of the policies and practices relating to current out-groups—such as sex offenders, suspected terrorists, those with severe mental illnesses, young offenders, and those deemed to be high-risk offenders—in the United States, Scotland, England, and Australia.

During the workshopping process, there were a number of discussions about the best ways in which to manage those considered to be dangerous and whether preventive detention could ever be considered justifiable. A number of themes emerged relating to *risk assessment and management* as well as *legal* issues. Of course, the judges, lawyers, forensic psychiatrists, forensic psychologists, social workers, corrective services personnel, and others who work in preventive detention contexts are interested in both categories of questions, so the distinction is only a convenient one and should not be overstated. A multiplicity of overlapping normative concerns and ethical challenges operate in the shared professional discourse that marks out the field of preventive detention.

In terms of structuring this book, we grouped this chapter and the ensuing ones into five parts as follows:

- *Parameters* in the general sense of the word as a boundary or limit. The chapters in this part explore the international human rights and legal limitations relating to preventive detention regimes.
- *Policy* in the sense of both governmental plans of action and the legislative objectives of regimes dealing with those considered dangerous. The chapters in this part deal with policies in relation to sex offenders, offenders with severe mental illnesses, and suspected terrorists.
- *Prediction* as it relates to determining who is likely to commit crimes in the future. The chapters in this part deal with assessing the risk of committing violent crimes in youth and in individuals with severe mental illnesses as well as some of the criticisms that may be made of risk assessment techniques.
- *Practice* as it relates to recent schemes in Scotland and England in relation to those considered at a high risk of reoffending.
- The *conclusion*, which sets out the challenges for future research in this field.

The rest of this chapter places the material that follows in context. It also outlines some of the problems that have arisen in relation to identifying the dangerous; explores the risk assessment, management, and legal issues alluded to above; then discusses the effectiveness of current policies and alternatives to post-sentence preventive detention.

Identifying "the Dangerous"

The title of this book pays homage to a collection of essays edited by Nigel Walker in 1996 and published in England titled *Dangerous People*. Some of that work focused on where the balance should lie between proportionality in punishment and public protection. In 1997, on the other side of the world, John Pratt's book *Governing the Dangerous* explored how certain offenders, thought to show a propensity to commit crimes, have generally been governed through some form of indeterminate prison sentence. These books were written when there was a focus on offenders being given indefinite prison terms *at the time* of sentence. Some 14 years on, offenders can now be "civilly" detained *after* their sentence has expired, which gives rise to a whole new set of issues.

It is interesting to note that while the literature may have moved beyond exploring the concept of dangerous people to identifying methods of assessing the risk of future harmful behavior, governments still couch their policies using the concept of dangerousness. In Australia, for example, certain legislation enabling preventive detention refers to those considered dangerous in statutory titles (for example, the Dangerous Prisoners (Sexual Offenders) Act 2003 (Qld), the Dangerous Sexual Offenders Act 2006 (WA)) and in England and Wales, there are programs specifically targeted at "Dangerous People with Severe Personality Disorder" (Ministry of Justice and Department of Health 2010).

But how do governments identify the dangerous people from whom society requires protection? The aforementioned catalog of preventive detention regimes only provides some clues. No one would dispute that a violent, recidivist sex offender who has given evidence that he plans to commit fresh offences should be subject to supervision, and even some form of preventive detention, in certain circumstances. Nigel Walker (1978: 40) has pointed out that there is a high degree of certainty in predicting that offenders who declare their intention of committing another criminal act will indeed do so. Such offenders may be considered dangerous because of the real threat they represent to the community if released or unsupervised.

However, people who arrive in a country without authority to seek asylum can hardly be called dangerous unless they carry disease or otherwise pose a threat to public safety or security. The evidence indicates that this is rarely the case (Blay et al. 2007). The maintenance of the integrity of an immigration system may require a limited period of detention to enable paperwork to be checked or to conduct health checks. But it is not justifiable on the ground that asylum seekers are, per se, dangerous people. In short not every variety of preventive detention responds to those considered dangerous.

It may simply be that the categories of those considered dangerous evoke strong emotional responses arising from fear or anger (Freiberg 2001). This may explain why of all the different varieties of dangerous people, the category that has received the most attention, at least until the terrorist attacks in the United States on September 11, 2001, has been that of sex offenders, particularly those who commit sex crimes against children. Edwin Sutherland (1950: 142) observed over half a century ago that "a community is thrown into panic by a few serious sex crimes, which are given nation-wide publicity; the community acts in an agitated manner, and all sorts of proposals are made; a committee is then appointed to study the facts and to make recommendations." This statement still applies today.

In 1990, Washington State responded to the brutal sexual assault of a child by a violent, recidivist sex offender with wide-ranging proposals for increasing criminal penalties for sex offences, the development of a sex offender registry, community notification powers, new measures to assist victims and also a new civil commitment system enabling the post-sentence preventive detention of sex offenders adjudged to be a high risk to the community if released (McSherry and Keyzer 2009: 2–6). The civil commitment regimes that have emerged in many of the states of the United States since 1990 provide the archetypal example of a shift from a post- to a "precrime society" (Zedner 2007). The rationale for these systems is that if certain individuals have demonstrated that they are incapable of being released into the community without a substantial risk existing that they will engage in sex offences, then it would be derelict of government not to take steps to protect the public against that risk.

The main challenge for policymakers is to find a midway point between assuming that all people in a certain group (sex offenders, suspected terrorists, young offenders, and so on) are dangerous in the sense that they are at a high probability of harming others and assuming that no one, even those who have declared their intentions of committing crimes, are a danger to others. A wealth of literature has emerged concerning the assessment of risk that attempts to identify the dangerous.

Risk Assessment and Management Issues

The assessment of risk is of such significance that it has been viewed as a core organizing concept of the Western world over the past two decades (Morgan et al. 1998; Rose 1998; Zedner 2009). During the early 1980s, the emphasis was on making clinical assessments of dangerousness, which did not provide a medical diagnosis, but involved "issues of legal judgment and definition, as well as issues of social policy" (Steadman 2000: 266).

Between the mid-1980s until the mid-1990s, the focus of mental health professionals shifted from assessing dangerousness to a focus on statistical or actuarial risk prediction. This shift to risk assessment and risk management has seen the rise of "scientific" literature examining a range of risk factors that have a statistical association to a future event.

In its current iteration, risk assessment involves the consideration of risk factors, harm, and likelihood. It combines both actuarial and clinical approaches to form what has been termed *structured professional judgment* (see, for example, Heilbrun et al. 1999). In Chapter 11 of this volume, Lorraine Johnstone refers to some of the problems that have been experienced with actuarial risk models and outlines how the structured professional judgment approach is now well established and how "a burgeoning literature attests to its utility in terms of its reliability, validity, and clinical utility." She is concerned, however, that available risk assessment approaches are not sufficiently sophisticated to enable them to be used in relation to young offenders.

As well as the move toward a structured professional judgment approach to risk, there has been a conceptual shift that can be identified in the past decade in the focus from risk *prediction* to risk *management* (Douglas and Kropp 2002; Hart et al. 2003). That is, various assessment tools have been viewed as appropriate guides for the overall level of risk management that might be required (for example, the greater the risk, the greater the necessary resources). However, there is a concern that they should not be used to predict offences for the purpose of preventive detention regimes or be used as guidelines for specific violence prevention strategies.

It has been the use of actuarial approaches by experts in the courtrooms that has caused perhaps the most concern in the literature on risk assessment. In Chapter 12 of this volume, David Cooke and Christine Michie raise serious questions about actuarial methods for violence risk assessment that are currently used in many forensic and adjudicative settings. Focusing on individual offenders (whether suffering from mental disorders or not), Cooke and Michie's contribution critically analyses these practices with the objective of yielding "useful, valid, ethically sound information that is probative and not prejudicial." According to Cooke and Michie, a focus on the individual is essential because "there is confusion in the literature about what information from groups can tell us about individuals."

Cooke and Michie detail the misuse of actuarial models, which they conclude is based on misplaced confidence in their reliability and accuracy. Actuarial risk assessment instruments involve the use of information about groups to make predictions about individuals. Using statistical methods, Cooke and Michie test actuarial risk assessment techniques and conclude that the ability to estimate the average risk for a group is not matched by any corresponding ability to predict which individuals are going to commit crimes in the future. They state that it "remains worrying that the significance of uncertainty in violence risk assessment based on ARAIs [actuarial risk assessment instruments] is not widely understood." The authors conclude that the employment of actuarial risk assessment instruments should be subject to greater judicial skepticism and more rigorous legal challenge by defence counsel.

Legal Issues

Laws settle a normative framework for human activity. The regimes for detaining and managing those considered to be dangerous raise a number of issues that touch on the scope and appropriateness of laws that curtail individual freedom. This section outlines some of the issues discussed in the ensuing chapters.

International Human Rights Law

International human rights standards embody the aspirations of the most people and justifiably claim the widest normative realm. The jurisprudence of the United Nations Human Rights Committee (HRC), particularly relating to Article 9 of the International Covenant on Civil and Political Rights (ICCPR), is significant in the preventive detention context as the pre-eminent statement of the human rights of all people who are subjected to civil or criminal confinement (Keyzer 2009b). The HRC's jurisprudence indicates that when a person is detained without charge or trial, he or she must be informed, at the time of the arrest, of the reasons for arrest and must be entitled to take proceedings before a court so that the court may decide without delay on the lawfulness of the detention. In addition, a person subjected to unlawful arrest or detention has an enforceable right to compensation in the domestic sphere (see Chapter 2 by Ronli Sifris in this volume).

It is important that Article 9 also protects people from detention that is inappropriate, unjust, unpredictable, inconsistent with principles of due process, unreasonable or unnecessary in the circumstances, and/or disproportionate to achieving its objectives (see Chapter 2; McSherry and Keyzer 2009).

Must nations abide by these standards? There is a substantial argument that the standards of lawfulness can only be settled at the international level, or else nation-states become the judges of their own laws (Blay and Piotrowicz 2001). Certainly, the 165 nations that are signatories to the ICCPR (including Australia, Canada, New Zealand, the United Kingdom, and the United States) must give serious consideration to the decisions of the HRC. But that does not mean that the covenant will be faithfully implemented. For example, Australia has adopted a policy of preventive detention of asylum seekers, and more recently a policy for the offshore detention of asylum seekers, that has been criticized as punitive in character, and which has been subject to repeated and sustained international criticism for that reason (Blay et al. 2007). A substantial number of the decisions of the HRC exploring the boundaries of Article 9 of the ICCPR have been decisions in response to communications by asylum seekers about Australian policies. But Australian governments have been slow to take steps to ameliorate the punitive character of these policies (the release of unaccompanied children from detention has only recently commenced).

Ultimately, even in those countries that have signed the First Optional Protocol to the ICCPR, which allows domestic complaints to be made to the HRC about breaches of human rights standards, the HRC does not operate as a court of appeal. Thus in recent years, a number of the Australian states have managed sex offenders considered to pose a high risk in the community by using prison as a venue for the preventive detention of sex offenders after the conclusion of their prison sentences. Two successful communications to the HRC made by Australian prisoners contesting these regimes found that the preventive detention regimes in these Australian states violated the ICCPR, which prohibits arbitrary detention, the retroactive infliction of increased punishment, and the use of prison for non-punitive objectives such as the preventive detention of high-risk offenders (see Chapter 3 by Patrick Keyzer in this volume). The Australian government had 180 days to respond to the committee's views, which were published in March 2010, but that period elapsed and over a year later, the government has done nothing to fulfill its human rights obligations in relation to preventive detention.

The Issue of Proportionality   The civil commitment of those considered to be sexually violent predators in many states of the United States also raises a number of legal issues. The principle of proportionality—the need to adopt proportionate responses to the risk that a person would pose to the community if released—is a central theme in the writing on the punishment and detention of offenders. Proportionality is also a central theme in the United States constitutional jurisprudence of due process.

In Chapter 4, Christopher Slobogin argues that properly contained, preventive detention might turn out to be a useful means of protecting society that imposes less harm on offenders than strictly punishment-oriented regimes. Invoking United States constitutional standards of substantive and procedural due process, Slobogin argues that proportionality principles can justify only the least drastic risk-reducing intervention in any disposition. In addition, proportionality must be the guiding principle at every stage of a legal disposition: when a standard of proof is applied, when risk is calculated, and when detention length is calculated.

However, while the proportionality principle typically is applied when formulating standards of proof applicable in preventive detention contexts (for example, by requiring only a probability of danger to self and others for short-term emergency commitment, but requiring proof beyond reasonable doubt that a person will commit a fresh sexual offence in sexually violent predator cases), courts have not applied proportionality principles to questions about the probability and magnitude of risk sought to be prevented, nor have they applied proportionality principles to determinations relating to incarceration.

Predictions of risk can have dire consequences, reinforcing concerns for due process and proportionate responses. Slobogin argues that proportionality should inform the evidentiary and procedural rules applied in cases where risk prediction may lead to preventive detention. For that reason, Slobogin adopts the controversial position that the state should be *required* to use actuarial instruments for the assessment of risk in any disposition adjudication, on the basis that actuarial risk assessment instruments are more reliable than clinical opinions. Evidence led by reference to actuarial risk assessment must be properly normed and demonstrably relevant to the prediction context. If the state cannot satisfy a minimum threshold warranting consideration of a preventive detention order (for example, that a person is high risk), then evidence drawn from (purely) clinical judgment should not be allowed. This position is controversial because, as outlined in the previous section, there has been growing criticism of the uncritical use of actuarial risk assessment instruments (see Chapter 12 by David Cooke and Christine Michie). Henry Steadman (2000: 268) has pointed out that although mental health professionals may have moved risk assessment beyond dichotomous thinking in relation to identifying whether a person is dangerous or not, "from the judicial perspective, [it is unclear] how much change has really occurred" in the forensic context.

Civil Commitment Regimes for the Dangerous

Assuming that a preventive detention system complies with international human rights standards and domestic constitutional standards, a range of questions arise about the appropriateness of the domestic institutional apparatus to ensure that rights standards are realized in practice. Ian Freckelton and Bernadette McSherry explore this issue in two diverse settings in their chapters in this volume.

Ian Freckelton (Chapter 8) surveys the legislative regimes dealing with the disposition of people found not guilty of serious criminal offences by reason of insanity or mental impairment in England and Wales, Canada, New Zealand, and the Australian states and territories. The Australian state of Victoria has adopted an approach of ensuring judicial review of indefinite detention orders made on these grounds. This approach contrasts with the approach adopted in many jurisdictions, which is to leave the power to alter dispositions to the executive government. Freckelton notes that the Victorian Supreme Court has adopted a conservative, gradualist approach to the revocation of indefinite detention orders, but has been "constructively informed by clinical opinion." The result has been that acquittees have been reintegrated into the community when it is clinically warranted, and in a staged process.

Do mental health professionals have any role to play in circumstances where a person does not have a diagnosable mental illness? Bernadette McSherry (Chapter 9) explores this issue in her contribution to this volume. Mohamed Haneef and Izhar Ul-Haque were arrested and subjected to detention and interrogations on the presumption that they possessed information about terrorist activities. Haneef was deported and his work visa was revoked on specious character grounds that were never properly explained by the Minister for Immigration at the time (Ewart 2009), with the Australian Director of Public Prosecutions later admitting that he should never have been charged. Ul-Haque spent six weeks in solitary confinement in a maximum-security prison before being released on bail. The Supreme Court of New South Wales ruled that evidence drawn from interviews conducted with him by the Australian Security Intelligence Organisation were inadmissible because they had been influenced by the oppressive conduct of the security officers. The trial was discontinued and the Court's decision was not appealed.

Australian antiterrorism legislation, which parallels that adopted in the United States, United Kingdom, and Canada after the terrorist attacks on the United States on September 11, 2001, has made provision for lengthy detention for questioning without charge, and detention that can be extended on a variety of grounds. Individuals can be detained, including people who are not suspected of any involvement with terrorism but who are believed, on reasonable grounds, to have information of use to the government in investigating terrorist activity. Confidentiality provisions limit the independent monitoring of these investigations and there is no capacity to seek judicial review of the validity or terms of an Australian Security Intelligence Organisation warrant.

McSherry writes in Chapter 9 that these measures, based on "reasonable suspicion" or "reasonable belief," completely bypass the need for risk assessments by mental health professionals that are characteristic of preventive detention regimes for high-risk offenders. Gisli Gudjonsson (2009) and Elaine Pressman (2009) observe that new, structured professional judgment tools could be developed to assess the risk of terrorist violence. Whether such tools should be developed is another matter, given the criticisms of the use of risk assessment tools in the forensic context outlined earlier. However, it is clear that there is a need for empirically-based evidence concerning who is at risk of engaging in terrorist activity to replace the existing recourse to presumptions in this regard.

The Effectiveness of Current Policies

Have preventive detention systems been successful in reducing risk in the community? Have these regimes made dangerous people less dangerous? In the sex offender context, a medical approach to the management of sex offenders released from prison has been replaced by a new civil commitment approach in both Australia and the United States. Commitments are not grounded in established diagnostic criteria or causal theories of conduct (see Chapter 5 by John La Fond in this volume). In addition, detention is not justified by reference to the application of proven treatment methods (see Chapter 6 by John Petrila in this volume).

Laws authorizing the civil commitment of sex offenders in the United States have imposed significant costs in relation to

- new bureaucracies;
- the conduct of clinical evaluations;
- litigation costs;
- the creation of civil commitment centers;
- the employment of appropriate staff; and
- the development of treatment programs.

The constitutional right to treatment that springs from due process guarantees under the United States Constitution has properly required that detainees have individual treatment plans, but these are expensive to administer. In practice, community release is rare, commitment rates exceed release rates by a considerable margin, and the aging population of detainees will impose an increasing economic burden on governments that have adopted this approach (see Chapter 5).

Do the costs outweigh the benefits? Societies should do whatever they can to lower the number of sex crimes and do this as efficiently as possible at the lowest possible cost. But there is no evidence that civil commitment systems are achieving this objective. In an environment of government budget deficits, precious resources are withdrawn from more critical needs. La Fond writes in Chapter 5 that the civil commitment approach to the management of sex offenders "has been an abysmal and costly failure" and "other countries should learn from our terrible mistakes."

In Chapter 7 in this volume, Eric Janus also argues that sexually violent predator civil commitment systems have failed and asks what went wrong. Why did the United States fail to adopt a public health model that is characterized by clinical interventions that have proven to be effective in reducing sexual violence? Janus offers a fascinating thesis to explain why the public health model was rejected. Empirical research preceding the passage of the United States Violence Against Women Act 1994 supported feminist theorizing about sexual violence; that it is ubiquitous in society, but that women are at greater risk of sexual violence in the home than they are in public. Janus argues that conservatives in the United States have employed civil commitment laws to reassert patriarchal perspectives on general relations and sexual violence—that women are safest in the home (and in marriage) and are most in danger in public. High profile episodes of sexual violence provided the opportunity for conservative politicians to reinforce a view that sexual violence is ordinarily committed by strangers, and that sexual violence could therefore be reduced by the preventive detention of sex offenders. In fact, sexual violence is most likely to be committed in the home by someone known to the victim.

According to Janus, civil commitment laws reinforce the conservative, antifeminist agenda by focusing on a small group of sexually violent predators who are publicly exiled to civil commitment centers. When released, these offenders are subject to registration and notification regimes that further accentuate their outsider status. This combination of policies diverts United States governments from addressing the cultural practices that flourish in a society where women and children are disempowered. Disproportionate energy has been placed on repunishing offenders rather than generating insights from empirical sources. The result has been a system that is at odds with the direction taken by the United States public mental health system over the last three decades (see Chapter 6).

On the flipside of this concentration on a small percentage of sex offenders, people with mental disorders are disproportionately represented in the criminal justice system and their access to mental health facilities is often denied. Diverse efforts across and within countries are generally united by a belief that people end up in the criminal justice system because they have not received necessary mental health services. In Chapter 10 in this volume, Jennifer Skeem, Jillian Peterson, and Eric Silver outline problems with this assumption. They write that "there is little compelling evidence that (a) mental illness directly causes criminal behavior for this population, or (b) that effective mental health services meaningfully reduce new crimes and victims."

Focusing on adult offenders with diverse, numerous, serious past offences adjudged to be a high risk to the community, Skeem, Peterson, and Silver argue that people with severe mental illnesses follow different pathways to criminal behavior. For one small subgroup, mental illness directly causes criminal justice involvement; for the second, the causal relationship is indirect, and for the third, mental illness is incidental to or independent from the criminal behavior. On that basis, Skeem, Peterson, and Silver argue that "a major task for future research will be to identify the specific moderator(s) that differentiates the subgroup for whom the effect of mental illness on criminal behavior is direct versus indirect/independent." This chapter indicates that diversion from the criminal justice system may not be appropriate for all offenders with severe mental illnesses; rather, a more nuanced approach is needed.

There are also concerns that current policies are failing certain groups of those considered at risk of future harm. In Chapter 11 in this volume, Lorraine Johnstone questions the assumption underlying contemporary penal policy for offenders who are under the age of 18 that it is possible to differentiate children who do from children who do not present an ongoing risk of serious harm to others.

Similarly, in Chapter 17, Caroline Logan draws attention to the need for more appropriate institutional and community treatment of people with severe personality disorders. Logan observes that personality disorders are common among offenders, common among violent offenders, and common among recidivists. Lindsay Thomson in her contribution to this volume (Chapter 13) observes that although many high-risk offenders have a personality disorder, in Scotland "mental health services generally, and forensic mental health services specifically, have been reluctant to offer services to individuals with a primary diagnosis of personality disorder." They are instead dealt with via the criminal justice system. Logan examines the following questions: Does a history of violence make a personality disorder diagnosis more likely, cause such individuals to be violent, or are personality disorder and violence linked through a third unknown variable? These are the types of basic research questions that need to be answered in preventive detention contexts.

Alternatives to Post-sentence Preventive Detention

What alternative strategies are there to current preventive detention and management regimes? In Chapter 5, John La Fond advocates risk management in the community supervised by specialist courts adopting measures "tailored to the level of the offender's risk and his pattern of offending" and proportionate to that risk.

In 2006, Scotland introduced a new system for the assessment, sentencing, and post-sentence management of sexual offenders and violent offenders considered to pose a risk of serious harm to others in the community (see Chapter 16 by Rajan Darjee and Katharine Russell; for the historical background see Chapter 15 by Innes Fyfe and Yvonne Gailey). This new system provides an extra sentencing option to the many that already existed as outlined by Thomson (Chapter 13). If a person is convicted of a sexual offence, a violent offence, an offence endangering life, or an offence that indicates a propensity to commit certain offences, and it appears that detailed risk criteria may be met, a court may make a risk assessment order. An offender subject to such an order is placed on pre-sentence remand of 90 or 180 days so that a risk assessment order can be prepared. A carefully structured, detailed risk assessment process using a structured professional judgment approach (not an actuarial approach) is undertaken at the time that an offender is sentenced (see Chapter 16; for this system's approach to young offenders, see Chapter 11).

The risk assessment report is considered by the High Court of Scotland, which then has the option of making a risk assessment order and/or making an order for lifelong restriction. Offenders subject to orders for lifelong restriction will be subject to risk management interventions throughout their life, first during their imprisonment (where it is ordered) and afterward in community settings. The order for lifelong restriction is available to cover a broad range of offences, targets offenders who are recidivists, and is ordinarily made when a person is judged to be high risk (see Chapter 15).

Unlike the systems that operate in Australia and the United States, the Scottish Risk Management Authority that conducts the assessment for sentencing purposes is an independent, multidisciplinary agency staffed by forensic experts focused on the comprehensive assessment of individuals and the minimization of the risk of serious violence and sexual offending (see Chapter 15). Steps have been taken to ensure that there is no overreliance on a particular assessment tool or diagnostic assessment (see Chapter 16). The Risk Management Authority develops a risk management plan for implementation first by the prison service and then in all other contexts (including hospitals and the community). Because the assessment is done at sentencing, this enables risk management strategies to be implemented from that point on. This is done through what are called *multiagency public protection arrangements*, which have been designed to ensure effective care coordination across agencies, a problem that has been identified in a number of other jurisdictions (see Chapters 11, 13, 16; McSherry and Keyzer 2009). The evidence suggests that the multiagency arrangements have indeed improved administration. The application of a human rights-based approach has allowed a focus on the individual. Systematic risk assessment is now the norm.

In Chapter 14 in this volume, Alex Quinn and John Crichton demonstrate aspects of the practical operation of risk management in Scotland in their description of the risk management traffic light system, a tool designed to assess risk contingencies in the forensic setting of managing high-risk offenders with mental disorders in Scotland. After tracing the historical development of policy in this context over the past 40 years, Quinn and Crichton describe the Care Program Approach and case management strategies presently operating in that jurisdiction. Quinn and Crichton outline the care coordination and communication problems that have likely increased the risk of released offenders committing violent offences in the community. Improved care meeting processes, guidelines for meeting operation, interagency communication protocols, and information sharing guidelines have aimed to address these problems. A system of amber and red light alerts have been adopted to reduce risk contingencies and to stimulate action by participating professionals.

There are thus alternatives to preventive detention being developed that are aimed at reducing recidivism and supervising those considered to be at high risk of future harm. The jury may be out as to the efficacy of some of these alternatives, but they do give policymakers a starting point beyond continued detention in prison or specifically built facilities.

Conclusion

In the final chapter, we explore some of the challenges that lie ahead in relation to the detention and management of those considered at risk of harming others. What is clear is that the dangerous individual still remains, in Mark Brown and John Pratt's terms, a "powerful ... icon in modern Western Societies" (2000: 1) and the concept of risk is central to classifying, punishing, detaining, and managing those deemed to be dangerous by governments.

The following chapters not only summarize current directions in policies and schemes aimed at protecting the community from those considered dangerous; they look to ways of improving those policies and schemes in order to provide legitimate and effective ways of protecting the community from harm.

2

An International Human Rights Perspective on Detention Without Charge or Trial

Article 9 of the International Covenant on Civil and Political Rights

RONLI SIFRIS

Introduction

This chapter provides a general overview of the approach of international human rights law to the issue of detention without charge or trial. Detention without charge or trial may take a number of forms and may be referred to using a multitude of terms. These include preventive detention, administrative detention, ministerial detention, and extrajudicial detention. There is significant overlap amongst these terms; therefore, for the purposes of this chapter, the term *detention without charge or trial* is used to include all these forms of detention. There are numerous circumstances in which a person may be detained without charge or trial. Examples include the mandatory detention of asylum seekers pending determination of their refugee status, quarantining of people with infectious diseases, involuntary commitment in psychiatric institutions, imprisonment of those suspected of involvement in terrorist-related activities, detention of members of the military for disciplinary purposes, and detention prior to extradition (Keyzer 2009a: 262; International Commission of Jurists 2005: 4; Figure 2.1). Another example is the detention of serious sex offenders following the serving of their sentences. This particular example is discussed at length in other chapters of this book. This chapter considers whether, and in what circumstances, detention without charge or trial is legal pursuant to international human rights law.

The discussion in this chapter is confined to Article 9 of the International Covenant on Civil and Political Rights (ICCPR). The first part of this chapter provides an overview of the international human rights framework and the positioning of Article 9 of the ICCPR within this framework. The second part of this chapter considers the legality of detention without charge or trial under Article 9(1) of the ICCPR, and the third part considers the procedural safeguards that Article 9 of the ICCPR provides for people who are detained without charge or trial. I discuss each paragraph of Article 9 separately and, with respect to each paragraph, refer to the commentary and jurisprudence of the Human Rights Committee (HRC).

It should be noted that Article 9 addresses solely the "fact of deprivation of liberty and the observance of the minimum guarantees specifically formulated in this context" (Nowak 2005: 212). It does not address the "manner in which liberty is deprived" or the treatment of detainees (Nowak 2005: 213). For example, if a person is arrested without being informed of the reasons for arrest, this constitutes a violation of Article 9, but if such a person is mistreated in the course of being arrested, such mistreatment is not a violation of personal liberty and therefore is not a violation of Article 9. Similarly, Article 9 does not address other detention-related issues such as conditions of detention or denial of contact with legal representation (Nowak 2005: 213). There are other binding and non-legally binding documents that address the treatment of persons detained without charge or trial as well as other articles of the ICCPR that expand on the

Detention without charge or trial… some examples…	asylum seekers
	people with infectious diseases
	involuntary commitment in psychiatric institutions
	suspected terrorists
	disciplinary purposes
	awaiting extradition
	high-risk offenders after sentence served
	drug addicts
	political opponents

Figure 2.1 Examples of detention without charge or trial.

Article 9 safeguards as regards the treatment of detainees. It is unfortunately not possible to go beyond the framework of Article 9 for the purpose of this discussion. Further, it should be noted that discussion of the status of detention without charge or trial under the various regional systems will also be left to another forum.

The International Human Rights Framework

The issue of detention without charge or trial is addressed at both the international and regional levels (see Figure 2.2). Each of the primary human rights treaties contains a specific article that defines the parameters of the right to liberty. As stated earlier, it is not possible to include a discussion of the approach of the regional human rights systems in this chapter. However, it should be noted that a state may be bound by treaties at both the international and regional levels. For example, the United Kingdom has ratified both the ICCPR and the European Convention for the Protection of Human Rights and Fundamental Freedoms; it is therefore bound by both of these treaties. Similarly, Argentina has ratified both the ICCPR and the American Convention on Human Rights; it is therefore bound by both of these treaties.

The ICCPR is the primary international law document that addresses the question of detention without charge or trial. It does so in Article 9, which is titled "Liberty and Security of Person." The ICCPR is a treaty, the international law version of a contract, meaning that it is legally binding on those states that have agreed to its terms (Smith 2007: 2). States agree to the terms of a treaty by signing and ratifying that treaty; the ICCPR has been ratified by the majority of states, therefore, the majority of states are bound by its provisions. The consequence of a state binding itself to the terms of the ICCPR is that the state is then required under international law to "translate the ICCPR guarantees into domestic rights for individuals" (Joseph et al. 2004: 14). In other words, once a state ratifies the ICCPR it undertakes to ensure that the rights enshrined in the covenant are respected.

In addition to binding those states that have agreed to its terms under international law, the ICCPR is also binding under the domestic law of many states. For a monist state, the ICCPR becomes binding under domestic law at the same time as it becomes binding under international law. This is because "in those States advocating a monist view to international law, international, regional and national law all form part of the same single legal system" in which "international law usually enjoys primacy over national law" (Smith 2007: 228). For a dualist state, the ICCPR is only binding under domestic law if specific action is taken by the state to incorporate the covenant into domestic law. This is because "dualist States maintain a distinction between international (usually including regional law) and national law. As the two systems are deemed to serve

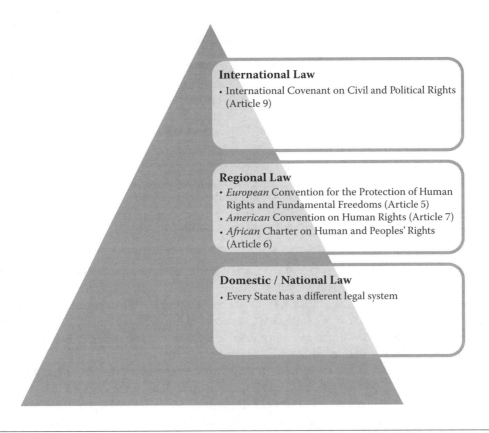

Figure 2.2 Relationship between international law, regional law, and domestic law.

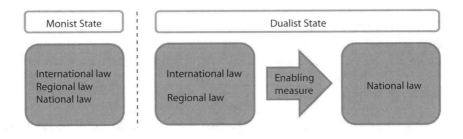

Figure 2.3 The monist versus dualist approach to incorporating international law into the domestic context.

different functions they are mutually exclusive" unless law is transferred from the international sphere into the national sphere with the explicit consent of the national legislature (Smith 2007: 228; Figure 2.3).

Part IV of the ICCPR establishes the HRC. The HRC is the body of independent experts that monitors implementation of the ICCPR by its states' parties. One of its functions is to examine individual complaints with regard to alleged violations of the covenant by states parties to the First Optional Protocol (a subsidiary treaty to the ICCPR). This process enables an individual to lodge a complaint against a state, alleging that the state has violated one or more of the rights enshrined in the covenant. The goals of the procedure are said to be to

identify steps that States should take to comply with their international legal obligations in the context of concrete individual situations. The procedures offer individual relief to victims of human rights violations and should stimulate general legal, policy and pro-gramme change. (Chairpersons of the Human Rights Treaty Bodies 2006: para. 9)

Through this mechanism the HRC has established a body of jurisprudence interpreting Article 9, which has had a "progressive influence on the legislation and practice" of states (Frankowski and Shelton 1992: 299).

The Legality of Detention Without Charge or Trial Under Article 9(1) of the ICCPR

As previously stated, discussion of the legality of detention without charge or trial under inter-national human rights law is centered on Article 9(1) of the ICCPR. Article 9(1) states that

> everyone has the right to liberty and security of person. No one shall be subjected to arbi-trary arrest or detention. No one shall be deprived of his liberty except on such grounds and in accordance with such procedure as are established by law.

Article 9(1) of the ICCPR is a more detailed version of Articles 3 and 9 of the Universal Declaration of Human Rights (UDHR). Article 3 of the UDHR states "everyone has the right to life, liberty and security of person" and Article 9 states "no one shall be subjected to arbitrary arrest, deten-tion or exile." Article 9 of the ICCPR has also been described as a fundamental human right and as enshrining a principle of customary international law (Keyzer 2009a: 265). Customary international law is an additional source of international law to treaty law; it is established by the general practice of states together with state acceptance of the practice as law (Henkin et al. 1987: 37). Certain customs are viewed as peremptory norms, meaning that they permit no dero-gation (Henkin et al. 1987: 67). In its General Comment discussing the ICCPR's non-derogable rights (which do not include Article 9) the HRC specifically stated that states may not invoke the fact that the ICCPR fails to categorize Article 9 as non-derogable in times of public emergency "as justification for acting in violation of humanitarian law or peremptory norms of international law, for instance … through arbitrary deprivations of liberty" (Human Rights Committee 2001: para. 11). In other words, although the ICCPR itself may not prohibit derogation from Article 9, such derogation is in practice prohibited under customary international law.

The first sentence of Article 9(1), written in the spirit of natural law, states that "everyone has the right to liberty and security of person" (Nowak 2005: 216). The term *liberty of person* refers to "the freedom of bodily movement in the narrowest sense" (Nowak 2005: 212). In other words, it refers to the right to be free from forceful detention in locations such as a prison, psychiatric facility, labour camp, or other type of detention facility (Nowak 2005: 212). The term *security of person* refers to the obligation of states parties to "protect the physical integrity of their citizens with positive measures" (Nowak 2005: 214). For example, in the case of *Delgado Paéz v Colombia* (1990) the HRC found a violation of Article 9(1) in circumstances where the state failed to take appropriate measures to protect a citizen against death threats.

It seems that the principle of legality enshrined in the third sentence of Article 9(1) refers to legality under domestic law (Nowak 2005: 224). Therefore, the question of whether detention without charge or trial is legal under international human rights law depends on the interpreta-tion of the second sentence of Article 9(1) of the ICCPR. The second sentence of Article 9(1) states that "no one shall be subjected to arbitrary arrest or detention." The phrase "arrest or detention" is interpreted broadly to include not only the traditional form of arrest on criminal charges, but also "the holding of minors, mentally ill persons, alcohol or drug addicts or vagrants, as well as deprivation of liberty by private persons" (Nowak 2005: 221). The word *arrest* refers to the act of depriving a person of their liberty and the word *detention* refers to the actual state of deprivation of liberty (Nowak 2005: 221). For the purpose of determining the legality of detention without charge or trial, the key word in this sentence is *arbitrary* (Figure 2.4). Thus when considering the

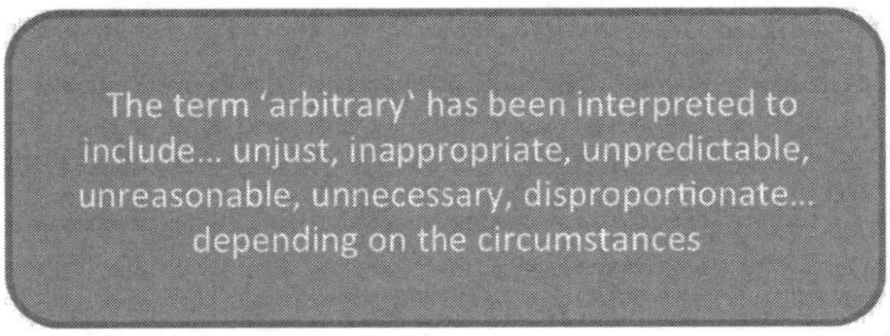

> The term 'arbitrary' has been interpreted to include... unjust, inappropriate, unpredictable, unreasonable, unnecessary, disproportionate... depending on the circumstances

Figure 2.4 Meaning of *arbitrary*.

legality of detention without charge or trial it is necessary to consider whether such detention constitutes arbitrary detention within the meaning of Article 9(1).

The *traveaux préparatoires* (preparatory works) of the ICCPR indicate that the drafters of Article 9 inserted the word *arbitrary* to ensure protection against unjust laws (Hassan 1973: 179). Thus according to Parvez Hassan:

> To most of the members who voted for its adoption in both the Commission and in the General Assembly, "arbitrary arrest or detention" implied an arrest or detention which was incompatible with the principles of justice or with the dignity of the human person irrespective of whether it had been carried out in conformity with the law. (Hassan 1973: 181)

Similarly, the HRC has confirmed that

> "arbitrariness" is not to be equated with "against the law," but must be interpreted more-broadly to include elements of inappropriateness, injustice, lack of predictability and due process of law. (*Mukong v Cameroon* 1994)

Thus detention will be deemed arbitrary not only if it is unlawful but also if it is unreasonable or unnecessary in the circumstances (International Commission of Jurists 2005: 166; *Van Alphen v The Netherlands* 1990). In addition, detention that is disproportionate to achieving a legitimate end of the state will also be considered arbitrary (Joseph et al. 2004: 319; Keyzer 2009a: 265).

If one accepts that the word *arbitrary* in Article 9(1) of the ICCPR does not simply mean "unlawful" but rather, is interpreted broadly, the next step is to consider whether detention without charge or trial falls within this broad interpretation of arbitrary. Phrased differently, it is necessary to consider whether detention without charge or trial constitutes "arbitrary detention" thereby contravening Article 9(1) of the ICCPR. According to Nowak, the *travaux préparatoires* indicate that the categories of detention explicitly sanctioned in the equivalent provisions of the European Convention for the Protection of Human Rights and Fundamental Freedoms and the American Convention on Human Rights will not be considered arbitrary in the context of Article 9(1) of the ICCPR. It is particularly relevant to this discussion that those categories of detention explicitly sanctioned in the regional conventions include

> confinement of a person of "unsound mind" to a psychiatric hospital, detention of persons for the prevention of the spreading of infectious diseases, detention of alcoholics, drug addicts and vagrants, detention of aliens in connection with immigration, asylum, expulsion, extradition and deportation matters. (Nowak 2005: 225–6)

These categories of detention are all different forms of detention without charge or trial. Thus although it may be the case that detention without charge or trial tends to lend itself to abuse (Frankowski and Shelton 1992: 10–11), there is nonetheless general agreement that detention without charge or trial does not per se constitute arbitrary detention and therefore does not per se violate Article 9(1) of the ICCPR (Office of the High Commissioner for Human Rights 2003: 175). Further, in its General Comment 8 the HRC clearly indicates that preventive detention is legal as long as it is not arbitrary and as long as the relevant state complies with the safeguards set out in the other paragraphs of Article 9 (Human Rights Committee 1982).

In a number of decisions addressing the issue of detention without charge or trial the HRC has found such detention to be lawful pursuant to Article 9(1). The following two decisions of the HRC in favor of New Zealand provide useful examples of the circumstances in which preventive detention may be viewed as conforming to Article 9(1). In *A v New Zealand* (1999) the HRC decided that the nine-year detention of a person pursuant to mental health legislation in circumstances where that person had engaged in "threatening and aggressive behavior" and where the order was based on the opinion of three psychiatrists (who continued to conduct periodic reviews of his mental state) "was neither unlawful nor arbitrary" and therefore did not violate Article 9(1) of the ICCPR (*A v New Zealand* 1999: para. 7.2). In the case of *Rameka v New Zealand* (2003), the complainants were convicted of separate crimes of serious sexual violence following which, in accordance with New Zealand law, they received sentences that included a preventive component. The HRC stressed that "detention for preventive purposes … once a punitive term of imprisonment has been served, must be justified by compelling reasons, reviewable by a judicial authority, that are and remain applicable as long as detention for these purposes continues." In this particular case the HRC concluded that the preventive detention was justified and that the relevant safeguards were in place, thus there was no violation of Article 9(1). In reaching this decision the HRC considered all of the circumstances, including the fact that the existence of "compulsory annual reviews by the independent Parole Board" were subject to judicial review (*Rameka v New Zealand* 2003: para. 7.3).

In contrast, the HRC has also issued a number of decisions to the effect that detention without charge or trial, in particular circumstances, does violate Article 9(1). By way of example, it is useful to consider the recent decisions of *Fardon v Australia* (2010) and *Tillman v Australia* (2010). These decisions are analyzed in Patrick Keyzer's chapter in this book, which considers the legitimate parameters for the preventive detention of serious sex offenders. Fardon served a 14-year sentence of imprisonment for rape, sodomy, and unlawful assault following which he continued to be detained pursuant to a Queensland law allowing a person who poses a serious danger to the community to be detained for an indefinite term. The HRC decided that preventive detention in such circumstances was arbitrary, in violation of Article 9(1). It provided a number of reasons for its decision including that Fardon continued to be detained after serving his initial sentence without being convicted for another offence. Elaborating on this point, it stated that imprisonment is penal in character and therefore can only be imposed following conviction; imprisonment cannot be imposed "in respect of predicted future criminal conduct which had its basis in the very offence for which he had already served his sentence." In addition, the HRC expressed the view that to avoid arbitrariness in circumstances where a court is charged with making a finding of fact as to whether a past offender poses a future risk to the community, the state must demonstrate that rehabilitation could not be achieved by "means less intrusive than continued imprisonment or even detention" (*Fardon v Australia* 2010: para. 7.4).

Tillman was convicted of sexual offences involving a child under the age of 10 and assault of a 15-year-old girl. After serving his sentence he continued to be detained pursuant to a New South Wales law directed at serious sex offenders, which enables the court to order the continued detention of a person it deems likely to commit a further serious sexual offence. It should be noted that the facts in both the *Tillman* and *Fardon* cases may be distinguished from those in *Rameka v New Zealand* (2003; discussed earlier) on the basis that in *Rameka* the preventive component was contemplated and included in the original sentence; it was not imposed after the sentence was served. In the *Tillman* decision, echoing its approach in *Fardon*, the HRC decided that Australia had violated Article 9(1) and that the provisions of the New South Wales law

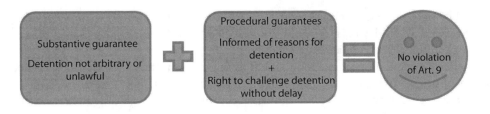

Figure 2.5 Article 9 ICCPR: substantive and procedural guarantees.

under which Tillman continued to be detained at the conclusion of his 10-year term of imprisonment were arbitrary. In providing the reasons for its decision the HRC stated that Tillman had impermissibly been subjected to a fresh term of imprisonment in the absence of a fresh conviction; in other words, he was subjected to a further term of imprisonment "in respect of predicted future criminal conduct which had its basis in the very offence for which he had already served his sentence." In addition, the HRC noted that Australia had not demonstrated that there was no less intrusive means to achieve the objective of protecting the community than continued imprisonment (*Tillman v Australia* 2010: para. 7.4).

To summarize the analysis so far, Article 9(1) of the ICCPR acts as a substantive guarantee that detention will not be arbitrary (Figure 2.5). Detention without charge or trial is not per se arbitrary but may be arbitrary depending on the circumstances of the specific detention in question. Nonetheless, even if a detention does not violate the substantive guarantee of Article 9(1), it must also comply with the procedural guarantees in the remaining paragraphs of Article 9 (Joseph et al. 2004: 304).

Safeguards Established Under Article 9 of the ICCPR

The preceding section of this chapter has discussed Article 9(1), pursuant to which detention without charge or trial is permissible under international human rights law as long as it is not arbitrary. The remaining paragraphs of Article 9 set out the procedural safeguards that must be observed when a person is detained. Articles 9(2), 9(4), and 9(5) apply irrespective of whether the person detained is charged or tried. This has been confirmed by the HRC in its General Comment 8 (Human Rights Committee 1982). Article 9(3) only applies where a person is "arrested or detained on a criminal charge." Therefore, Article 9(3) is not relevant to this discussion and this chapter will consequently confine itself to discussion of the procedural safeguards contained in paragraphs 2, 4, and 5 of Article 9.

Article 9(2) of the ICCPR

Article 9(2) of the ICCPR states:

> Anyone who is arrested shall be informed, at the time of arrest, of the reasons for his arrest and shall be promptly informed of any charges against him.

Thus pursuant to Article 9(2) a person who is detained without charge or trial has a right to be informed of the reasons for his or her arrest (Human Rights Committee 1982).

One question of interpretation that has arisen in connection with Article 9(2) concerns the meaning of "at the time of arrest." This requirement that the reasons for arrest be provided in a timely fashion exists to enable the detainee to effectively challenge the detention within a short period of time pursuant to Article 9(4) (Nowak 2005: 228). It is unclear precisely at what point a delay in informing a detainee of the reasons for detention becomes a violation of the "at the time of arrest" component of Article 9(2). Although each case must be determined according to its own facts, the jurisprudence of the HRC indicates that a three-hour delay is reasonable (*Hill v*

Spain 1997) but a three-day delay (*Ashurov v Tajikistan* 2007; *Komarovski v Turkmenistan* 2008) and certainly a seven-day delay (*Grant v Jamaica* 1996) in informing a detainee of the reasons for detention constitute a violation of Article 9(2).

Another question of interpretation that has arisen in connection with Article 9(2) concerns the level of specificity required in the reasons provided to the detainee. A person detained without charge or trial must be provided with sufficient information regarding the reasons for the detention to enable him or her to challenge the lawfulness of the detention pursuant to Article 9(4). Thus in *Drescher Caldas v Uruguay* (1983) the HRC held that

> Article 9(2) of the Covenant requires that anyone who is arrested shall be informed sufficiently of the reasons for his arrest to enable him to take immediate steps to secure his release if he believes that the reasons given are invalid or unfounded. (*Drescher Caldas v Uruguay* 1983: para. 13.2)

Thus it is not sufficient for a detainee to merely be told of the legal basis for detention, he or she must be able to discern "the substance of the complaint" (*Drescher Caldas v Uruguay* 1983). Nonetheless, it seems that Article 9(2) does not require the obtaining of a written arrest warrant. Further, it does not require a complete explanation in the language of the detainee (Nowak 2005: 228–9). What it requires is that the detainee is able to understand the specific legal charges at issue (Carlson and Gisvold 2003: 84). In addition, a state is not absolved of its obligation to inform a detainee of the reasons for detention simply because it assumes that the detainee knows the reasons (*Grant v Jamaica* 1996); nonetheless if a person surrenders to police it would be difficult to argue a lack of awareness of the reasons for arrest (*Stephens v Jamaica* 1995).

Article 9(4) of the ICCPR

Article 9(4) of the ICCPR states:

> Anyone who is deprived of his liberty by arrest or detention shall be entitled to take proceedings before a court, in order that that court may decide without delay on the lawfulness of his detention and order his release if the detention is not lawful.

Thus pursuant to this paragraph, a detainee has the right to challenge the lawfulness of his or her detention without delay and, if the court finds the detention to be unlawful, it must order the immediate release of the detainee (Figure 2.6; Carlson and Gisvold 2003: 85). As stated earlier, Article 9(4) applies to all forms of detention, including detention without charge or trial. According to Nowak (2005: 235), this paragraph is particularly relevant to "preventive cases of deprivation of liberty beyond that required for criminal justice, such as detention of vagrants, drug addicts, the mentally ill and aliens." This paragraph of Article 9 essentially encapsulates the principle of habeas corpus; it exemplifies the notion that the executive remains accountable to the judiciary; it cannot act outside the law. In fact, the HRC has found a violation of Article 9(4) in numerous circumstances where states have denied persons deprived of their liberty the opportunity of seeking a writ of habeas corpus (*Valcada v Uruguay* 1979).

In addition to being a fundamental right, this right must also exist as a real right that can be exercised in practice, rather than merely a theoretical right. For example, the HRC has held that Article 9(4) is violated where a person is held incommunicado and is therefore "effectively barred from challenging his arrest and detention" even if in theory that person is entitled to challenge his or her detention (*Barbato et al. v Uruguay* 1982: para. 10). Similarly, in *Berry v Jamaica* (1994) the HRC found a violation of Article 9(4) in circumstances where the complainant had no access to legal representation despite the fact that, in theory, he could have challenged the lawfulness of his detention. Nonetheless, in circumstances where a complainant has had access to legal representation and has still failed to challenge the detention, the HRC has found no violation of

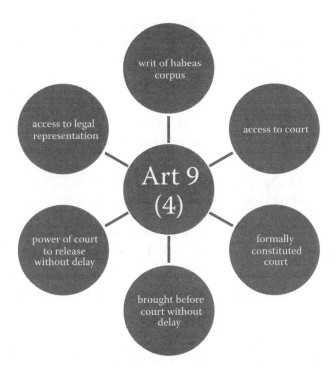

Figure 2.6 Interpretation of Article 9(4) ICCPR.

Article 9(4) on the basis that the State cannot be held responsible for a person's failure to exercise his or her Article 9(4) right (*Stephens v Jamaica* 1995). Thus it seems that pursuant to Article 9(4) a state is obligated to provide a detainee with legal representation and to afford the detainee the opportunity to challenge the lawfulness of detention, but once legal representation has been made available the state is not obligated to ensure that the detainee exercises the opportunity to challenge the detention.

One of the questions that arises in connection with this paragraph of Article 9 is the meaning of "proceedings before a *court*." Rodley and Pollard (2009: 466) point out that "the authority in question is nothing less than a formally constituted court." An authority or institution does not constitute a court merely because it "reviews detention according to established legal procedures" (United Nations Centre for Human Rights 1994: 40). To constitute a court, the review body must possess the "requisite judicial character" (Carlson and Gisvold 2003: 86). Thus review by a superior military officer (*Vuolanne v Finland* 1989) or the Minister of Interior (*Torres v Finland* 1990) has been viewed as failing to comply with Article 9(4).

Another question that arises in connection with this paragraph of Article 9 is the meaning of "without delay." How soon after being arrested must a person be brought before a court? A delay of several days has been found to violate Article 9(4) (*Torres v Finland* 1990) as has a three-day delay resulting from the detainee being held in incommunicado detention (*Hammel v Madagascar* 1987). However, in *Portorreal v Dominican Republic* (1987) the HRC decided that there was no violation of Article 9(4) in circumstances where the complainant was detained for 50 hours without being given the opportunity to challenge his detention before a court. Thus, as discussed earlier with respect to Article 9(2), it is unclear precisely at what point a delay in enabling a detainee to challenge the lawfulness of the detention becomes a violation of the "without delay" component of Article 9(4); each case must be assessed individually (*Torres v Finland* 1990). Further, pursuant to this requirement, it is not sufficient for a detainee to be allowed to challenge his or her detention without delay but the court must decide the lawfulness of the detention without delay (Office of the High Commissioner for Human Rights 2003: 206). Where detention is unlawful the court must have the power to order the immediate release of the detainee (Nowak 2005: 236).

Yet another question arises in connection with Article 9(4): What is the content of the court's power pursuant to Article 9(4)? In *A v Australia* (1997) the relevant legislation allowed the court to determine whether a person was a "designated person" under the legislation. If the person was a designated person the court had no power to order his or her release. In finding a violation of Article 9(4) the HRC stated:

> Court review of the lawfulness of detention under article 9, paragraph 4, which must include the possibility of ordering release, is not limited to mere compliance of the detention with domestic law … article 9, paragraph 4, requires the court to be empowered to order release, if the detention is incompatible with the requirements in article 9, paragraph 1, or in other provisions of the Covenant [*sic*]. (*A v Australia* 1997: para. 9.5)

In this case, the fact that the court was limited to determining whether the detainee fell within the relevant definition of delegated person in the domestic legislation, and in such a case had no power to declare the detention unlawful, was found to violate Article 9(4). Thus it seems that in the context of Article 9(4), *lawfulness* means lawfulness under the ICCPR rather than lawfulness in domestic law (Joseph et al. 2004: 342). Consequently, a court must have the power to release a person if the detention is found to be incompatible with the requirements of the ICCPR (Nowak 2005: 236; Rodley and Pollard 2009: 466–7).

Article 9(5) of the ICCPR

Article 9(5) of the ICCPR states that "anyone who has been the victim of unlawful arrest or detention shall have an enforceable right to compensation." Thus Article 9(5) provides for a right of compensation to all who have been "unlawfully deprived of their liberty of person" (Joseph et al. 2004: 345). The HRC has repeatedly confirmed that compensation pursuant to Article 9(5) is payable upon a breach of any paragraph of Article 9 (Joseph et al. 2004: 345). While Article 9(5) does not specify the process for claiming compensation, the term "enforceable right" implies enforcement via a domestic authority (Nowak 2005: 239). Further, the amount of compensation may take into account both pecuniary and non-pecuniary damage to the victim (Dinstein 1981: 135; Nowak 2005: 239).

In the context of Article 9(5), "unlawful" has traditionally been interpreted as unlawful under a state's own domestic law as well as "contrary to the ICCPR" (Macken 2005: 27). This interpretation was confirmed in *A v Australia* (1997). The HRC's decision in *Chambala v Zambia* (2003) threw some doubt on this interpretation given that, in this case, the HRC decided that the complainant should only be paid compensation for the portion of the period of detention that contravened domestic law, even though the entire period of detention contravened Article 9(1). However, in the decision of *Marques v Angola* (2005) the HRC specifically referred to the decision in *A v Australia* (1997), stating that Article 9(5) "governs the granting of compensation for arrest or detention that is 'unlawful' *either* under domestic law *or* within the meaning of the Covenant" (*Marques v Angola* 2005: para. 6.6).

Conclusion

This chapter has endeavored to provide a general overview of the approach of international human rights law to the issue of detention without charge or trial. Article 9 of the ICCPR is the core legally binding international human rights provision that addresses this issue. Detention without charge or trial is not per se illegal under international human rights law, but it is illegal if it constitutes "arbitrary arrest or detention" pursuant to Article 9(1). Thus it is necessary to consider the circumstances of each case to determine whether the detention in question constitutes arbitrary detention, thereby violating Article 9(1). However, even in circumstances where detention does not violate Article 9(1) of the ICCPR, to be legal it must still comply with the procedural safeguards contained in the remaining paragraphs of Article 9. Thus, when a person is detained without charge or trial, he or she must be "informed, at the time of the arrest, of the reasons" for arrest and must be entitled to take proceedings before a court so that the court may decide "without delay" on the lawfulness of the detention. In addition, a person subjected to unlawful arrest or detention has an enforceable right to compensation. Thus when a person is detained without charge or trial in violation of Article 9 of the ICCPR, that person is entitled to claim compensation in the domestic sphere.

3

The International Human Rights Parameters for the Preventive Detention of Serious Sex Offenders

PATRICK KEYZER

In Australia, four states enable the continued detention of serious sex offenders in prison, rather than a purpose-designed facility, after the conclusion of their prison sentences. This chapter considers two 2010 decisions of the United Nations Human Rights Committee (HRC) that have designated new parameters for the preventive detention of serious sex offenders—*Fardon v Australia* (2010) and *Tillman v Australia* (2010). In *Fardon* and *Tillman*, the HRC found that the detention regimes in two (and by implication all) of the Australian states that adopt the continued detention in prison approach violate human rights enshrined in the International Covenant on Civil and Political Rights (ICCPR): the prohibition against arbitrary detention (Article 9), the guarantee of due process (Article 14), and the prohibition on the retroactive infliction of punishment (Article 15).

This chapter explores these decisions and their significant implications in the context of the preventive detention of serious sex offenders. To date, the response of the Australian states to the challenge of managing serious sex offenders after the conclusion of their prison sentences has been, in a great many cases, to subject these offenders to further imprisonment. The HRC has said that this practice is inconsistent with international human rights, and Australia must take steps to change this practice. Significantly, the HRC has also said that Australian policies must not be characterized by further retribution but should emphasize rehabilitation in the community. I explore the implications of the HRC's approach for contemporary Australian practice, particularly when courts order supervision in the community. It is clear that the Australian regimes will require significant reform to comply with the human rights criteria set out in the HRC's decision.

Continued Detention in Prison: Is It Punitive?

In Australia, four of the six states have enacted legislation that authorizes the Supreme Court of each state to order the continuing imprisonment of a serious sex offender (referred to as *continuing detention*) after the conclusion of their prison term if the offender is judged to be an unacceptable risk to the community if released:

- Dangerous Prisoners (Sexual Offenders) Act 2003 (Queensland; Qld), sec. 50
- Dangerous Sexual Offenders Act 2006 (Western Australia; WA), sec. 17
- Crimes (Serious Sex Offenders) Act 2006 (New South Wales; NSW), sec. 20
- Serious Sex Offenders (Detention and Supervision) Act 2009 (Victoria; Vic), sec. 42

The procedure contemplated by the legislation bears little resemblance to a criminal trial (Keyzer et al. 2004). The legislation does not require courts to be satisfied that the risk that a person will represent to the community meets the criminal standard of proof, beyond reasonable doubt. That is the standard required in United States civil commitment statutes (*Kansas v Hendricks* 1997: 353; *Kansas v Crane* 2002; see John Petrila, Christopher Slobogin and Eric Janus's chapters in this volume). Instead, a civil standard of proof applies in three of the four Australian states that have adopted this approach (see NSW, sec. 17(2); Qld, sec. 13; WA, sec. 7). The courts in these states must be satisfied to a "high degree of probability" that the offender is likely to commit a further sexual offence. In Victoria, the Supreme Court may determine "that an offender poses an unacceptable risk of committing a relevant offence even if the likelihood that the offender will commit a relevant offence is *less than a likelihood of more likely than not*" (Vic, sec. 35(4); emphasis added).

The Australian preventive detention systems do not require a finding of mental illness or mental abnormality as is the case with detention regimes in the United States (see Christopher Slobogin's chapter in this volume). As Queensland Attorney-General Robert Welford said in his Second Reading Speech introducing the Dangerous Prisoners (Sexual Offenders) Bill to the Queensland Parliament on 3 June 2003:

> The scheme of this bill is however not part of the sentencing process but a separate process for detaining persons who are seriously dangerous, convicted, violent sex offenders and whose risk of reoffending demands that the community be protected. It is akin to the detention authorised under mental health laws, except that the protection provided to the public by this new law is founded not on the mental illness of a person but on a different though equally sound principle of public policy. That principle is the priority that must be given to protecting the public, our families and children from the serious danger that a person, having already been convicted and imprisoned for committing offences of a violent sexual nature, poses to the community because of their propensity for committing such an offence again.

The other Australian states have likewise included no requirement that an offender be found to have a mental abnormality, let alone a mental illness (McSherry and Keyzer 2009).

A repeat sex offender named Robert Fardon brought a constitutional challenge to the Queensland legislation. Fardon was serving a 14-year sentence for rape, sodomy, and unlawful assault on a female committed in October 1988 when he was subjected to an order under the Queensland regime. It was argued on behalf of Fardon that Australian courts cannot authorize the civil commitment of a person to prison; imprison a person on the basis that they are at risk of reoffending in the future; imprison a person for putatively therapeutic reasons without a finding of mental illness; authorize punishment, by way of reimprisonment, of a class of prisoners; or authorize double punishment (Keyzer et al. 2004; McSherry 2005).

It was argued that although there are no express constitutional principles protecting due process in the Australian Constitution it would be repugnant to the role of any institution called a court to imprison a person twice for a crime for which they have already been tried and punished. This argument had succeeded in an earlier case involving legislation that named a particular offender and engineered his reimprisonment without a criminal trial (*Kable v Director of Public Prosecutions (NSW)* 1996: 96–97, 106, 120, 132; Gray 2005; Keyzer 2008).

A majority of the High Court rejected these arguments in *Fardon v Attorney-General (Qld)* (2004: 592, 597, 610, 647, 654), holding that Queensland's legislation was valid on the ground that it was enacted for the "non-punitive" purpose of rehabilitating sex offenders, and therefore did not effect double punishment. Chief Justice Gleeson characterized the legislation as authorizing preventive detention, not punitive detention (2004: 592). Justice McHugh stated that

> the Act is not designed to punish the prisoner. It is designed to protect the community against certain classes of convicted sexual offenders who have not been rehabilitated during their period of imprisonment. (p. 597)

Justice Gummow, with whom Justice Hayne agreed (p. 647), pointed out that

> the making of a continuing detention order with effect after expiry of the term for which the appellant was sentenced in 1989 did not punish him twice, or increase his punishment for the offences of which he has been convicted. (p. 610)

Justices Callinan and Heydon stated that

> the Act, as the respondent submits, is intended to protect the community from predatory sexual offenders. It is a protective law authorising involuntary detention in the interests of public safety. Its proper characterization is as a protective *rather than a punitive enactment*. (p. 654)

The foundation for the conclusion reached by the majority was that in a constitutional system that does not have a bill of rights, it is appropriate to be guided by the legislature's description of its policy objectives in determining whether a law is constitutionally valid. The legislation was intended to protect the community, and it was asserted that further detention of serious sex offenders adjudged to be a high risk to the community if released from prison would achieve that objective. Since no principles of "due process" are constitutionally enshrined in Australia, the characterization of the legislation as punitive arguably had no bearing on the resolution of the constitutional question whether the law was a valid act of the Queensland Parliament. Chief Justice Gleeson observed (p. 586):

> There are important issues that could be raised about the legislative policy of continuing detention of offenders who have served their terms of imprisonment, and who are regarded as a danger to the community when released. Substantial questions of civil liberty arise. This case, however, is not concerned with those wider issues.

Justice Kirby, in the sole dissenting judgment, adopted the written submissions of Fardon and emphasized that civil commitment to prison of those who have not been convicted of a crime is repugnant to the exercise of judicial power. In particular, he stated (2004: 636–7):

> Simply calling the imprisonment by a different name (detention) does not alter its true character or punitive effect. Least of all does it do so in the case of an Act that fixes on the subject's status as a "prisoner" and "continues" the type of "detention" that previously existed, that is, punitive imprisonment. Such an order, superimposed at the end of judicial punishment for past crimes, must be distinguished from an order imposing imprisonment for an indeterminate period also for past crimes that is part of the judicial assessment of the punishment for such crimes, determined at the time of sentencing. There, at least, the exercise of judicial power is addressed to past facts proved in a judicial process. Such a sentence, whatever problems it raises for finality and proportionality, observes an historically conventional judicial practice. It involves the achievement of traditional sentencing objectives, including retribution, deterrence and incapacitation applied prospectively. It does not involve supplementing, at a future time, a previously final judicial sentence with new orders that, because they are given effect by the continuation of the fact of imprisonment, amount to new punishment beyond that already imposed in accordance with law (internal references omitted).

It is difficult to understand how the majority of the Australian High Court reached the conclusion that the Queensland law was not punitive in nature, given that the detention authorized by the legislation takes place in a prison. As Justice Kirby also observed in his dissenting judgment (pp. 643–4):

> The Act under consideration includes amongst its objects "care" and "treatment" of a "particular class of prisoner to facilitate their rehabilitation" (DPSOA, s 3). However, in the scheme of the Act, this object obviously takes a distant second place (if any place at all) to the true purpose of the legislation, which is to provide for "the continued detention in custody ... of a particular class of prisoner" (section 3(a)). If the real objective of the Act were to facilitate rehabilitation of certain prisoners retained in prison under a "continuing detention order," significant, genuine and detailed provisions would have appeared in the Act for care, treatment and rehabilitation. There are none. Instead, the detainee remains effectively a prisoner. He or she is retained in a penal custodial institution, even as here the very prison in which the sentences of judicial punishment have been served. After the judicial sentence has concluded, the normal incidents of punishment continue. They are precisely the same.

In 1974, the Australian High Court had stated that its members "cannot understand how ... imprisonment, either with or without hard labour, can, however enlightened the prison system is, be regarded as otherwise than a severe punishment (*Power v The Queen* 1974: 627; see also *Witham v Holloway* 1995). Similarly, in *Kable v Director of Public Prosecutions (NSW)* (1996), a majority of the High Court indicated that one of the grounds of constitutional invalidity in that case was that the legislation inflicted punishment in prison without a predicate criminal trial (Gray 2005; Keyzer 2008).

Within the narrow moral compass of Australian constitutionalism, the decisions of the majority justices were perfectly open to them. Still, it is remarkable that the justices in the majority in *Fardon v Attorney-General (Qld)* decided to resolve the case, at least in part, on the basis that prison is not punitive if a legislature says that it is not. A prison does not stop being punitive because a parliament characterizes its purpose as non-punitive (Keyzer 2008). Australian prisons are, on any sensible view, punitive environments. They are often characterized by overcrowding, substandard facilities, and climactic extremes. There is a lack of appropriate accommodation for differently classified inmates, particularly people who are mentally ill or have intellectual disability (Edney 2000). Psychiatric services are often inadequate or unavailable (Pereira 2001). Australian prisoners are routinely denied human rights (Edney 2002).

Even if Australian prisons were characterized by decent conditions, they would still be punitive. It may be acknowledged that there is no generally accepted theory of punishment, but there is no doubt that imprisonment is one variety of it. The deprivation of liberty in punitive conditions is what makes prison punitive. At any rate, the question of whether a person's circumstances are properly characterized as punitive ought not be definitively resolved by the legislature authorizing the detention. The question must always be resolved by reference to the actual facts of a situation. In constitutional democracies, the power to determine the facts upon which the exercise of judicial power depends is always a matter for the courts (*Wilson v Minister for Aboriginal and Torres Straits Islander Affairs* 1996: 10–11).

It is plain that the Australian law of civil liberties has been retarded by the absence of a constitutionally entrenched (let alone a statutory) bill or charter of rights (O'Neill 1987). In the present context, this has meant that unlike in countries where constitutional or supranational guarantees of civil rights and liberties impose some conditions on system design, the Australian states have had carte blanche when it comes to the preventive detention of high-risk offenders. This has allowed them to produce systems that (Keyzer et al. 2004; McSherry and Keyzer 2009)

- authorize the reimprisonment of a person without a fresh crime;
- authorize the reimprisonment of a person without a criminal trial;
- punish a person twice for a previous offence;
- distort sentencing principles by effectively lengthening them, breaking the nexus between community censure as a component of a sentence and the crime for which a sentence is imposed;
- distort sentencing principles by altering the deterrence value of a sentence, rendering sentences for sex offences, essentially, indeterminate;
- remove certainty from sentencing; and
- disturb the calculation of proportionality that takes place in sentencing by creating a system that enables them to be lengthened indefinitely.

The United Nations Human Rights Committee Decisions

In 2010, the HRC handed down its decisions in response to two communications brought by prisoners incarcerated under the Queensland and New South Wales regimes: *Fardon v Australia* (2010) and *Tillman v Australia* (2010). Ken Tillman was serving a 10-year sentence for sexually assaulting a minor when he was subjected to an order under the New South Wales regime. Both Fardon and Tillman filed communications with the HRC in 2007, and the HRC delivered its views in March 2010.

The communications both raised arguments that the regimes inflict arbitrary detention contrary to Article 9(1), double punishment contrary to Article 14(7), and a retroactive infliction of further punishment contrary to Article 15(1) of the ICCPR. Australia is a signatory to the ICCPR and its First Optional Protocol, which allows its citizens to make communications to the HRC to determine whether Australia (or its states) have breached the ICCPR. The HRC admitted the communications and decided that they should be determined on their merits.

Arbitrary Detention

Article 9 of the ICCPR provides that "no one shall be subjected to arbitrary arrest or detention." Fardon and Tillman pointed out that the HRC and the House of Lords have described this as a fundamental human right (*Kurt v Turkey* 1997: para. 122, 123; *A v Secretary of State for the Home Department* 2004: para. 36). It is also a principle of customary international law (Lillich and Hannum 1995: 136), and a well-established principle of the common law (see the cases referred to by Justices Brennan, Deane, and Dawson in *Chu Kheng Lim v Minister for Immigration* 1992: 25–28).

In their communications, Fardon and Tillman pointed out that the HRC had previously stated that detention will be arbitrary and contrary to Article 9 if it is not reasonable, necessary in all the circumstances of the case and proportionate to achieving the legitimate ends of the state party (*A v Australia* 1997: para. 9.2, 9.4; *C v Australia* 2002: para. 8.2; *Baban v Australia* 2003: para. 7.2; *D and E v Australia* 2006: para. 7.2; *Bakhtiyari v Australia* 2003: para. 9.2 and 9.3; *de Morais v Angola* 2005: para. 6.1; *Taright v Algeria* 2006: para. 8.3; *Shafiq v Australia* 2006. See also *A v Secretary of State for the Home Department* 2004: per Lord Bingham). The HRC has stated that the "drafting history of article 9, paragraph 1" of the ICCPR "confirms that 'arbitrariness' must be interpreted broadly to proscribe detention that is inappropriate, unjust and unpredictable" (in *van Alphen v The Netherlands* 1990: para. 5.8). The sanctity of personal liberty has been recognized as requiring the strict construction of provisions authorizing exceptions to that principle (see *van Alphen v The Netherlands* 1990: para. 5.8). This provision does not prohibit state parties to the ICCPR from authorizing their courts to order indefinite sentences that contain a preventive component (*Rameka v New Zealand* 2002: para. 7.2 and 7.3; Keyzer and Blay 2006). But, importantly, if a state party is able to achieve its legitimate ends by less invasive means than that of detention, detention will be considered to be arbitrary.

Fardon and Tillman argued that although there can be no doubt that the objective of rehabilitation and treatment of sex offenders is a legitimate one, the use of reimprisonment to achieve it is not reasonable, nor is it necessary or proportionate to that objective (Keyzer 2009a). Australia could provide special facilities for offenders requiring preventive detention, in the cases where that is required (Keyzer and Coyle 2009).

The HRC, in an 11–2 ruling, upheld Fardon's and Tillman's complaints that the Queensland and New South Wales legislation respectively was (and, at the time of writing, presently is) contrary to Article 9. Before setting out the HRC's reasons, it is convenient to outline Fardon's and Tillman's arguments under Articles 14 and 15 of the ICCPR. Article 14(7) prohibits double punishment, and Article 15(1) prohibits the retrospective infliction of punishment.

Double and Retrospective Punishment

In *Rameka v New Zealand* (2002), a case in which an indefinite sentence including a "preventive" component was under challenge, four members of the HRC, in a minority opinion, had observed:

> It is the very principle of detention based solely on potential dangerousness that [we] challenge, especially as detention of this kind often carries on from, and becomes a mere and, it would not be going too far to say, an "easy" extension of a penalty of imprisonment … While often presented as precautionary, measures of this kind in question are in reality penalties, and this change of their original nature constitutes a means of circumventing the provisions of articles 14 and 15 of the ICCPR.

The principles enunciated by the four members of the HRC in their minority opinion in *Rameka v New Zealand* (2002) applied directly to the circumstances of Fardon and Tillman (Keyzer and Blay 2006). Fardon and Tillman adopted the minority's remarks in *Rameka's* case and argued that the Queensland and New South Wales legislation inflicts double punishment and a retrospective increase in their punishment.

Australia, for its part, advanced the following argument in its submissions to the HRC in defense of the state regimes (Keyzer 2009b):

> The complainant argues that the mere fact that the detention takes place in a prison gives it a predominantly punitive character and that detention would need to take place in a special mental facility or hospital to avoid this … The Australian Government submits that this is not the case. As stated above, the complainant has access to the best available rehabilitative resources and facilities within the prison system. This enables the government to achieve the dual goals of ensuring the safety of the community through detention in a secure facility and rehabilitation by providing the individual with the most appropriate therapy.

The HRC observed that Australia had pointed to what it characterized as the "stringent test" to be applied by a court: that a court must be satisfied to a "high degree of probability" that the offender is likely to commit a further sexual offence. The court could take into account psychiatric reports and other evidence, including evidence relating to the likelihood of recidivism, the offender's willingness to participate in rehabilitation programs, and any patterns of offending.

Australia argued that a supervision order would be inappropriate for Fardon or for Tillman, "for reasons of safety of the community and his own protection." In prison, Fardon and Tillman would have access to rehabilitation services that they would not have access to in the community. Australia argued that detaining these men for the purpose of ensuring they had access to rehabilitative programs was reasonably proportionate to the rehabilitative objectives of the legislation. Furthermore, the legislation contemplated periodic independent review by a court (*Tillman v Australia* 2010: para. 4.4).

A majority of 11 of the 13 members of the HRC did not accept this submission. The HRC declined the opportunity to apply Article 14(7), concluding instead that the New South Wales and Queensland preventive detention regimes (and by implication, the functionally identical regimes of Western Australia and Victoria) were inconsistent with Articles 9, 14, and 15 of the ICCPR. The HRC accepted the arguments of Fardon and Tillman that they were subject to the same regime of imprisonment as if they had been convicted of a criminal offence (for example, *Tillman v Australia* 2010: para. 5.3). Fardon and Tillman argued that their cases differed fundamentally from the *Rameka* decision and decisions of the European Court of Human Rights (*Mansell v United Kingdom* 1997; *De Wilde, Oms and Versyp v Belgium* 1971; *Iribarne Pérez v France* 1995), in which courts had ordered the imprisonment of a person for preventive reasons at the time of sentencing. The imposition of further imprisonment after a person has served their original sentence constituted double punishment. This reimprisonment was independent of the initial criminal trial, took place after completion of a finite sentence, and without a finding of criminal guilt or any fresh crime. Furthermore, the HRC observed (in *Tillman v Australia* 2010: para. 5.5, and in like terms in *Fardon v Australia* 2010):

> Mr Tillman reiterates that he neither disputes the lawfulness of his continuing detention order, nor the legitimacy of the legislative objective to protect the community from harm. Mr Tillman disputes that utilization of re-imprisonment to achieve the objectives of the CSSOA, in particular the objective of rehabilitation. He claims that rehabilitation can only be tested when a person has (some) liberty …. He maintains that imprisonment is not necessary to achieve the legitimate objective of rehabilitation of a person in the interest of the protection of the community, which could be achieved by psychiatric and psychological services in a community setting which balances the safety of the community with the rehabilitative needs of the former offender. He submits that the CSSOA inflicts arbitrary detention contrary to article 9, paragraph 1, of the Covenant because it inflicts imprisonment on the basis of what a person might do rather than on what a person has done.

After setting out the arguments put by Fardon and Tillman, the majority of the HRC stated it had come to the conclusion that the continuing detention of these men under the Australian regimes was arbitrary and therefore violated Article 9(1) of the ICCPR. This was so "for a number of reasons, each of which would, by itself, constitute a violation" (2010: para. 7.4):

> (1) Mr Tillman has already served his 10 year term of imprisonment and yet he continued, in actual fact, to be subjected to imprisonment in pursuance of a law which characterizes his continued incarceration under the same prison regime as detention. His purported detention amounted, in substance, to a fresh term of imprisonment which, unlike detention proper, is not permissible in the absence of a conviction for which imprisonment is a sentence prescribed by law.
>
> (2) Imprisonment is penal in character. It can only be imposed on conviction for an offence in the same proceedings in which the offence is tried. Mr Tillman's further term of imprisonment was the result of Court orders made, some 10 years after his conviction and sentence, in respect of predicted future criminal conduct which had its basis in the very offence for which he has already served his sentence. This new sentence was the

result of fresh proceedings, though nominally characterized as "civil proceedings," and fall within the prohibition of Article 15, paragraph 1, of the Covenant. In this regard, the Committee further observed that, since the [New South Wales Act] was enacted in 2006 shortly before the expiry of the author's sentence for an offence for which he had been convicted in 1998 and which because an essential element in the Court order for his continued incarceration, the [Act] was being retroactively applied to the author. This also falls within the prohibition of article 15, paragraph 1, of the Covenant, in that he has been subjected to a heavier penalty "than was applicable at the time when the criminal offence was committed." The Committee therefore considers that detention pursuant to proceedings incompatible with article 15 is necessarily arbitrary within the meaning of article 9, paragraph 1, of the Covenant.

(3) The [Act] prescribed a particular procedure to obtain the relevant Court orders. This particular procedure, as the State party conceded, was designed to be civil in character. It did not, therefore, meet the due process guarantees required under article 14 of the Covenant for a fair trial in which a penal sentence is imposed.

The Implications of the *Fardon* and *Tillman* Decisions

The *Fardon* and *Tillman* decisions reinforce the purely utilitarian rationale for preventive detention outside the criminal sentencing context; they require a focus on the policies and practices that should be applied to achieve therapeutic and rehabilitative objectives. The Australian states, should they wish to honor the ICCPR, will need to devise new strategies for the management of released offenders that do not employ reimprisonment. In *Tillman* (2010: para. 7.4, and in similar terms in *Fardon v Australia* 2010), the HRC stated:

(4) The "detention" of the author as a "prisoner" under the [New South Wales Act] was ordered because it was feared that he might be a danger to the community in the future and for the purposes of his rehabilitation. The concept of feared or predicted dangerousness to the community applicable in the Case of past offenders is inherently problematic. It is essentially based on opinion as distinct from factual evidence, even if that evidence consists in the opinion of psychiatric experts. But psychiatry is not an exact science. The [Act], on the one hand, requires the Court to have regard to the opinion of psychiatric experts on future dangerousness but, on the other hand, requires the Court to make a finding of fact of dangerousness. While Courts are free to accept or reject expert opinion and are required to consider all other available relevant evidence, the reality is that the Courts must make a finding of fact on the suspected future behavior of a past offender which may or may not materialize. To avoid arbitrariness, in these circumstances, the State party should have demonstrated that the author's rehabilitation could not have been achieved by means less intrusive than continued imprisonment or even detention.

The HRC's use of the disjunctive word *or* in the last line of this quotation indicates that even civil detention regimes such as those that exist in the United States should they emerge in Australia in the light of these decisions as an alternative to the use of prison as a venue for preventive detention will need to incorporate genuine rehabilitative and therapeutic measures in order to realize the obligation arising under Article 10(3) of the ICCPR to take steps to rehabilitate offenders. Article 10(3) provides that the "penitentiary system shall comprise treatment of prisoners the essential aim of which shall be their reformation and social rehabilitation."

Australia is under no legal obligation to comply with the decisions of the HRC. The HRC's opinions are not legally binding on the Australian government (Blay and Piotrowicz 2000). It is not a court of appeal. However neither can a state party "invoke the provisions of its internal law for its failure to perform a treaty" (Brownlie 1998: 35; *Vienna Convention on the Law of Treaties* Article 27). As Sam Blay and Ryszyard Piotrowicz have asked (2000: 14):

> Does it mean that, in the context of the ICCPR, a state can adopt any legislation in munici-pal law regarding detention, for instance, and argue that its obligations are met if such legislation is in accordance with its legal system?

Blay and Piotrowicz, after considering this question in the light of other decisions of the HRC concerning Article 9, and the Australian practice of detaining asylum seekers pending determi-nation of their status, conclude that "the standard for assessing whether the state has in fact met its obligations remains in the domain of international law" and cannot be determined by refer-ence to local (Australian) standards (Blay and Piotrowicz 2000: 18). In short,

> the standard for assessing the state's conduct is not to be calculated by reference only to what it does within its own jurisdiction; to do so would render the essence of its interna-tional obligations meaningless.

If the foregoing analysis is correct, then the Australian states that have adopted reimprison-ment policies will now need to devise and implement policies for the management of serious sex offenders that are genuinely aimed at rehabilitation and in the community.

What Does Australia Need to Do to Comply with the Human Rights Committee's Decisions?

It looks as if there is a lot of work ahead for the four states that have implemented these regimes. The cases indicate that (McSherry and Keyzer 2009: 70–76)

- sex offender treatment programs are only available to a limited number of prisoners;
- sex offender treatment programs are only available in a limited number of prisons;
- waiting lists are long;
- there is limited availability of sex offender treatment maintenance programs in the community; and
- sex offender treatment maintenance programs are only available in urban areas.

Administrative oversights by corrective services departments in rationing access to treat-ment programs would be laughable if they were not so serious. *Gough v Southern Queensland Regional Parole Board* (2008) illustrates the problem. In this case, a sex offender, representing himself, brought an application in the Supreme Court for judicial review of a decision by the parole board to deny him parole. Gough had been sentenced in November 2006 to four and a half years imprisonment and was given a parole eligibility date of 24 February 2008. On 25 October 2007 the parole board received an application for parole from the prisoner, who indi-cated that he had "continually and persistently lobbied prison authorities to be permitted to participate in appropriate intervention courses" but his pleas had "fallen on deaf ears" (at 2008: para. 2). The Supreme Court observed (at 2008: para. 6):

> For reasons that are unexplained by the evidence, Queensland Corrective Services ("QCS") did not offer the applicant one of the intervention programs that the applicant was prepared to undertake so as to enable him to commence, let alone complete, the programs prior to his application for parole being considered in late 2007 and prior to his parole eligibility date of 24 February 2008. In the result, the applicant, through no fault of his own, was unable to rely in his application to the Board upon the results of his participation in such programs. The relapse prevention plan that the applicant submitted was not enhanced by any benefits that such programs may have provided to him.

The Queensland Department of Corrective Services had provided no evidence to the Court that it was not practicable for the prisoner to enter and complete the recommended programs prior to his parole eligibility date (*Gough* 2008: para. 57). Yet the parole board had stated in its reasons for denying parole that the prisoner lacked insight regarding his pattern of offending behavior and that this "was to be expected, given that he had not completed any interventions" (at 2008: para. 61). Justice Applegarth concluded that the parole board erred in law by reaching its conclusion to deny parole without any regard to why the applicant had yet to complete the programs (2008: para. 72).

Other problems that have been identified with Australian preventive detention regimes include

- inadequate employment and social services;
- an absence of substance abuse relapse prevention planning (see McSherry and Keyzer, 2009: 75–76); and
- a lack of funding.

Planning for transition to the community, and the provision of community-based supports, has been poor (McSherry and Keyzer 2009: 75–83). There is a high correlation between the lack of post-release housing options and recidivism (see John Petrila's chapter in this volume). But the cases indicate that often the housing that is available is utterly inappropriate (*Attorney-General (Qld) v Fardon* 2007: para. 29; *Attorney-General (Qld) v Toms* 2007: para. 15–16; *Attorney-General (Qld) v Yeo* 2007: [42]). The Queensland Department of Corrective Services has offered "accommodation" on the prison property at Wacol Correctional Centre that is located only 20 meters from the prison and is surrounded by a 10-meter-high barbed wire fence (Keyzer and Coyle 2009). Twenty-four-hour closed-circuit television and floodlights have been installed. A dog squad officer has also been placed just outside the new facility as an added security measure. All residents are given a security classification rating before moving into the precinct and are required to carry Queensland Corrective Services identification cards at all times. Similar accommodation is provided at Victoria's Ararat Prison.

Justice Chesterman described the Wacol Prison Reserve in the following terms (*Toms* 2007: para. 15):

[Toms] was moved to accommodation at Wacol near the prison which was far less suitable. One of his neighbours was a notorious criminal and paedophile with whom the respondent was thrown in contact. The location is isolated and offers no opportunity for positive social interaction or employment. The respondent told Dr James that his location at Wacol made his anticipated rehabilitation into society more difficult and he found the consumption of alcohol alleviated his sense of isolation and rejection.

Therapeutic interventions do not appear to be the focus of activity in the Prison Reserve. In *Attorney-General (Qld) v Currie* (2009: para. 13), the director of the High Risk Offender Management Unit within the Queensland Corrective Services Department (QCS) gave evidence that

whilst some initial support is offered on a case by case basis, offenders are expected to live independently and are responsible for their own reintegration activities in accordance with the conditions of their order … The precinct does not provide an intensive personal support program and does not include such activities as escorted leave.

The Supreme Court has exhorted the QCS to find better accommodation meeting the recommendations of psychiatrists "as a matter of urgency" (*Toms* 2008: para. 23). However, for an increasing number of prisoners there appears to be no other option for them than the Wacol Prison Reserve (see *Attorney-General (Qld) v George* 2009: para. 41). Developing a sensible and properly funded policy for pre-release planning and post-release housing and community support for people who are released from prison is in the best interests of the community, and would therefore help to realize the scheme's paramount concern for the protection of the community (Dangerous Prisoners (Sexual Offenders) Act 2003 (Qld) sec. 13(6)).

It is difficult to avoid the conclusion that the principal objective of the Australian states has been to maintain control of offenders who have served their sentences, with positive therapeutic outcomes being at best an afterthought (*Fardon v Attorney-General (Queensland)* 2004: 640). Indeed, this conclusion is reinforced when one considers the objects clause of the legislation in each of the states, which refers to "care, control or treatment" (Dangerous Prisoners (Sexual Offenders) Act 2003 (Qld) sec. 3). Although the courts have urged a reading of the legislation that emphasizes its therapeutic objectives, it must be recognized that the objects clause of the legislation in these states indicates that the formal intention of the legislation is the "control, care *or* treatment" of offenders. As the Supreme Court of Queensland observed in *Attorney-General (Qld) v Downs* (2008), as a matter of ordinary language, these objects must be read disjunctively. In other words, it is open to a court to make an order that has nothing to do with the care or treatment of an offender, and instead is *only* based on the need to control him (for example, see *Attorney-General (Qld) v Lawrence* 2008; *Attorney-General (Qld) v Hynds* 2007).

Conclusion

To respond to the HRC's decision, the Australian government, in partnership with the four states that have adopted this technique of preventive reimprisonment, will need to work out what to do with the offenders who are currently in prison under these laws who, in the HRC's opinion, should not be. These prisoners may have been judged to be high risk by the state Supreme Courts, so there is a need for suitable facilities that are not prisons to provide accommodation for these offenders while efforts are made to assist them with transition to the community.

Perhaps the United States civil commitment model could provide a short-term solution to this problem, and a longer-term solution for "the worst of the worst." However the very strident criticisms of the United States systems considered elsewhere in this volume (see the chapters by Eric Janus, Christopher Slobogin, John La Fond, and John Petrila) need to be borne in mind by Australian policymakers. The HRC has expressly indicated that rehabilitation needs to be the fundamental objective, not punishment. A secure hospital incorporating a graduated release program with support in the community is warranted.

Second, state governments need to think quickly but also carefully about what they will do after that. Sooner or later most offenders are released. In addition to securing accommodation options in the community (a foundation for other community-based services), released sex offenders need access to treatment programs run by well-qualified professionals who can work with offenders so that they can learn how to reintegrate into society and live crime-free lives. Released offenders need access to employment opportunities, substance-abuse relapse-prevention programs, and to undertake healthy leisure activities. For some offenders, antilibidinal medication may also be required. Again, all of these services need to be provided by well-qualified professionals, ideally by an agency that is independent of government and committed to the maintenance of high standards. Scotland has started promising experiments in this area that are considered by others in this volume (see the chapters by Innes Fyfe and Yvonne Gailey, and Raj Darjee and Katharine Russell).

Third, state governments need to review prison-based systems for sex offender treatment and risk management. There is evidence of mismanagement and also poor funding. Treatment programs are only made available to a limited number of prisoners in a limited number of prisons. Offenders should not have to beg to be included in these programs.

Plainly, the HRC's decisions in *Fardon* and *Tillman* also have significant implications for the preventive detention of serious sex offenders in countries other than Australia, particularly those countries that have signed the First Optional Protocol to the ICCPR, which contemplates that citizens of those countries can file communications with the HRC. Further consideration of these international implications is outside the scope of this chapter, but the implications are considered to some extent in the chapter by Ronli Sifris in this volume. It is notable that neither the United States nor the United Kingdom has signed the First Optional Protocol although freedom from arbitrary detention is guaranteed under the European Convention for the Protection of Human Rights and Fundamental Freedoms.

4

Legal Limitations on the Scope of Preventive Detention

CHRISTOPHER SLOBOGIN

Preventive detention is a deprivation of liberty, instigated by the government through incarceration or other means, which is based on an assessment that the person deprived of liberty represents a risk of harm to society. So defined, preventive detention takes place in a number of contexts, sometimes explicitly, sometimes implicitly. Moving from the least intrusive to the most intrusive examples, explicit preventive detention occurs in connection with police stops and frisks; civil commitment; pre-trial detention; quarantine; indeterminate sentence and parole decision-making; sexually violent predator statutes; detention of enemy combatants and "terrorists;" and administration of the death penalty (when dangerousness is a designated aggravating factor). Preventive detention goals can be implicit in connection with arrests for various crimes such as loitering, possession of drugs or weapons, conspiracy and attempt; sentences within a determinate range; three-strikes statutes; and the death penalty (when dangerousness is not a designated aggravating factor).

Scholars have inveighed against preventive detention, in particular open-ended preventive detention that occurs in lieu of or after a criminal sentence, on a number of grounds (see the chapters by Eric Janus, John La Fond, and John Petrila in this volume). But the practice appears to be firmly in place in most, if not all, of the contexts described earlier. On the assumption that preventive detention will continue to be a popular means of dealing with antisocial behavior, in previous work I have examined the limitations that first principles might place on this form of government coercion (Slobogin 2006: 103–77; 2007: 99–130). This chapter summarizes this work, and also notes its intersection with international legal doctrine and with policies in the countries featured in this book (the United States, England, Scotland, and Australia).

Seven principles or rules are set out and defended:

1. the principle of legality, which requires commission of a crime or immently risky conduct before preventive detention takes place;
2. the proportionality principle, which requires that government prove a probability and magnitude of risk proportionate to the duration and nature of the contemplated intervention;
3. the related least drastic means principle, which requires the government to resort to the least invasive means of accomplishing its preventive goals, including community treatment;
4. the principle of criminal justice primacy, which requires that systems of preventive detention separate from criminal justice be limited to detention of those who are unaffected by even a significant prospect of serious criminal punishment;
5. the evidentiary rule that, when government seeks preventive confinement, it may only prove its case using actuarial-based probability estimates;

6. the evidentiary rule that the subject of preventive detention may rebut the government's case concerning risk with clinical risk assessments, even if they are not as provably reliable as actuarial prediction;

7. the procedural principle that risk and risk management plans must be periodically reviewed using procedures that assure voice for the subject and avoid executive branch domination of the decision-making process.

Substantive Limitations on Preventive Detention

The Act Requirement: A Crime or Imminently Risky Conduct

As an empirical matter, almost all individuals who are considered a serious risk to others are likely to have committed at least one previous criminal act. In theory, however, an assessment of risk does not require a predicate crime. The right combination of psychological or physiological condition (for example, psychopathy) and situation (for example, the imminence of gang warfare) might permit a fairly robust prediction that violence will ensue without such an act.

Even if the prediction is highly accurate, however, preventive detention should not take place in the absence of antisocial conduct. This conclusion flows from the principle of legality, which applies in both the criminal and civil contexts, and in the United States stems from the due process clause. The principle of legality posits, inter alia, that the basis for depriving individuals of life, liberty, or property may not be so vague or so broadly framed that government officials can intervene regardless of what the individual does. Thus, for instance, the United States Supreme Court has struck down a loitering statute because it "contains no standard for determining what a suspect *has to do* in order to satisfy (its) requirements," and therefore "vests virtually complete discretion in the hands of the police to determine whether the suspect has satisfied the statute" (*Kolender v Lawson* 1983: 358; emphasis added). International law barring "arbitrary detention" could be interpreted to require the same result (see Ronli Sifris's chapter in this volume).

If the government could intervene based solely on the nature of one's thoughts, condition, or environment, individuals with the relevant status-based risk characteristics would have no way of avoiding the intervention, at least when those characteristics are either unchangeable or cannot realistically be changed. Further, the government would have carte blanche to arrest such individuals whenever it wanted to do so. The practical consequence of the legality principle is that preventive detention may not occur unless the individual has committed a crime or has engaged in conduct that is imminently risky, as when police have reasonable suspicion that the person is about to engage in criminal activity (see *Terry v Ohio* 1968) or a person with a communicable disease enters the public domain. On the same reasoning, once detention takes place the imposition of new or greater restrictions on liberty is prohibited unless additional criminal or imminently risky conduct occurs.

The legality principle also mandates a clear statement as to the nature of the conduct that justifies intervention (*Connally v General Construction Company* 1926: 391). The legality principle has long required that crimes be defined by statute. Ideally "imminently risky conduct" would also be defined beforehand, via a court or legislative rule, inclusion in risk assessment instruments, or some other vehicle. If the relevant triggering conduct is for some reason not identified ex ante, the person detained should be able to obtain an ex post check on the government's decision as soon as possible.

The Risk Necessary for Intervention: The Proportionality Principle

The most important substantive question raised by preventive detention is the degree of risk necessary to justify intervention or, in the case of sentencing, prolongation of the intervention. At one extreme, society could decide that, once a person meets the act predicate, a person could be preventively detained upon any showing of risk for any type of antisocial behavior. At the other extreme, society could prohibit intervention until the government adduces proof beyond a reasonable doubt that the person will commit a serious, violent crime. However, neither of these positions is consistent with long-standing justice principles. Instead, the law has taken a contextual approach. For instance, as interpreted by the United States Supreme Court in *Jackson v Indiana* (1972: 738), the due process clause of the Fourteenth Amendment mandates that "the nature and duration of commitment bear some *reasonable relation* to the purpose for which the individual is committed" (emphasis added). In essence, *Jackson* announces a proportionality principle in the preventive detention context. This principle can also be derived from Article 9 of the International Convention of Civil and Political Rights, which has been interpreted to provide that "detention ... disproportionate to achieving a legitimate end of the State will ... be considered arbitrary" (see the chapter by Ronli Sifris in this volume).

In the criminal justice system, punishment is generally supposed to be proportionate to desert (culpability). In a preventive detention regime dispositions should be proportionate to risk. Risk can be measured along a number of dimensions, but the two most important are the probability that harm will occur and its magnitude (Brooks 1974: 143). While a high probability and magnitude of harm might justify serious preventive measures, including long-term confinement, of minimal probability, and magnitude of harm should never be the basis for significant preventive intervention.

American law has long implicitly recognized this proportionality principle. Preventive intervention always requires some justification and that justification becomes more onerous as the intervention becomes more significant. Even a brief detention on the street requires reasonable suspicion that criminal activity is occurring or is imminent. Short-term emergency civil commitment requires probable cause to believe a person is a danger to others, and pre-trial detention requires a preponderance showing or clear and convincing evidence that a felony will otherwise occur. Moving up the ladder, long-term civil commitment requires clear and convincing evidence that hospitalization is needed to prevent serious bodily injury. Sexually violent predator commitment usually requires proof beyond a reasonable doubt that another sex offence will be committed and a death sentence usually requires proof beyond a reasonable doubt that a violent crime will otherwise be committed (Slobogin 2006: 143). A version of the proportionality principle is also recognized in connection with detention of enemy combatants, where courts have held that "evidence that may have justified the initial detention will not serve in retrospect to convince a court to bless it" (Wittes et al. 2010: 24–25).

Unfortunately, while the typical *standards of proof* reflect proportionality analysis, many statutes and courts fudge the intervention-threshold issue by failing to adhere to proportionality reasoning in defining the *legal standard*—that is, the probability of risk and the magnitude of risk. Under Texas's death penalty statute, for instance, an offender is considered eligible for the death penalty when the state can show beyond a reasonable doubt "a probability that the individual will commit criminal acts of violence that constitute a continuing threat to society" (Texas Code Criminal Procedure 2010, art. 37.071 §2(b)(1)). While dangerousness so defined must be proven under the reasonable doubt standard—which sounds consistent with proportionality reasoning—the statute defines dangerousness itself in terms of "a probability." Thus, a Texas prosecutor seeking a death sentence need only show a *probability* of harm beyond a reasonable doubt. Furthermore, the magnitude of harm described in this statute—a criminal act of violence—is extremely vague and, to the extent an assault is considered violent, insufficiently proportionate to the preventive intervention at stake. Together, the probability and magnitude elements of this statute mean that the dangerousness aggravator under Texas death penalty law is proven even if there is less than a 50 per cent chance that the offender will commit another crime and even if that crime is only a simple assault.

Similarly vague formulations are found in other countries. For instance, in Scotland an Order for Lifelong Restriction, which can result in prolonged confinement and permanent supervision by the state, can be imposed if "there is a *likelihood* that (the individual), if at liberty, will seriously endanger the lives, or physical or *psychological well-being*, of members of the public at large" (emphasis added; see the chapter by Innes Fyfe and Yvonne Gailey in this volume). The Imprisonment for Public Protection Sentence in England and Wales permits preventive detention of those who pose a "significant risk of causing serious harm to members of the public" (see the chapter by Innes Fyfe and Yvonne Gailey in this volume). The detention of insanity acquittees in Victoria, Australia, usually ends only if courts can be assured that the risk of violent reoffending is remote, insignificant, or non-existent (see the chapter by Ian Freckelton in this volume).

If the proportionality principle underlying *Jackson v Indiana* (1972) were taken seriously, these types of practices could not continue. In the United States, the anchor for proportionality analysis should be the reasonable suspicion required for a police stop, because that legal standard is mandated by the Fourth Amendment's stipulation that seizures be reasonable (*Terry v Ohio* 1968). Reasonable suspicion has been quantified at approximately a 20 per cent to 30 per cent level of certainty that the person stopped is about to engage in some sort of criminal activity (McCauliff 1982: 1327–8), and under the United States. Supreme Court's case law that level of risk permits a detention on the street of no more than 20 minutes (*United States v Sharpe* 1985). Using that rule as a baseline for proportionality reasoning, *incarceration* for preventive purposes should require proof of a higher degree of risk, perhaps at the 50 per cent level (analogous to the probable cause required for an arrest). If confinement becomes prolonged, it should require increasingly higher showings of risk, both in terms of probability and magnitude, while the death penalty could be imposed only upon sufficient proof of near certainty that the person will commit a seriously violent felony.

If implemented in the manner described, the proportionality principle requires a level of proof that, compared to current preventive detention practices, will reduce false positives (people declared to be a legally sufficient risk but who are not), but will also probably increase false negatives (people who do not pose a legally sufficient risk but who in fact will recidivate if released). The trade-off between false positives and false negatives need not be a zero-sum game, however. Although reducing either rate below 25 per cent is very difficult, researchers have been able to develop prediction techniques that come close to this goal. As illustrated in Figure 4.1, an AUC—or Area Under (the receiving operating characteristic) Curve—value of .78, a not-uncommon AUC value for actuarial risk assessment instruments, can provide a cut-off score that produces a 30 per cent false positive rate and a 20 per cent false negative rate. Note also that failing to meet the higher proof standards merely means the government cannot *confine* the individual. There are often less restrictive ways of reducing risk that can limit the number of false negatives (see Slobogin and Fondacaro 2009) and that may even be mandated under the next principle to be discussed.

Disposition: The Least Drastic Risk-Reducing Intervention

Assume now that a person has committed the necessary predicate act and that the degree of risk necessary to justify some sort of state intervention has been shown. The next issue that arises is the type of disposition that the government may impose on the individual. Here again substantive due process plays a significant role. It is a constitutional axiom under American law that if the government deprives an individual of a fundamental right, such as liberty, it must do so in the least drastic manner necessary to achieve its aim (*Lawrence v Texas* 2003: 593). This principle is also clearly recognized in international law (see Patrick Keyzer's chapter in this volume; *Tillman v Australia* 2010: para. 7.4) and in the policies of various jurisdictions (see Alex Quinn and John Crichton's chapter in this volume).

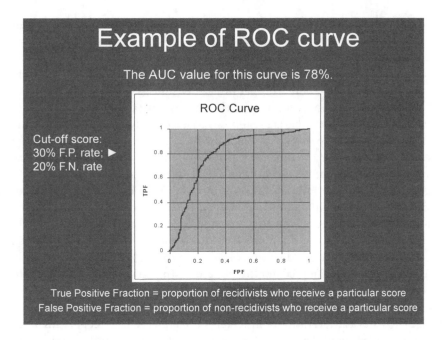

Figure 4.1 Sample receiving operating characteristic curve.

The government's goal in this setting is prevention of harm to others. Thus, in the dispositional context the least drastic means principle means that, even if risk sufficient to justify confinement has been proven, confinement may occur only if necessary to achieve prevention of harm, and may continue only if it remains necessary to achieve that aim. In *Jackson v Indiana*'s wording, confinement must bear a "reasonable relationship" to the government's need to protect society, or it is not permissible (1972: 738).

Jackson v Indiana's (1972) language, echoed in other United States Supreme Court decisions such as *Youngberg v Romeo* (1982) and *Seling v Young* (2001), has one other important implication for the dispositional consequences of a finding of risk. If available treatment will reduce the duration of the government's intervention and the individual is willing to undergo it, that treatment must be provided. As *Youngberg* put it, "liberty interests require the State to provide minimally adequate or reasonable training to ensure safety and *freedom from undue restraint*" (*Youngberg v Romeo* 1982: 319). Decisions from other countries and the United Nations Human Rights Committee appear to recognize the same principle (see Patrick Keyzer's chapter in this volume).

Thus, for instance, a person committed to a mental institution on dangerous-to-others grounds has a right to treatment with antipsychotic medication if medication would reduce the time in confinement and is medically appropriate. Similarly, a person committed as a sexually violent predator may not be confined if less restrictive options, including community registration and notification laws, ankle bracelets, or community treatment, can adequately protect society. Most dramatically, the least drastic means principle means that the death penalty can never be used as a method of prevention, even if the high degree of risk necessary to justify it is proven, because the option of confinement can achieve the government's goal equally effectively (Slobogin 2009).

Criminal Justice System Primacy: The Undeterrability Predicate

Preventive detention can take place within the criminal justice system or outside of it. Pre-trial detention, indeterminate sentencing, and capital sentencing are triggered by the commission of or conviction for a crime, and may occur only if a culpable mental state has been proven. In contrast, numerous other preventive detention regimes—quarantine, civil commitment, commitment of people found not guilty by reason of insanity, commitment of sexually violent offenders after they have served their sentence, and detention of enemy combatants—are, according to the United States Supreme Court, non-criminal in nature (*Kansas v Hendricks* 1997; *Boumediene v Bush* 2008). With the possible exception of the enemy combatant situation, the deprivation of liberty that occurs via these separate regimes is based entirely on an assessment of what the person will do, not what the person has done. Although, as noted earlier, the legality principle mandates a predicate act in these situations, that requirement exists solely as a side constraint on government power; it is not the *justification* for the intervention.

This distinction between criminal and non-criminal prevention is important because it triggers application of one more limitation on preventive detention, a limitation that might prohibit intervention even when the government can demonstrate the requisite risk and a readiness to implement the least drastic disposition necessary to contain it. The limitation comes from the United States. Supreme Court's holding in *Kansas v Hendricks* (1997), which dealt with the constitutionality of sexually violent predator (SVP) statutes. In that case, the petitioner argued that his SVP commitment after he had served his sentence for child molestation violated substantive due process, for the simple reason that he was not seriously mentally ill. Hendricks's lawyers pointed out that, historically, civil commitment had been reserved for people with psychosis and similar mental problems and that the SVP statute expanded this traditional role by permitting commitment of people with personality disorders. The Supreme Court refused to strike down the SVP law. But it did signal that dangerousness is insufficient, on its own, to justify preventive detention outside the criminal justice system. Without admitting it was doing so, the Court amended the SVP statute at issue in *Hendricks* by stating that the law required the government to show not only that the person is dangerous but also that he has great difficulty in controlling his behavior; as the Court put it, the person must be "dangerous beyond (his) control" (*Kansas v Hendricks* 1997: 357). In *Kansas v Crane* (2002: 415), the Court reiterated that holding, while also stating that there may be "considerable overlap" between difficulty in controlling behavior and "defective understanding or appreciation."

The Court has never provided a clear rationale for this lack of control or lack of appreciation limitation on preventive detention. But a rationale does exist, if one assumes that individuals who have difficulty controlling or appreciating the nature of their conduct are very hard to deter. On this assumption, the criminal justice system is powerless to protect society from these people and the government is justified in establishing a preventive regime for them separate from the criminal process. In other words, the state may resort to a system other than the criminal justice process to deal with behavior that is harmful to others when, and only when, the individual is characteristically unaffected by the prospect of serious criminal punishment—that is, when the person is truly "undeterrable" by the criminal sanction (Slobogin 2006: 129–41).

At least four categories of people might be considered eligible for detention in a non-criminal system on the ground that they are undeterrable by criminal sanctions. The first category consists of those offenders who are seriously mentally ill. People with psychosis who commit crimes often do not know they are doing so or think they are acting in self-defense. Fear of the criminal law can have no impact on their actions. On this view, a separate preventive detention system for insanity acquittees or a civil commitment system for people who suffer from psychosis is justifiable.

Second, some offenders with severe impulse control problems, although not as compromised as people with psychosis, might be said to be undeterrable at the time of their crime. As Justice Scalia stated in *Kansas v Crane* (2002: 420), if SVP laws make sense, it is because "ordinary recidivists choose to re-offend and are therefore amenable to deterrence through the criminal law," whereas "those subject to civil commitment under (SVP laws) … are unlikely to be deterred." However, the degree of undeterrability must be significant or this reasoning could easily end up justifying preventive intervention against ordinary recidivists as well. As the Minnesota Supreme Court held in *In re Blodgett* (1994: 913), sex offender commitment requires proof not only of risk but also of "an utter lack of power to control sexual impulses" (see also *Thomas v Missouri* 2002; *In re WZ* 2002).

The third category of individuals who might qualify for preventive intervention outside the criminal justice system is comprised of enemy combatants. Of course, these individuals are typically neither mentally ill nor severely compromised volitionally. But they are under orders to harm innocent citizens; their entire existence is devoted to killing others, upon pain of sanctions and perhaps death. For that reason many enemy combatants might also be considered undeterrable. In fact, in recent years most American judges who have addressed the issue of when a person fits this category have focused on "whether the individual functions or participates within or under the command structure of the organization, that is, whether he receives and executes orders or directions" (*Hamlily v Obama* 2009: 70–78). Those who do not meet this test may not be preventively detained, even if there is evidence that they have supported terrorist efforts. But those who do meet it may be detained until the "cessation of hostilities" or at least until government demonstrates that they do not pose a risk to innocent citizens. The United Kingdom and Australia appear to take a similar approach (see Bernadette McSherry's chapter in this volume).

The final category of individuals who could be said to be undeterrable consists of those who endanger others simply through the act of remaining free within the jurisdiction. Individuals with highly communicable diseases are illustrative. The harm to others presented by such people when they are in the public domain is literally unstoppable. Unlike the ordinary recidivist who can choose to avoid harm to others, contagious individuals usually have no control over when and whom they harm, unless they are confined.

Procedural and Evidentiary Limitations on Preventive Detention

Proof of Risk: Probability Estimates

Under the proportionality principle, the government is required to prove a high degree of risk in order to justify confinement. A very important question is how the government can meet its burden of proof in preventive detention cases. Traditionally, evidence of risk was clinical in nature. The best evidence of this sort relies on intensive interviews with the subject of the risk assessment and scrutiny of third-party records and witnesses, designed to discern patterns of antisocial behavior, the degree of impulsivity, typical responses to perceived slights, and the like. More recently, researchers have devised actuarial instruments that allow evaluators to place a given individual within a numerical risk category. For instance, the Violence Risk Appraisal Guide relies on 12 variables found to be predictive of risk (for example, degree of psychopathy, elementary school misconduct, *Diagnostic and Statistical Manual of Mental Disorders* (*DSM*) diagnosis; age at time of offence, history of alcohol abuse) in producing a score that can then be correlated with recidivism rates of people who received similar scores. Structured professional judgment (SPJ) approaches are less statistical in orientation, but can still produce individual scores, which in turn have been associated with statistical risk estimates (Slobogin 2007: 101–6).

In the United States, courts are still in a state of flux as to which type of risk assessment they prefer. The United States Supreme Court has made clear that, as a *constitutional* matter, the government may rely on even the most suspect type of prediction testimony in proving risk (*Barefoot v Estelle* 1983). However, the rules of evidence still govern matters of proof in a given jurisdiction. In *Daubert v Merrell Dow Pharmaceuticals Inc* (1993) and its progeny (see especially *Kumho Tire Company v Carmichael* 2000), the Supreme Court has construed the rules applicable in federal courts to prohibit expert testimony unless its basis has been subject to some sort of verification process, ideally including the generation of error rates that provide the fact finder with a sense of how much weight to give to the testimony. Further, even if expert testimony is sufficiently probative under the *Daubert* case, it is still inadmissible if it has the potential for prejudicing, biasing, or overinfluencing the jury—a consideration applicable to all evidence, expert and lay (Federal Rules of Evidence 2010: 401, 403). Although few courts have excluded expert prediction testimony under these rules, they are beginning to pay closer attention to the analysis.

In other work, I have argued that, under the balancing analysis required under the federal evidence rules (an analysis similar to that used in other countries with an adversarial tradition), government experts should be limited to statistically-based probability estimates of the type most commonly produced by actuarial instruments, unless the defense opens the door to use of clinical or SPJ risk assessment testimony (Slobogin 2007: 122–9). Actuarial prediction testimony is clearly superior to unstructured clinical prediction testimony, with respect to both the probative value and prejudice inquiries. First, research has firmly established that predictions based on the clinical method, while typically better than chance, are less valid than actuarial predictions by a significant magnitude (Janus and Prentky 2003). Second, clinical predictions are very hard to assess in terms of error rates, since the clinical method varies from evaluator to evaluator; in contrast, actuarial-based predictions provide standardized error rate information. Third, while actuarial prediction testimony identifies a quantified probability estimate that can be compared to the standards of proof described earlier, experts relying on clinical prediction can at most make general statements about risk, such as "the offender poses a higher than average risk" or "the respondent represents a low risk." These latter types of statements can mean very different things to different evaluators, and in any event are not susceptible to verification.

These considerations mean that actuarial evidence has much greater probative value than unstructured clinical prediction testimony. With respect to the prejudice inquiry, laboratory research and evidence from actual cases indicates that, despite its more questionable reliability, clinical prediction testimony presented by the government is extremely influential with judges and juries, much more so than actuarial prediction (Slobogin 2007: 122–4). Clinical testimony that a person is likely to be violent is difficult to rebut even with effective cross-examination and opposing witnesses (Diamond 1996: 52–53). The danger is great that fact finders attribute too much weight to this type of testimony precisely because it is so vague.

Unless associated with probability estimates, opinions derived from SPJ assessments suffer from the same evidentiary deficiencies that afflict unstructured clinical assessment. SPJ is apt to be more closely focused on relevant risk and protective factors than any other approach, and it is very useful in developing risk management plans once preventive detention or an indeterminate sentence is authorized (see Lorraine Johnstone's and Lindsay Thomson's chapters in this volume). But because it *only* generates information about risk management, it does not provide the court with an empirically-based assessment of an individual's degree of risk.

Only actuarial-based predictions provide the latter type of information. It may be true that, as later chapters in this book suggest (see chapters by David Cooke and Christine Michie, and Caroline Logan), data about groups cannot provide provably accurate information about individual risk levels. But that conceptual conundrum does not change the well-documented fact that actuarial prediction produces relatively low false positive and false negative rates and favorable AUC values of 0.7 to 0.8 (Mossman 2009: 132). Furthermore, even SPJ and clinical assessments are ultimately based on assumptions about individuals developed from study of or experience with other individuals, so those methods of assessment do not avoid the group-to-individual prediction problem. When the issue at hand is whether the state may deprive an individual of liberty, actuarial risk assessment provides the most probative and least prejudicial information.

Accordingly, in those cases where the government must prove risk, it should be required to rely on statistical probability estimates based on actuarial or structured professional judgment evaluation procedures, unless it can show that such estimates are not possible. The latter situation might arise for at least two reasons. First, actuarial instruments might not be properly validated; the Violence Risk Appraisal Guide (VRAG) was initially devised based on studies of predominantly white Canadians and thus, until it had been cross-validated on various other populations, was of limited use. Second, statistical estimates might be based on outcome variables that are of questionable worth in court. For instance, the researchers who developed the VRAG defined *violent recidivism* to include two simple assaults within a seven-year period (Rice et al. 2010: 102). This information is arguably irrelevant in both a death penalty proceeding (which ought to be focused on seriously violent recidivism) and a civil commitment proceeding (which ought to be focused on imminent harm). In these types of situations, judges might decide to exclude actuarial prediction testimony.

Even if relevant actuarial information is unavailable, however, government should not be permitted to use clinical prediction testimony in its place, given the reliability and prejudice problems noted earlier. Rather, the court should consider two options. The first option is simply to find that the state cannot prove its case with admissible evidence. The second is to permit the state to prove risk based on prior antisocial behavior of a type that is relevant to the proceeding. If a risk assessment must be made in the absence of statistical probability estimates, prior behavior provides the most probative, least prejudicial, and most helpful method of providing evidence of risk (Monahan 2006: 423).

Monahan goes so far as to argue that, in the criminal justice setting and perhaps in the SVP context as well (to the extent it is really criminal in nature), *only* past acts may be used in assessing risk. Although recognizing that the effect of this limitation would be to render most risk assessments modalities useless in these contexts, Monahan reasons that the criminal justice system is based on the premise that punishment is deserved only in response to choices offenders have made. Thus, he argues, risk assessments in the criminal system cannot be based on conditions such as diagnosis, or traits such as age or gender (Monahan 2006: 427–32). But as I have noted, "if the relevant law permits sentences to be based on dangerousness, it does not undermine the criminal justice system's 'premise of self-determination' (a premise that has already been honored at trial) to permit predictions based on immutable or quasi-immutable factors;" further, "as a practical matter, it is hardly protective of the individual's interests to make prediction a sentencing issue and then deny the fact finder the best means of making the prediction" (Slobogin 2007: 114).

Individualization: The Subject-First Rule

Assume now that the government has proven the requisite degree of risk with statistically-based probability estimates. Certainly the offender or respondent (henceforth called the "subject" of the preventive detention proceeding) can respond in kind. But the subject should also be able to respond with clinical prediction testimony, despite the more questionable probative value of that type of evidence. Predictions based on clinical assessment are still, on average, better than chance selection, and thus have some probative value (Mossman 1994: 789). Furthermore, actuarial-based probability estimates often do not capture all of the individual protective factors that might reduce risk, which clinical prediction testimony can provide. Most important, clinical prediction testimony presented by the defense does not have the potentially prejudicial impact that such testimony has when it is presented by the government. The defense position on risk at a sentencing or commitment hearing is that the subject will not repeat what the judge or jury has just decided the subject recently did. Under such circumstances, defense testimony about risk is not particularly likely to overinfluence the jury and should be admissible whether relying on actuarial, structured professional judgment, or unstructured clinical assessment.

Thus, the courts should adopt a "subject-first" rule with respect to clinical prediction evidence. Generally, this type of evidence should not be admissible. But if the subject wants to use such evidence in an effort to individualize the prediction, he or she should be allowed to do so. At that point, the prosecution should be able to respond in kind. This proposal is analogous to the familiar character evidence rule that prohibits, out of fear it will otherwise prejudice the fact finder, prosecution introduction of prior bad acts unless and until the defense "opens the door" by introducing evidence of good character (*Federal Rules of Evidence 2010*; r404(a)).

Procedures: Periodic Review and Due Process

In order to ensure that the proportionality and least drastic means principles are implemented properly, preventive regimes must routinely reconsider both the nature of the risk posed by individuals detained and whether their current disposition is necessary to achieve the government's goals (the latter an inquiry that includes an assessment of whether alternative treatment regimens would be more effective at reducing recidivism). *Hendricks* made clear that such periodic review is *required* for preventive regimes outside the criminal justice system (*Kansas v Hendricks* 1997: 363). This requirement should also be imposed on prevention decisions within the criminal process, for the same reasons. Decisions about pre-trial detention and indeterminate sentences both need to be revisited on a frequent basis to ensure adherence to the proportionality and least drastic means principles and to ascertain the effects of risk management.

As to the procedures that should apply in preventive detention and periodic review hearings, one central point about the applicable American law must be emphasized. Although the Sixth Amendment's guarantees of notice, counsel, confrontation rights and public jury decision-making do not attach in non-criminal proceedings such as commitment hearings (*Kansas v Hendricks* 1997), the Fourteenth and Fifth Amendments' stipulation that deprivations of life or liberty may not occur in the absence of due process of law do still apply. Depending on the circumstances, due process may impose some or all Sixth Amendment-type rights on noncriminal prevention proceedings. Given the technical nature of risk assessment, the criminal procedure right most vulnerable to being discarded in its entirety in such proceedings is the jury trial, but even that guarantee could be considered a key procedural protection in some circumstances (for example, SVP hearings). The overarching goal in constructing a procedural framework in the preventive context should be the same one that drives the Sixth Amendment: executive branch decisions should be subject to meaningful challenge and monitoring whenever they threaten liberty.

Conclusion

Preventive detention continues to be an extremely controversial exercise of state power. This chapter does not address those controversies. Rather it assumes that governments will continue to implement preventive goals through deprivations of life and liberty and describes how constitutional, evidentiary, and international legal principles limit the state's preventive efforts.

In summary, the government may restrict a person's liberty for the purpose of detention only under the following conditions. First, it must demonstrate that the person has been convicted of a crime or engaged in imminently risky conduct. Second, both before the initial intervention and periodically thereafter, the government must demonstrate, at proceedings consistent with procedural due process, that the intervention is both proportionate to the probability and magnitude of the risk (as proven by appropriately normed probability estimates) and the least drastic means of achieving the government's prevention goal. Finally, when the intervention occurs outside the criminal justice system, the government must prove that the person is very unlikely to be deterred by the prospect of serious criminal punishment.

II
Policy

5

Sexual Offender Commitment Laws in the USA

The Inevitable Failure of Misusing Civil
Commitment to Prevent Future Sex Crimes

JOHN Q. LA FOND

In the late 20th century the American public and policymakers abruptly decided that too many dangerous sex offenders were being released from the American criminal justice system after serving their prison sentences and, after their release, committing horrendous sex crimes against vulnerable victims, especially children (La Fond 2005; Scheingold et al. 1992). Spurred by tragic sex crimes and murders committed by these offenders and sensationalized by the media, the public demanded that these dangerous criminals be confined indefinitely to prevent them from sexually reoffending.

The United States Constitution, however, prevented the government from extending their prison terms (see Patrick Keyzer's chapter in this volume for a description of this issue in Australia) or from detaining them indefinitely solely because they might be dangerous (see Christopher Slobogin's chapter in this volume for a general discussion of this problem). The only available authority for incapacitating sex offenders for an indefinite period was the state's civil power to commit mentally ill persons for control and treatment (La Fond 1992b). In theory general civil commitment laws were available to commit sex offenders; in practice, however, they could not be used for most of these offenders and, even if available, they could not assure long-term confinement.

Civil Commitment Laws in the United States

General Civil Commitment Laws

Every state in the United States has a general civil commitment law that allows compulsory hospitalization for persons with medically recognized mental illness. They generally require proof of a serious mental disorder recognized by mental health professionals that causes the individual to be imminently dangerous to themselves or others. The government usually must prove that the person engaged in recent behavior manifesting his or her dangerousness. Commitment is for a short time period, subject to periodic renewal. There is a constitutional right to treatment, which requires the government to spend significant funds on institutions and personnel. Drug treatment is the most common form of therapy. This medical model of civil commitment has been used in the United States for over a century and is still available today (La Fond and Durham 1992).

However, policymakers decided that general commitment laws were not adequately protecting the community from dangerous sex offenders being released from prison. Most sex offenders did not suffer from a recognized mental illness nor did their recent behavior manifest imminent sexual dangerousness since most candidates for commitment were confined in secure prisons. Moreover, these laws emphasized short-term hospitalization for intensive treatment, provided generous judicial review of continued hospitalization, and encouraged timely release into the community.

Sexual Psychopath Laws

States had previously used their general civil commitment authority to pass specialized commitment laws, called sexual psychopath laws, for sex offenders. In 1937 the first sexual psychopath law was passed in the United States. By 1980 more than half of the states had a sexual psychopath law. These statutes generally required the government to prove the offender had committed a *recent* sex crime and suffered from a condition that made it very difficult to control his sexual behavior. Many sexual psychopath laws also required a determination that the individual would benefit from treatment. In addition, commitment for treatment was in lieu of punishment. After conviction, the government had to send the offender to prison for punishment or send him to a secure facility for treatment. Insight and talking therapy provided in groups was the primary mode of treatment (La Fond 2005: 131–3).

As noted in the Criminal Justice Mental Health Standards in 1989, these laws rested on several crucial assumptions:

> (1) there is a specific mental disability called sexual psychopathy ... (2) persons suffering from such a disability are more likely to commit serious crimes, especially sex offences than normal criminals; (3) such persons are easily identified by mental health professionals; (4) the dangerousness of these offenders can be predicted by mental health professionals; (5) treatment is available for the condition; and (6) large numbers of persons afflicted with the designated disabilities can be cured. (American Bar Association 1989: 457–8).

These assumptions were not validated by experience. By the mid-1980s virtually every state in the United States had repealed its sexual psychopath law or no longer used it. Policymakers had concluded that sex offenders were not mentally ill; they were simply bad people who chose to commit crimes. Lawmakers had also concluded that treatment for sex offenders did not reduce sexual recidivism. And, too often, some serious sex offenders committed as sexual psychopaths spent less time in custody than if they had been sent to prison. In many cases, they avoided punishment altogether (La Fond 1992b: 667–9). Consistent with the law and order ideology then sweeping the United States, punishment—not rehabilitation—was the appropriate social response. Henceforth, all sex offenders in the United States would be punished like any other criminal (La Fond 1992b: 670).

Modern Sex Offender Civil Commitment Laws in the United States

In 1990 Washington State was the first state to enact a unique sex offender commitment law to solve the problem of confining dangerous sex offenders about to be released from prison. It allowed the government to civilly commit sexually violent predators (SVPs) who had served their full prison term and were about to be released back into the community. Prosecutors had to prove the individual had committed a qualifying sex crime and suffered from a mental abnormality or personality disorder that makes them likely to commit another serious sex crime (Predators and Politics 1992). Subsequently, the United States Supreme Court has required the government to also prove that the individual suffers from a condition that makes it "difficult, if not impossible for the person to control their dangerous behavior" (*Kansas v Hendricks* 1997: 358). Commitment can only be sought *after* the individual has served his or her criminal sentence and is about to be released (or has actually been released) from prison. These laws, in effect, require the government to punish sex offenders *before* they can seek involuntary treatment. Since then at least 19 states as well as the federal government have passed similar laws.

Supporters argued that the law cannot be powerless to prevent the release of a clearly dangerous sex offender to commit a serious sex crime. And, the state's power to civilly commit sex offenders was a clearly established constitutional authority; it was, in fact, the only available legal strategy that could be used to confine sex offenders otherwise entitled to their liberty after serving their criminal sentences (Boerner 1992).

Powerful Criticisms of Sexually Violent Predator Laws

Unlike general commitment laws, these novel sex offender commitment laws do not rest on a medical model of illness, established diagnostic criteria or causal theories of conduct, proven treatment and sufficiently accurate predictions of dangerous behavior. Consequently, they are implausible, incoherent, and inconsistent. Not surprisingly, they overconfine and fail to treat or release most sex offenders subjected to these laws, thereby wasting scarce resources that could be used to prevent more sex crimes. (For other criticisms of SVP laws see the chapter by Eric Janus in this volume.)

Expansive Universe

Any individual convicted of a single qualifying sex crime presently confined in the criminal justice system (or the juvenile justice system in most states) is subject to commitment under these laws. Some states even allow commitment of sex offenders who have served their criminal sentence, have not committed another sex crime, and are living in the community. Thus, the universe of sex offenders potentially subject to commitment is vast.

Valid Medical Diagnosis not Required

Most sex offender commitment laws require proof that the individual suffers from a mental abnormality or personality disorder. Though there are a limited number of recognized mental disorders involving sexual deviance, including pedophilia, which could be applicable in some cases (American Psychiatric Association 2000: 571–6), these diagnoses are generally not used in most SVP cases. Instead, most experts use the statutory terms for their diagnoses.

There is no medically recognized definition of *mental abnormality*. Thus, each clinician must construct his or her own operational definition. There is, on the other hand, a recognized definition for *personality disorder*. However, the most commonly used one is anti-social personality disorder, which is based primarily on past antisocial behavior, especially committing crimes (American Psychiatric Association 2000: 701–6.) Consequently, the operational diagnostic terms allow for inevitable indeterminacy, clinician bias, and inconsistent application. To compound the epistemological confusion, the United States Supreme Court effectively determined that civil commitment did not require a definition of mental disease or disorder recognized by the medical profession. Rather, this definition is essentially a political decision *(Kansas v Hendricks* 1997; *Kansas v Crane* 2002).

Tautological Definitions

These laws require the government to prove that the individual suffers from a mental condition that causes significant volitional impairment that makes future sex offending likely. Past sex offending is the primary evidence used to establish each of these elements. Simply put, the very same evidence that qualified the offender for conviction and punishment in the first instance is also used to civilly commit him or her.

No Expertise on Volitional Impairment

Ironically, policymakers in the United States had previously concluded that mental health professionals simply did not possess sufficient expertise to determine whether any individual, even if mentally ill, could not control his or her behavior or simply chose not to do so. In 1982–83 the American Psychiatric Association and the American Bar Association recommended the elimination of the volitional prong of the American Law Institute insanity defense, on the ground that experts could not make this determination. At about the same time at least eight states and the federal government eliminated volitional impairment as an excusing condition in their insanity tests (La Fond and Durham 1992: 60–65). Yet, SVP laws assume that mental health experts had suddenly developed the ability to identify individuals who could not control their criminal behavior.

Convenient Onset of Mental Abnormality

Every sex offender subject to commitment as a SVP was previously convicted of a crime and held fully responsible for his sexual behavior. During the course of their incarceration the government cannot seek involuntary treatment under SVP laws for their dangerous sexual behavior based on an underlying condition. Only at the end of their imprisonment can their underlying mental condition and its resulting dangerousness be detected and involuntary treatment provided. In sum, these individuals are considered bad and then mad! Of course, all experts agree that treatment for sexual misbehavior is much more effective if it is not delayed for years or decades. Delay allows offenders to deny the severity of their crimes and to construct rationalizations that justify or excuse their conduct (Wettstein 1992).

Predictive Model Inaccurate

These laws also rely primarily on past historical data (essentially the individual's record of sex offending) to make an open-ended prediction that the individual is—at some future indeterminate time—likely to reoffend. (For a critique of how experts make predictions about dangerousness, see the chapter by David Cooke and Christine Michie in this volume.) More recent behavior that is indicative of safety is generally discounted because the individual is usually in prison. Nor is aging itself given much weight in the evaluation process. Virtually no consideration is given to whether the individual is likely to reoffend if subject to risk-appropriate supervision in the community when released from prison. Moreover, there is no valid or reliable research method (such as a double-blind study) politically viable to determine if the most dangerous sex offenders are, in fact, confined under SVP laws. In sum, these laws simply do not allow accurate identification of those relatively few sex offenders who are unable to control their sexual appetites and are truly dangerous.

Treatment Efficacy not yet Fully Established

Current treatment for sex offenders focuses primarily on cognitive-behavioral therapy that emphasizes relapse prevention. Treatments include redirecting sexual preference, cognitive restructuring, victim empathy, developing social competency, stress and anger management, and relapse prevention. Medical approaches include medication designed to reduce the production or uptake of testosterone, thereby diminishing the male sex drive, and, in rare cases, surgical castration. Drugs that modify compulsive behavior may also be used (La Fond 2005: 59–83).

These treatment approaches for sex offenders are promising, but their efficacy has not been firmly established. An international study published in 2002 found that current sex offender treatment significantly reduced sexual recidivism (from 17 to 10 per cent) and general recidivism (from 51 to 32 per cent). The study cautiously concluded: "the balance of available evidence suggests that current treatments reduce recidivism, but that firm conclusions await more and better research" (Hanson et al. 2002: 187). In sum, it is not clear whether treatment for sex offenders committed under these new laws holds realistic and sufficient promise for reducing sexual recidivism. Of course, treatment efficacy is even more problematic when imposed coercively, as it is for SVPs. If treatment proves ineffective, then it is very likely that most of these individuals will remain committed for as long as they live.

Costs of Implementing Sexually Violent Predator Laws

New Bureaucracies

States have had to create new bureaucracies to implement these laws. Personnel must review the records of sex offenders about to be released from prison to determine if they qualify for commitment and if their commitment should be sought. New software must be developed to assist in this process. As of 1 December 2009, California alone had reviewed 30,504 individual case records to determine if those sex offenders might qualify for commitment (California Department of Mental Health 2010).

Clinical Evaluations

Qualified clinicians must be hired either as permanent staff or retained on a case-by-case basis to evaluate those sex offenders for potential commitment, prepare written reports, and, if necessary, to testify at trial. These costs are significant.

California, for example, requires that two separate evaluators must conclude the individual is a SVP before commitment proceedings can be initiated. If the initial two evaluators disagree, a third evaluation must be conducted. In 1997–98 evaluators were paid $100 per hour for evaluations, report writing, testifying in court, and travel time. In addition, prisoners are often held beyond their end of sentence for evaluation, requiring additional incarceration costs. During that same time period California appropriated $7,221,000 to provide assessment by state employees, contract clinical staff, and temporary holds (La Fond 1998). As of 1 December 2009 California had evaluated 8,798 sex offenders. It found 1,725 positive evaluations and 7,073 negative evaluations (California Department of Mental Health 2010). California spent more than $24 million on clinical evaluations in 2007 (Piller and Romney 2008a). Evaluation costs, of course, are ongoing as the state continues to screen and commit sex offenders in its prison system.

Litigation Costs

SVP laws confer on defendants a right to a trial to determine if they satisfy the legal requirements for commitment. Either the prosecutor or the defendant can request a jury trial and prosecutors often do. Thus, juries must be assembled. Indigent defendants also have a right to a court-appointed attorney, as well as an independent expert to evaluate the offender and to assist at trial. Most individuals are indigent since they have been in prison prior to commitment. These trials often take several days or longer and consume significant resources. Defendants also have a right to appeal their commitment. Most SVP laws also allow for periodic review of the initial commitment, thereby often requiring additional trials, including additional evaluations by mental health professionals and, in many cases, jury trials. In 1997 Minnesota officials estimated the costs of conducting a SVP trial to be about $100,000 (La Fond 1998: 485).

A Constitutional Right to Treatment

The United States Constitution guarantees a right to treatment for individuals civilly committed for care and treatment. Courts have held that this right also protects individuals committed under these new statutes (*Turay v Weston* 1994). Generally speaking, the government must provide humane and therapeutic facilities, an adequate number of professionally qualified staff, and individual treatment plans for all committed individuals. It must also provide a transitional program, such as secure halfway houses, which allows sex offenders to be released safely into the community (La Fond 1998).

Facility Costs

As a result of this constitutional right to treatment, the state must provide separate facilities to house and treat SVPs. Because of their special condition, they cannot be placed either with prisoners who are not mentally ill or with the general civil commitment population for safety and other reasons. Thus, they cannot be put in prisons or in hospitals used to house and treat those committed under the general civil commitment law. SVP commitment includes juveniles and women. These groups must be housed and treated separately from other SVPs, increasing facility and treatment costs. Because SVPs are considered both sick and dangerous, the state must also ensure that these facilities are secure. Simply put, states must pay for both a prison and a hospital.

In many cases states have had to construct new stand-alone facilities at significant cost. California, for example, spent $388 million to build a new facility in Coalinga. This will allow commitment of up to 1,500 SVPs. Many states, including Florida, Minnesota, Nebraska, Virginia, and Wisconsin, are still adding SVP beds to their current facilities (Davey and Goodnough 2007).

Facing what may be the worst budget crisis in Kansas history, legislators balked at a 2009 request to build a 90-bed expansion to house SVPs at Larned, Kansas, that would cost $2.5 million to plan and $40 million to construct. Budget cuts had already been made in community mental health centers (Rothchild 2009).

Staff Costs

States must hire sufficient numbers of professionally qualified staff to treat SVPs confined in these special facilities. In many cases, staff shortages are experienced and this is underpinned by a number of reasons, including the limited supply of such professionals, the location of SVP facilities, and the nature of the treatment population.

Treatment Costs

States must provide state-of-the-art treatment programs for SVPs. This requires hiring and retaining staff to develop and provide programmatic treatment for all SVPs who choose to participate. Although the hours spent in treatment in SVP programs vary from state to state, on average offenders who did participate received less than 10 hours a week of treatment (Davey and Goodnough 2007). A survey in 2002 found that 12 per cent of SVPs suffered from serious psychiatric problems like schizophrenia and bipolar disorder. Appropriate psychiatric treatment, including medications, must also be provided to these individuals. Of course, many of these men cannot participate in SVP treatment because of their illnesses (Davey and Goodnough 2007).

It is not unusual for staff to fail many SVPs during a treatment phase, thereby requiring them to start over. Only 50 SVPs had been released completely from commitment in the United States as of March 2007 because clinicians or state-appointed experts considered them ready for release (Davey and Goodnough 2007). This abysmal lack of treatment progress and final release results in even more costs, a loss of trust in the staff, and a disinclination to participate or continue in treatment because there is little chance of being released.

Individual Treatment Plans

The right to treatment also requires staff to prepare individual treatment plans for each SVP. These plans set treatment goals and provide measurement of progress toward these goals. These plans require significant time and energy to prepare and to revise.

Geriatric Population

Because of the reluctance to release SVPs once committed, the inevitable trend is for this population to include many older individuals who suffer from illnesses typical of a geriatric population. More than 400 SVPs were 60 or older in 2007. The oldest SVP in Arizona was 68. The oldest in Florida was 87. In Wisconsin a 102-year-old SVP was unable to participate in treatment because of memory lapses and poor hearing. States must spend even more money on wheelchairs, walkers, high blood pressure, and senility (Davey and Goodnough 2007). Even though studies indicate a significant drop in sexual recidivism for this group, states are reluctant to release them. The cost of providing normal health care for all SVPs will increase as this institutional population continues to age and new members join their ranks.

Community Release Facilities

The right to treatment also includes a graduated release program that allows SVPs to move from a high-security facility to a less restrictive facility to assist in a safe transition back into the community. (Courts often call these placements in secure or unsecure community facilities least restrictive alternatives or LRAs for short.) Such a placement allows offenders to apply the strategies of relapse prevention that they have learned. It also permits the state to observe the offenders in a community setting and to make more realistic assessments of how much risk each individual poses to the community.

Most states have had to build new facilities or extensively renovate older facilities for this purpose. Usually these facilities must provide sufficient security to protect the community, while also allowing SVPs to obtain work and receive treatment. Not surprisingly, community security goals can be inconsistent with therapeutic goals, making placement of LRAs very difficult.

Most communities have vigorously resisted the locations of such LRAs. Some state legislatures have passed laws limiting where these facilities can be located. These efforts have delayed the development of LRAs (often for a very long time) and have frequently resulted in their being located far from jobs and therapists. After intense community resistance, Washington State spent $1.7 million converting a warehouse into an LRA facility. It is also expensive to operate. It has 26 monitoring cameras, a dozen workers, and other expensive security devices. As of 2007 only two men lived there (Davey and Goodnough 2007).

Without LRAs, many SVPs languish in secure (and usually more costly) SVP institutions or, in many cases, in county jails while they await the development of an LRA. California made 269 attempts to find housing for a 77-year-old SVP without success. In some cases California required SVPs conditionally released from the secure treatment center to live in trailers next to prisons. After numerous failed attempts to place Mr. Hendricks, a Kansas SVP, in a community placement, he was moved to a facility on the grounds of a state mental hospital. For all of these reasons LRA facilities are extremely costly to build and operate.

Commitment Rates Exceed Release Rates

Most states have committed far more sex offenders as SVPs than initially projected. Many policymakers believed that the due process protections (including a right to a lawyer, an independent expert to evaluate and testify, jury trial, and judicial review) would result in many individuals not being committed as SVPs. This assumption has not been borne out in practice. The government wins most cases it brings.

To compound matters, states are releasing far fewer SVPs than initially projected. As of 2007 about 250 SVPs had been released unconditionally nationwide. About half of these releases were based on legal or technical grounds unrelated to treatment (Davey and Goodnough 2007). Many SVPs do not participate in treatment and there is no way to force them to participate. As of March 2007 approximately 75 per cent of SVPs in California were not participating in treatment. In Minnesota only 40 per cent had participated in treatment in August 2003. Lawyers often advise sex offenders held pending trial not to participate in treatment, fearing their statements would be used at trial to commit them. Some committed SVPs do not trust the treatment providers; they assume that any information they disclose in treatment will be used to extend their confinement. Others see no point in participating since so few SVPs have been released. Staff members generally do not recommend transfer of SVPs who have not participated in treatment to a community release facility. Even when staff does recommend release of SVPs who have successfully progressed through the treatment program to a community facility or unconditional release, prosecutors often object and insist on a jury trial to determine if the offender should continue to be confined in a secure facility. And, as noted earlier, juries are reluctant to release convicted sex offenders back into the community, fearing they may commit another terrible sex crime.

The math is simple: Commitment rates are far higher and release rates are far lower than projected. As a result, state SVP populations have been swelling since these laws were first enacted. As of March 2007 approximately 2,700 sex offenders were being held indefinitely, either pending commitment proceedings or committed as SVPs. Since 1990, when Washington passed the first SVP law, almost 3,000 sex offenders have been committed. In 18 of the 19 states with such laws about 50 sex offenders have been finally released from commitment because clinicians considered them no longer to be SVPs. Another 115 offenders have been released because of court rulings, terminal illness, or old age. Only Arizona has had greater success releasing SVPs. As of March 2007 it had released 81 offenders. More SVPs, 189 as of March 2007, have been released into community facilities as part of an LRA placement (Davey and Goodnough 2007).

On average it costs more than $100,000 per year to confine and treat SVPs. This is about four times more than it costs to keep these offenders in prison. It costs the state of Kansas about $185,000 each year to confine Leroy Hendricks, the sex offender who spawned *Kansas v Hendricks* (1997). This amount is about eight times more than it would cost to keep him in prison. It is not surprising then that states spent almost $450 million on SVP programs as of 2007.

Costs of these commitment schemes are sure to increase as patient populations increase. Since 2003 the Minnesota budget for its SVP program has increased by almost 400 per cent, ballooning from $18.5 million annually to $71.6 million annually in just six years (Demko 2009). An audit of the Kansas SVP program concluded: "Unless Kansas is willing to accept a higher level of risk and release more sexual predators from the program, few options exist to curb the growth of this program" (Davey and Goodnough 2007).

Given the inevitable increase in SVP numbers, states can expect to spend even more money implementing SVP laws. This comes at a time when states are experiencing record deficits and, because states are required to have balanced budgets, are cutting funding for education, health care, and other vital public services (see also the chapter by John Petrila in this volume).

Implications for Mental Health Professionals

There are psychological costs to consider. Surely, many mental health professionals who work in SVP programs must feel discouraged. Often their jobs are moved to remote locations as some states build or locate SVP facilities in rural areas. This patient population is extremely varied with multiple mental and physical health issues and, increasingly, medical problems related to an aging population. The non-participation in treatment by so many SVPs cannot be encouraging for mental health professionals or contribute to a therapeutic culture. The absence of success—at least as measured by the release of SVPs into community facilities and eventual discharge— must be disheartening. And, the increasing scarcity of resources cannot be welcome. Mental health professionals working in other public health systems may see their resources reduced to pay for escalating SVP costs. This can create stress and frustration.

Current State Budget Deficits

Forty-eight states in the United States projected budget deficits for 2010. Only one state with a SVP law does not project a budget deficit—North Dakota. Wisconsin, another state with a SVP law, initially projected a \$3.2 billion deficit for 2010, but has taken steps designed to cover that shortfall (Center on Budget and Policy Priorities 2010b). State expenditures implementing SVP laws are not discretionary. Failure to provide adequate funding will result in lawsuits seeking to enforce the constitutional right to treatment. These suits often succeed in requiring states to spend more money on these programs (La Fond 1998). Thus, states with SVP laws are effectively subject to a constitutional mandate to provide increasing funding for these programs as the populations increase. This can mean decreased funding for other vital public services, such as education, health care, and infrastructure.

Alternative Strategies

Prediction Model

SVP laws use a prediction model of dangerousness and prevention. A decision is made at one moment in time, usually at trial, that a particular sex offender is very likely to commit another sex crime sometime in his or her lifetime if no additional steps are taken to prevent it. The only solution available under most SVP laws is total confinement for an indefinite period until the individual proves he or she is safe to be released into an LRA.

Most other sex offenders are released into the community from prison subject only to a duty to register their current residential address and other personal information with the police. In many states this information is made available to the public. The police may actively disseminate the information or the public may have to seek it out. Though registration and notification laws can create much anxiety in the community, no valid research has shown they prevent sex crimes. Thus, a relatively small number of sex offenders are confined as dangerous for many years after they serve their prison sentences, whereas most sex offenders are released without significant control in the community (La Fond 2005: 85–125).

Building more high-cost secure and therapeutic facilities both for confinement and for community transition and release, staffing them with adequate numbers of qualified mental health professionals, and preparing and implementing individual treatment plans is not a realistic or cost-effective strategy for preventing sex crimes.

Risk Management

A more effective strategy for reducing sexual recidivism is available: risk management. Under this model, risk is assessed periodically and control measures appropriate to the measured risk are implemented to prevent harm (see the chapter by Caroline Logan in this volume). Applied to sex offenders, this means that an initial risk assessment for each individual about to be released from prison, using state-of-the-art actuarial instruments and other techniques, including polygraph testing (which, admittedly, has its critics), is conducted. This will provide a more realistic estimation of how likely the person is to commit another sex crime and also provide more information about what pattern of behavior leads to his or her criminal conduct. Control measures tailored to the level of the offender's risk and his or her pattern of offending can then be imposed as a condition of his or her release from prison. For example, the offender may be required to not consume alcohol and drugs, avoid being alone with children, and participate in treatment. Specially trained parole officers can monitor the offender's compliance with these conditions.

Periodically, new assessments of risk can be made. This could include polygraph testing, as well as reports from parole officers and treatment providers. This allows the level of risk to be redetermined and the level of control to be increased or decreased in light of this new and current information. If the offender has complied with the conditions of release, made appropriate progress in treatment, and no longer manifests the types of behavior that led to his or her sex offending in the past, then control measures can be reduced. If, on the other hand, the level of risk has increased, the level of control can be increased. He or she might be required to live in a halfway house and to use GPS technology showing their real-time location. If necessary, the person can be incarcerated. Colorado relies on this type of strategy and calls it community containment (English et al. 2003).

Scholars have also proposed specialized courts, called sex offender reentry courts, to manage the risk posed by releasing sex offenders back into the community. These special courts that try, sentence, and release sex offenders can harness the power of therapeutic justice (Wexler and Winick 1991) with risk management to start the process of cognitive restructuring essential to reducing sexual recidivism even earlier. Under this legal regime, specially trained judges would preside over trials of sex offenders. Pre-trial treatment would be encouraged and plea bargaining available as a means of setting treatment goals and encouraging treatment participation for the offender. If successful, sex offenders would spend less time in prison and be released safely into the community (La Fond and Winick 2003).

Preventing More Sex Crimes: More Prevention for More Sex Offenders

There are, of course, other risk management approaches that can also be used to prevent sexual recidivism. Because it costs far less than SVP commitment, society's limited resources can be applied more effectively through risk-management strategies to a larger number of sex offenders. This, in turn, should reduce sexual recidivism more than SVP laws do. (For further discussion of the risk management approach for offenders in the community see the chapters by Alex Quinn and John Crichton; Jennifer Skeem, Jillian Peterson, and Eric Silver; and Lorraine Johnstone in this volume).

Mismatch of Models to Reality

SVP laws deliberately misuse the state's civil commitment authority to warehouse sex offenders for as long as possible. Most sex offenders do not suffer from a recognized mental disorder. What causes sex offending is still not known. More likely than not, there are a number of causes. Treatment shows some promise—at least for voluntary patients—but the jury is still out. In any event, many states are simply not providing the resources necessary for effective treatment. Experts are better at predicting dangerousness than they are at predicting safety because predictions of the former are based primarily on fixed, historical factors that do not change; whereas predictions of the latter are based primarily on current, dynamic factors that can change. Thus, it is far easier to commit sex offenders initially as SVPs than it is to release them (La Fond 2005).

But Do SVP Laws Work?

We know that more than 3,000 men, women, and juveniles are being confined in expensive facilities for an indefinite period. We do not know if these are the most dangerous offenders among those eligible for civil commitment. We do not know how many sex crimes they would have committed if released at the end of their prison term or how many crimes they would have committed if they had been subjected to appropriate community supervision and treatment. We do know that there is no end in sight to the exploding costs associated with SVP laws and that states, now in dire financial situations, will have to spend money on these laws rather than on other more critical needs.

In short, the critiques that lead to abandoning sexual psychopath laws in the United States in the 1980s still apply with equal force to SVP laws. The future is clear: far more sex offenders will be warehoused at exorbitant cost in ever-expanding facilities, growing older and requiring more medical treatment every year.

A Better Approach

It is generally agreed that society has a moral obligation to prevent as many sex crimes as possible with the limited resources available. Risk management fits the problem of sexual recidivism much better than civil commitment. It costs less, can be applied to many more sex offenders, and ensures appropriate level of control and treatment in the community. It will prevent more sex crimes and protect more victims. Predictably, the American SVP experiment has been an abysmal and costly failure. Other countries should learn from our terrible mistakes.

6

Sexually Violent Predator Laws

Going Back to a Time Better Forgotten

JOHN PETRILA

In Miami, a causeway in the middle of Biscayne Bay has become home to one of the country's least desirable populations: sex offenders ... What was once a collection of tents has become a small village ... Right now, 67 people live here. And nearly every week, probation officers drop off sex offenders, recently released, who have nowhere else to go ... [State Senator] Aronberg says the [residency restriction] laws as currently written make little sense. He asks, "How is it that an army of homeless sex offenders who are roaming our streets [makes] us safe?"

—**Greg Allen,**
"Sex Offenders Forced to Live Under Miami Bridge,"
National Public Radio, 20 May 2009

While we have upheld state civil commitment statutes that aim both to incapacitate and to treat ... we have never held that the Constitution prevents a State from civilly detaining those for whom no treatment is available, but who nevertheless pose a danger to others. A State could hardly be seen as furthering a "punitive" purpose by involuntarily confining persons afflicted with an untreatable, highly contagious disease. Similarly, *it would be of little value to require treatment as a precondition for civil confinement of the dangerously insane when no acceptable treatment existed.* To conclude otherwise would obligate a State to release certain confined individuals who were both mentally ill and dangerous simply because they could not be successfully treated for their afflictions.

—**Kansas v Hendricks (1997),**
p. 366; emphasis added

There are more than 700,000 registered sex offenders in the United States (National Center for Missing and Exploited Children 2010). More than 3,000 individuals are confined indefinitely to institutions, usually after the expiration of a prison sentence, under sexually violent predator (SVP) statutes (Davey and Goodnough 2007). Approximately 20 states have a version of an SVP statute, as does the federal government. These populations are likely to continue growing.

Registration laws and indefinite confinement are not restricted to the United States, although as is the case with incarceration and various forms of community control, the United States has higher rates of use. (For a comparison of United States and Canadian sex offender laws, see Petrunik, Murphy, and Federoff 2008; for a comparison of Germany and United States laws, see Hammel 2006; for a comparison of Scotland, United States, and Australian laws, see McSherry and Keyzer 2009).

SVP and registration laws have been adopted because of concerns regarding public safety. The laws raise questions over the application of important constitutional principles, including bans on ex post facto punishment and double jeopardy. However, both federal and state courts have rejected constitutional challenges to SVP laws, asserting that the statutes are not punitive in nature, that they serve an important goal in incapacitating dangerous individuals, and that the states have broad authority in writing and implementing such laws. There have been some restrictions placed on legislative authority. For example, the United States Supreme Court has ruled that the federal Sex Offender Registration and Notification Act, which mandates that sex offenders register with state and national databases, cannot be applied to individuals convicted before enactment of the statute (*Carr v United States* 2010). However, at the same time, the Court ruled that Congress had the authority to create a civil commitment law that resulted in the indefinite confinement of sex offenders (*United States v Comstock* 2010). In addition, a recent decision by the Georgia Supreme Court (*Rainer v Georgia* 2010) held that individuals could be required to register as sex offenders even if their offence did not have a sexual component.

These decisions leave little doubt about the basic constitutionality of SVP laws. They also appear to provide broad legislative authority to detain people indefinitely who meet statutory criteria, at least for the purpose of incapacitation, if not for retribution or deterrence. The institutions that have been created for these individuals are often run by the state mental health agency, rather than the correctional department, despite the fact that these institutions are designed for long-term preventive confinement. In addition, the institutions are expensive; for example, Virginia spends $140,000 per year to confine a sexual offender, six times the annual cost of incarcerating a prisoner (Geissenhainer 2008). However, despite their expense, no state that has adopted one of the current generations of SVP laws has moved to repeal it and it is difficult to imagine, even in times of severe economic strain, that any politician would risk a career by advocating repeal of such a statute or closure of an institution confining sexual offenders (Janus 2004).

What then are we to make of SVP statutes? They can be criticized on many grounds: they are a form of preventive detention that can lead to the erosion of liberty guarantees for all (La Fond 2008; also see the chapters by Christopher Slobogin, Eric Janus, and John La Fond in this volume); they undermine the ethical integrity of the justice system by blurring the line between the criminal and civil law (Cantone 2009; see also Pfaffenroth 2003); and they violate notions of substantive due process because they are punitive in character though characterized as a form of civil commitment (Janus and Logan 2003). Some have argued that SVP laws are best understood in the context of a pendulum effect in mental health law that swings between civil liberty concerns and public protection (Brakel and Cavenaugh 2000). However, judicial disinterest in civil liberties claims made by SVP committees is particularly troubling given the larger context of debates over preventive detainment as a tool in combating terrorism (see the chapter by Bernadette McSherry in this volume).

SVP laws have another important effect that has been commented on less frequently. As written and as applied, these statutes are fundamentally at odds with the direction taken by the United States public mental health system over the last three decades. This is the focus of the rest of this chapter.

The Evolution of Public Mental Health and the Destructive Nature of SVP Laws

The public mental health system in the United States has four distinguishing characteristics relevant here. First, civil commitment laws today focus on serious mental illnesses for which potential treatment exists. Second, in large part as a response to consumer advocacy, it is assumed that people with mental illnesses, with appropriate treatment, can recover from their illnesses. Third, the use of state hospital care has been minimized, there have been significant efforts to improve conditions in the state institutions that remain, and hospitalization, whether in state or community hospitals, is typically of short duration. Finally, while the financial bases potentially available for mental health treatment have expanded, investment in mental health services has not kept pace with health care spending generally, and in fact in some states has lessened over the years. SVP laws fly in the face of the first three developments and threaten to significantly exacerbate the last.

Civil Commitment and Mental Illness

Lawyers challenged civil commitment laws in the 1960s and 1970s because they permitted indefinite, involuntary confinement based on a person's mental illness with little else required (Melton et al. 2007). As a result of federal lawsuits based on constitutional law principles, state civil commitment laws were significantly revised, to incorporate new requirements that the person be dangerous as well as mentally ill. This litigation was anchored in assumptions that the diagnosis of mental illness was idiosyncratic at best. Some argued that mental illness was a social construct designed to segregate the undesirable (Szasz 1961) and even for those who granted the existence of mental illness, there were fundamental validity and reliability issues with diagnosis (see Kirk and Kutchins 1994).

While arguments regarding diagnostic nomenclature and the processes by which it is revised continue (for example, see Francis 2009), state legislatures over the years have refined statutory definitions of mental illness to make them more precise. In doing so, many legislatures have excluded specific diagnostic categories as a predicate for involuntary civil commitment. For example, Florida civil commitment law defines mental illness as

> an impairment of the mental or emotional processes that exercise conscious control of one's actions or of the ability to perceive or understand reality, which impairment substantially interferes with a person's ability to meet the ordinary demands of living, regardless of etiology. For the purposes of this part, *the term does not include retardation or developmental disability …, intoxication, or conditions manifested only by antisocial behavior or substance abuse impairment.* (Florida Mental Health Act, sec. 394.455 (18); emphasis added)

The Alabama definition has similar exclusions for substance use and developmental disabilities; "mental illness" is

> a psychiatric disorder of thought and/or mood which significantly impairs judgment, behavior, capacity to recognize reality, or ability to cope with the ordinary demands of life. Mental illness, as used herein, specifically *excludes the primary diagnosis of epilepsy, mental retardation, substance abuse, including alcoholism, or a developmental disability.* (Code of Alabama, sec. 22-52-1.1; emphasis added)

These legislative efforts are designed to more closely align civil commitment law with diagnostic nomenclature so that civil commitment will be used only for those with an identifiable mental illness. The exclusions are important, not only because they limit the reach of civil commitment laws but because they impose limits on the treatment responsibilities of the mental health system. Many states, like Florida, have excluded psychopathy and antisocial personality disorder from the mental disorders that can lead to civil commitment, in part based on the assumption that difficulties in providing adequate treatment should preclude hospital admission (Appelbaum 2005). Legislative proposals to open up involuntary hospitalization to people with personality disorders, for example, in the United Kingdom, have been opposed in part because they would permit hospitalization for individuals many believe cannot be treated with current treatment modalities (Appelbaum 2005). In many jurisdictions, the mission of the public mental health system has been increasingly defined as first serving those with serious mental illnesses; definitions of mental illness used in state civil commitment laws at least to some degree reflect that mission, both by what they include and what they exclude.

As has been discussed extensively elsewhere, SVP laws detach the law from professional notions of mental illness. Rather, in using terms such as *mental abnormality*, defined in terms such as a "congenital or acquired condition affecting the emotional or volitional capacity which predisposes the person to commit sexually violent offences" (*Kansas Statutes*, sec. 59-2902(b)), legislatures have significantly broadened the actual and potential reach of civil commitment statutes. The United States Supreme Court has endorsed this, with Justice Thomas noting in *Kansas v Hendricks* (1997: para. 359) that

> Indeed, we have never required State legislatures to adopt any particular nomenclature in drafting civil commitment statutes. Rather, we have traditionally left to legislators the task of defining terms of a medical nature that have legal significance… As a consequence, the States have, over the years, developed numerous specialized terms to define mental health concepts. Often, those definitions do not fit precisely with the definitions employed by the medical community. The legal definitions of "insanity" and "competency," for example, vary substantially from their psychiatric counterparts.

Justice Thomas is correct of course, when he notes that definitions of insanity and competency are not always congruent with psychiatric definitions. It would also be problematic to insist that legal definitions must be internally consistent with psychiatric definitions, given continuing disputes over diagnostic reliability and validity and given that whether a person meets legal criteria is more than simply a clinical judgment. However, in practice, legal decision-making is rooted in psychiatric definitions of illness. For example, few defendants are found incompetent to stand trial or not guilty by reason of insanity absent an underlying diagnosis or history of a psychotic disorder (Cooper and Zapf 2003), and in states like Florida, which has an SVP law, the statutory definition of mental illness governing treatment of individuals found incompetent or legally insane is the same used in the civil commitment law (Florida Statutes, 916.106(13)); only the SVP provisions substitute the term *mental abnormality* (Florida Statutes, 394.912(5)) for *mental illness.*

By resorting to ill-defined terminology as a predicate for the civil commitment of sex offenders, state legislators have eroded a decades' old trend of attempting to mold more precise, clinically informed definitions of mental illness. In doing so, legislatures have also effectively expanded the mission of public mental health agencies charged with the administration of SVP programs to include the care of those assumed (whether correctly or incorrectly) to be untreatable.

SVP Laws as Written and Applied Are at Odds with the Philosophy of Recovery That Guides Public Mental Health Systems Today

One of the most significant developments in mental health treatment and policy in the last two decades has been the emergence of recovery as an achievable treatment goal. Michael Hogan, who chaired the President's New Freedom Commission on Mental Health in the United States, described recovery in this way:

> Although recovery is often thought of as an end state of complete wellness and freedom from illness, a more universal idea of recovery emerged from testimony and input from individuals with mental illness, who tended to describe recovery as a process of positive adaptation to illness and disability, linked strongly to self-awareness and a sense of empowerment. (Hogan 2003: 1469)

The United States Surgeon General, in a 1999 report, wrote:

> Recovery is variously called a process, an outlook, a vision, a guiding principle. There is neither a single agreed-upon definition of recovery nor a single way to measure it. But the overarching message is that hope and restoration of a meaningful life are possible, despite

serious mental illness [references omitted]. Instead of focusing primarily on symptom relief, as the medical model dictates, recovery casts a much wider spotlight on restoration of self-esteem and identity and on attaining meaningful roles in society. (p. 97)

Recovery as a treatment goal and as an organizing principle for policymakers is not a United States specific phenomenon. One can find discussions of the impact of recovery in many places, for example, Canada (Piat et al. 2010), the Slovak Republic (Hyun et al. 2008), Norway (Borg and Kristiansen 2004), the United Kingdom and Australia (Ramon et al. 2007), and for European members of the World Health Organization (World Health Organization Europe 2005).

The embrace of recovery rests in part on the optimism and sense of possibility it brings to treatment of the most serious mental illnesses. Recovery moves far beyond the stigmatizing view that symptom reduction is the most realistic treatment goal. Contrast that with the Kansas legislature's description of the treatability of sex offenders:

The legislature finds that a small but extremely dangerous group of sexually violent predators exist who *do not have a mental disease or defect that renders them appropriate for involuntary treatment* pursuant to the treatment act for mentally ill persons ... which is intended to provide short-term treatment to individuals with serious mental disorders and then return them to the community. In contrast to persons appropriate for civil commitment ... sexually violent predators generally have antisocial personality features which are *unamenable to existing mental illness treatment modalities* and those features render them likely to engage in sexually violent behavior. The legislature further finds that sexually violent predators' likelihood of engaging in repeat acts of predatory sexual violence is high ... therefore a civil commitment procedure *for the long-term care and treatment of the sexually violent predator* is found to be necessary by the legislature. (*Kansas Statutes*, 59-29a01; emphasis added)

Other state SVP statutes use identical or similar language. The legislative message is unmistakable: people meeting SVP criteria are not treatable, regardless of rhetorical commitments to providing treatment. SVP statutes typically promise that treatment will be provided in anticipation of legal challenges asserting that the statutes, while designated civil rather than criminal, are retributive in nature. Justice Thomas, writing for the majority in *Kansas v Hendricks* (1997: 366), seemed satisfied that a legislative nod in the direction of treatment satisfied state obligations not to use civil commitment for retribution or deterrence: "we have never held that the Constitution prevents a State from civilly detaining those for whom no treatment is available, but who nevertheless pose a danger to others." Nonetheless, despite legislative assumptions regarding untreatability, offenders will be committed indefinitely for long-term care and treatment.

The point here is not whether people committed as sexually violent predators are treatable by existing treatment modalities or not. There are a number of reviews of the efficacy of sex offender treatment and reviews of the methods used in studies (for example, see Grossman et al. 1999; Hanson et al. 2002; Harkins and Beech 2006). (For a review of treatment issues generally, including advances in treating correctional populations, see the chapter by Jennifer Skeem in this volume.) The evidence is mixed, and it is difficult to find a definitive answer to the question of treatability because people committed under SVP statutes are seldom if ever discharged from custody. There is also little consensus over recidivism rates among sex offenders (see Cantone 2009).

The general conclusion that may be drawn from these reviews is that there is some evidence that in the right conditions some types of treatment might have positive effects but that the impact on long-term risk is very difficult to measure for people committed as SVPs because discharge other than through death is such a rare event.

It is also true that civil commitment rests on the state's police power as well as its parens patriae power. While civil commitment laws have become more "medicalized" at least in the United States in recent years, the thank you theory proffered by Alan Stone (1975) and Loren Roth (1979), which argued that civil commitment should be used only if treatment was available for the person's illness, has never been adopted, in part because of its perceived paternalism and in part from a desire to retain police power commitments.

Granting uncertainty about the effectiveness of sex offender treatment, and granting the state's long-standing authority to commit people in the interest of public safety, legislative assumptions that a class of people is simply not treatable is a profoundly pessimistic conclusion that runs counter to the general optimism that characterizes mental health treatment today. This is not the only area where legislative and judicial assumptions of non-treatability, often fueled by clinical opinion, prevail. The ongoing debate over whether treatment can make a difference with people who meet various measures for psychopathy is another example where individuals are confined for long periods of time for the protection of the public, based on assumptions that psychopaths can't be treated (see Skeem et al. 2009). If only people in a narrowly homogeneous group were committed under SVP statutes, and if the scientific evidence proved that all treatment was useless in changing behavior, then characterizing that group as untreatable might be justifiable. However, given the heterogeneous nature of SVP populations, differences in the risk of recidivism, and differences in responsiveness to treatment among groups of sex offenders in other settings, the legislative characterization and the policies that result from it are unwarranted. They also put public mental health systems in the position of holding people simply for incapacitation, something that strikes at the heart of the core tenet of recovery.

The Return of the State Psychiatric Warehouse

SVP legislation is disingenuous at best, cynical at worst, in promising treatment on the one hand while labeling the subjects of the legislation untreatable. The result in some states has been the incipient return of the state psychiatric warehouse, a development that vaults public mental health policy backward at least 30 years in time.

Much mental health law developed in response to conditions in state psychiatric institutions. Those institutions were often little more than warehouses, grossly overcrowded, understaffed, and unsafe. Many were located far from major population centers, which exacerbated difficulties in staffing them in the best of times. Many state institutions, including psychiatric hospitals, facilities for people with developmental disabilities and prisons, ended up under the continuing jurisdiction of federal courts, mandated to conform to far-reaching judicial decrees regarding the most basic conditions.

One of the contributing factors in the deinstitutionalization of state hospitals was the expense of complying with these judicial orders. The decline in census has been dramatic, and the population in many state hospitals today is largely forensic in composition. While many state institutions have continuing problems, state hospitals today tend to be far less overcrowded, better staffed, and committed to active treatment while minimizing the use of restraint and seclusion. In addition, treatment in one's community has become a central tenet of mental health treatment in the publicly funded system; segregation in large, remotely located institutions is viewed today as one of the cardinal failings of the state hospital-dominated mental health systems of the 1950s–1980s.

State facilities for people committed under SVP statutes are throwbacks to an era of state psychiatric institutional care that state public mental health systems have spent decades trying to put to rest. The mission of SVP institutions is unclear, torn between correctional and treatment goals with incapacitation the clear legislative and public expectation. In testifying before a

Florida legislative committee about the many problems at Florida's SVP facility, a vice president for the company then administering the program said

> There's a little bit of confusion … What is this place? Is it a prison? Is it a mental health center? A residential treatment facility where people are clients? What is it? We ask that question sometimes too. We really don't have a lot of guidance around what it is the state wants the facility to be, and we would encourage the state to look at that. (Goodnough and Davey 2007: 3)

A mental health counselor described the facility more succinctly, characterizing it as "like walking into a war zone … The residents in that place ran the whole facility" (Goodnough and Davey 2007). Other observers wrote "most of the centers tend to look and feel like prisons, with clanking double doors, guard stations, fluorescent lighting, cinder-block walls, overcrowded conditions and tall fences with razor wire around the perimeters" (Davey and Goodnough 2007).

One might argue that the lack of clarity regarding mission is only apparent, that the real mission, as John La Fond (2008: 169) asserts elsewhere, is "preventive detention masquerading as involuntary treatment." However, even assuming the good faith of treatment staff, other basic issues compromise efforts to ensure a therapeutic emphasis. A majority of residents simply refuse treatment. In Florida, for example, only 17 per cent of 283 detainees (those awaiting the outcome of the civil trial that would determine whether they met the Florida SVP statutory criteria) were participating in treatment, while 46 per cent of the 322 committed as SVPs after hearing were in treatment (Florida Office of Program Policy Analysis and Government Accountability 2008). Similar rates of nonparticipation have been noted in other states as well (La Fond 2008). A major incentive to participate in treatment does not exist, because few people are released, and for many, indefinite confinement may become lifelong confinement (Davey and Goodnough 2007).

It is not surprising in such settings that staff issues arise as well. Recruiting and retaining qualified treatment and security staff is a significant issue, in part because like many state hospitals, SVP facilities may be located in remote locations and in part because of pay and quality of work environment issues (Gold and Romney 2007). As a result of these difficulties in hiring qualified staff, employees themselves may cause major problems. In Florida, a 2005 account of a raid on Florida's treatment center for sex offenders by nearly 400 law enforcement officers described conditions in this way:

> Though the raid exposed a number of issues, the five year old commitment center has been beset by management problems almost from its inception. They include: female staff having sex with residents, rampant alcohol and drug use with the staff's knowledge, racism, nepotism, sexual harassment, unchecked violence between residents, falsified reports and convicted criminals on staff. (Pinkham 2005: 1)

It is difficult enough to maintain staff morale in the best run psychiatric facilities. In facilities in which most people refuse to participate in treatment, the success of treatment modalities for those who do participate is unclear, and where even those who participate in treatment may never be released, the impact on staff morale, recruitment, and retention is likely to multiply over time.

Right to treatment litigation ultimately had an impact on census, conditions, and staffing in large psychiatric institutions. Could the same happen with facilities housing SVP detainees and committees? It is not impossible: commentators have argued, with varying degrees of persuasiveness, that individuals held under SVP statutes have a right to institutional (Janus and Logan 2003; Smith 2008) and community treatment (Cornwell 2004) and there have been interesting discussions on managing the risk and treatment of offenders in community settings

(Harris 2006; La Fond and Winick 2004). Indeed, in 1994, in *Turay v Seling* (2000) a federal jury found that the Washington State facility violated constitutional norms in a number of ways, and a federal judge later entered sweeping injunctive relief against the state. However, while the litigation resulted in some improvements, a series of status hearings over the years found that the state continued to violate significant portions of the decree. Despite continuing violations, a judge subsequently assigned to the case after 15 years vacated the decree, stating "this case has been troublesome to the Court in that there seems to be no right answer, and no good fix for the situation" faced by residents at the state facility (Smith 2008: 1388–9).

One can read the *Turay* litigation optimistically, for the proposition that the federal judiciary's interest in remediating unconstitutional conditions for even the most undesirable of populations retains some life. Or one can read it more pessimistically, and probably more correctly, as an aberrant case in a judicial environment where early federal court activism in addressing right-to-treatment claims against state hospitals has been long dampened by a United States Supreme Court intent on remaking federal–state relationships and restricting the role of the federal judiciary.

In the end, the courts may circumscribe the growth of SVP facilities, not through right to treatment litigation, but because of judicial caution regarding the ultimate intrusion of the state's civil power in situations where criminal law is more properly applied. Justice Kennedy expressed this concern in *Kansas v Hendricks* (1997). In voting to uphold the constitutionality of the Kansas SVP law, he wrote a concurring opinion in which he noted that the Kansas statute as implemented could cross constitutional lines if "civil confinement were to become a mechanism for retribution or general deterrence, or if it were shown that mental abnormality is too imprecise a category to offer a solid basis for concluding that civil detention is justified" (*Kansas v Hendricks* 1997: 373).

Regardless of the ultimate outcome of judicial challenges, SVP facilities today, in their characteristics, if not their size, have taken on the trappings of old-style state hospitals. In this respect, SVP facilities, like SVP laws, hearken to a time most United States public mental health policymakers would prefer to leave in the past.

The Escalating Costs of SVP Facilities Compound the Problem of Insufficient Public Investment in Mental Health Treatment

SVP facilities are expensive to build and to operate. In 2007, an examination of SVP programs in the United States reported that states had spent nearly $450 million on such programs in that year (Davey and Goodnough 2007). A number of states have built or anticipate building new facilities for populations that have grown much faster than anticipated. The growth is not surprising. If a facility cannot release anyone and lengths of stay become years, one can either shut the facility front door (not politically possible, at least today, in states with SVP legislation) or add additional beds. Other issues also contribute to the "bed blocking;" a Florida review found that 303 individuals who had been detained pending the outcome of their civil commitment hearing were released without being committed. Their average length of stay as detainees was 760 days at an average cost of over $80,000 (Florida Office of Program Policy Analysis and Government Accountability 2008: 3). In addition, more than one-third of the nearly 13,000 individuals referred for evaluations under the SVP legislation in the five years prior to the review were referred after expiration of sentences of less than 545 days. In other words, it was not unusual for a detainee waiting the outcome of a commitment hearing to be confined in the Florida SVP facility longer than he had been confined in prison after sentencing.

While legislatures invest in SVP programs that are likely to continue to grow in size, investments in public mental health care are eroding. State governments have a number of core obligations. Some are non-discretionary. Medicaid, a mixed federal–state funded program to provide health care services for people meeting its disability and income criteria, is largely non-discretionary because of federal rules and constitutes approximately 21 per cent of spending by state governments in the United States (Marton and Wildasin 2007). Approximately one-quarter of state spending goes to education, with another 5 per cent historically going to adult and juvenile corrections; however, correctional spending in some large states such as California and Florida is now closer to 10 per cent, outstripping spending on state university systems (Center on Budget and Policy Priorities 2010a).

Sources of payment for mental health services in the United States are varied and diffuse. For many years, state governments bore the bulk of financial responsibility for the care of people with serious mental illnesses, but Medicaid, Medicare, private insurance, and other payment sources have become available since the mid-1960s. However, although the number of payment sources has increased, mental health spending as a share of national income has not grown for more than 30 years (Frank and Glied 2006b) and increases in mental health spending have been attributable largely to expenditures for psychotropic medications (Frank et al. 2009).

In addition, mental health has been an inviting target for budget cuts in states looking for funds for politically more popular or non-discretionary programs. Budget cuts have affected access to newer medications for Medicaid recipients as well as community mental health programs (Frieden 2003; Mildwurf 2009). While the recession that began in December 2007 has exacerbated funding reductions, even during more economically stable times, mental health expenditures have not kept pace with need. It is estimated that only about one-quarter to one-third of people with a diagnosable mental disorder in a particular year receive treatment in that year (United States Surgeon General 1999: chap. 2). In fact, from 1981 through 2005, state mental health expenditures as a percent of total state government expenditures declined, and per capita spending, when adjusted for inflation, stayed flat during those years (Lutterman 2007).

As a percentage of all public expenditures on mental health in the United States, the several hundred million dollars spent on SVP facilities may be a comparatively small amount of money. However, in a nation where most people with mental illnesses go untreated, where state mental health budgets are cut year after year, and where virtually all cuts at this point have a programmatic impact, the investment in SVP facilities draws money from other, more pressing needs. As a practical matter, SVP facilities play a role in confining people that can be played more cheaply, per person, by state departments of corrections. Instead, SVP facility budgets are often located in state mental health budgets. As a result, people with serious mental illnesses are deprived of resources that potentially might go for treatment of serious illness, rather than for warehousing people with mental abnormalities.

Summary

SVP laws are designed primarily to protect the public by incapacitating sexual offenders in institutions. They are part of a much larger effort to protect the public that includes registration of sex offenders and restrictions on domicile. The laws erode traditional constitutional guarantees, procedurally and substantively. They permit indefinite confinement and only nod rhetorically at the possibility of treatment that legislatures do not believe in.

As a result of these laws, there are now groups of sex offenders living under bridges and in forests in the United States, and there are several thousand people confined to institutions with little chance of eventual freedom. Although few would argue that many of those committed under SVP statutes are risk free, it is not yet clear where the courts might ultimately draw boundaries around the authority of states to confine people without a real effort at rehabilitation. While we wait for the answer to that question, most people in SVP facilities go untreated, by choice or because of inadequate investment in treatment.

SVP laws have many collateral effects. One of the most significant is that they stand at odds with some of the most important gains in public mental health in the last 30 years. They presage a return to the days of chaotic state hospitals, where institutional budgets caused community investments to seriously lag need. They also emphasize the police power of state mental health authorities, at a time when most public mental health administrators would prefer to focus scarce resources on the treatment needs of people with serious mental illnesses. And in articulating a legislative belief that whole groups of people are untreatable, they undercut a hard won belief in recovery as the ultimate purpose of mental health intervention and care.

7

Sexual Violence, Gender Politics, and Outsider Jurisprudence

Lessons from the American Experience in Prevention

ERIC S. JANUS

Introduction

The prevention of sexual violence—in contrast to its detection and punishment—has emerged in the past two decades as a primary motif for public policy in the United States. In the hands of American policymakers, this undoubted public good has gone badly astray. This chapter attempts to learn some lessons by identifying the reasons why.

As a tool for social control, traditional criminal law seeks to solve crimes and punish criminals, accomplishing prevention of future crime only indirectly, through the deterrence and incapacitation that are the by-products of punishment. Beginning in the late 1980s in several United States jurisdictions, social control policy began to take a very different turn, claiming prevention as a primary goal and situating itself explicitly outside of the criminal justice paradigm. The new direction manifested first in so-called sexually violent predator (SVP) laws that adopted the form of civil mental health commitments to confine in secure treatment centers mentally "abnormal" offenders who were "too dangerous" to release from prison. Twenty states and the federal government have enacted SVP laws (Janus and Prentky 2008: 91). These laws were followed by registration and community notification laws (collectively known as Megan's laws). Pushed by strong incentives from the federal government, all 50 states have enacted some form of registration and notification requirements (Logan 2009). Finally, many states and local jurisdictions have enacted, or considered, a mélange of other preventive measures, including residential restrictions (Landers 2008; Laney 2008: 18–26), and other temporal and spatial restrictions such as prohibitions on sex offenders using storm shelters (Associated Press 2005) or going outside on Halloween (Chaffin et al. 2009; Grinberg 2009), and disqualifications from various government benefits (Associated Press 2009a). These laws all share a central feature: in order to evade the strict constitutional guarantees constraining criminal punishments, they all claim a regulatory label and a non-punitive purpose.

It is my premise in this chapter that these preventive laws—which I will refer to collectively as *sexual predator laws*—have had, overall, an increasingly negative impact on the project of preventing (or decreasing) sexual violence. Though I will sketch out the factual basis for this premise, my focus here is not to prove these bad effects, but instead to ask, if I am correct, why American prevention policy has for two decades veered increasingly out of balance, allowing for expansive reforms that neglect empirical understandings instead of seeking a more balanced and effective approach to prevention.

How Has United States Prevention Policy Gone Wrong?

To understand what is wrong with United States prevention policy, one must begin by asking what prevention could have been. Many government agencies (Miller et al. 2007: 5), scholars (Vieth 2006), and advocacy groups (Minnesota Department of Health 2009: app. 5–6) make a convincing case that a public health model is the proper approach to a problem as widespread and harmful as sexual violence. The public health model prescribes interventions that are comprehensive, systematic, and deliberately designed based on empirical knowledge. It would evaluate promising programs and approaches and seek to replicate those that prove to be effective at reducing sexual violence. The principle of comprehensiveness would dictate interventions at all stages of the stream of violence. The public health model would implement primary prevention programs designed to intervene upstream by identifying root causes, and changing the societal attitudes and values that allow sexual violence to flourish. But it would not neglect downstream programs aimed at prison populations and others at very high risk for offending. Being a systematic approach, it would seek to anticipate and minimize unintended negative consequences of its prevention programs. Through careful evaluation and empirical assessment, the public health model would attempt to balance the mix of interventions to achieve ever-improving prevention effects.

Departing in almost all particulars from a public health approach, American prevention policy has become strongly antiempirical, driven instead by virulent political considerations. Valorizing a view of sexual violence that is at odds with empirical evidence, the American approach has increasingly distorted the allocation of prevention resources. American prevention policy is interstitial rather than systemic, reactive rather than comprehensive. It has pushed our attention away from root causes and biosocial understandings and toward actuarial methods that are etiologically agnostic. Primary and many secondary approaches are neglected and underfunded, while tertiary programs aimed at the ritual exile of the "most dangerous" offenders consume disproportionate resources and incorporate vastly overbroad restrictions that lump teenage streakers together with serial pedophiles (Sakry 2009). Expensive programs ignore the great bulk of sexual violence, while approaches that cost little but impose restrictions indiscriminately are shown to have counterproductive, if unintended, consequences (Janus 2006: 60–72).

As time has passed, preventive approaches have become more expensive, more extreme, less effective, and less connected to empirical knowledge. Sexual predator laws have grown beyond all estimates, and absorb protection resources vastly disproportionate to their benefits. The confined population of Minnesota's SVP program (MSOP) increased 24 per cent from 190 in 2003 to 235 in mid-2004 (Janus 2006: 62). In the six years since, it has nearly doubled, reaching 550 in early 2010 (Demko 2010a). Officials estimate that its population will double again in seven years (Kaszuba 2010). Since 2004, the cost for the MSOP has more than tripled, from $20.4 million to $64.8 million (Demko 2010b). Missouri's program has grown from 68 residents with a budget of $3.8 million in 2002, to 162 residents and a budget of $11.3 million in 2008 (Retka 2009). In Virginia, the cost of the SVP program has grown from $2.7 million in 2004 to $24 million in 2010 and is projected to exceed $32 million in 2011. The number of commitments has increased from one per month to five (Potter 2010). No residents have been released in Missouri, Minnesota, or Iowa (Retka 2009). Florida's sex offender registry has increased nearly 50 per cent in five years, exceeding 53,000 names at present (Jagirdar 2009).

National, well-respected antiviolence organizations, such as the Jacob Wetterling Foundation, warn against residency restriction laws, pointing out that they are "ineffective at preventing harm to children, and may indeed actually increase the risks to kids" by providing "a false sense of security while sapping resources that could produce better results used elsewhere" (Jacob Wetterling Resource Center 2010; Duwe et al. 2008). But states and local jurisdictions continue to enact residency restrictions. The Council for State Governments, reporting that 24 states have passed "blanket residency restrictions," found that "pressure on state legislators for tougher sex-offender laws had increased, even as the efficacy of residency restrictions was called into question" (Landers 2008). In study after study, residential restrictions have been shown to inhibit re-entry and law enforcement, by increasing dislocation and homelessness among released sex offenders (Associated Press 2009b; Lantigua 2009; Mercado 2009). Studies identify the "collateral damage" to families of sex offenders caused by registration, notification and residential restriction laws (Levenson and Tewksbury 2009). These unintended consequences include increased frequency of housing crises, financial difficulty, and mental health issues (Levenson and Tewksbury 2009). Community notification has made it all but impossible to release offenders from SVP treatment facilities, even when the risk they pose has moderated (Prescott and Rockoff 2008; Simerman 2010; Vielmetti 2010). But even where doubts have arisen as to the wisdom of such laws, politicians consider the political pressure too great to dial them back (Frank 2010).

Despite this aggressive prevention push, studies fail to show a correlated decrease in sexual violence (Frank 2010; Fry-Browers 2004: 913–15; Zevitz 2006; Zgoba and Witt 2010: 47). In a study conducted in 2003, I compared changes in forcible rape rates in states that had SVP laws with the national change in the rate of forcible rape. Almost half of the SVP states did worse than the national average, suggesting that SVP laws have little effect on actually reducing this type of violence.

Nonetheless, while SVP programs consume increasing budgets, other forms of prevention, such as domestic violence services, child protection services, sexual violence education, police services, parole and probation, and victim services, are starved for funding (Potter 2010; Schoenmann 2009; Washington State Strategic Plan for Victim Services 2005: 5). The budget overrun of Virginia's SVP program is escalating, and "legislative leaders say that if they can't find ways to trim the program's budget, they will be forced to take money from other programs, many of which received dramatic cuts last winter when legislators trimmed billions in core services such as education and health care to balance the state's budget" (Potter 2010). California spends $55 million a year on GPS tracking of sex offenders released from prison, but has "largely ignored treatment" (Simerman 2010), despite broadly accepted evidence that treatment, coupled with supervision, reduces recidivism (Janus 2006: 126).

An additional harm resides in the model of sexual violence that is reinforced by these laws and in turn shapes developments in public policy. This "tabloid model" portrays sexual violence as aberrational and abnormal, emphasizing a psychological model of sexual violence over social and normative explanations (Janus 2006: 76). By designing legislation to respond to rare but horrific crimes, lawmakers act as if prevention were a matter of closing the loopholes, and sexual violence could be successfully prevented if only we could identify the most dangerous individuals and design policies to separate them from us. Influenced by the tabloid model, these laws embody an interstitial approach to prevention, addressing the most visible resources at a small, atypical part of the problem of sexual violence. With an emphasis on the ritual exile of sexual predators (Chaffin et al. 2009; Janus 2006), these laws portray sexual violence as separable, rather than entangled with, mainstream "normal" life. Despite their exorbitant price tag, they do little to prevent harm to those they seek to protect. They suggest that sexual violence is stranger violence, and that the solution is to separate out the abnormal people rather than to change the normal values.

Why This Unfortunate Trajectory?

Despite the cost and obvious failures of SVP schemes, policymakers have neither learned nor adjusted, allowing the pendulum of public opinion and policy making to swing in one direction only. One simple explanation is that everyday politics, combined with the salience of violent sex in the media, produce a push toward excess. As Dr. Michael Miner (2007) said in a recent editorial:

> In general, these laws are based on public fear and misperception of both the nature of sexual crimes and the risk that is posed by convicted sexual offenders.

But this observation leaves more basic questions unanswered: Why has sexual violence produced such hot salience in politics and the media? Why have our leaders felt so free (or perhaps so compelled) to reject, even condemn, scientific information about sexual violence, boasting, along with Rep. Matt Salmon (R. Arizona), "I don't want to understand pedophiles, I want to put them in prison" (O'Meara 1999).

The problem is not simply that the political process is poor at self-regulation. To understand this point, compare briefly the American policy response to domestic violence, a problem causing at least as much harm as sexual violence to women and children. Experts estimate that "40 to 50 of the 60,000 to 70,000 arrests each year for sex crimes against children involve homicide" (Koch 2005), and that there are about 160 sex-crime-related killings annually in the United States (Zimring 2004: 26). Compare the 1,000 to 1,600 deaths of women attributable annually to United States domestic violence (Websdale 2003: 2). Despite the magnitude of the problem, public policy approaches to domestic violence have not careened out of control even when horrendous murders occur that might have triggered a flurry of legislative activity had they fit the sexual predator mold (Backus 2010). As Philip Jenkins (2009: 38) puts it in his exploration of why some social problems get constructed as "moral panics" while others do not, "these potentially sensational cases provide no springboard for wider rhetoric" (Jenkins 2009: 38).

One might also contrast American responses to drunk driving, seat-belt use, smoking, and, more recently, texting while driving. Although each of these threats produces harm on the same (or higher) order of magnitude as sexual violence, the approaches taken have been relatively balanced, with a robust mix of primary and secondary approaches to prevention. Contrast, finally, the rather cautious approach to sexual violence taken by Canada, with "the swift, aggressive approach taken in the United States" (Petrunik 2003: 44).

Gender Politics and Outsider Jurisprudence

This comparative approach allows us to see that two factors account for the problematic trajectory of American sex-violence prevention policy: the first is the antifeminist agenda comprising the politically conservative side of the gender politics that is reflected in the culture wars festering in the United States during the two decades in which these laws have developed. The second is the decision to place antisexual violence measures outside of the criminal justice paradigm. It is these two factors and their sequelae working synergistically that have pushed sexual violence policy further out of balance.

As I explain in more detail later, situating the prevention agenda outside of the criminal justice system has had two main consequences. The first is the principle of exceptionalism, (Agamben 2005: 1–6; Ericson 2007: 26) and the second is the adoption of risk as the predicate for intervention. Together these have created and reinforced an archetype for sex offenders that has come to be known as the sexual predator, a label that has experienced a meteoric rise in the news media. See Figure 7.1.

Gender Politics In turn, the paradigmatic sexual predator has resonated with social conservatives, providing a powerful vehicle to push back against a rising tide of feminist reforms. The feminist revolution began to touch public policy regarding sexual violence in the mid-1970s. Inspired by feminist theory, legislators broadened definitions of rape and sexual assault, and

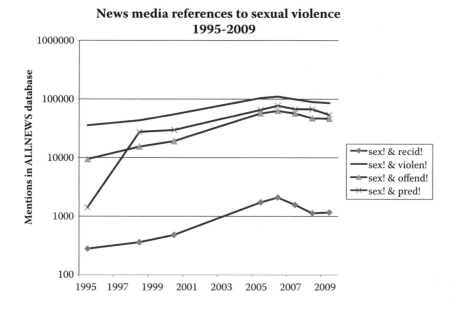

Figure 7.1 News media references to sexual violence. Source: Westlaw ALLNEWS Database, March 26, 2010.

modified procedural rules in order to root out traditional assumptions about the nature of sexual violence, often referred to as rape myths. These broadly held traditional societal attitudes portrayed sexual violence as the product of aberrational psychology; doubted women's claims of rape, placing on them the burden to disprove acquiescence and provocation; and generally asserted that women were safest at home and in marriage, and most in danger in public (Janus 2006: 84).

In contrast to these traditional views, feminist theorists posited that rape was deeply rooted in the patriarchal values and structures of the society, and therefore was the product of societal rather than biopsychological causes. Empirical research supported feminist theory, showing sexual violence to be much more ubiquitous and more a characteristic of intimate relationships than portrayed in the traditional view (Bachman and Paternoster 1993). In short, feminist theorists claimed, and researchers proved, that "collectively, women are more at risk of violence in intimate relations than in public spaces" (Stanko 2000: 150).

The grand narrative inherent in the feminist reforms presumed a revolutionary rejection of the patriarchal order and was therefore anathema to the social conservative movement. Some conservative writers tried to push back against the feminist framing of sexual violence (Sommers 1994), but their critique foundered because it was contradicted by authoritative empirical data and could be interpreted as hostile to the protection of women and children (Evans 2003; Haaken and Lamb 2000). In a further blow to the conservative agenda, passage of the Violence Against Women Act (VAWA) in 1994 was seen as giving official recognition to the feminist-inspired highlighting of the social and political nature of sexual violence.

For conservatives, it became imperative to find a way to reassert the traditional patriarchal view of sexual violence, without appearing to be soft on sexual crime. The newly emerging sexual predator laws provided a paradigm suited to this conservative agenda. It provided a safe and powerful way to turn the tide in antiviolence policy in a direction much more compatible with the traditional patriarchal views of gender relations and sexual violence.

The new sexual predator laws provided an appropriate vehicle because they were based on, and over time strengthened, an archetype that reflected and reinforced traditional views of gender and sexual violence (Janus 2006: 85). The genesis for the laws set their trajectory. Widely reported, recidivist, stranger violence in Minnesota and Washington became the template against which reform was evaluated (deFiebre 2004; La Fond 1992: 771). Task forces in both states settled on the civil commitment model as the primary vehicle to respond to this recidivist violence. Five years later, a grass-roots push in New Jersey—again responding to similar violence—led to the highly visible adoption of laws requiring registration and community notification for sex offenders (Filler 2001).

For a variety of reasons, both of these legal responses to sexual violence were situated outside of the criminal justice system. As suggested earlier, this has had two key consequences that have allowed for the synergistic interaction with social conservatism: these are the reliance on the principle of exceptionalism and the elevation of risk as the key predicate for the deprivation of liberty. I address the idea of exceptionalism first.

The Principle of Exceptionalism   Civil commitment involves a "massive curtailment of liberty" (*Humphrey v Cady* 1972: 509). It thus requires justification in two distinct senses. First, there must be some proportionality between the harm to society and the deprivation to the individual (Frase 2005; Richards 1989). No one doubts that the harm of sexual violence can be sufficiently severe to justify liberty deprivation. The second axis is more problematic, because it demands a justification for civil commitment's departure from the criminal law paradigm, the normal means of dealing with antisocial behavior. To justify this adoption of an alternative system of justice, the state must demonstrate that the circumstances requiring liberty deprivation are exceptional (Hudson 2009). Though there are, in law, a number of ways of satisfying this exceptionalism criterion (for example, intense social disorder, wartime, epidemic contagion), a traditional and well-used line of justification in American jurisprudence is that the target of the alternative system of justice is, in some sense, an outsider. Thus, a key consequence of the adoption of the non-criminal template is the characterization of sexual offenders as different in kind from the rest of us (*State of Minnesota ex rel. Pearson v Probate Court of Ramsey County* 1939: 299). The mental disorder predicate built into the civil commitment template flows from this justification imperative (*Kansas v Crane* 2002: 413), and subsequently supports and strengthens the archetype of the sexual predator as a mentally disordered, aberrational outsider.

The outsider template is echoed and reinforced in Megan's laws and residential restrictions, which are premised on the assumption that offenders are strangers (and otherwise unknown to parents), and that their threat can be addressed by physical separation (O'Brien 1998). Gradually, the archetypal figure, the sexual predator, takes on this outsider characteristic, and the aberrational, disordered feature of sexual violence is strengthened at the expense of a systemic, empirically-based understanding of sexual violence as tied in strong ways to normal societal values.

Sexual predator laws reinforce the conservative antifeminist agenda by performing a ritual exile of sexual violence, sending the offenders from our midst. Having performed this "cleansing ritual," in the words of Karen Franklin, we can tell ourselves that the larger society has fulfilled its obligation for protection, and this obligation required no change in our values or ownership of the origins of sexual violence (Franklin 2010; Janus 2006: 89). Contrary to the feminist notion that patriarchal values and attitudes allow sexual violence to flourish (Dworkin 1993: 14), the repeated ritual exile of archetypal predators reassures us that the problem is them, not us; we reinforce that mantra by framing the problem—and therefore the solution—as a matter of identifying and segregating these outsiders, monsters who are different from us.

Risk   The adoption of non-criminal regulatory approaches to prevention establishes risk, as opposed to guilt, as the primary predicate for state intervention. The new focus on risk has had some salutary effects, spurring a serious and concerted effort to develop empirically-based and more rigorously vetted methods for assessing an individual's risk of reoffending (Hanson and Thornton 2000). But it has had at least three consequences that contribute to the lack of balance in sexual violence policy. First, risk, a continuous variable, replaces a binary attribute (guilty–not guilty) as the predicate for state intervention, thus removing a key bright-line boundary on expansion of state deprivation of liberty. Especially when combined with the politics of sexual violence, this lack of natural taxonomic thresholds for state intervention invites, or perhaps demands, continual net widening (Janus 2004).

Second, guilt and risk function differently as anchors in the calculus of proportionality. Guilt is a normative concept, and thus is commensurate with an assessment of how much punishment—measured largely as a function of time incarcerated—an offender deserves. Risk is largely seen as a natural or scientific quality, and thus the cumulative time-dependent measure of confinement gives way to a moment-by-moment assessment of whether current risk justifies constraints on liberty. Length of confinement thus becomes a quasi-scientific, rather than normative, decision.

Last, the banishment of morality and normative judgment from the most visible official discourse justifying the fight against sexual violence suggests that sexual violence is a fact of nature, a result of aberrant psychology, rather than a cultural practice that flourishes because of (moral) choices that individuals and societies make. Yet changing the societal conditions that allow sexual violence to flourish requires just such normative judgments.

Recidivism as the Key Metric   The centrality of risk reflects and supports the emergence of recidivism as the major metric in defining the problem of sexual violence. The modern sexual predator laws had their genesis as a reaction to recidivist crime. The public outrage in Washington State, Minnesota, and New Jersey in the late 1980s and early 1990s was directed not simply at horrendous crimes, but particularly at horrendous recidivist crimes (*Smith v Doe* 2003: 103).

There are two aspects of the current laws that strengthen the role of recidivism as a key measure of sexual violence. First, from a scientific point of view, recidivist crime is much more predictable than non-recidivist crime, because the base rate of (future) sexual offending is higher among individuals with a prior record of sexual violence than among those without (Lanagan et al. 2003).

Second, the current SVP laws require an outsider group as the target. Recidivists, who by definition have been convicted of a sexual offence, provide a politically safe outside group. This point can be seen clearly by contrasting an early sex psychopath law in Iowa, where the targets were not recidivists but rather homosexual men—a group whose outsider status was unexceptional in the 1950s but unacceptable, as well as unconstitutional, now (Miller 2009; *Lawrence v Texas* 2003: 564).

The consequences of the prominence of the recidivism frame are serious. The frame pushes our public policy strongly in an antifeminist direction, away from the kind of comprehensive, public-health-inspired approach advocated by many experts and antiviolence groups. Especially coupled with the development of actuarial risk assessment tools to quantify risk, the recidivism metric encourages a focus on individual risk and on the identification of the worst of the worst, at the expense of systemic understandings of societal patterns of risk.

Recidivism is inherently a downstream concept; as recidivism becomes our primary measure for sexual violence, our public policy focus becomes narrower. First, recidivist crime represents only a small sliver of sexual violence. Of individuals imprisoned for a sex offence, only about one in seven (Greenfield 1997:22) or, in at least one study, as few as one in 10, had a previous conviction for a sex offence (California Sex Offender Management Board 2008: 53). Of sex offence convictions among individuals released from prison, only about 13 per cent of the sex crimes were committed by released sex offenders (Lanagan et al. 2003).

Further, SVP laws address only a fraction of this fraction. Even in states with SVP laws, most of the "future recidivists" set for release from prison will be released to the community, not committed to the SVP program (Janus 2003). For example, using the cut-score recommended by the developers of the Minnesota Sex Offender Screening Tool–Revised (MnSOST-R) risk assessment tool for SVP commitments, 84 per cent of recidivists are likely released to the community rather than committed (Epperson et al. 2003).

Recidivism is not an irrelevant metric. But under the influence of the twin drivers of the sex predator laws, it has come to occupy a large part of the field of vision, accounting in large measure for the misdirection of contemporary American prevention policy.

Good Prevention; Bad Prevention

How can we differentiate between good and bad prevention policies? What lessons can we learn from the United States experience with prevention?

I have suggested that the consequences of the regulatory nature of prevention, coupled with the sexual politics of the culture wars, have given American sexual violence policy a persistent lack of balance. To bring the point home, let us return to the contrast between sexual violence and domestic violence policy. Why has the former, rather the latter, been the site of such energy and imbalance?

In the 1970s and 1980s, feminist theory and research shed new light on both domestic violence and sexual violence. This new understanding led directly to empirically grounded legislative reforms aimed at both forms of violence against women. But sexual violence policy diverged in the early 1990s, adopting the antiempirical, counterproductive path described earlier.

Empirical growth in the domestic violence area can be seen when examining historical developments in research and subsequent changes in the law. One early and notable body of research that influenced domestic violence policy came from feminist and psychologist Lenore Walker, who studied a collection of interviews of battered women and focused on the commonalities among their stories (Walker 1979). Her work led to the notion that battered woman syndrome could explain the dynamics that give rise to and maintain abusive relationships and that a specific cycle of violence is present in many such relationships (Rothenberg 2002: 84–85; Walker 1979). Further empirical research was done to confirm her anecdotal evidence (Rothenberg 2002: 96). Policymakers responded to Walker's findings and by 1997 at least 22 states had adopted legislation that recognized battered woman syndrome (Rothenberg 2002: 91).

Advocacy and research developments again "led to dramatic changes in law enforcement's domestic violence policies across the country" when many states adopted mandatory or warrantless arrest policies after a 1984 study gave empirical support to the use of such methods (Sack 2004: 1669–70). The federal government also addressed the issues unearthed by the women's movement when it enacted VAWA. Passed in 1994 after decades of fervent political and scholarly work, VAWA served as national recognition of the essence of feminist reforms, making domestic violence a federal crime and acknowledging it as a civil rights issue (Crais 2005: 406; Violence Against Women Act 1994).

Sexual violence reforms initially followed a similar path, incorporating changes in the definition of criminal sexual conduct and in law enforcement procedures that reflected the new understandings of sexual violence (Janus 2006: 81–82). But sexual violence policy has diverged in the past two decades, leaving behind reliance on empiricism as it embraced the sexual predator paradigm (Janus 2006; Russakoff 1998).

Nothing could symbolize the divergence more starkly than the practice of naming sexual violence laws — but not domestic violence laws — after specific victims. For instance, just 89 days after New Jersey child Megan Kanka was raped and murdered by a convicted pedophile who was living in her neighborhood, the legislature in her home state passed Megan's law, which requires that people be notified about the presence of sex offenders within their community (Janus 2006: 15–16; Russakoff 1998). All other states have passed similar legislation and the term *Megan's law* is now used to refer to this type of law generally (Janus 2006: 20). Jessica's law followed the tragic murder of nine-year-old Jessica Lunsford in Florida (Janus 2006: 156; Carpenter 2010: 24). The Adam Walsh Act, named in honor of a young child who was kidnapped and murdered in 1981 (Enniss 2008: 701), also contains several sections named after other victims of high-profile sex-crimes cases. It also bears noting that only those victims who are viewed as particularly tragic because their race, youth, and gender make them archetypes of innocence are memorialized through the naming of these laws (Carpenter 2010: 24; Russakoff 1998).

Domestic violence laws, in contrast, tend to bear very generic titles such as the Violence Against Women Act. The difference, I suggest, represents divergent conceptualizations of victimhood. Those who experience domestic violence become part of a broad and unremarkable category of victims, whereas those who experience atypical sexual violence at the hands of strangers become individually memorialized (Carpenter 2010: 24).

The divergence underlines the outsider jurisprudence that has come to characterize sexual violence policy but not domestic violence policy. Domestic violence is, of course, by definition not outsider violence. But sexual violence has both intimate and stranger manifestations. The adoption of the regulatory model of prevention demanded an outsider model of sexual violence. Conservative politics, anxious to push back against feminist theory, welcomed and strengthened this outsider framing. In fact, one might speculate that the imperviousness of domestic violence to patriarchal revisionism provided part of the energy that has kept sexual violence policy so far off balance. In other words, the success of the domestic violence model, with its fidelity to the feminist understanding of risks to women, puts additional pressure on the SVP model to serve as a vehicle to strengthen the conservative, outsider archetype of gender violence.

Self-Correction?

I have argued here that the confluence of gender politics and outsider jurisprudence can explain the uncorrected excesses of American sexual violence policy. I want to end this chapter by suggesting that there may be mechanisms that can bring the system back into a more balanced mode, though there are dangers inherent here too.

The SVP laws have been upheld by the courts on the grounds that they are bona fide civil commitment laws, with a non-punitive purpose, as manifested by the provision of treatment and the release of detainees when their risk no longer justifies confinement. But in many states, a decade and a half of executive implementation has failed to release any detainees, and many believe that treatment is an empty promise (Demko 2009). It is possible that courts will someday recognize the pretexuality of the claim of non-punitiveness, striking down the SVP laws and ordering the wholesale release of detainees (cf. *In re Travis* 2009; *Seling v Young* 2001; Janus and Bolin 2008). In a somewhat similar vein, Philip Jenkins reports on the collapse of what could have been a "vast and successful" child pornography prosecution because it was based on an "egregious fiction," which surfaced in court (Jenkins 2009: 40). Such a collapse might restore balance to public policy. More likely, it would demoralize the antiviolence effort, while flooding communities with unsupervised, angry, institutionalized offenders.

A second potential brake on the excesses of United States policy may have its seeds in the outsider jurisprudence that constructs sex offenders as the degraded other, outside of the normal protections of the law. The construction of sexual offenders as predators who are different from us allows policymakers to avoid the political repercussions that excessive regulation would otherwise provoke. But if the outsider group begins to appear excessively expansive, encroaching on people who are quite obviously not different, the public may begin to push back. Already, there appears to be some movement in this direction, as overbroad laws routinely lump teenage streakers and sexters with serial rapists, and even some politicians publicly remark on the counterproductive consequences of residential restriction laws.

Third, the foundation for sexual predator laws may be deeply weakened because of the fundamentally contradictory views of children and sexual abuse that these laws advance. On the one hand, the laws are based on a model of child innocence (Finkelhor 1994: 42) that portrays child sexual abuse as invariably and unquestionably severely harmful to children. At the same time, most perpetrators of sexual abuse against children are themselves juveniles (Snyder 2000), and these child offenders are increasingly included as the targets of harsh sexual predators laws (Walsh and Velazquez 2009). It is not clear that the law can sustain a system that treats children as pure and innocent victims, while reserving its harshest, most punitive responses for adolescent behavior that, for many, is not unrelated to the offender's previous sexual victimization (Garfinkle 2003: 191).

Conclusion

The distortions in American sexual violence prevention policy are driven by two factors: situating it outside the criminal justice paradigm and conservative gender politics. The former encouraged the development of an outsider jurisprudence, which in turn supported, and was amplified by, conservative gender politics. Together, these forces have created a broken system, investing resources without attention to empirical information, in an increasingly unwise and out-of-balance approach. The challenge is to take the intense energy and expansive resources directed at exiling sexual predators and redirect it in a more comprehensive, empirically-based public-health-oriented approach to preventing and reducing sexual violence.

8

The Preventive Detention of Insanity Acquittees

A Case Study From Victoria, Australia

IAN FRECKELTON

Introduction

Legislative regimes dealing with the dispositions given to those found not guilty of serious criminal offences by reason of insanity (NGRI) or mental impairment (NGRMI) have been controversial and in flux for over a quarter of a century. Across countries and within Australia they vary in significant respects. Traditionally, and still in some jurisdictions, the prediction of risk in respect to the release of persons found NGRI or NGRMI remains the province of the executive upon advice from mental health professionals which may or may not be taken (*Re VAS* 2010). The risk in this scenario is that politicization of the process can lead to decision-making that is extremely risk averse, cautious, and not adequately informed by clinical experience. The consequence can be that acquittees spend inappropriately long periods in confinement or under supervision. In some other jurisdictions, the task has been remitted either to the courts that, but for the NGRI/NGRMI verdict, would have sentenced the accused or to a multi-disciplinary tribunal constituted for this specialist purpose.

This chapter reviews the legislative underpinnings for a number of the different approaches and then scrutinizes the substantial risk prediction jurisprudence that has evolved in Victoria, Australia, a jurisdiction that has opted for the Judiciary taking over the functions of the Executive to decide upon the release of persons found NGRI and NGRMI. It argues that although there is much to be said in principle for specialist tribunals discharging such a role, the experience of a little over a decade in Victoria of the judiciary undertaking the risk-prediction exercise justifies reasonable confidence in the informedness of a fair and evidence-based decision-making process in this context on the part of judges.

Approaches to NGRI and NGRMI Disposition

This section outlines some of the approaches that have been taken in some common law countries to the disposition of individuals found NGRI or NGRMI.

England and Wales Major changes have taken place in England in the aftermath of the Criminal Procedure (Insanity) Act 1964 (England and Wales), which required a hospital order with restrictions without limit of time for those found NGRI. The Criminal Procedure (Insanity and Unfitness to Plead) Act 1991 (England and Wales) introduced greater flexibility of dispositions (Fennell 1992). When a person is found NGRI, the court can order the person to be admitted to a designated hospital, guardianship or a supervision and treatment order (sec. 5; see for example *R v Grant* 2008). Consignment to a hospital if the person has committed a serious crime and the decision for release is that of the secretary of state.

Canada In Canada, upon an accused person being found not criminally responsible by reason of mental disorder (Criminal Code, sec. 672.34), the equivalent to NGRI, a court may, or, if there is an application by the accused or the prosecutor, must hold a disposition hearing (Criminal

Code, sec. 672.45). At such a hearing the court may make a disposition, if satisfied that it can readily do so and that a disposition should be made without delay (sec. 672.45). It or the review board may order the least onerous and restrictive option to the acquittee of the following:

- absolute discharge, if the acquittee if considered not to be a significant threat to public safety;
- conditional discharge; or
- detention in custody in hospital, subject to conditions, taking into consideration the need to protect the public from dangerous persons, the acquittee's mental condition and the objective of reintegrating the acquittee into society, as well as his or her other needs (sec 672.54).

When detention in hospital is ordered, the review board is obliged to review the acquittee's status every 12 months (sec. 672.81). Otherwise, the review board can extend the detention of the acquittee if satisfied that the condition of the person is not likely to improve and that detention remains necessary for the period of the extension (sec. 672.81(1.2)(c)).

New Zealand   Under the Criminal Procedure (Mentally Impaired Persons) Act 2003 (NZ), when a person is found NGRI (sec. 20), a court must order (sec. 24) the person to be detained as a "special patient" under the Mental Health (Compulsory Assessment and Treatment) Act 1992 (NZ); in a secure facility as a "special care recipient" under the Intellectual Disability (Compulsory Care and Rehabilitation) Act 2003 (NZ); as a jailed prisoner; or that the person be released absolutely.

Where the person is detained, the period is indefinite in duration. However, the burden of this is alleviated by the fact that at any time while the order continues in force, a certificate may be given under the Mental Health (Compulsory Assessment and Treatment) Act 1992 (or the Intellectual Disability [Compulsory Care and Rehabilitation] Act 2003) indicating that the acquittee's continued detention under the order is no longer necessary to safeguard the acquittee's own interests or the safety of the public or of a person or class of person. If such a certificate is given, the Minister of Health is obliged to consider whether, in the Minister's opinion, the acquittee's continued detention is no longer necessary to safeguard those interests. If this is the conclusion reached by the minister, he or she must direct that the acquittee be held as a patient or, as the case requires, as a care recipient, or be discharged. If the person is directed to be held as a patient, he or she has the status of a civilly committed patient under a compulsory treatment order for the purposes of the Mental Health (Compulsory Assessment and Treatment) Act 1992 (sec. 33) (Skipworth et al. 2006).

Australia   Under the Commonwealth Crimes Act 1914 a court may order that a person found not guilty by reason of mental impairment be released absolutely, be released subject to conditions for up to three years, or be detained in safe custody in prison or hospital for a specified period (sec. 20BJ). If the acquittee is detained, the attorney general must reconsider the acquittee's release at least every six months, taking into account relevant expert material and representations on behalf of the acquittee. On the basis of such material the attorney general can order the acquittee's release (sec. 20BL). Thus under both New Zealand and Australia's Commonwealth legislation, decision-making about release of NGRI acquittees remains the prerogative of the executive.

In the Australian Capital Territory there is a different approach. Where there is a special verdict of not guilty because of mental impairment, the Supreme Court is obliged to order that the acquittee be detained in custody until a tribunal, the Australian Capital Territory Administrative Tribunal (ACAT), orders otherwise unless it is satisfied that it is more appropriate to order that the accused submit to the jurisdiction of the ACAT to enable the ACAT to make a mental health order (Crimes Act 1900 [ACT], sec. 323), which can be in the form of a psychiatric treatment order (Mental Health (Treatment and Care) Act 1994 (ACT), sec. 26), a community treatment order (sec. 36), or a restriction order (sec. 30, 36B).

In New South Wales, when a person is found not guilty by reason of mental illness, the court may order that the person be detained in such place and in such manner as the court thinks fit until released by due process of law or may make another order (including an order releasing the person from custody, either unconditionally or subject to conditions) as the court considers appropriate (Mental Health (Forensic Provisions) Act 1900 (NSW), sec. 39(1)). The person is then subject to the jurisdiction of the Mental Health Review Tribunal, which must not make an order for release of the person unless it is satisfied, on the evidence available to it, that the safety of the person or any member of the public will not be seriously endangered by the person's release, and other care of a less restrictive kind, that is consistent with safe and effective care, is appropriate and reasonably available to the patient, or that the person does not require care (sec. 43). The Tribunal must review the case of each such person every 6 months but if he or she is subject to a community treatment order or are detained at a correctional center it must do so every 3 months (sec. 46).

In the Northern Territory, if a person is found NGRMI, the court must either release the person unconditionally or declare him or her liable to supervision (Criminal Code Act 1983 (NT), sec. 43I(2)). Supervision orders are for indefinite terms (sec. 43ZC) and can be custodial or non-custodial (sec. 43ZA). In considering whether to make an order in relation to an acquittee, including his or her release, a court must have regard to whether the supervised person concerned is likely to, or would if released be likely to, endanger himself or herself or another person because of his or her mental impairment, condition, or disability; the need to protect people from danger; the nature of the mental impairment, condition, or disability; the relationship between the mental impairment, condition, or disability and the offending conduct; whether there are adequate resources available for the treatment and support of the supervised person in the community; whether the supervised person is complying or is likely to comply with the conditions of the supervision order; and any other matters the court considers relevant (sec. 43ZN(1)).

In Queensland a person found not guilty by reason of insanity under sec. 647 of the Criminal Code (Qld) must be ordered by the court to be kept in strict custody, in such place and in such manner as the court thinks fit, until the person is dealt with pursuant to the Mental Health Act 2000 (Qld). If the minister is satisfied it is necessary for the proper treatment or care of the person, then he or she may direct by a forensic order that the person be admitted to, and detained in, a stated high security unit. If, however, the minister is satisfied the person can be safely detained in an authorized mental health service other than a high-security unit, he or she may direct that the person be admitted to a stated authorized mental health service (Mental Health Act 2000 (Qld), sec. 302).

Thereafter the status of the person is subject to the Mental Health Review Tribunal, which must review the person's mental condition at least every six months (sec. 200(1)). In deciding whether to revoke or confirm the person's forensic order, the tribunal is obliged to have regard for the patient's mental state and psychiatric history; each offence leading to the patient becoming a forensic patient; the patient's social circumstances; and the patient's response to treatment and willingness to continue treatment (s 203(6)).

In South Australia a similar scheme to that in the Northern Territory exists with a court able to release an acquittee found NGRMI unconditionally or on a supervision order or subject to license or conditions for a period equivalent to the term of imprisonment or supervision that could have been imposed had the person been found guilty of the criminal offence (Criminal Law Consolidation Act 1935 (SA), sec. 269O). The court retains jurisdiction to vary or revoke a supervision order (sec. 269P) and in making a decision is obliged to have regard to the nature of the acquittee's mental impairment; whether the acquittee is, or would if released be, likely to endanger another person, or other persons generally; whether there are adequate resources available for the treatment and support of the acquittee in the community; whether the acquittee is likely to comply with the conditions of a license; and other matters that the court thinks relevant (sec. 269T(1)).

In Tasmania a court finding a person NGRI can make a restriction order; release the acquittee and make a supervision order; make a continuing care order; release the acquittee and make a community treatment order; release the acquittee on such conditions as the court considers appropriate; or release the acquittee unconditionally (Criminal Justice (Mental Impairment) Act 1999 (Tas), sec. 21). A restriction order, only able to be made by the Supreme Court, requires the person to be admitted to and detained in a secure mental health unit until the court otherwise orders (sec. 24). In making a decision about the revocation of a restriction order a court must, in addition to applying the least restrictive principle, have regard to largely the same principles as those in South Australia.

In Western Australia when a person is found NGRMI of a serious offence, the court must make a custody order (Criminal Law (Mentally Impaired Accused) Act 1996 (WA), sec. 21) under which the acquittee must be detained in an authorized hospital, declared place, detention center, or prison, as determined by the Mentally Impaired Accused Review Board (sec. 24). The board must submit a report on the acquittee within eight weeks of the making of a custody order and thereafter at least once each year to the minister (sec. 33). The board does not have determinative powers, only being able to make recommendations about release, taking into account the degree of risk that the release of the acquittee appears to present to the personal safety of people in the community or of any individual in the community; the likelihood that, if released on conditions, the acquittee would comply with the conditions; the extent to which the acquittee's mental impairment, if any, might benefit from treatment, training, or any other measure; the likelihood that, if released, the acquittee would be able to take care of his or her day-to-day needs, obtain any appropriate treatment and resist serious exploitation; the objective of imposing the least restriction of the freedom of choice and movement that is consistent with the need to protect the health or safety of the acquittee or any other person; and any statement received from a victim of the alleged offence in respect of which the acquittee is in custody (sec. 33(5)).

This overview of regimes in some common law jurisdictions shows that the disposition of individuals found NGRI or NGRMI is strongly controlled. This reflects the notion that such individuals may be dangerous in the future if no such controls are in place (see the introductory chapter by McSherry and Keyzer in this volume).

The Victorian Experiment

By legislation, in 1999, Victoria initiated its own experiment in managing those found NGRMI or unfit to stand trial. Its legislation bears many features in common with that in South Australia. Victoria's legislative provisions were promulgated in the Crimes (Mental Impairment and Unfitness to be Tried) Act 1997 and were the product of a report by the Community Development Committee of the Victorian Parliament (Parliament of Victoria 1995). A shift was undertaken from decision-making about such persons' ongoing detention from the Executive (see *R v Judge Martin; Ex parte Attorney-General* 1973: sec. 342–50) to the courts that had dealt with such acquittees.

There were said to be two principal advantages of the new system. First, it created the potential for depoliticized legal decision-making (see *Re M* 1998) in relation to a category of persons who had previously often been detained preventatively for periods generally regarded as being far in excess of what was necessary to address the symptomatology that had played a role in their offending or in rendering them so unwell that they could not participate in the criminal proceedings brought against them (Delaney 1998; Freckelton 2003; Lightfoot 1998; McSherry 1999). Second, it was anticipated that the change would result in shorter periods of confinement for such persons when release was clinically justified.

Thus, the Victorian initiative has eschewed "expert" decision-making by a tribunal, as is employed in England and Wales, Canada, the Australian Capital Territory, New South Wales, and Queensland. The experiment has vested responsibility and an ongoing predictive role in the court that originally heard the charges (the County Court or the Supreme Court for homicide charges), with the responsibility for evaluation being that of a judge, assisted by expert evidence from treating clinicians and, occasionally, second-opinion psychiatrists and psychologists commissioned by the acquittee.

The rest of this section outlines how the Victorian system works toward releasing back into the community persons found not guilty by reason of mental impairment. The remainder of the chapter reviews a little over 10 years of jurisprudence on the prediction of risk in the context of persons whose pathology has been proved to have exercised a major effect upon their commission of criminal offences or their capacity to participate effectively in their own trials. It also scrutinizes the reasoning processes that have characterized the modest number of decisions by the Victorian Supreme Court to revoke acquittees' supervisory status.

The Supervision Orders System   When a person in Victoria is found not guilty of murder by the Supreme Court by reason of mental impairment, he or she is made subject to supervision orders (Crimes (Mental Impairment and Unfitness to be Tried) Act 1997, sec 18 or 23). These can be custodial or non-custodial, but, as elsewhere, the vast majority of circumstances initially are custodial, meaning that the acquittee is consigned either to Victoria's forensic psychiatric institution, Thomas Embling Hospital, or occasionally to prison (sec. 26(2)). The duration of such orders is indefinite, although an order can be made by the court for a review at any prescribed time (sec. 27). The court must set a nominal term, which is 25 years for murder and half the maximum sentence for other serious offences (sec. 28).

The standard procedure within Thomas Embling Hospital is for persons on custodial supervision orders to be trialed with on-ground supervised and then unsupervised leave, and then with off-ground supervised and then unsupervised leave. Next along the road to recovery of autonomy by the acquittee are three different forms of status, all of which exist pursuant to court order:

- extended leave orders;
- non-custodial supervision orders; and
- revocation orders.

Under section 57 of the Act, the court that made a custodial supervision order can grant an application for extended leave if satisfied on the evidence available that the safety of the person or members of the public will not be seriously endangered. Extended leave orders can be easily suspended at any time if the chief psychiatrist is satisfied the safety of the person or members of the public will be seriously endangered if a suspension is not continued (sec. 58).

An acquittee can apply for a downgrading of a custodial supervision order to a non-custodial order. This enables greater freedom for an acquittee than if under an extended leave order pursuant to a custodial supervision order. There can be no variation of a custodial supervision order unless the acquittee has had at least 12 months extended leave (sec. 32(3)(a)). In addition, the court considering the issue must take into account the acquittee's compliance with conditions of extended leave (sec. 32(3)(b)).

Under section 32 of the Act, a court must not vary a custodial supervision order to non-custodial during the nominal term unless satisfied that the safety of the person or of members of the public will not be seriously endangered as a result of the release on a non-custodial supervision order.

The Review Process   Three months before the expiry of the nominal term and after that at least every five years, the court that made a supervision order (or that sentenced the offender earlier, if that occurred prior to 1997) must undertake a major review of the acquittee's status. At such a review, if the order is custodial the court must vary it to a non-custodial supervision order unless satisfied that the safety of the person or of members of the public will be seriously endangered by release (sec. 35). This provides a forensic advantage for the acquittee in terms of securing a change of status in that he or she does not bear the onus of proof.

In any order relating to supervision, a court is obliged to have regard to

- the nature of the person's mental impairment or other condition or disability;
- the relationship between the impairment, condition, or disability and the offending conduct;
- whether the person is, or would if released be, likely to endanger themselves, another person, or other persons generally by reason of their mental impairment;
- the need to protect people from such danger;
- whether there are adequate resources available for the treatment and support of the person in the community;
- any other matters the court thinks relevant (sec. 40; cf. Criminal Justice (Mental Impairment) Act 1999 (Tas), sec. 34, and Criminal Law Consolidation Act 1935 (SA), sec. 269T).

Table 8.1 illustrates the number of acquittees on custodial supervision orders, extended leave in the community, and on non-custodial supervision orders. Table 8.1 and Table 8.2 have been compiled from information in Forensicare Annual Reports, as well as with the assistance of Janet Ruffles who is collecting data in this regard for her doctor of psychology thesis (Ruffles 2010). Table 8.2 shows that modest numbers of persons have had their supervisory status revoked. Thus, 22 revocations in total were made (by both the County and Supreme Courts) between 1997 and 2008/2009.

By far the greater percentage of persons on supervision orders have schizophrenia, many of them paranoid schizophrenia. However, some have been diagnosed as having disorders with a mood component, which have resulted in psychotic symptoms—schizoaffective disorder, bipolar disorder, or a major depressive disorder. A small number of acquittees have been diagnosed as having a personality disorder, as against a mental illness. Most notable among these is Derek Percy (*Re Major Review of Percy* 1998; *In the Matters of Major Reviews of Percy, Farrell and RJO* 1998; *Percy Derek Ernest, In the Matter of a Major Review* 2004) who was found guilty of a sexually deviant murder of a young girl some 40 years ago and has been investigated for involvement in a series of other comparable homicides (Marshall 2009; Whitticker 2008; *Priest v Deputy State Coroner* 2010). Another such offender is RC (2009), who has been diagnosed as having a mixed personality disorder with narcissistic and borderline traits (see also *Re IT* 1999).

The Concept of Serious Endangerment   At the core of all decision-making concerning ongoing supervision of acquittees is the notion that they may constitute a serious ongoing risk to

Table 8.1 Persons on Custodial Supervision Orders, on Extended Leave, and on Non-custodial Supervision Orders

Order	2003	2004	2005	2006	2007	2008	2009
Custodial	40	48	52	60	66	67	72
Extended Leave	4	6	6	4	7	6	10
Non-custodial	23	33	40	43	50	68	64

Table 8.2 Supervision Order Revocations

Year	Revocations
1997	0
1998	2
1999	1
2000	1
2001	0
2002/2003	2
2003/2004	3
2004/2005	1
2005/2006	6
2006/2007	1
2007/2008	1
2008/2009	4

members of the public or themselves (see for example *Re SKD* 2009). In Victoria judicial interpretation of the term *serious endangerment* has shown the concept to be somewhat elastic, determined as it must be in the context of a person who has already committed an offence of extreme violence while symptomatic with mental illness or, less commonly, who has committed a serious offence when unwell.

It has been held that the potential for endangerment can be relatively remote in likelihood but if the consequences are very serious this will still constitute a serious endangerment. For instance, Justice Eames in the first major decision on the Act (*In the Matter of Major Reviews of Percy, Farrell and RJO* 1998) observed that in the cases coming before the Supreme Court could not be eliminated entirely but that the court should undertake a balancing exercise, included within which is an assessment of the likelihood of risk as well as the seriousness of the harm that would be caused if the relatively unlikely risk came to fruition:

> It would be most unlikely that Parliament intended that where a significant chance of a serious violence to members of the public was perceived by a judge, but was assessed to involve less than a 50-50 chance of its occurrence, such a conclusion would not be capable of constituting satisfaction that the public would thereby be "seriously endangered," should the reviewee be released. (*In the Matter of Major Reviews of Percy, Farrell and RJO* 1998: para. 61; see also *Re GBS* 1999: para. 32)

Similarly Justice Ashley in *Re RC* (1998: para. 46) held that a risk may be considered really significant even though it could not be said that it will inevitably or even probably translate into an occurrence—"the concept of serious endangerment involves issues of fact and degree." He denied that the least restrictive alternative provision in section 39 of the Act gave any "warrant for adopting a weak position when the safety of the applicant and other members of the public is under consideration" (*Re RC* 1998: para. 46).

In practice, before a significant downgrading in supervisory status by the Supreme Court will be made, there must be substantial and credible reassurance by mental health professionals that the chances of the acquittee offending violently again are remote, very low, slight, insignificant, or non-existent. Not surprisingly, this evaluation has consistently been justified by judges in terms of the need to protect the community against recidivism on the part of the acquittee (see for example *Re PL (No 4)* 2004; *Re MS* 2010). In an early decision Justice Cummins framed the jurisdiction as "protective":

The court examines the treatment, insight and progress of the applicant and considers expert evidence from very experienced medical and other professionals. It calls upon its own experience of human behaviour and of recidivism and reformation. Thus the court proceeds with as much responsible data as reasonably can be obtained, to seek to ensure community safety as contemplated by the Act. However, it must be remembered that applicants found not guilty by reason of mental impairment (or previously insanity) have not been convicted of a crime. Characteristically, they have suffered from a mental illness. The court's jurisdiction in that respect is protective. It should be remembered that ultimately the best protection for the community is that persons found not guilty by reason of mental impairment are able to return to the community as useful citizens. (*Re PL* 1998: para. 15)

The challenge for the acquittee seeking a downgrading in supervisory status or revocation lies in part in the fact that many psychiatric disorders are lifelong (see *Re NR* 2000: para. 23) or at least long-term disorders. As it is the disorders in this context that are presumed to have constituted a causal factor in the index offending, this has required close scrutiny by judges. The focus has generally been on the status of the disorder at the time of the review, its continuing symptomatology, especially any continuing delusions or hallucinations, the insight of the acquittee into relevant matters, and his or her history of compliance with prescribed treatment. These latter matters are considered to be predictive of later ongoing adherence to the pharmacotherapies and monitoring that constitute protections against relapse and further offending. In addition, the likelihood of fast onset of dangerous symptomatology upon relapse has been taken into account as a factor relevant to the exercise of judicial caution (see for example *Re PL* 2004: para. 50).

A further difficulty for acquittees' progress through the supervisory system has proved to be that downgrading in status requires the court to be persuaded of a negative—an absence of serious endangerment (see *Re PSG* 1998: para. 7). Reservation, hesitation, or uncertainty of any significant kind on the part of the court will lead to a disinclination to change the status quo. This has been particularly problematic at two phases—that of moving from the relatively stringent status of an acquittee being on extended leave and applying for a non-custodial supervision order and, particularly, when an acquittee applies to graduate from a non-custodial supervision order to revoked status.

A number of judges have queried in the context of residual concerns about the risk posed by the acquittee why the change in status is particularly important, given the modest requirements made of many acquittees on either extended leave or a non-custodial supervision order. In short, the temptation toward conservative decision-making is very high, and it has been necessary for acquittees to establish by evidence why the symbolism of downgrading in supervisory status is of consequence for their health or reintegration into the community. Even then it has been common for judges to speak in terms of the need for the exercise of caution. Thus, in *Re SKD* (2009: para. 7; see also *Re VAS* 2010) Justice Whelan observed that:

Revocation of a non-custodial supervision order is a particularly serious step. The principal consideration is the protection of the community and the applicant. The Court is entitled to take a cautious approach, as each case is demonstrative of the terrible tragedy that could occur if a revocation was ordered without sufficient care. (citing *Re PSG* 2005: para. 44 and *Re TDD* 2004: para. 27)

To similar effect Justice Kaye commented in *Re PL (No 4)* (2004: para. 45):

I would not be disposed to grant the application unless I was satisfied on cogent evidence, and to a comfortable degree, that the applicant would not endanger himself, or other members of the community, should I revoke the non-custodial supervision order.

Examples of Revocation Decisions As is evident from Table 8.2, only a small number of decisions have been made to revoke the supervisory status of persons found not guilty by reason of insanity or mental impairment. It is difficult to explore every such instance because almost all of the decisions in this context are restricted to facilitate reintegration of persons into the general community without sensationalist publicity. This section of the chapter therefore reviews a selection of such decisions by the Supreme Court.

In *Re NC* (2009) the acquittee had attempted to kill his wife in 2002 while in a manic phase of bipolar affective disorder. He had been found not guilty by reason of mental impairment. Doctors reported his mental state to have been stable for some seven years and that he had been compliant with visits to his psychiatrist and with taking the tetracyclic antidepressant, Mirtazapine. He had reconciled with his wife and was described by his psychiatrist as no danger to anyone. He had a good understanding of the warning signs of any relapse and the revocation application made by him was not opposed by the attorney general. It was allowed by Justice Coghlan.

In *Re RC* (2009) the acquittee, when 39 years of age in 1974, had killed his father and attempted to kill his mother. Upon being found not guilty of the crimes by reason of insanity, he was detained at the Governor's pleasure and spent 18 years in various prisons in Victoria. In 1992 he was transferred to the precursor to the Thomas Embling Hospital, Rosanna Forensic Psychiatric Centre. In 2000, RC's deemed custodial supervision order was varied to a non-custodial supervision order. This status was confirmed on a major review in 2003. The Attorney General did not oppose RC's application for revocation, which was supported by his psychiatrist who expressed the view that there was a low likelihood of his endangering himself or others. RC had become prepared and able to discuss the sexual fantasies, which had related to the commission of his offences. RC's diagnosis was of a mixed personality disorder with traits of narcissism and borderline personality disorder. He had a history of compliance with treatment, which was mostly non-pharmacotherapeutic, and had developed strategies for dealing with stress, which he acknowledged was his main risk factor. The evidence before the Supreme Court was that he could be adequately treated by his general practitioner and that revocation of his supervisory status would carry a number of therapeutic consequences. His order was revoked by Justice Curtain.

In *Re WN* (2009), the Victorian Supreme Court heard an application for revocation by a man who, when 37 in 1999, had committed a series of serious non-fatal offences when psychotic. He had been found not guilty by reason of mental impairment and treated with antipsychotics. The clinical evidence before the Court was that the risk that he posed to himself and others was low. His non-custodial supervision order was revoked by Justice Cummins.

In *Re LN* (2006), the Supreme Court dealt with a revocation application by a man who, in 1995, killed his wife in horrific circumstances when psychotic as a result of paranoid schizophrenia. He was found not guilty by reason of insanity and detained at the Governor's pleasure. In 2000 his deemed custodial supervision order was changed to a non-custodial supervision order with positive results. The expert evidence was that he had been highly compliant with what was asked of him by his treating team, and was very insightful about his illness and the circumstances of his offending. He had experienced no relapses for over a decade and was currently in full remission from his symptoms. His order was revoked by Justice Harper.

In *Re SDK* (2000), the Supreme Court dealt with an application for revocation from a mother who had killed her five-year-old daughter to spare her when SDK was deeply depressed as a result of bipolar disorder. The evidence was that she had been highly cooperative with treatment and had acquired good insight into the circumstances of her offending. Her prognosis was good. There was no or only a slight risk of her reoffending. Justice Hedigan concluded that she had "an unusually high level of insight into the necessity for her to maintain her controlling medication and is in a very low risk group, that is slight or no risk. … [It] would be harsh, even verging on the perverse not to revoke her supervision order" (*Re SDK* 2009: para. 29). He revoked the order (see also *Re JG* 1998).

An Overview of Revocation Decision-Making

As previously indicated, a substantial jurisprudence has developed in Victoria in relation to prediction of risk in respect of those on supervisory orders. It bears some similarities with the jurisprudence developed by Victoria's Mental Health Review Board and, on appeal, by the Victorian Civil and Administrative Tribunal in relation to the involuntary status of psychiatrically unwell patients—as inpatients or mandated outpatients on community treatment orders. However, what distinguishes the Supreme Court jurisprudence is that it is relatively unguided by statute, and all acquittees have committed significant acts of violence, generally a homicide or homicides, when mentally ill. Thus far, cases involving intellectual disability and brain injuries have not figured prominently. Nor have cases involving persons found unfit to stand trial. The Supreme Court jurisprudence is not easily accessible and is not substantially cross-referenced, cases being principally dealt with on the basis of their own facts. It is likely that the relative inaccessibility of decisions has affected the capacity of counsel to refer the court to relevant cases and thus a limited tendency of the court to cite other cases.

Decision-making by the Supreme Court, especially as to revocation, has, understandably, been conservative, gradualist (see for example *RDM v Director of Public Prosecutions* 1999: para. 97), and cautious (see for example *Re SKD* 2009: para. 7; *Re VAS* 2010)—looking carefully to how acquittees have performed on step downs of supervisory status. This has involved scrutiny of issues such as relapses, even many years before development of rapport with clinicians, coping with change, and drug and alcohol ingestion habits. Thus, for instance in *Re NR* (2000: 24), Justice Kellam concluded in respect of a person who had killed his mother while psychotic and heavily intoxicated, that his alcohol consumption needed to be addressed before serious consideration could be given to revocation of his non-custodial supervision order.

The views of psychiatrists, and, to a lesser degree, psychologists and case managers, not surprisingly have been highly influential on the Supreme Court's decision-making. For the most part (although there have been exceptions) downgrading in supervisory status has not occurred save upon the advice of, and with the reassurance of, clinicians. Nonetheless, it has been emphasized by a number of judges that decision-making is their non-delegable responsibility and that the practice in other contexts that where expert evidence is cogent and unchallenged "a judge should ordinarily be slow to depart from the risk assessment which the expert has made" does not apply in the context of supervision order revocations (*Re VAS* 2010: para. 33 applying *RDM v Director of Public Prosecutions* 1999: para. 287). This has meant that in spite of the support of clinicians on a number of occasions for downgrading or revocation of supervisory status, the court has decided against such a step.

Another dynamic that has affected decision-making by Supreme Court judges is that some psychiatrists have tended to be risk averse in their evaluation of the degree of danger of relapse and therefore the potential consequences of such relapse for acquittees and those with whom they have contact; others have been more optimistic. When this has occurred, their reservations have tended to be adopted by the court.

Given that many of the acquittees dealt with by the Supreme Court have schizophrenia, frequently paranoid schizophrenia, the tendency of the court has been to inquire into the nature of the delusions or hallucinations experienced by the acquittee around the time of the crime and into the persistence of such symptomatology in the acquittee. If bizarre ideas about a particular person, category of persons, or a specific issue have persisted in spite of treatment, this has been regarded as a major danger factor in relation to the potential for further offending. If, however, such primary symptoms have attenuated significantly to a point where the person is no longer preoccupied by such concerns and not troubled about them even if some such cognition continues to have elements of the delusional or the perplexed, this has not been viewed as so serious. The same can be said of continuing elements of secondary symptomatology in those with schizophrenia, such as amotivation, anhedonia, and the like, as these do not constitute particular risk factors for reoffending, save if they contribute to a lack of treatment adherence.

Much has depended for clinicians and for the Supreme Court on the degree of insight (Amador and David 1998; Dawson and Mullen 2008; Diesfield 2003; Freckelton 2005) on the part of the acquittee and on the acquittee's adherence to recommended treatment. The insight looked for is in relation to having a mental illness, what its symptoms are, the need to take medication prescribed (if any) and for monitoring, as well as for capacity to identify and respond to relapse signs. Absence of one or other of these aspects of insight is not disastrous but it has been found relevant to judges' decision-making. The substantial absence of insight is not necessarily the last word. Possession of insight is not a statutory precondition to downgrading in supervisory status, any more than it is for release from involuntary status in the civil context (Freckelton 2010). The Supreme Court has held that the major question is whether the acquittee will continue to take the medication that has the potential to keep him or her well. If he or she is likely to do so because of a deferential and cooperative disposition, or even a fear of being returned to strict custody, the relevant outcome is the safety that ensues from treatment adherence, not the degree of sophistication of insight into the nature of the illness and what needs to be done to address its symptomatology. As Justice McDonald observed in *Re DGC* (1998: para. 25) of a patient who had little by way of insight into having a mental illness or requiring medication but had a history of cooperation:

> It is in consequence of this that he accepts the prescribed treatment and by accepting the same the treatment had the effect as sought by his treating psychiatrist. This demonstrates that the applicant has in this respect insight. He appreciates that it is necessary to be compliant with treatment to be able to live in the circumstances that he currently enjoys.

Thus, treatment adherence, also often referred to as compliance with treatment, has emerged as a significant issue for supervision order clinicians and for the Supreme Court. This can be a complex matter because antipsychotics and treatment for both bipolar disorder and for depression all have side effects, some of them significant for at least some patients. Understandably, drugs like Clozapine, which carry the potential for serious blood dyscrasias and require ongoing blood testing, are not acceptable to some patients, although they can be very effective for treatment-refractory schizophrenia. Depot medications such as Risperidone (although it can also be administered orally) are deeply resented and viewed as demeaning by some patients. In addition, drugs like Zyprexa and Lithium can engender substantial weight gain, which is distressing and discommoding.

For many legitimate reasons, patients can be loathe to take medications that cause them ill effects. Patients with bipolar disorder can also be highly ambivalent about losing the highs, which they can perceive as facilitating their creativity (Jamison 1993, 1995). These observations aside, if a precondition to wellness of a patient, or at least reduction to acceptable levels of positive symptoms, is the taking of a medication or class of medications, it is proper and orthodox that the Supreme Court has looked carefully to the reliability of patients' complying with what is prescribed for their condition.

The attitude of the Attorney General, particularly if in opposition to downgrading supervisory status, is a factor the Supreme Court has taken into account. However, it has not been determinative and there have been instances in which judges have inquired both as to the reasons for the attorney general's stance and as to why he has not supported a downgrading or revocation if he has adopted a position of not expressing a view to the court.

Another relevant factor has been the attitude of surviving relatives of victims or of the victims themselves. This has the potential to be advantageous, as well as disadvantageous, for acquittees.

On occasions, as noted earlier, acquittees have reconciled with victims. On other occasions, victims' relatives have identified that a crime, for instance, homicide, has been committed by a person affected by a serious mental illness and, if they are reassured that this is well addressed, are not averse to the downgrading of the acquittee's supervisory status.

On other occasions, more often, relatives of a deceased person are passionately opposed to the supervisory order over the person being revoked and are fearful of the consequences for themselves or others if that course is adopted by the court. These sentiments and the genuineness of their fears, as well as the degree to which they are well founded, are factors that are often referred to by Supreme Court judges. Under section 42 of the Act, reports can be provided to the court by family members and this happens quite frequently.

The Supreme Court has tended to be more liberal in downgrading supervisory status from custodial to non-custodial than in revoking supervisory status absolutely. This is because of the continuing capacity that the court retains to order acquittees to return to inpatient status if they are on a non-custodial supervision order and have significantly deteriorated in mental state and breached the terms of a non-custodial supervision order (see sec 29(1) of the Act). By contrast, if the court revokes an acquittee's supervisory status, he or she reverts to being simply another patient in the community with a diagnosis of a mental illness.

There have been many inquiries into the extent to which the area mental health system or a private practitioner (either a psychiatrist or a general practitioner) will be able to deal with any reemergence of psychotic symptomatology and the likelihood of their becoming aware of such reemergence in the first place. Different attitudes have been taken, based upon the evidence adduced in specific cases. On some occasions, the court has been troubled about the sufficiency of likely response. For example, Justice Smith stated in *Re SS* (2000: para. 20):

> There is often a tendency on the part of those treating someone to err on the side of optimism in supporting the person. In addition, the harsh reality of the provision of services of the kind in question in our community, at present, is that these services have been and remain under stress because of lack of resources and the demand for those services. It is likely, also, that responsibility will be divided. (See also Gillard J in *Re TDD* 1998: para. 18.)

On other occasions, the court has been satisfied that an acquittee is sufficiently monitored for any relapse signs, that the treatment regime in place adequately recognizes the risks and is in a position to respond adequately and promptly (see for example *Re JG* 1998). This is a sensitive issue for some acquittees because it generally takes many years for them to be able to live down their crime and to be released from the fetters of the forensic system. If they are the subject of a red flag within the civil mental health system (after release from the forensic system) by reason of their criminal conduct many years before, as is sometimes proposed, this can be keenly felt and quite countertherapeutic. This proposition was accepted by Justice Warren in *Re JG* (1998: para. 40) when he observed that "persons such as the applicant experience an enormous sense of release and freedom when a supervision order or court order controls are eventually put behind them."

A result of all of these considerations is that there have been modest numbers of successful applications for revocation of supervisory orders. This is especially so in the Supreme Court. The approach of the Supreme Court has been gradualist, requiring the passage of significant time on supervisory status and the management by the acquittee of different vicissitudes so as to give confidence that they will cope with other potential precipitants to relapse in the future without the safety net (*Re PL (No 4)* 2004: para. 53) of supervisory status.

It is rare for an application for revocation to succeed on the first occasion. This is hard both for acquittees, who often find the experience of appearing before the Supreme Court a traumatic experience that requires them to relive their index offending in a countertherapeutic way, and for relatives of victims who also reexperience extremely traumatic and often life-changing events with each further hearing about the acquittee's supervisory status. This observation is made not to suggest that the process needs to be changed but to acknowledge the highly emotionally charged context of the court's decision-making and the consequences for acquittees and relatives of victims alike.

While at the five-year mark of the legislation, there was reason to be concerned about the difficulties for acquittees to proceed to revocation (Freckelton 2003), and whether this outcome was significantly the province of females found not guilty by reason of depression of neonaticide offences, the passage of over a decade gives more cause for optimism. A cohort of Supreme Court judges, at first led by Justice Kellam, has acquired real expertise in this complex area of dangerousness prediction. Acquittees are relatively rarely expected themselves to give evidence and, if they do, are usually treated with dignity and circumspection by cross-examiners. When they testify and perform adequately, this can be a forensic advantage for them. The current Attorney General, too, is tending to take a less oppositional role in cases where clinicians identify some merit in revocation, leaving the decision to the court without himself expressing a view through counsel.

On a number of occasions, revocation orders have been made in relation to acquittees with schizophrenia and with personality disorders. A jurisprudence, albeit not very accessible, has evolved that focuses upon clinically informed risk-prediction factors. Insight has tended not to be unduly elevated to a stand-alone extralegislative factor, but questions of relevant symptomatology and treatment adherence have regularly figured prominently in decision-making. The views of treating clinicians are extremely, and properly influential, but not determinative. Judges' decision-making is conservative and cautious, but reasonably so. Some judges require more reassurance about the level of risk posed by an acquittee than others, but a number have been prepared, when adequately satisfied about the reasonable absence of the risk of serious endangerment, to take the step into the unknown of releasing an acquittee from supervisory status and entrusting him or her to the area mental health system or to the treatment of a private psychiatrist or general practitioner.

There is an important caveat that needs to be made in relation to this optimism. The positive comments in this chapter apply principally to those found by the Supreme Court to be NGRMI of homicide offences. It can now be said that, where acquittees are responsive to and cooperative with treatment, there is the prospect that they will spend significantly less time in custody than they would have done had they pleaded guilty to murder or manslaughter. However, this depends on the degree of the responsiveness of their condition to treatment. There still remain persons with personality disorders and refractory schizophrenia who have spent in the order of 40 years in custody and there appears little likelihood of their ever emerging from it (see for example Re RJO 2008: para. 12). From a forensic perspective, there is a real gamble in an accused's plea of NGRMI to a homicide because release from confinement and progression by the person through the supervisory system will depend upon his or her actual symptoms and their amenability to pharmacotherapy. This cannot easily be forecast at the time of decision-making about a plea.

This dilemma is exacerbated in the County Court of Victoria and is starkly exposed in the Magistrates' Court. In the County Court, where the sentences are for the most part much lower than in the Supreme Court, which deals with homicide offences, the balance may shift with the person likely to serve longer in confinement in the forensic mental health system than they otherwise might in the penal system. This is a problem for those representing accused persons who have responsibility for advising on pleas. If the result of a plea of NGRMI is that acquittees spend a long period in psychiatric confinement by reason of their ongoing symptomatology and their risk of relapse and dangerous reoffending, there can be much to commend such an outcome. From the point of view of acquittees, what they wish, understandably enough, is to minimize their period of confinement and supervision—whether it be in the penal or forensic mental health systems.

Conclusions

Further monitoring and evaluation of the shift of responsibility in Victoria from the executive to the judiciary for the release back into the community of persons found NGRMI is required. So too is comparison between the Victorian experiment and the system in jurisdictions in which decision-making about the reintegration of NGRI and NGRMI acquittees into the community is undertaken by multidisciplinary tribunals. Additional reflection also needs to be devoted to the potential relevance of the process for the Magistrates' Court in relation to persons found NGRMI after their commission of less serious forms of criminal offending.

For the present, what can be said of the Victorian experiment in relation to risk evaluation by the Supreme Court, rather than by the executive, is that it has been constructively informed by clinical opinion. There remains cautiousness in decision-making but that is justified in most instances given the violence engaged in by acquittees and their illness course. Depoliticization of the process has not wholly avoided risk aversion in assessment or decision-making, but it has resulted in a significant improvement in the quality and fairness of predictions of risk to self and others in relation to a particularly complex category of offenders. The result is that while there is much to be said in principle for giving the role of decision-making about those found NGRI or NGRMI to an expert tribunal appointed specifically for the purpose, as occurs in a number of jurisdictions, the Victorian experiment in a little over its first decade has suggested that Supreme Court judges for the most part have undertaken the risk-assessment process in a clinically informed and considered way. The outcome has been reintegration of acquittees into the community in a staged process attended by the exercise of caution, but caution that generally has been clinically warranted.

9

The Preventive Detention of Suspected Terrorists
Better Safe than Sorry?

BERNADETTE McSHERRY

Introduction: Two Australian Cases

Preventive detention schemes for sex offenders, explored elsewhere in this book, generally come into play post-conviction (and in some jurisdictions post-sentence) and have generally been justified on the basis of the utilitarian approach that regards the protection, and subsequent happiness, of the majority as overriding any individual right to liberty (Mill 1863). A similar argument has been used to justify powers for the preventive detention of suspected terrorists and pre-charge detention for the purposes of investigation. However, such powers go even further than those enabling the preventive detention of sex offenders because no offence need ever have been committed at all for a person's liberty to be taken away.

This chapter examines the issues related to the preventive detention of suspected terrorists and raises the issue as to whether mental health professionals should play a role in identifying those who may be considered at risk of taking part in terrorist activities. Two Australian cases are outlined to explore how powers to detain suspected terrorists based on the concept of a belief or suspicion on "reasonable grounds" rather than the assessment of risk can lead to errors of judgment.

Dr. Mohamed Haneef

On 29 June 2007, two car bombs were defused in London and on 30 June, there was a car bomb attack on Glasgow Airport. On 2 July 2007, Dr. Mohamed Haneef, a 27-year-old Indian doctor who had been working at a Gold Coast hospital pursuant to a work visa, was arrested without warrant at Brisbane Airport under section 3W(1) of the Crimes Act 1914 (Commonwealth; Cth) (a detailed account of the Haneef enquiry can be found in Ewart 2009). A central requirement of section 3W(1)(a) is that at the time of the arrest, the relevant police officer must believe "on reasonable grounds" that the arrested individual has committed or is committing an offence. The main evidence upon which such a belief was based was a report to the Australian Federal Police (AFP) by a member of the Metropolitan Police Service in London that a mobile telephone subscribed in Haneef's name was of significance in their investigation (Clarke 2008: 46). There are separate provisions governing how long and on what grounds an individual may continue to be detained and these are outlined later in the chapter.

Haneef's detention was widely reported in the media. He was charged 12 days later with recklessly providing assistance to a terrorist organization by giving a mobile phone SIM card to his cousin, Sabeel Ahmed. (Ahmed was not in fact directly involved with the bombing, but he later pleaded guilty to withholding information about his brother's involvement in the attack.)

On 16 July 2007, after being granted bail by a Brisbane magistrate, Haneef had his work visa revoked by the then Immigration Minister Kevin Andrews, and was detained in prison (Haneef elected to stay in prison rather than immigration detention) pending his committal hearing. On 27 July, the Commonwealth Director of Public Prosecutions Damien Bugg QC (Queen's Counsel), withdrew the charge on the basis that there was insufficient evidence to proceed with a prosecution. The Immigration Minister returned Haneef's passport and Haneef flew to India the following day. The Director of Public Prosecutions later admitted that Haneef should never have been charged (Marr 2007).

A subsequent inquiry into the matter led by the former New South Wales Supreme Court Justice John Clarke QC found that Haneef was neither associated with nor had foreknowledge of the terrorist events (Clarke 2008: vii). Haneef's lawyers have subsequently filed proceedings for defamation against the former immigration minister as well as proceedings for unlawful arrest and misconduct in public office against the federal government (Gregg 2010).

Izhar Ul-Haque

In March 2003, Izhar Ul-Haque, an Australian citizen and medical student at the University of New South Wales, returned to Sydney from Pakistan. Upon arrival in Sydney, his baggage was searched and customs officers found written material about events in Afghanistan and information about oil and gas pipelines in Central Asia. There was also a letter by him addressed to his family stating that he was going to Kashmir for jihad and that he intended to join the organization, Lashkar-e-Taiba. This organization is based in Lahore, Pakistan, and has as its main goal the ending of Indian rule in Kashmir.

This material was confiscated but Ul-Haque was not subject to any further action at that stage. On 6 November 2003, Ul-Haque, accompanied by his 17-year-old brother, Izaz, arrived at Blacktown, New South Wales, train station where he had parked his car on his way home from university. Three officers from the Australian Security Intelligence Organisation (ASIO), referred to subsequently in a pre-trial hearing as B14, B15, and B16, stopped him. B15 identified himself as a member of ASIO and reportedly said: "You are in serious trouble. You need to talk to us and you need to talk to us now." Ul-Haque said he was told to accompany them and when he asked about his brother he was told to "give the keys to him." When he said his brother couldn't drive, he was told he could sit in the car and wait. (Izaz later found his own way home.)

Ul-Haque was then seated in the back seat of a vehicle between two of the officers and driven to a park. There, he was told to get out of the car. B15 testified that he had said: "You're in a substantial amount of trouble. We are conducting a very serious terrorist investigation at the moment and that investigation had led us to you. We have many means of investigation and we hold considerable information about you. What we now require from you is your full cooperation." He then drew a figure y in the gravel with his foot. He pointed to the intersection of the y and said: "We are here … We've got two choices. We can go down the difficult path or the less difficult path."

Ul-Haque was then told his house was being raided. His reaction to these statements was as could be expected from a 21-year-old (*R v Ul-Haque* 2007: 363):

> I never thought I had a choice because I believed I was under arrest and that if I did not comply with whatever they asked me that they will either use physical violence or take me to a more sinister place to interrogate me, or, you know, do something to my family or deport me, or lots of other things were going on in my mind, and the thought of choice never really occurred because I was under extreme pressure or stress.

The ASIO officers took Ul-Haque back to the house that he shared with his mother and three brothers (his father being in Pakistan at the time) where around 20 ASIO officers and five AFP officers were in the process of executing a search warrant. At around midnight, Ul-Haque was taken into a bedroom at the front of the house and was interviewed again until 3:45 a.m., with four short breaks in between. During this interview, a member of the AFP was present as a passive observer.

Some months later, in 2004, Ul-Haque was charged under section 102.5 of the Criminal Code (Cth) with receiving training from a terrorist organization between 12 January 2003 and

2 February 2003. At the time it was alleged that Ul-Haque had undergone training, Lashkar-e-Taiba was not a specified terrorist organization under the Criminal Code and the prosecution had the onus of proving that it was a terrorist organization in January 2003.

Ul-Haque spent six weeks on remand, in solitary confinement at Goulburn's "supermax" prison before being released on bail on 27 May 2004. At his trial, which took place in 2007, Justice Adams of the Supreme Court of New South Wales ruled that the evidence from the interviews conducted on 7 and 12 November 2003 and on 9 January 2004 was inadmissible because it had been influenced by the "oppressive conduct of ASIO" (*R v Ul-Haque* 2007: 384).

Justice Adams was of the opinion that on 6 November 2003 the ASIO officers "conveyed to the accused that he was obliged to accompany them, knowing that this was false" (*R v Ul-Haque* 2007: 384). According to Justice Adams, the officers had accordingly committed the offences of false imprisonment and kidnapping. The inadmissibility of these interviews left the prosecution with very little choice but to discontinue the trial. Prosecutor Geoff Bellew SC (Senior Counsel) told the court on 12 November 2007 that the Commonwealth Director of Public Prosecutions would not appeal the decision and there would be no further action (Scheikowski 2007).

Detention and Investigation of Suspected Terrorists

The cases of Mohamed Haneef and Izhar Ul-Haque have been summarized here to highlight some of the problems that can occur with detention and investigation regimes in relation to individuals who are suspected of terrorist activities. They are not isolated cases. Justice Coghlan of the Supreme Court of Victoria has criticized the AFP concerning its tactics in an investigation of three Australian men who were thought to be members of the Tamil Tigers, a separatist group in Sri Lanka: *R v Rajeevan, Vinayagamoorthy and Yathavan* (2010). Serious terrorism charges were subsequently dropped and the men pleaded guilty to a lesser offence of sending money to a terrorist organization. They were sentenced to suspended jail terms, and released on condition they pay $1,000 bonds and be of good behavior.

There are also indications of overzealous policing of terrorism offences in other countries. A 2007 report found that in the United Kingdom, of 1,166 arrests since 11 September 2001, only 40 led to convictions under anti-terrorism legislation (Press Association 2007). The Independent Reviewer of Terrorism has also criticized counter-terrorism police for failing to consult prosecution lawyers when arresting 12 terrorism suspects in Liverpool and Manchester (Laville 2009). The 12 men were all later released without charge.

In addition to increased investigatory powers, there are broad legislative powers now available in most common-law countries for preventive detention of suspected terrorists for the purposes of community protection rather than for the purposes of investigation and questioning. The Australian powers are outlined later in this chapter.

The next section focuses on Australian anti-terrorism laws in relation to detention for investigation purposes that provided the context for the two investigations outlined earlier.

The final section draws out some themes highlighting the similarities and differences in preventive detention regimes for high-risk offenders and suspected terrorists, and raises the issue as to whether risk assessment may provide a better model for investigation than the concept of a belief or suspicion on reasonable grounds.

Powers of Pre-charge Detention of Suspected Terrorists

A senior counterterrorism officer with the Australian Federal Police, federal agent Kemuel Lam Paktsun, testified during a pre-trial hearing in the Izhar Ul-Haque case (Neighbour 2007):

> At the time, we were directed, we were informed, to lay as many charges under the new terrorist legislation against as many suspects as possible because we wanted to use the new

legislation … So regardless of the assistance that Mr. Ul-Haque could give, he was going to be prosecuted, charged, because we wanted to test the legislation and lay new charges, in our eagerness to use the legislation.

The new legislation referred to was a package of statutes prohibiting terrorist organizations and creating special terrorism offences and antiterrorism financing provisions (Hancock 2002). This reform paralleled developments in other common-law jurisdictions such as the United States, United Kingdom, and Canada (Ramraj 2002). Subsequent legislation has amended the powers of investigation and surveillance by both federal and state police as well as by members of ASIO.

The Anti-Terrorism Act 2004 (Cth) amended certain provisions of the Crimes Act 1914 (Cth) in relation to investigations of suspected terrorists. Table 9.1 summarizes the provisions under which Mohamed Haneef was detained.

Table 9.1 shows that although the time for investigation is capped at four hours, this can be extended by 20 hours on multiple grounds and there is no limit placed on dead time or down

Table 9.1 Pre-charge Detention for Investigation in Australia: Crimes Act 1914 (Cth)

Grounds for arrest without warrant	Constable believes on reasonable grounds person has committed or is committing an offence	
In general	Person arrested for terrorist offence may be detained for four hours for questioning and investigation about their involvement in any terrorist offence the investigating officer reasonably suspects the person to have committed	23CA
Option 1: Extension	Extends period of investigation by up to 20 hours (24 hours total)	23DA(7)
Grounds for extension	• Offence is a terrorism offence • Further detention of the person is necessary to preserve or obtain evidence or to complete the investigation into any terrorism offence • The investigation into the offence is being conducted properly and without delay • Person, or their lawyer, has been given a chance to make representations re application	23DA(4)
Option 2: Dead time	Specifies time of reasonable suspension or delay which can be disregarded from maximum detention time (dead time)—no limits	23CA(8) 23CB
Grounds for declaring dead time	• Appropriate to do so, having regard to (i) the application, (ii) any representations made by the person, or their lawyer, about the application, and (iii) any other relevant matters • Offence is a terrorism offence • Detention of the person is necessary to preserve or obtain evidence or to complete the investigation into the offence or into another terrorism offence • The investigation into the offence is being conducted properly and without delay • The person, or his or her legal representative, has been given the opportunity to make representations about the application	23CB(7)
Issuing authority	• Magistrate • Justice of the peace • Bail justice	23CB(3) 23DA(2)

time when a person is not being questioned. This approach was criticized by John Clarke QC in his inquiry into the circumstances surrounding Haneef's detention (Clarke 2008). He stated (Clarke 2008: 249):

> I believe the concept of uncapped detention time is unacceptable to the majority of the community and involves far too great an intrusion on the liberty of citizens and non-citizens alike ... There is a powerful argument in favour of remedying the situation in Australia—not only to limit the length of detention but also to ensure that an investigation is carried expeditiously and with a sense of the need to act with urgency.

It should be noted that while the language used for arrest without warrant is a belief on reasonable grounds, continued detention for investigation purposes rests on the concept of reasonable suspicion. As well as granting these powers under the Crimes Act 1914 (Cth), the Australian government decided to increase ASIO's intelligence-gathering powers. The Australian Security Intelligence Organisation Legislation Amendment (Terrorism) Bill 2002 (Cth) originally contained powers to strip-search and detain both children and adults who might have information about terrorism for two-day periods, which could be renewed indefinitely. Severely criticized by two parliamentary committees, the Bill stalled and was replaced by a second version, which was enacted in June 2003.

The Australian Security Intelligence Organisation Act Amendment (Terrorism) Act 2003 (Cth) introduced a power (under Section 34HC) to detain individuals for questioning without charge for renewable periods of seven days, with the maximum time allowable being 28 days. It is a criminal offence for a detainee to refuse to answer a question and he or she has no right to seek judicial review of the validity or terms of the ASIO warrant. There are also confidentiality provisions that limit the independent monitoring of the use of these ASIO questioning and detention powers by the media, lawyers, and academics. Table 9.2 summarizes the key elements of this legislation.

The current powers enable the detention for up to 28 days of individuals who are not suspected of any involvement with terrorism but who are believed on reasonable grounds to have information of use to the government. This means that a person who is not suspected of committing any offence can potentially be detained for longer than a person who is suspected of terrorist activity.

Andrew Lynch and George Williams (2006: 39) state that between the enactment of these powers in June 2003 and November 2005, 13 people had been detained, but it is difficult to obtain accurate data because of the non-disclosure provisions. Paddy Hillyard (1987) has made the point in the context of Northern Ireland that "temporary" emergency laws dealing with terrorism are rarely repealed but tend to become normalized over time. It is interesting to note that there was a three-year sunset clause for the ASIO powers, but this was extended for a further 10 years by the Australian Security Intelligence Organisation Legislation Amendment Act 2006 (Cth).

Lynch and Williams (2006: 40) state that the "possibility that expansive powers might be abused by intelligence agencies is very real" and point to the 2002 finding that the Federal Bureau of Investigation (FBI) and the United States Justice Department supplied false information in relation to more than 75 applications for search warrants and wiretaps for suspected terrorists. The two cases outlined earlier certainly indicate that a culture of testing such powers to the limit can easily develop, although, ironically, such a culture can lead to the failure of investigations through the judicial process. As Arie Freiberg (2000: 58) has pointed out in another context, judicial responses to laws concerning the dangerous generally have been prescient and cautious.

Table 9.2 ASIO Detention for Intelligence Gathering: Australian Security Intelligence Organisation Act 1979 (Cth)

What does warrant authorize?	• Immediate arrest by police officer • Immediate appearance before a prescribed authority for questioning • Detention for a prescribed period • Contact with limited identified persons at specified times
Issuing authority	Federal magistrate or judge appointed by the minster
Prescribed authority	Generally, an ex-judge of a superior court who served for five years, appointed by the minister. May also be a current: • State/territory judge of supreme or district court who has served for five years • AAT president/deputy enrolled as legal practitioner of Federal/Supreme Court for at least five years
Grounds	First warrant: • *Reasonable grounds to believe* the warrant will substantially assist the collection of intelligence that is important in relation to a terrorism offence Further warrants: • New or different information arises since the request for the last warrant's issue and • The person is not being detained in connection with an earlier warrant
Duration	• 168 hours (seven days) maximum continuous detention; renewable (see above) • Warrant may remain in force for 28 days max
Contacting others	During detention, detainee must be allowed to contact: • Inspector general of intelligence and security • Ombudsman • Person referred to in s 40SB(3)(b) of the Australian Federal Police Act 1979 • A lawyer of the detainee's choice Detainee may be allowed to contact a family member
Disclosure offences	Offence to recklessly disclose, while warrant in force and without permission: • That a warrant has been issued • Anything relating to the content of the warrant, the questioning or detention under the warrant • Operational information (information held by ASIO, including source, or operational information of ASIO) obtained as a result of the issue of the warrant, doing something authorized under the warrant or a direction of the prescribed authority or by another provision under the division Offence to disclose without permission, within two years of the warrant's expiry, operational information obtained as a result of the issue of the warrant, doing something authorized under the warrant or a direction of the prescribed authority or by another provision under the division Penalty: Imprisonment for five years **Strict liability for detainee and their lawyer

This pattern appears once more to be emerging in relation to increased powers of detention for investigation and intelligence gathering.

Pre-charge Preventive Detention for Community Protection

The most far-reaching legislative powers in relation to suspected terrorists that have been introduced in common-law countries relate to pre-charge preventive detention. These powers enable an individual to be detained for community protection purposes rather than for the traditional processes of investigation and questioning.

Table 9.3 sets out the relevant powers that exist in Australia in this regard.

The introduction of these powers has been subject to criticism about their derogation from established legal values (Head 2004, 2005; Joseph 2004; Kerr 2004; Lynch and Williams 2006; MacDonald and Williams 2007; Michaelsen 2008; Palmer 2004). A private member's Bill, the Anti-Terrorism Law Reform Bill 2009, sought to limit the maximum time for ASIO detention to 24 hours, but after being referred to the Senate's Legal and Constitutional Affairs Committee, has not found government support.

As highlighted in Table 9.3, the key terms justifying preventive detention are generally that of a suspicion on reasonable grounds that the individual concerned is a terrorist or will engage in a terrorist act. This differs slightly from the requirement of a belief on reasonable grounds for arrest without warrant under the Crimes Act 1914 (Cth), but reflects the concept of reasonable suspicion in that act for continued detention for investigation purposes. What is meant by a belief or suspicion on reasonable grounds is open to debate. There have been some judicial opinions on the concept of reasonable suspicion in criminal cases. The following are samples from the case law:

1. "Suspicion" is "a conception of the imagination. It is not a physical fact" (*Dunleavy v Dempsey* 1916: 92 per Justice Burnside).
2. "Suspicion can take into account matters that could not be put into evidence at all" (*Hussein (Shabaan Bin) v Kam (Chong Fook)* 1969: 1631–2 per Lord Denning).
3. The word "suspicion" is "intended to indicate a minimum and not a maximum as regards proof" (*R v Carter* 1978: per Chief Justice Street).
4. "Suspicion" carries less conviction than belief. A reasonable suspicion "does not necessarily imply that it is well-founded or that the grounds for suspicion must be factually correct" (*Tucs v Manley* 1985: 461 per Justice Jacobs).
5. "Suspicion is not to be confused with proof" (*R v Chan* 1992: 437 per Justice Abadee).

From these statements, it can be gleaned that the word *suspicion* has been interpreted as describing a mental state that need not be based on "proof," but is tempered by an objective gloss, that of "reasonableness." Of course the latter term has been criticized as meaning different things to different people at different times. Geoffrey Alpert and William Smith (1994) have argued that the police have not been aided by vague standards of reasonableness in guidelines concerning in relation to the use of force. The same can be said of reasonableness in relation to a suspicion or a belief. A reasonable belief may impose a higher threshold, but it still does not necessarily reach the civil standard of proof on the balance of probabilities (Clarke 2008: 234).

What is important to note here is that there is no mention of risk. Precautionary measures such as detention based on reasonable suspicion completely bypass the need for risk assessments by mental health professionals. This marks an important difference in the regimes of preventive detention of high-risk offenders and preventive detention of suspected terrorists. This is explored in the next section.

Precautionary Politics and the Role of Mental Health Professionals

Preventive detention regimes in the context of terrorism target individuals suspected of being in some way involved in a future terrorist act. In relation to the response to terrorism, Dan Gardner (2008: 4) points out that the statistics dealing with deaths from terrorist acts suggest that the chance of dying as a result of a terrorist act is miniscule, yet the irrational fear of planes being targeted led to the death of 1,595 Americans when they made the mistake of switching from planes to cars after the September 11 terrorist acts in the

Table 9.3 Preventive Detention in Australia

Who can make a PDO (preventive detention order)	Supreme Court	ACT sec. 18(1); New South Wales sec. 26H; Tasmania s 7(1); Victoria sec. 13E
	Former judge appointed by minister/ governor	Australia (Fed) sec. 105.2; Queensland sec. 7(2); Western Australia sec. 7
	Current judge appointed by minister/ administrator/ governor/lord chief justice	Australia (Fed) sec. 105.2; Northern Territory s 21C; Queensland sec. 7(2); South Australia sec. 4(1)(2); Western Australia sec. 7
	AAT president/deputy president	Australia (Fed) sec. 105.2
	Senior police officer (initial order or in urgent circumstances)	Australia (Cth) sec. 100.1(1), 105.8; Queensland sec. 7(1); South Australia sec. 4(3); Tasmania sec. 7(1)
Grounds for making an order	• *Reasonable grounds to suspect* that detainee: will engage in a "terrorist act"; possesses a thing connected with preparation/engagement in a terrorist act or; has done an act in preparation for a terrorist act • Would substantially assist in preventing terrorist act • Period of detention under PDO is reasonably necessary • The terrorist attack must be imminent (next 14 days)	Australia (Cth) sec. 105.4(4)(5); Queensland sec. 8(3)(4); New South Wales sec. 26D(1); Northern Territory sec. 21G(1)(a); South Australia sec. 6(3)(4); Tasmania sec. 7(1)(a); Victoria sec. 13E(1)(a) ACT sec. 18(4): test is "reasonable necessity" not "substantial assistance" Also PDO is least restrictive means Western Australia sec. 13(1)(b)(i): except no requirement that period of detention be reasonably necessary
	• Terrorist act occurred in the last 28 days • Detention is necessary to preserve evidence of, or relating to, the terrorist act • Period of detention under the PDO is reasonably necessary to preserve the evidence	Australia (Cth) sec. 105.4(6); Queensland sec. 8(5); New South Wales sec. 26D(2); Northern Territory sec. 21G(1)(b); South Australia sec. 6(5); Tasmania sec. 7(1)(b); Victoria sec.13E(1)(b) ACT sec. 18(6): Also detention under PDO is only effective way to preserve the evidence Western Australia sec. 13(1)(b)(ii): Except no requirement that period of detention be reasonably necessary
Duration: Initial/ interim	No initial/interim orders	Northern Territory; South Australia; Western Australia
	24 hours (including extensions)	Australia (Cth) sec. 105.10(5); ACT sec. 20(6), 23(3); Queensland sec. 17(5)
	48 hours (no possible extensions)	New South Wales sec. 26L; Tasmania sec. 9(3); Victoria sec. 13G(2)
Maximum duration: Final	24 hours, where issued by senior police officer	South Australia sec. 10(5)(a); Tasmania sec. 9(1)
	48 hours	Australia (Cth) sec. 105.14(6)
	7 days	ACT sec. 21(3)(a)
	14 days	New South Wales sec. 26K(2); Northern Territory sec. 21K(1); Queensland sec. 25(6), 31(3); Victoria sec. 13G(1); Western Australia sec. 13(3); ACT sec. 21(3)(b), total under any PDOs; South Australia sec. 10(5)(b); Tasmania sec. 8(3), 9(2), where issued by judge

Table 9.3 Preventive Detention in Australia (Continued)

Disclosure offences—Detainee	None	ACT; Queensland; New South Wales; UK Australia (Cth) sec. 105.41(1); South Australia sec. 41(1)
	Detainee cannot, while in detention, disclose to another that: • they are under a PDO • they are being detained • period of detention	
	Detainee cannot, while in detention, intentionally disclose to another without entitlement that they are: • under a PDO • being detained • under a prohibited contact order	Victoria sec. 13ZJ(1); Tasmania sec. 38(1); Western Australia sec. 46(1) Northern Territory sec. 21ZO(1): Also cannot disclose where detained
Disclosure offences—Third parties	None	ACT; New South Wales; UK Australia (Cth) sec. 105.41,105.35; Queensland sec. 64–68; Northern Territory sec. 21ZO(2)–(9); South Australia sec. 41(2)–(7); Tasmania sec. 38(2)–(7); Victoria sec. 13ZJ(2)–(10); Western Australia sec. 46(2)–(9)
	Offences replicated for: • Lawyer contacted by the detainee • Parent/guardian of detainee who discloses to another person who is not entitled to have contact with the detainee (including another parent/guardian who has not had contact with the detainee). Parent/guardian can tell another person that the detainee is safe but not contactable • Interpreter monitoring the detainee's contact with another person • Recipient of information obtained improperly under this act • Monitor monitoring the detainee's contact with another person Exceptions arise for proceedings, applications and complaints about the PDO, treatment of the detainee or the performance of the PDO etc. Generally, it is permissible to inform others that detainee is safe but not contactable	
Closed proceedings	Yes	Queensland sec. 76; New South Wales sec. 26P; Northern Territory sec. 21U(2); South Australia sec. 47; Tasmania sec. 50; Western Australia sec. 53
	No	Australia (Cth); ACT; Victoria

Commonwealth: Criminal Code (Cth) Division 105
ACT: Terrorism (Extraordinary Temporary Powers) Act 2006 (ACT)
Queensland: Terrorism (Preventative Detention) Act 2005 (Qld)
New South Wales: Terrorism (Police Powers) Act 2002 (NSW)
Northern Territory: Terrorism (Emergency Powers) Act 2003 (NT)
South Australia: Terrorism (Preventative Detention) Act 2005 (SA)
Tasmania: Terrorism (Preventative Detention) Act 2005 (Tas)
Victoria: Terrorism (Community Protection) Act 2003 (Vic)
Western Australia: Terrorism (Preventative Detention) Act 2006 (WA)

United States. Despite terrorist acts occurring rarely, Western neo-liberal countries continue to broaden powers of investigation and monitoring on the basis of what has been termed the *precautionary principle.*

This principle stems from environmental science and posits that where the risk of harm (such as through a terrorist attack) is unpredictable and uncertain, and where the damage wrought will be irreversible, any lack of scientific certainty in relation to the nature of the harm or its consequences should not prevent action being taken (Aradau and Van Munster 2007; Ericson 2007; Stern and Weiner 2006; Sunstein 2005). Thus, when translated to pre-crime tactics, the precautionary principle ousts risk-based or evidence-based approaches to public policy (Goldsmith 2008).

One suggestion for curbing the rise of precautionary politics has been to call for more empirical data to inform legal responses to terrorism. Christopher Harding (2002: 17) has stated:

> the whole subject [terrorism] is beset by an obscure and uncertain state of knowledge and understanding and it is disappointing that social scientific and legal evaluation has done little so far to penetrate some of these issues.

Mental health professionals are now publishing some material about how the risks of terrorism may be reduced (for example, Stout 2004), but what is striking about preventive detention of suspected terrorists is the lack of attention to risk terminology that is so common in preventive detention regimes for convicted offenders. Rather, as outlined earlier, the emphasis is on reasonable suspicion or belief.

Jeff Victoroff (2005) in an extensive review of psychological explanations for terrorism has concluded that the majority of studies in this area have lacked a sound empirical basis, with many approaches being based on the subjective interpretation of anecdotal evidence. There now seems to be a move toward encouraging mental health professionals to develop tools and techniques that provide a better evidence base for the identification and preventive detention of suspected terrorists. Gisli Gudjonsson (2009: 519) posits that "psychology has a great deal to offer in providing meaningful conceptual and theoretical frameworks for the risk assessment of terrorist offenders, which can guide research and individual assessments."

Elaine Pressman (2009) has argued that current risk assessment tools are of questionable relevance for identifying the risk posed by suspected terrorists because the factors used do not include the background and motivations of such individuals. She has proposed that a specific structured professional judgment tool titled the Violent Extremism Risk Assessment (VERA) be introduced to assess the risk of violence from certain individuals. The factors to be assessed include attitude items (such as attachment to an ideology justifying violence), contextual items (such as the use of extremist websites), historical items (such as state-sponsored military or paramilitary training), protective items (such as the rejection of violence to achieve goals), and demographic items (Pressman 2009: 34). Pressman (2009: i) points out that the VERA is still a "conceptual 'research' tool intended to generate debate and discussion." How such a tool could be tested for reliability and validity is left open. Models for prediction have typically been developed for use with specific populations such as serious sexual offenders—it is debatable whether a group that can be labeled as "terrorists" even exists, given the considerable controversy about what the term terrorism actually means (McSherry 2004: 358).

Even if a risk assessment tool such as the VERA proves to be of some benefit, there is a question as to who would be best placed to use it. Mats Dernevik, Alison Beck, and colleagues (2009: 512) point out that "mental health professionals are not likely to have training in certain areas which are crucial to terrorist violence, such as political and cultural science or social and political psychology." They suggest that collaboration is needed between mental health professionals and individuals with expertise in "areas of political science, anthropology, cultural diversity, and so on" (2009: 512).

Lazar Stankove, Derrick Higgins, Gerard Saucier, and Goran Knežević (2010) provide an example of one interdisciplinary research team working on constructing scales based on linguistic and traditional psychometric approaches to measure the mindset of militant extremism. There may also be some promise in collaborative teams exploring behavioral rather than psychological traits to construct a picture of those likely to be involved in terrorist activity (Victoroff 2005; Wilson 2008).

The use of risk assessment tools and techniques in relation to suspected terrorists is thus in its infancy, but it may be that this is a field that is worth exploring in collaboration with experts from across the humanities and social sciences.

Conclusion

In 2007, the then Australian Prime Minister John Howard was quoted as saying "when you are dealing with terrorism, it's better to be safe than sorry" (Smiles and Marriner 2007). Pre-charge preventive detention of suspected terrorists for investigation or community protection marks a change from risk-based approaches as underlying preventive detention to precautionary measures based on reasonable suspicion or reasonable belief rely largely on police officers' and intelligence operatives' intuitive responses that are uninformed by evidence-based approaches.

The cases of Mohamed Haneef and Izhar Ul-Haque highlight some of the problems that can occur with detention and investigation regimes in relation to individuals who are suspected of terrorist activities. These two cases were ultimately tempered by prosecutorial and judicial adherence to due process considerations, but this is undoubtedly of little comfort to the individuals concerned.

It would seem that the lack of empirically-based evidence concerning who is at risk of engaging in terrorist activity has left a gap that is currently filled by recourse to presumptions in this regard. The use of risk assessment tools and techniques in relation to suspected terrorists might be worth exploring with appropriate caution. The limitations of risk assessment tools are explored in the chapter by David Cooke and Christine Michie in this volume, but it may well be that the language of risk has more to offer policymakers and law enforcement officers when it comes to suspected terrorists, than the language of belief or suspicion on reasonable grounds.

III
Prediction

10
Toward Research-Informed Policy for High-Risk Offenders With Severe Mental Illnesses

JENNIFER SKEEM, JILLIAN PETERSON, and ERIC SILVER

People with mental illnesses are disproportionately represented in the criminal justice system (Fazel and Danesh 2002). Approximately one in seven men (15 per cent) and one in three women (31 per cent) detained in jails in the United States suffer from severe and often disabling illnesses, such as schizophrenia, bipolar disorder, and major depression (Steadman et al. 2009). The majority experience co-occurring substance abuse disorders (see Prins and Draper 2009). Many of these men and women become inextricably entangled in the criminal justice system. Compared to their relatively healthy counterparts, offenders with mental illnesses are incarcerated longer and placed in supermax or solitary confinement more often (Lovell et al. 2007; Toch and Adams 2002; for a review, see Fellner 2006). After they are released from prison, these offenders are two times more likely to be reincarcerated than offenders without mental illnesses (Eno Louden and Skeem, in press).

This problem "not only takes a toll on people with mental illness, their families, and the community in general, it also threatens to overwhelm the criminal justice system" (Council of State Governments 2002: 6). In an effort to improve criminal justice's response to people with mental illnesses, policymakers and practitioners in the United States have launched numerous federal initiatives and local programs for this population (see Skeem et al. in press). Similar movements inspired by large populations of offenders with mental illnesses are apparent across the United Kingdom and Australasia (for example, Beyond Bars Alliance 2007; Mullen 2001; Rethink and Sainsbury Centre for Mental Health 2010).

These efforts are diverse, both across and within countries. Nevertheless, they are united by the belief that these individuals wind up arrested and under correctional supervision because they have not received the mental health services they require. They view criminal justice involvement as the direct product of mental illness, and linkage with mental health treatment as the solution. Contemporary policy underlying these efforts relies heavily on the notion of diversion, seeking to replace involvement in the criminal justice system with (greater) involvement in the mental health system. In this chapter, we outline problems with the conceptual model that underpins this policy; present an alternative model that is more firmly rooted in research; and explain the implications of this alternative model for sentencing, treating, and supervising the heterogeneous group of offenders with severe mental illnesses.

Throughout this chapter, our primary focus is on adult offenders with serious, diverse, and numerous past offences and a high estimated risk of repeated criminal behavior. We focus on this population because intervention programs for high-risk offenders are significantly more effective in reducing recidivism than those focused on low-risk offenders (Lowenkamp et al. 2006a). Focusing supervision and intervention efforts on high-risk offenders will maximize returns in public safety. We specifically focus on high-risk offenders with severe mental illnesses (schizophrenia spectrum disorders, bipolar disorder, or major depression), and co-occurring substance abuse problems who have been convicted of crimes or arrested and diverted from jail (rather than those deemed not guilty by reason of insanity). We emphasize the context of community corrections (probation and parole) rather than institutions (jail and prison) because most offenders are supervised in the community and the bulk of work on evidence-based corrections focuses on that context. The model we present focuses on criminal behavior; we set aside criminal justice involvement that reflects stigma, paternalism, and decision-making biases against those with mental illnesses (for a review, see Skeem et al. in press) that are independent of unlawful behavior.

Contemporary Policy: The Direct Cause Model

The Model and Programs

The perceived root of the problem is simple and literal: the widely held belief is that people with mental illnesses are disproportionately represented in the criminal justice system because mental illness causes criminal behavior. In theory, psychiatric services have become unavailable, fragmented, or inadequate, so individuals with mental illnesses are deteriorating and committing crimes that should have been prevented or managed through treatment. Sometimes, a person would be arrested for violence that is the direct "product of the person's untreated mental illness" (Torrey et al. 2002: 48). A person with paranoid delusions, for example, may assault his perceived persecutor. More often, a person with a mental illness would be arrested for a minor crime, perhaps in an effort to secure treatment in jail (see Lamb and Weinberger 1998). For example, someone displaying psychotic behavior on the street may be arrested for disturbing the peace.

What types of programs have been developed for offenders with mental illnesses? In the United States, there are two general classes of programs. The first class is derived from general criminal justice models and focuses on a particular stage of case processing (for example, pre-booking jail diversion and post-booking jail diversion; specialty probation and parole caseloads; jail transition and prison reentry). For example, mental health courts are post-booking jail diversion programs that involve a specialized court docket and ongoing judicial supervision of community-based treatment plans. Mental health courts have spread prolifically in the United States over recent years (Bureau of Justice Assistance 2009), with some recent uptake in Australasia (Richardson and McSherry 2010), but little or none in the United Kingdom. The second class of programs is derived from mental health models: forensic assertive community treatment (FACT) and forensic intensive case management (FICM). FACT and FICM are relatively intensive community treatment and service linkage models that may be used either independently or in conjunction with criminal-justice-derived programs (for example, a mental health court). FACT and FICM were adapted from the most extensively studied and perhaps most resource-intensive mental health service, assertive community treatment (ACT; Morrissey et al. 2007; Osher and Steadman 2007). Treatment development efforts for this population, then, have involved adapting services that have been shown to improve patients' clinical outcomes (for example, reduced hospitalization) rather than services that have been shown to reduce offenders' recidivism (for example, reduced arrests).

Despite differences both within and among programs, virtually all are designed to link offenders with mental illnesses to community treatment services. Indeed, there has been a "proliferation of case management services as the policy response" (Draine et al. 2007: 161) for this population. The chief policy goal of these programs is to reduce the likelihood of recidivism. This mostly means protecting public safety by minimizing new crimes and new victims (Keiser 2009). The technique for reaching that goal generally focuses on a single dimension: mental illness. Criminal justice involvement is used to mandate or link the individual to psychiatric treatment (for example, a probationer is required to abide by a special condition to participate in treatment) and treatment is thought to reduce the risk of recidivism. Given that (untreated) mental illness is perceived as the root of the problem, access to effective mental health services has been cast as the lynchpin to successful response (for example, Council of State Governments 2002: Policy Statement #1 and chap. 7).

Problematic Assumptions of the Model

When evaluated against empirical evidence, the direct cause model is underpinned by two problematic assumptions. That is, there is little compelling evidence that (a) mental illness directly causes criminal behavior for this population, or (b) that effective mental health services meaningfully reduce new crimes and new victims. Although a comprehensive review of this literature is beyond the scope of the present chapter, each assumption will be briefly addressed here (for more information, see Skeem et al. in press).

Mental Illness Directly Causes Criminal Behavior   Violence is a form of criminal behavior that laypeople often (erroneously) attribute to severe mental illness. A large body of research indicates that "risk of violence is modestly elevated for people with mental disorder, particularly those who misuse substances" (Silver 2006: 685). Still, most people with mental illnesses are not violent, most violent offenders are not mentally ill, and the strongest risk factors for violence (for example, past violence) are shared by those with and without mental illnesses. The link between psychosis and violence is particularly weak among offenders (for example, Bonta et al. 1998; Quinsey et al. 2006), perhaps because the base rate of violence is high and the strongest risk factors are well represented, leaving little room for the modest role that mental illness plays in other contexts (see Buchanan 2008). Based on a meta-analysis of 204 diverse studies and samples, Douglas, Guy, and Hart (2009) found no meaningful correlation between psychosis and violence for offenders with mental illnesses ($r = .00$ or $OR = 0.91$) and general offenders ($r = .01$ or $OR = 1.27$).

Setting aside violence per se, there is little evidence that offenders with mental illnesses recidivate because of (uncontrolled) symptoms or other clinical factors. For example, in a meta-analysis of 58 prospective studies of offenders with mental illnesses (70 per cent with schizophrenia), Bonta et al. 1998 found that clinical variables (for example, diagnoses and treatment history) did not meaningfully predict a new general offence ($r = -.02$) or a new violent offence ($r = -.03$). Instead, the strongest predictors of a new violent offence ($r > .20$) were antisocial personality, juvenile delinquency, criminal history, and employment problems—risk factors that this population shares with offenders who are not mentally ill.

Despite the consistency of these findings, recent evidence collected in the United States argues that the direct cause hypothesis should be scaled back rather than wholly discarded. Among the heterogeneous population of offenders with mental illnesses, a small but important subgroup may become involved in the criminal justice system as a direct result of their symptoms (Junginger et al. 2006; Peterson in press; see also Monahan et al. 2001). A handful of individuals (perhaps 1 in 10) seem to be arrested because their hallucinations or delusions lead to (seemingly irrational) violence or because they cause a public disturbance by being psychotic at the wrong place at the wrong time. However, the rest—perhaps nine in 10—seem to have lifetime patterns of crime that are indistinguishable from those of general offenders.

Peterson et al. (in press) studied lifetime patterns of offending among a matched sample of 221 parolees with and without severe mental illnesses. The modal diagnosis in the sample was schizophrenia or another psychotic disorder (52 per cent). This study indicated that the pattern of offending for the vast majority of parolees—mentally ill (90 per cent) or not (68 per cent)—reflected trait anger and impulsivity. Only five per cent of parolees with mental illness manifested a pattern that was attributable to psychotic symptoms and only two per cent fell in the disadvantaged or survival crime group. Thus, although most had offence patterns similar to those without mental illnesses, a minority (seven per cent) of the mentally ill sample fit the direct cause model. Remarkably similar findings emerged in a study of less serious offenders and in a study of violence among psychiatric patients. Based on a sample of 113 inmates deemed eligible for a jail diversion program (34 per cent of whom had a schizophrenia spectrum disorder), Junginger et al. (2006) found that 8 per cent had been booked for offences that their psychiatric symptoms probably-to-definitely caused, either directly (four per cent) or indirectly (four per cent). Based on a sample of over 608 violent incidents that involved psychiatric patients enrolled in the MacArthur Violence Risk Assessment study, 11 per cent were rated as having occurred while patients were delusional or hallucinating (Monahan et al. 2001). Thus, in the United States, there is evidence that mental illness directly causes violence and other crime for a small but important minority of this population (about 10 per cent). The size of this subgroup in other countries remains to be determined. To the extent that individuals with mental illnesses are, for example, more likely to be acquitted by reason of insanity, this subgroup in countries outside the United States may be smaller.

Psychiatric Services Directly Reduce Criminal Behavior   The aforementioned data suggests that psychiatric symptoms are a direct or leading cause of criminal behavior for only a small minority of offenders with mental illnesses. At the group level, there is little evidence that mental illness directly led this population into jail or prison (see Juninger et al. 2006). Even so, the second assumption of the current policy model could still be correct. Is it? That is, do psychiatric services meaningfully reduce criminal behavior for this population?

Although one can never prove the null hypothesis, the answer provided by the most rigorous controlled studies is probably not. In a review of these studies, Skeem et al. (in press) distilled evidence that contemporary programs often successfully link offenders with psychiatric treatment and sometimes reduce their symptoms and distress; but this rarely translates into fewer new crimes and new victims. This is particularly true of the mental-health-based models (FACT, FICM; see Morrissey et al. 2007) and of jail diversion programs that rely heavily on case management (without judicial, probation, or other ongoing supervision). This pattern raises a question about the wisdom of prioritizing psychiatric service linkage if the chief goal is to reduce recidivism.

One might argue that the policy model is correct, but merely poorly implemented. That is, contemporary programs may be linking offenders with psychiatric services, but they will fail to meet the policy goal unless those psychiatric services are effective. Although intuitively appealing, this argument rests on little evidence. In rigorous experiments, even evidence-based mental health services that reliably affect clinical outcomes (that is, assertive community treatment and integrated dual diagnosis treatment) do not affect criminal justice outcomes like arrest (for example, Calsyn et al. 2005; Chandler and Spicer 2006; Clark et al. 1999).

Moreover, in the few studies indicating that some contemporary programs are meeting the chief policy goal, Skeem et al. (in press) could find no evidence that recidivism reduction was mediated by mental health services or symptom improvement. For example, Skeem et al. (2009) have been studying the outcomes of 360 offenders with severe mental illnesses placed on either specialty mental health or traditional probation. The two samples of probationers have been rigorously matched, both methodologically and statistically, and followed for over one year. Compared to traditional probationers, specialty probationers received more treatment services, exhibited better treatment adherence, and were substantially less likely to have their probation revoked ($d = .74$). Nevertheless, trajectories of symptom change over one year were unrelated to the probability of revocation. Moreover, there were no differences between the two groups in the number of new crimes and new victims, based on within-offender changes in the number of arrests from the two years before to the two years after probation placement. These findings resonate with others. Based on over 1,000 participants in a multisite jail diversion study, Steadman et al. (2009) found no significant relationship between symptom reduction and the number of re-arrests over time. Broadly, then, offenders who show symptom improvement during a program (for whatever reason) are no less likely to recidivate than those whose symptoms remain unchanged or worsen.

As a group, these studies suggest that the issue lies less in fidelity to the current policy model than in problems with the model itself. At a more fundamental level, additional research indicates that the availability, organization, and financing of psychiatric services in a given locale is unrelated to incarceration rates for individuals with mental illnesses (for a review, see Skeem et al. in press). In fact, there is little evidence that the risk of incarceration has uniquely increased for those with mental illnesses. Based on a careful analysis of living arrangements for people with severe and persistent mental illness (SPMI) in the United States from 1950 to 2000, Frank and Glied concluded "it would be a mistake to attribute the increase in … incarceration among people with SPMI directly to the experience of deinstitutionalization" (2006a: 128); instead, the increase in this "undesirable circumstance" seems shared with the general population.

Toward a Research-Informed Policy

The research reviewed so far suggests that for most offenders with mental illnesses, the current focus on linkage with psychiatric services may poorly match the chief policy goal of reducing criminal behavior. Plausible alternatives to the direct cause model assume that the etiology of criminal behavior largely is shared by offenders with and without mental illnesses. In this section, we review evidence suggesting that these offender groups are more alike than different in their patterns of risk and present a theory that links mental illness with criminal behavior. In the next section, we explain implications of this theory for developing policy that will better reduce recidivism for offenders with mental illnesses.

More Alike than Different

Particularly for offenders at high estimated risk of repeated criminal behavior, there is substantial overlap in contextual or distal risk factors and characterological or proximal risk factors between those with and without severe mental illnesses. This overlap is captured by a criminological perspective that spans sociological, economic, and psychological (including social psychological) disciplines.

Contextual or Distal Risk Factors One dimension of similarity between offenders with and without mental illnesses involves exposure to contextual or distal risk factors. For example, individuals with a low position in the social hierarchy are at risk for crime and other deviant behavior. Poverty is an indicator of low social class. Poverty can force people to live with other marginalized citizens in settings rife with illegal substances, health problems, underemployment and unemployment, child abuse and neglect, domestic violence, family breakdown, and crime (Fisher and Drake 2007). Thus, it may be that people with mental illnesses engage in criminal behavior "not because they have a mental disorder, but because they are poor. Their poverty situates them socially and geographically, and places them at risk of engaging in many of the same behaviors displayed by persons without mental illness who are similarly situated" (Fisher et al. 2006: 553).

Although poverty is but one of several distal risk factors, this contextual perspective enjoys some indirect empirical support. That is, offenders with mental illnesses are particularly likely to live in disadvantaged neighborhoods (Dickinger et al. 2008); be under or unemployed (see Prins and Draper 2009); have histories of child abuse and victimization (Prins and Draper 2009); abuse substances (Abram and Teplin 1991; Abram et al. 2003); and associate with people who have criminal histories, drink heavily, and use drugs (Skeem et al. 2009).

Characterological or Proximal Risk Factors   A second dimension of shared risk is characterological or proximal risk factors for crime. From a social psychological perspective, criminal behavior largely is learned through patterns of early modeling and reinforcement, and maintained by proximate risk factors like criminal attitudes (for example, Andrews and Bonta 2006; Gendreau and Goggin 1997). According to this perspective, people with mental illnesses engage in criminal behavior not because they are mentally ill, but because they have developed factors like "antisocial cognition, antisocial personality pattern, and substance abuse" (Andrews et al 2006: 10). Of course, one need not adopt this particular theoretical approach to recognize that there are strong individual, characterological, or proximal risk factors for criminal behavior. Although these factors may be caused by learning, it seems more plausible that they reflect an interaction between learning and innate tendencies or temperaments.

Painted broadly, this view enjoys some indirect support. That is, there is evidence that offenders with mental illnesses are at disproportionate risk of criminal behavior because they have even more proximal risk factors for recidivism than their relatively healthy counterparts. According to one model, the big four risk factors for crime are an established criminal history (with an early onset and diverse pattern), an antisocial personality pattern (stimulation seeking, low self-control, hostility-antagonism), antisocial cognition (attitudes, values, and thinking styles supportive of crime), and antisocial associates. Four additional, moderate risk factors include substance abuse, employment instability, family problems, and low engagement in prosocial leisure pursuits. Together, these risk factors have been called the central eight and are assessed by a risk-needs tool called the Levels of Services/Case Management Inventory (LS/CMI; see Andrews et al. 2004).

Based on a matched sample of 221 parolees with and without mental illnesses, Skeem et al. (2008) found that those with mental illnesses obtained significantly higher scores on the LS/CMI (*eta* = .20), particularly on the antisocial pattern subscale (for example, early or diverse criminal behavior, criminal attitudes, pattern of generalized trouble). Similarly, based on a sample of 600 probationers, Girard and Wormith (2004) found that those with mental health problems (*n* = 169) obtained higher scores on the LS/CMI than those without such problems. In turn, the LS/CMI predicts recidivism equally well for those with and without mental illnesses (Andrews et al. 2004; Girard and Wormith 2004), and perhaps better than risk assessment tools that reference clinical factors (Skeem et al. 2008). These LS/CMI results are in keeping with a finding that offenders with mental illnesses obtain scores on a validated measure of antisocial cognition or criminal thinking that are similar to, or higher than, those obtained by offenders without mental illnesses (see Morgan et al. 2010).

As a more general point, when one isolates the policy-relevant group of high-risk offenders, one obtains a relatively homogeneous group. This point is illustrated by Kroner, Mills, and Reddon (2005), who used a large sample of general offenders to examine their score patterns across four alternative tools that often are applied to estimate recidivism risk. They found that (a) offenders' scores on the alternative tools were strongly correlated (for example, LSI-R and PCL-R, r = .77), and (b) new tools created by randomly selecting items from the original tools performed as well as the originals in predicting new convictions and revocations. This suggests that the instruments are an interchangeable means of tapping overlapping risk factors (for example, criminal history, antisocial lifestyle). Thus, high-risk offenders (whether mentally ill or not) are likely to share robust risk factors for recidivism that can and should be targeted in supervision and intervention.

Theory: Three Pathways to Criminal Behavior   Skeem et al. (in press; see also Peterson et al. in press) integrated the dominant psychiatric perspective (aka, direct cause model) with criminological perspectives to develop a provisional model to guide research and improve the effectiveness of correctional policy for offenders with mental illnesses. Their analysis suggests that those with severe mental illnesses follow one of three different pathways to criminal behavior.

For the small subgroup described earlier (approximately one in 10), mental illness directly causes criminal justice involvement. For example, paranoid delusions and acute feelings of threat may lead to assault of perceived persecutors. For this subgroup, the current policy focus on effective mental health services should be the solution. The vast majority, however, will fall in the two remaining subgroups. For these subgroups, mental illness does not directly cause criminal behavior. Instead, contextual or characterological are leading causal risk factors for crime that either fully mediate—or are independent of—the effect of mental illness. For them, the current policy focus will not effectively reduce recidivism risk. Potential foci for each subgroup are outlined next.

For the second subgroup, mental illness indirectly causes criminal behavior by exposing individuals to contextual risk factors for crime. Borrowing from the criminological perspectives outlined earlier, mental illness may lead to substance abuse and downward socioeconomic drift, exposing individuals to modeling and reinforcement patterns that establish proximal risk factors for crime like criminogenic attitudes. Similarly, the onset of psychosis during late adolescence may cause some to gravitate toward social networks and disadvantaged environments that model, reinforce, and create opportunity for criminal behavior. For the indirect subgroup, prevention efforts that target risk factors that lie directly downstream from mental illness (for example, social-occupational dysfunction; substance abuse) may be most effective. If opportunities for prevention are missed, intervention arguably should target proximate risk factors for criminal behavior. Why? The factors that caused criminal behavior may differ from those that maintain it. It seems unlikely that psychiatric services and symptom improvement will change "personal attitudes and values supportive of criminal behaviour" (Bonta et al. 1998: 138).

For a third subgroup, mental illness is incidental to or independent of criminal behavior. Here, exposure to contextual or characterological risk factors would have occurred even if the individual was not mentally ill. For example, growing up in a chaotic, disadvantaged environment with an abusive parent may establish a hostile attributional style that leaves one prone to violence and other dysregulated behavior. Or, a disinhibited temperament combined with poor parenting and supervision may lead to criminal behavior. In both of these examples, criminogenic processes are independent of and, at best, run parallel to mental illness. For this group, evidence-based treatment for general offenders that targets criminal thinking and attitudes may be most effective for recidivism reduction.

As explained later in this chapter, a major task for future research will be to identify the specific moderator(s) that differentiates the subgroup for whom the effect of mental illness on criminal behavior is direct versus indirect or independent. A simple marker with promise is age of onset for criminal behavior. Those who begin antisocial behavior early in childhood, well before the onset of psychosis or other severe mental illnesses, may belong to the indirect or independent group. In contrast, those who begin criminal behavior after the onset of severe mental illness may belong to the direct group (see Hodgins 2000). As explained by Silver, "the heart of the distinction between early- and late-start offenders is that early start offenders are, from the beginning, more deeply embedded in and exposed to criminogenic risk factors both in themselves and in their social environments" (2006: 700). For late starters, mental illness seems to play a more causal role in offending. There is some support for this distinction, particularly for violent behavior (for example, Swanson et al. 2008; for a review, see Hodgins 2008).

Implications for Sentencing and Programs

Theory and evidence reviewed thus far suggest that contemporary policy for offenders with mental illnesses is too strongly driven by a one-size-fits-all approach. As shown in Figure 10.1, although

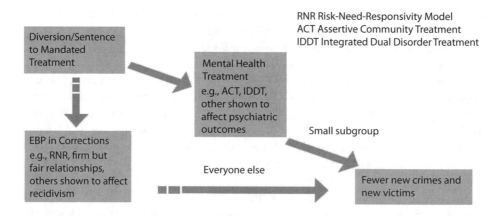

Figure 10.1 Toward a more valid model of what works to reduce criminal behavior.

linkage with psychiatric services is likely to reduce criminal behavior for a very small but important subgroup of offenders with mental illnesses, it is unlikely to do so for the vast majority.

Most high-risk offenders with mental illnesses share robust (and changeable) risk factors for crime with their relatively healthy counterparts. It may be that their most immediate pathways to criminal behavior are much the same as those without mental illnesses. If so, it would be wise to leverage evidence-based correctional programs to reduce their recidivism.

In this section, we address three policy-relevant questions about this population. First, is the current exceptionalist approach appropriate, or should offenders with mental illnesses be more mainstreamed with other offenders? Second, what is the appropriate role of psychiatric treatment in policy for this population? Third, how can evidence-based correctional programs and principles be bridged to these offenders to reduce their risk? In this section, we address each question in turn.

To Divert or Not to Divert?

As noted earlier, many programs for this population in the United States and beyond revolve around the concept of diversion. Diversion means change, alteration, or departure. Theoretically, diversion programs would release offenders from the criminal justice system and admit them to the mental health system. Practically, this rarely happens.

Arguably, diversion (in the true sense) is appropriate for only two small subgroups of offenders with mental illnesses. Legal mechanisms have long been in place to effect diversion for the first subgroup of offenders. That is, individuals who are not criminally responsible for their actions because of a severe mental illness are acquitted by reason of insanity and appropriately diverted from the criminal justice system. Diversion also seems appropriate for the small subgroup of offenders with mental illnesses who actually fit the current direct cause model. For these individuals, psychiatric symptoms have motivated criminal behavior (but perhaps not enough to meet the criteria for insanity) or become crimes themselves (for example, psychotic behavior becomes disturbing the peace). Channeling these individuals out of the criminal justice system and into mental health treatment arguably amounts to correcting a system sorting error. Providing them with effective psychiatric treatment should ameliorate what was masquerading as criminal behavior.

For the vast majority of offenders with mental illnesses, however, the notion of diversion does not seem particularly appropriate. If these offenders' criminal actions reflect risk factors that are shared with their relatively healthy counterparts and will not be effectively addressed through psychiatric treatment, then it is senseless to divert them from the criminal justice system to the mental health system. Here, diversion simply seems a misnomer for mandated treatment. Rather than signaling immediate egress from the criminal justice system, it signals that psychiatric treatment is going to be mandated within the correctional system. The goal is more to recognize that offenders are mentally ill and need appropriate treatment than to leverage them out of correctional supervision altogether. Remarkably, most jail diversion programs in the United States are post-booking programs that mandate treatment within the correctional system. Arguably, it would make sense to stop calling these diversion programs.

What Role Should Psychiatric Treatment Play?

Like the direct cause model itself, the role of psychiatric treatment in policy for offenders with severe mental illnesses should be contextualized, not jettisoned. Although effective mental health services will reduce criminal behavior for only a small minority of offenders with severe mental illnesses, we believe that they all should receive such services. First, even if mental health services have no effect on recidivism, they may achieve crucial public health outcomes for this group (for example, reducing symptoms, substance abuse, and hospitalization). For example, an assertive community treatment team may not reduce recidivism but is quite likely to reduce repeated hospitalizations. Second, prisoners have a constitutional right to adequate health care, including mental health care (*Estelle v Gamble* 1976; *Ruiz v Estelle* 1980). For probationers and parolees, we assume that sentencing bodies will continue mandating psychiatric treatment when mental illness has been identified (see Skeem and Eno Louden 2008). Third, and perhaps most important, correctional intervention programs have been shown to be more effective in reducing recidivism when services are responsive to the abilities, styles, and needs of offenders (see Andrews et al. 2006). Effective psychiatric treatment may complement correctional treatment by, for example, reducing hallucinations that interfere with an offender's ability to attend to, and benefit from, cognitive behavioral sessions that target criminal thinking. Regardless of whether the relationship between an offender's mental illness and criminal behavior is direct, indirect, or independent, psychiatric treatment can play some role in correctional interventions.

How Can We Better Leverage (or Make Explicit) Evidence-Based Corrections?

Correctional policy for offenders with mental illnesses should not stop at linkage with psychiatric services because doing so will fail to meet the chief policy goal for the vast majority (perhaps 90 per cent) of that population. Beyond sharing risk factors for criminal behavior with their relatively healthy counterparts, there is preliminary evidence that (as a group) offenders with mental illnesses respond to similar principles of risk reduction. Earlier, we mentioned randomized controlled trials indicating that ACT and IDDT do not meaningfully improve criminal justice outcomes. Given such results, scholars have cautioned that positive outcomes observed for evidence-based mental services (for example, reduced hospitalization, improved symptoms) will not necessarily extend to criminal behavior, and have called for "interventions that specifically target reduction of criminal behavior" (Calsyn et al. 2005: 245). This is the reason for our model, shown in Figure 10.1.

Adapting Formal Evidence-Based Correctional Programs   Correctional principles and interventions that have been shown to reduce criminal behavior among general offenders are readily available. In particular, cognitive behavioral treatment (CBT) that explicitly targets criminal thinking is consistently ranked "in the top tier with regard to effects on recidivism" (Lipsey and Landenberger 2006: 57). Although several specific brands of CBT are available (for example, reasoning and rehabilitation, moral reconation therapy, and thinking for a change), they all seem to be about equally effective in reducing recidivism (Aos, Miller, and Drake 2006; Landenberger and Lipsey 2005).

Remarkably, Skeem et al. (in press) could locate only one small controlled outcome study for offenders with mental illnesses that included any emphasis on criminal thinking. Specifically, Sacks et al. (2004) studied a subsample of these offenders who had participated in a prison-based therapeutic community program in the United States. Of these offenders, 43 chose to complete a residential aftercare program in the community and 32 did not. The aftercare program was intensive and multidimensional, targeting mental illness, substance abuse, unemployment, and criminal thinking. Over one year, those who chose the aftercare group were less likely to be reincarcerated than those who did not (five per cent versus 16 per cent). Although these results seem promising, the possibility of selection bias prevents any conclusion that the program reduced recidivism. Moreover, the multidimensional nature of the program prevents attribution of any recidivism reduction to reduced criminal thinking.

Only one true or more narrowly packaged CBT program for offenders with mental illness has been systematically studied. The program is Reasoning and Rehabilitation 2 for Mentally Disordered Offenders (Young and Ross 2007). Although it was adapted to be responsive to the cognitive limitations of some offenders with mental illness, it retains validated techniques like relapse prevention to target general criminogenic needs (for example, criminal values, impulsivity, hostility). Although each has methodological problems, four small controlled studies conducted on inpatient forensic psychiatric units in the United Kingdom and Germany provide preliminary evidence that this program increases motivation to change and reduces criminal thinking. Antonowicz (2005) reviews the three smallest studies (treatment group, $ns < 15$). In the fourth study, Young et al. (2010) compared 22 offenders with mental illness who completed this CBT program (out of 34 who began the program) with 12 wait-list controls. The authors found that the CBT group showed greater reductions in both pro-violence attitudes and disruptive behavior on the unit than the control group. Sadly, the effect of this CBT treatment on the outcome of interest (that is, recidivism) is unknown; all investigations to date have focused on inpatient forensic wards. In future research and practice, it will be vital to examine the extent to which CBT treatment reduces criminal behavior for offenders with mental illness, compared to psychiatric treatment as usual.

Making Evidence-Based Correctional Principles Explicit   The nature and prevalence of programs for offenders with mental illnesses in the United States, United Kingdom, and Australasia is unclear. A survey that described these programs would be helpful. In the absence of such a survey, the literature seems to suggest that formal CBT programs are rarely applied to offenders with mental illness, particularly in the United States, and particularly in community settings. Nevertheless, there is evidence that informal principles of evidence-based corrections sometimes infiltrate programs for offenders with mental illness—even in community-based programs in the United States driven by the direct cause model. In addition to better implementing formal CBT programs for offenders with mental illness, we believe that the next step in research and policy for this population is to make these principles explicit, practice them consistently, and evaluate their effect on recidivism. We suspect that existing programs work with this population—when they work—in some of the same ways that programs for general offenders work.

What is the preliminary evidence that these principles have infiltrated programs driven by the dominant direct cause model? In the study of 360 probationers with mental illnesses described earlier, Skeem et al. (2009) found that the effect of specialty mental health probation in reducing revocation was fully explained by the quality of officer-probationer relationships (not by symptom reduction, as the model that drives the program would assume). Specifically, firm but fair officer-probationer relationships characterized by caring, fairness, trust, and an authoritative (not authoritarian) style significantly protected against both re-arrest and revocation over a one-year period (see also Skeem et al. 2007). This finding is in keeping with the general literature on offenders, where some describe such relationships as the most important component of effective correctional practice. In one meta-analysis, Dowden and Andrews (2004) found that staff behaviors that are predictive of outcome include conveying an enthusiastic, warm, and personally respectful style, making program rules clear and exerting their authority without being authoritarian, frequently praising offenders for pro-social behavior, and structuring offender learning into concrete, graded steps. Moderate to large correlations resulted when programs incorporated some of these characteristics, compared to none.

It may also be the case that some staff intuitively target criminogenic needs, or changeable risk factors that relate closely to crime, rather than focus exclusively on mental health. Our encounters with practitioners across the United States provide some anecdotal accounts of staff members in mental health courts and other programs that naturally target factors that really get an offender in trouble (for example, hanging out with her drug-dealing cousin). To the extent that they do so, they are (accidentally) applying a well-validated principle of effective correctional treatment called the need principle (Lowenkamp et al. 2006a, 2006b). The effectiveness of correctional programs in reducing recidivism is positively associated with the number of criminogenic needs they target (that is, dynamic risk factors for crime, like pro-criminal attitudes), relative to non-criminogenic needs (that is, disturbances that impinge on an individual's functioning in society, like depression; Andrews and Bonta 2006). Because mental illness is a criminogenic need for only about one in 10 offenders with severe mental illness (that is, those in the direct subgroup), it seems important to target stronger risk factors for crime.

Although little data is available on this issue, Eno Louden et al. (2010) coded audiotapes of 83 interactions between specialty probation officers and supervisees with severe mental illnesses. They found that, although officers tended to focus heavily on general mental health issues (discussed in 66 per cent of meetings), they also discussed supervisees' criminogenic needs, including attitudes supportive of crime (36 per cent of meetings). In research with general offenders, Bonta et al. (2008) found that the amount of time officers spent discussing criminogenic needs was inversely related to the risk of recidivism.

The Message Although there is evidence that a few programs for offenders with mental illnesses occasionally work to reduce recidivism, there is no evidence that they do so for the reasons assumed (Skeem et al. in press). An important goal for future research is to identify the mechanisms by which programs reduce recidivism. Understanding what is critical to treatment and how it operates will help develop fewer, more efficient, and more effective interventions for offenders with mental illnesses (see Kazdin 2007). The current wealth of program operationalizations only underscores the need to identify change mechanisms and bring greater parsimony to the field. This is essential for developing model programs that can be widely disseminated. At a more local level, in today's economic environment, policymakers should insist on knowing why programs work because this will enable them to streamline programs while protecting their most essential elements.

Conclusion

To establish more effective policies for high-risk offenders with severe mental illnesses, it seems necessary to avoid approaching mental illness as the master status that uniformly defines it, and begin to attend to the criminogenic risk factors and needs that are shared with other high-risk offenders. Severe mental illness may relate directly, indirectly, or not at all to criminal behavior. This chapter provides a theoretical model to test in future research that can help shape policy toward recidivism reduction for this group as a whole.

11

Assessing and Managing Violent Youth
Implications for Sentencing

LORRAINE JOHNSTONE

Contemporary penal policy for offenders who are under the age of 18 (referred to interchangeably in this chapter as juvenile, child, or youth offenders), including the use of dangerous offender provisions, is predicated on the assumption that it is possible to differentiate children who do from children who do not present an ongoing risk of serious harm to others. Several protocols purport to provide an evidence-based framework for identifying high-risk youth and legal decision-making is heavily influenced by them.

This chapter explores the validity of this assumption that differentiation is possible and the utility of the methods used to assess risk. Considerable challenges are identified and the implications for sentencing are discussed. To set the scene, the chapter opens with an overview of the problem of youth violence and illustrates some of the current legislative responses that exist in an attempt to manage this issue. In the next section an overview of some of the most widely used risk assessment protocols is given. This is followed by a more detailed discussion of the range of conceptual, methodological, and developmental challenges that remain to be overcome. The chapter concludes by highlighting some of the implications for sentencing options for high-risk youth and makes some suggestions about how assessors might achieve defensible decisions while we await more sophisticated approaches.

Youth Violence: The Problem

Most, if not all, societies bear the scars of those rare but profound events where children perpetrate acts of incomprehensible violence: in the second half of the 19th century in the United States, serial killer Jesse Pomeroy; and in England, in the 1960s, 10-year-old killer Mary Bell; and of course, in England in the 1990s, the killing of James Bulger by two 10-year-old boys, Robert Thompson and Jon Venables, are poignant examples. However the 1980s and 1990s saw what was described as an epidemic of youth violence. According to some studies, the United States saw a 150 per cent increase in child-perpetrated homicide (DiIulio 1995; Federal Bureau of Investigation 1999; Snyder et al. 1996).

At the same time, the realization that children were not only victims but were perpetrators of sexual violence began to dawn. For example, Barbaree and Marshall (2006) reported that adolescent males were responsible for around 20 per cent of rapes and between 30 per cent and 50 per cent of child sexual assaults. Such findings led scholars to warn of a future where societies would be scourged by the juvenile "superpredator" (DiIulio 1995). A moral panic ensued.

Notwithstanding these findings concerning sexual violence, since the mid-1990s the United States has observed decreasing rates of youth violence (Thomas 2005), but rates remain high (Office of the Surgeon General 2001). From an international perspective, countries such as the United Kingdom, the Netherlands, Sweden, Italy, Austria, France, Denmark, Switzerland, and Poland are recording increasing levels of youth violence (Petrila 2009). Clearly, the problem of youth violence demands a response.

The Legal and Policy Response

Legal and policy responses were once guided solely by the parens patriae or welfare approach. Most jurisdictions adhered to the philosophy that children who perpetrated serious crimes were as vulnerable as they were culpable. This meant that, wherever possible, children were diverted away from the criminal justice system and interventions revolved around rehabilitation and support, with the child's best interests paramount to the process. In contrast, contemporary penal philosophies reflect the get tough on crime and a no more excuses doctrine. There has been a shift toward a punitive and deterrent philosophy, where public protection takes center stage (Scott and Steinberg 2008). Most Western jurisdictions now legislate for children to be transferred to adult courts for trial and disposal—a process colloquially referred to as the "adult crime, adult time" approach (Bouhours and Daly 2007; Grisso 1996, 1998).

Children may be subject to a range of measures that, in broad terms, are conceptualized under the heading "dangerous offender provisions." Dangerous offender provisions include: indeterminate sentencing, supervision via community notification or registration, and forms of preventive detention (John Howard Society of Alberta 1999; McSherry et al. 2006; McSherry and Keyzer 2009). In order to reach decisions about sentencing and detention, courts will often require opinions from mental health professionals on the level of dangerousness and risk posed by the child. Space precludes a comprehensive description of all the relevant laws and legal processes in this paper. However, some examples are provided next.

United States

In terms of its processes for dealing with children who perpetrate crimes resulting in serious harm, the United States has been unique in that, until the *Roper v Simmons* ruling in 2005, it was still held as constitutional to execute a minor. Nowadays, the legal response is to impose an indeterminate sentence of life without parole. Life means life in this context. There is no possibility of release. According to a recent analysis published by Amnesty International and Human Rights Watch (Parker 2005) there were 2,225 people incarcerated in the United States who had been sentenced to life without parole for crimes they had committed as children. Most often these sentences were imposed for homicide; but some children had received this sentence for other violent crimes including assault, attempted murder, kidnapping, grand larceny, or sexual offences against children. Fifty-nine percent had received this sentence for their first offence. In addition to custodial sentences, community notification and registration can be applied to children. According to Prentky et al. (2010), of the 11 states that have civil commitment laws for sex offenders, all have provisions for the civil commitment of adjudicated youth. Taking Michigan as an example, according to online sources, in February 2010 there were around 3,500 children listed as sex offenders. The youngest registrant was aged nine (Garcia 2010).

United Kingdom

The United Kingdom has also enacted dangerous offender provisions for children. In England and Wales the introduction of the Criminal Justice Act 2003 resulted in two major changes for sentencing offenders aged between 10 and 17 years. An order called *detention for public protection*, an indeterminate sentence, is used for offenders deemed to be dangerous and convicted of a serious, specified offence such as manslaughter, kidnapping, false imprisonment, causing explosions and endangering life or property, infanticide, aggravated burglary, hijacking, rioting, sexual assaults such as intercourse, or other sexual contacts with a male or female child under 13 years of age. An *extended sentence for public protection* may be used for offenders convicted of a specified offence such as malicious wounding, assault with intent to resist arrest, racially or religiously aggravated assaults, administering drugs to facilitate intercourse, soliciting, abusing a position of trust in relation to sexual activity with a child, and adjudged to be dangerous.

In its deliberations over which sentence to impose, the sentencing judge has access to opinions on risk provided by Youth Offending Teams. Youth Offending Teams use a procedure called ASSET (Youth Justice Board for England and Wales 2000; see later for details). Once incarcerated, the parole board will not recommend the release of a young person until a full risk assessment— method unspecified—confirms that the offender no longer poses a significant risk of harm to the public. After the changes to the Criminal Justice Act 2003, by December 2009, a total of 58 children were serving indeterminate sentences in England and Wales (Ministry of Justice 2010a). (This figure does not account for those detained without limit of time under the old system.)

In Scotland there are two different legal procedures by which a child can be given an indeterminate sentence. Under section 205(2) of the Criminal Procedure (Scotland) Act 1995, children can be sentenced to an indefinite period of incarceration in a secure residential setting. For example, children convicted of murder can be detained without limit of time and, while a tariff will be set, they will only be liberated once they are able to demonstrate that they no longer pose an unacceptable level of risk. To the writer's knowledge, the use of formalized risk assessment procedures for children is not consistent or routine in aiding these decisions; processes and procedures seem to be ad hoc, inconsistent and not evidence-based.

Another provision that can result in an indeterminate sentence for a child is Section 210 of the Criminal Justice (Scotland) Act 1995. This permits a judge to impose an Order of Lifelong Restriction. An order of lifelong restriction is in force for the entire duration of the offender's life (see Rajan Darjee and Katharine Russell's chapter in this volume). After serving the punishment part of their sentence in prison, if adjudged to pose a manageable risk, offenders can be released back into the community. Risk assessment is firmly embedded in this process. Risk opinions are provided to the court by accredited assessors and must conform to the structured professional judgment approach (see later for details). Unlike other sentencing options where the judge has discretion, if, on the basis of the risk assessment report and other evidence, the court is satisfied on the balance of probabilities that the risk criteria are met, it must impose an order of lifelong restriction. At the time of writing, five minors had received an order of lifelong restriction since the enactment of this legislation; at least one was for a first offence. All of these individuals currently remain incarcerated.

Other Jurisdictions

Similar policies on youth justice are used elsewhere. For example, in Canada indeterminate sentencing and community registration are used for managing even very young children. Barbados allows for the indeterminate sentencing of children and across the Western world there are many examples where legal decision-making about children is heavily influenced by opinions on risk. In the following sections the challenges of reaching risk decisions about youth are discussed.

Violence Risk Assessment for Youth

It is important not to underestimate the influence of risk assessments. Erroneous opinions can have devastating consequences for both victims and perpetrators. In the pursuit of accurate and defensible practice, major advances have been made and the extant literature denotes an evolutionary pathway involving three main approaches to risk assessment, which are briefly outlined next.

Models and Methods

The unstructured clinical judgment approach, also referred to as first-generation methods, relies on the experience and skill of the user. There is no structure to the approach. Despite their widespread use, the methods used under this approach have been heavily criticized for lacking transparency, consistency, reliability, and validity (Borum 1996; Grove and Meehl 1996; Monahan 1981) and would not achieve today's standards for forensic assessment.

Eager to compensate for these problems, psychologists produced a second-generation of risk assessment, the actuarial method approach (see, for example, Hanson and Thornton 1999; Quinsey et al. 1998). Actuarial risk tools include a set of risk factors derived from either theoretical or empirical procedures. Risk factors are selected and weighted in terms of importance. Items are scored numerically and the offender's total score is compared to the standardization sample, which is used to provide a percentage likelihood that the offender will recidivate within a given time period. Actuarial tools have face validity and provide a transparent and conceptually appealing process, as well as an easy-to-use method of assessing risk. They are open to a range of professions and are cost efficient. However these methods have been subject to considerable criticism, due to the overemphasis on historical items, the lack of concern for risk management, and the appropriateness of some of the items (Douglas and Kropp 2002). In addition, a fundamental and arguably fatal flaw is that any opinion on risk stemming from the use of an actuarial procedure fails to generalize to the individual case, and thus renders any statistically derived opinion meaningless (Hart et al. 2007; see also David Cooke and Christine Michie's chapter in this volume).

Mindful of these problems, other scholars have attempted to develop the field by making a conceptual shift in the focus from risk prediction to risk management (Douglas and Kropp 2002; Hart et al. 2003).

Third- and fourth-generation methods, or the structured professional judgment (SPJ) model, involve several key steps: (1) the assessment of personal history and psychosocial functioning, including a detailed analysis of psychological disturbance, mental health and psychopathology; (2) rating an evidence-based set of risk factors for presence and relevance, facilitated by reference to one or more sets of manualized guidelines; (3) risk formulation; (4) scenario planning; (5) risk management interventions; (6) risk communication; and (7) reassessment. In the SPJ approach, risk is not seen as an all-in-one entity; dynamic factors are included in the evaluation. The SPJ model is well established and a burgeoning literature attests to its utility in terms of its reliability, validity, and clinical utility. Guidelines exist to ensure that assessors conduct comprehensive evaluations (see Hart et al. 2003 for details).

Attempts have been made to extend the successes observed by using the SPJ model as it applies in adults downward to young offenders, and several protocols now exist which purport to assess the likelihood of violent and sexually violent behavior in children. As well as ensuring the fundamental legal principle of proportionality, having access to accurate methods of risk assessment for children could yield multiple gains across the personal, social, economic, and legal domains (Welsh et al. 2008). A brief overview of the available procedures for assessing violence and sexual violence is given below, and a summary of the item content of each is presented in Tables 11.1 and 11.2. Several guidelines exist for assessing risk of violence and offending behaviors. The Early Assessment Risk List for Boys (EARL-20B; Augmeri et al. 2001) and the Early Assessment Risk List for Girls (EARL-20G; Levene et al. 2001) are SPJ guides for evaluating known risk factors for antisocial behavior in children under the age of 12 years. The EARLS reflect the first systematic attempts to provide practitioners with a framework for organizing their assessments, in terms of method and coverage, when assessing pre-adolescent children.

The Structured Assessment of Violence Risk in Youth (SAVRY; Borum et al. 2003, 2006), also a SPJ model, was devised to assist clinicians in the evaluation of risk for violence, including sexual assault, in male and female adolescents aged between 12 and 18 years. The Youth Level of Service/Case Management Inventory (YSL/CMI; Hoge and Andrews 2002) is an adjusted-actuarial tool. It was designed to assess risk of general reoffending in 12- to 17-year-old children.

Table 11.1 Item Content for Protocols for Assessing Violence Risk

EARL-20 B	SAVRY	ASSET	YLS/CMI
Family (F) Items	Historical Risk Factors	Section 1: Offending Behavior	Part 1: Assessment of Risk and Needs
F1. Household circumstances	1. History of violence		1. Prior and current offences/dispositions
F2. Caregiver continuity	2. History of non-violent offending	Section 2: Risk Factors	2. Family circumstances/parenting/care arrangements
F3. Supports	3. Early initiation of violence	1. Living arrangements	3. Education/employment
F4. Stressors	4. Past supervision/intervention failures	2. Family and personal relationships	4. Peer relations
F5. Parenting style	5. History of self-harm or suicide attempts	3. Education, training, and employment	5. Substance abuse
F6. Antisocial values and conduct	6. Exposure to violence in the home	4. Neighborhood	6. Leisure/recreation
	7. Childhood history of maltreatment	5. Lifestyle	7. personality/behavior
Child (C) Items	8. Parental/caregiver criminality	6. Substance use	8. Attitudes/orientation
C1. Developmental problems	9. Early caregiver disruption	7. Physical health	
C2. Onset of behavioral difficulties	10. Poor school achievement	8. Emotional and mental health	Part 2: Strengths Factors
C3. Abuse/neglect/trauma		9. Perception of self and others	1. Family
C4. Hyperactivity/impulsivity/ attention deficits (HIA)	Social/Contextual Risk Factors	10. Thinking and behavior	2. Education
C5. Likeability	11. Peer delinquency	11. Attitudes toward offending	3. Peers
C6. Peer socialization	12. Peer rejection	12. Motivation to change	4. Substance use
C7. Academic performance	13. Stress and poor coping		5. Leisure
C8. Neighborhood	14. Poor parental management		6. Personality
C9. Authority contact	15. Lack of personal/social support		7. Attitudes/orientation
C10. Antisocial attitudes	16. Community disorganization		
C11. Antisocial behavior			Part 3: Assessment of Other Needs/Special Considerations
C12. Coping ability	Individual Risk Factors		1. Family/parents
	17. Negative attitudes		2. Youth
	18. Risk taking/impulsivity		

(Continued)

Table 11.1 Item Content for Protocols for Assessing Violence Risk (Continued)

EARL-20 B	SAVRY	ASSET	YLS/CMI
Responsivity R Items	19. Substance use difficulties		
R1. Family responsivity	20. Anger management problems		
R2. Child responsivity	21. Low empathy/remorse		
	22. Attention deficit/hyperactivity difficulties		
	23. Poor compliance		
	24. Low interest/commitment to school		
	Protective Factors		
	P1. Pro-social Involvement		
	P2. Strong Social Support		
	P3. Strong attachments and bonds		
	P4. Positive attitude toward intervention and authority		
	P5. Strong commitment to school		
	P6. Resilient personality		

Table 11.2 Item Content for Protocols for Assessing Sexual Violence

The ERASOR	J-SOAP	MEGA	SHARPS	AIM
1. Deviant sexual interest	Scale 1: Sexual Drive/ Preoccupation Scale	Aggregates	Domain 1. Sexually Harmful Behavior	Sexual and Non-sexual Harmful Behaviors
2. Obsessive sexual interests	1. Prior charged sex offence	1. Family love map aggregate	1. Situational dynamics of sexually harmful behavior	Static Concerns
3. Attitudes supportive of sexual offending	2. History of predatory behavior	2. Sexual incident aggregate	2. Victim characteristics	1a. Evidence of previous contact sexually abusive behaviors
4. Unwillingness to alter deviant sexual interests/ attitudes	3. Evidence of sexual preoccupation	3. Relationship (Predatory Elements) aggregate	3. Age difference between abuser and victim	1b. Sexually abused a stranger
	4. Duration of sex offence history	4. Coercion aggregate	4. Location where sexually harmful behavior occurred	1c. Used or threatened violence during sexual assault
5. Ever sexually assaulted 2 or more victims		5. Neuropsychological aggregate	5. Severity of sexually harmful behavior	1d. Previous non-sexual offences
6. Ever sexually assaulted the same victim 2 or more times	Scale 2: Impulsive, Antisocial Behavior Scale	6. Antisocial aggregate	6. Nature of aggression used during sexually harmful behavior	1e. Previously been significantly sanctioned for sexually abusive behavior
7. Prior adult sanctions for sexual assault(s)	5. Caregiver instability	7. Stratagem aggregate		1f. Abused one or more victims on more than 2 occasions
8. Threats of, or use of, excessive violence/weapons	6. Ever arrested before the age of 16 years	Scales	7. Onset and duration of sexually harmful behavior	1g. History of aggressive (non-sexual) behavior
9. Ever sexually assaulted a child	7. School behavior problems	1. Risk	8. Frequency of sexually harmful behavior	1h. History of cruelty to animals
10. Ever sexually assaulted a stranger	8. School suspensions or expulsions	2. Dynamical	9. Escalating pattern of sexually harmful behavior	1i. Sexually abused 2 or more victims
11. Indiscriminate choice of victims	9. History of conduct disorder	3. Principles	10. Established/emerging pattern of harmful sexual behavior	1j. Has sexually abused males
12. Ever sexually assaulted a male victim	10. Multiple types of offences	4. Static		
13. Diverse sexual-assault behaviors	11. Impulsivity	5. Protective risk		
14. Antisocial interpersonal orientation	12. History if alcohol abuse	6. Female		
	13. History of parental alcohol abuse			

(Continued)

Table 11.2 Item Content for Protocols for Assessing Sexual Violence (Continued)

The ERASOR	J-SOAP	MEGA	SHARPS	AIM
15. Lack of intimate peer relationships/Social isolation	Scale 3: Clinical/Treatment Scale		Domain 2. Antisocial Behavior	1k. Abusive behavior included penetration or attempted penetration
16. Negative peer associations and influences	14. Accepts responsibility for sexual offences		1. History of violent behavior/criminal convictions	1l. Previous allegations of sexually abusive behaviors (but no conviction or admission)
17. Interpersonal aggression	15. Internal motivation for change		2. History of delinquency/criminal convictions	1m. Offence(s) appear based on grievance or revenge
18. Recent escalation in anger or negative affect	16. Understands sexual assault cycle		3. Substance misuse/dependency	
19. Poor self-regulation of affect and behavior (impulsivity)	17. Evidence of empathy, remorse, guilt		Domain 3. Adverse Life Experiences	Dynamic Concerns
20. High-stress family environment	18. Absence of cognitive distortions		1. History of childhood sexual victimization	2a. Cold, callous attitude toward sexual offending
21. Problematic parent–offender relationships/parental rejection	Scale 4: Community Stability/Adjustment Scale		2. History of childhood physical victimization	2b. Sadistic or violent sexual thoughts
22. Parent(s) not supporting sexual-offence-specific assessment/treatment	19. Evidence of poorly managed anger in the community		3. Exposure to sexual abuse/sexual violence	2c. Self-reported sexual interest in children
23. Environment supporting opportunities to reoffend sexually	20. Stability of current living situation		4. Peer victimization	2d. Beliefs that minimize or support sexually abusive behaviors
24. No development or practice of realistic prevention plans/strategies	21. Stability of school		Domain 4. Sexual Development and Adjustment	2e. Obsessive/preoccupation with sexual thoughts/pornography
25. Incomplete sexual-offence-specific treatment	22. Evidence of support systems in the community		1. Unmet need for sexual contact/experience with a peer	
	23. Quality of peer relationships		2. Motive underpinning sexually harmful behavior	
			3. Nature of reinforcement from sexually harmful behavior	
			4. Pornography misuse/dependency	
			5. Sexual learning experiences	
			6. Sexual fantasies	

Developmental Concerns

Static Concerns

3a. Previous drop out from treatment programs to address abusive behaviors

3b. Formal diagnosis of conduct disorder

3c. Experienced significant physical, emotional, sexual abuse or neglect

3d. Witnessed domestic violence

3e. Early onset (pre 10 years) of severe non-sexual behavioral problems

3f. Ever had a diagnosis of depression or other serious mental health problem

3g. Ever had a diagnosis of attention deficit hyperactivity disorder (ADHD)

3h. Problematic sexual behaviors commenced pre-puberty and continued into adolescence

7. Sexual Preferences

8. Sexual Orientation/relations with same-sex peers

9. Cognitive rules underpinning sexually harmful behavior

10. Attitudes and beliefs underpinning sexually harmful behavior

11. Heterosocial competency/ relations with opposite-sex peers

12. Heterosexual/dating experiences

Domain 5. Social Development and Adjustment

1. Social competency
2. Social integration
3. Social immaturity
4. Social delinquency

Domain 6. Emotional Development and Adjustment

1. Emotional dysregulation
2. General/victim empathy deficits

(Continued)

Table 11.2 Item Content for Protocols for Assessing Sexual Violence (Continued)

The ERASOR	J-SOAP	MEGA	SHARPS	AIM
			3. Emotional immaturity	Dynamic Concerns
			4. Attachment difficulties	4a. Generally highly impulsive or compulsive
			Domain 7. Personality Development and Adjustment	4b. Difficulties emotionally regulating
			1. Emerging personality disorder	4c. Emotional congruence/identification with young children
			2. Psychopathy rating	4d. Poor general capacity for empathy (not just in relation to victims)
			Domain 8. Mental Health Development and Adjustment	4e. Poor assertiveness skills (overly passive or aggressive style)
			1. Childhood and adolescent psychiatric disorders	4f. Distorted self-image (extremely negative or narcissistic)
			2. Childhood and adolescent psychiatric symptoms and deficits	4g. General socially isolated (emotionally lonely)
			Domain 9. Cognitive Development and Adjustment	4h. Unresolved trauma (PTSD)
			1. Intellectual disability and cognitive deficits	4i. Pervasive anger
			2. Social-Cognitive information processing deficits	4j. There has been a recent escalation in the young person's aggression or hostility toward others
				4k. Young person currently engages in substance misuse
				4l. The young person displays non-compliance toward supervision

Domain 10. General Self-Regulation and Level of Independence
1. General self-regulation and coping deficits
2. Level of independence

Domain 11. Environment Risks
1. Family environment and opportunities for sexually harmful behavior
2. Neighborhood environment and opportunities for sexually harmful behavior
3. School environment and opportunities for sexually harmful behavior

Domain 12. Motivation and Compliance
1. Family acceptance/compliance/responsivity
2. Young person's manageability/treatability/responsivity

Family Issues
Static Concerns
5a. Early years or most of life in highly dysfunctional family
5b. The most significant adults in the young person's life (e.g., parents, carers) have a history of not addressing their own traumas/problematic behaviors

Dynamic Concerns
6a. The most significant adults in the young person's life express anger toward or blame the victim(s)
6b. The most significant adults in the young person's life deny, minimize, or justify the index offence
6c. Young person is currently experiencing a life crisis such as family rejection or death of a significant family member
6d. Family members do not support or actively undermine professional intervention

(Continued)

Table 11.2 Item Content for Protocols for Assessing Sexual Violence (Continued)

The ERASOR	J-SOAP	MEGA	SHARPS	AIM
				Environmental
				Static Concerns
				7a. Pattern of discontinuity of care
				7b. Previously been excluded from school or employment
				7c. Young person has abused or attempted to abuse another person in their current living environment
				Dynamic Concerns
				8a. Peer group predominantly pro-criminal
				8b. Local community is hostile toward the young person
				8c. Current carers are not support of professional intervention
				8d. Young person currently has little daily structure or pro-social activities in his life
				Strengths: Sexually and Non-sexually Harmful Behaviors

Static

9a. Referral behavior appears to be experimental

9b. Abusive behavior appears to be peer influenced

9c. Abusive behavior ceased when the victim demonstrated non-compliance or distress

Dynamic

10a. Accepts responsibility for the index offence (low level of denial)

10b. Regrets having sexually offended

10c. Willing to address sexual behavior problems

Developmental Issues

Static

11a. Healthy physical developmental history

11b. Above average intelligence

(Continued)

Table 11.2 Item Content for Protocols for Assessing Sexual Violence (Continued)

The ERASOR	J-SOAP	MEGA	SHARPS	AIM
				Dynamic
				12a. Positive talents and/or leisure interests
				12b. Good negotiation/problem solving skills
				12c. Developmentally appropriate level of sexual knowledge
				12d. Positive realistic goals/plans
				12e. Good communication skills
				Family Issues
				Static
				13a. Grown up with consistent and positive relationship with at least one adult
				Dynamic
				14a. The most significant adults in a young person's life (e.g., parents, foster carers) demonstrate good protective attitudes and behaviors
				14b. The most significant adults in young person's life (e.g., parents, carers) demonstrate positive emotional coping strategies

14c. The most significant adults in young person's life (e.g., parents, carers) have a positive support network

14d. The most significant adults in young person's life (e.g., parents, carers) are generally healthy

Environmental Issues

Dynamic

15a. The young person uses at least one emotional confidant

15b. Positive evaluation from work/educational staff (e.g., of behavior, attendance, application to activities)

15c. Positive relationships with professionals

15d. Young person feels emotionally and physically safe within their current environment

15e. Makes positive use of social support network

15f. Current carers/living environment can maintain appropriate level of supervision

ASSET (Youth Justice Board for England and Wales, 2000) was developed for use by the Youth Justice Board for England and Wales. It exists to facilitate an assessment of violence risk in 10- to 17-year-olds.

Several protocols have been developed specifically for evaluating sexually harmful behavior/sexual violence. The AIM (Assessment, Intervention and Moving-on; Youth Justice Board for England and Wales 2004) exists to assess children aged 10 to 17 years. The AIM employs an actuarial method for calculating risk estimates. The Multiplex Empirically Guided Inventory of Ecological Aggregates for Assessing Sexually Abusive Adolescents and Children (MEGA; Miccio-Fonseca 2006a, 2006b; Miccio-Fonseca and Rasmussen 2006) was developed to assess sexual violence risk in children aged 19 and younger. It is a 75-item tool designed for use by clinicians and non-clinicians. The Estimate of Risk of Adolescent Sexual Offence Recidivism Version 2.0 (ERASOR; Worling and Curwen 2001) was developed to assess the short-term risk of sexual recidivism in juveniles aged 12 to 18 years who have previously committed a sexual assault. It is a 25-item tool. Items are evaluated using qualitative ratings, and evaluators are required to make a structured clinical assessment regarding the level of risk that is present.

The Juvenile Sex Offender Assessment Protocol (J-SOAP-II; Prentky and Righthand 2003) was developed for assessing sexual violence risk in adolescents aged between 12 and 18 years. The first version was designed as an actuarial instrument but the most recent version is described as a structured decision-making tool. The Sexually Harmful Adolescent Risk Protocol (SHARP; Richardson 2009) assesses 50 factors that might be relevant to understanding sexually harmful behavior in children.

It is encouraging that research efforts have been directed into developing evidence-based protocols for assessing youth. However, this does not ensure that they will have utility. The utility and validity of a risk assessment procedure can be adjudged by its performance across a range of criteria, such as its methodological, conceptual, empirical, and developmental properties, as well as other practical concerns such as assessment time, competencies required, and so on. It is important for practitioners, policymakers and legal decisionmakers to be clear about the extent to which their opinions have validity. Taking a broad-based approach to evaluating practice in youth risk assessment, it is apparent that there are significant limitations associated with these protocols. A brief discussion of the main concerns is given next.

Utility of the Available Protocols

Actuarial Models

The problems associated with the actuarial and adjusted-actuarial approach have been discussed earlier and in other papers (see Hart et al. 2007, and see David Cooke and Christine Michie's chapter in this volume). Suffice to say it is of serious concern that these models continue to hold such prominence in the field of youth justice. It is incumbent on practitioners, policymakers, and decisionmakers to review the appropriateness and acceptability of these approaches.

Narrow Conceptualizations of the SPJ Model

Although many of the youth risk assessments described above claim to be developed according to SPJ guidelines, a review of their user instructions revealed that they offer little or no guidance beyond Step 2 of the sequence of assessment articulated in the SPJ model. For example, assessors are not told how to interpret their findings to ensure an individualized case conceptualization or formulation. which is a fundamental step toward understanding and managing risk (Logan and Johnstone 2010; Risk Management Authority 2006a). Furthermore, anecdotal evidence suggests that where risk factors are rated on a numerical scale, assessors simply cannot resist drawing inferences from the score. This increases the likelihood of the ecological fallacy—the belief that the group average describes the individual—and could lead to false conclusions.

Cumulative risk models say nothing about how a particular risk factor operates (Sanson and Prior 1999). A key challenge for assessors is to move beyond a simple listing of risk factors to a more integrative analysis (and narrative discussion) of what, why, and how these particular risk factors might be relevant to a particular time in a particular context in relation to a particular behavior. This process enhances the likelihood of individualized interpretations of nomothetic data.

Risk Specificity

A third concern is that the available protocols are lacking in terms of risk specificity. A wide range of antisocial conduct—not necessarily violence of a nature or degree that would warrant dangerous offender provisions—is assessable according to these guides. For example, the EARL-20 (Augmeri et al. 2001: xii) was designed to assess "the potential for antisocial, aggressive or violent conduct." This includes a vast range of behaviors, from swearing and shoplifting to serious aggression. The SAVRY (Borum et al. 2003, 2006) also includes a broad definition of antisocial conduct.

The specificity of effects and sensitivity of the protocols for serious violence will be difficult, if not impossible, to discern as they currently are. If risk assessment is to have utility, it is important to distinguish between different forms of risk, that is the topographical analysis, as well as the relationship between a wide range of different cognitive and behavioral mediators and mechanisms, that is, risk formulation. Thus it is unclear how useful the content is for identifying those children who present an ongoing risk of serious harm to the safety of the public at large, and who therefore require restrictive legal sanctions, as opposed to those who pose a risk of frequent nuisance but low-harm behaviors. This concern applies across all risk outcomes. Prentky et al. (2000) and Epps and Fisher (2004) cautioned that, as a group, juvenile sex offenders are characterized as high in general delinquency and antisocial behavior and lack of impulse control. Thus it is possible that the literature (and therefore risk assessment guides) is simply picking up on the likelihood of delinquency and not the risk of serious sexual harm per se.

Psychometric Properties

A third issue is that the extant literature fails to provide compelling evidence of their psychometric properties. Space does not permit a detailed discussion of each study here, but in general terms it can be concluded that although several studies report statistically significant findings with regard to the reliability and validity of many of the measures, across contexts and countries (see Burman et al. 2007 for a review; Miccio-Fonseca 2009), there are several concerns.

First, the predictor and outcome variables are diverse across studies, and it is not possible to extrapolate from the findings the extent to which they identify risk of serious harm. Second, some protocols, such as the SAVRY (Borum et al. 2003, 2006) and the Youth Level Service/Case Management Inventory (CMI; Hoge and Andrews 2002) have been studied far more than the other measures. Third, there are inconsistent and concerning results. For example, Elkovitch (2008) found that raters were not able to identify detected cases of either sexual recidivism or non-sexual violent recidivism above chance when their conclusions were aided by the SAVRY and J-SOAP-II (Prentky and Rightland 2003). Of particular concern, a high level of rater confidence was not associated with accuracy. Fourth, it cannot be assumed that because a protocol shows predictive validity at a group level it will generalize to individuals who present with low base rate complex risks and psychopathologies. This presents a key challenge to current methods of establishing the utility of risk assessment methods.

Reliance on Delinquency and Criminogenic Models

A fourth observation is that the conceptual underpinnings of risk assessment are heavily weighted toward delinquency and criminogenic models, where methodologies typically utilize broadly defined criterion variables—often including any type of antisocial, violent, aggressive, or sexually inappropriate behavior. It is possible, if not likely, that the overreliance on such models will limit the utility of these protocols. Very serious crimes perpetrated by children do not always conform to these frameworks. Forensic mental health and adolescent psychiatry settings bear testament to this fact. For some young people, major mental illnesses and symptoms associated with other forms of mental disorders (such as autistic spectrum disorders, mental retardation, personality problems, trauma, dissociation, and so on) can be the critical—and sometimes the only—risk factor. In addition, delinquency studies and models are biased in that there is an overrepresentation of male Caucasian children included in samples. Thus, the generalizability of these models to girls, minority groups, cultures, and so on is far from established.

Developmental Sensitivity

Acquiring a developmentally sound framework for risk assessment is a significant challenge, particularly because human development is a metamorphic process, which is likely to be at its most energetic during the formative years. The specialism of developmental psychopathology therefore provides a useful framework from which to adjudge the utility of youth violence risk models and procedures. A key objective in this field is to gain "a process-level understanding of how, why and in what ways individual differences in normal and abnormal social, emotional, cognitive and behavioural development emerge, interact, and develop across the lifespan" (Richters 1997: 198). Concepts such as heterogeneity versus homogeneity, equifinality versus multifinality, change and stability, transient developmental phenomena, homotypic versus heterotypic continuity, and the direction of effects in causal models are all relevant to reaching reliable assessments of risk. The relevance of these concepts to risk assessment is considered next. Richters (1997) referred to these issues collectively as the developmentalist's dilemmas.

Heterogeneity and Homogeneity   The principles of heterogeneity and homogeneity refer to the fact that because a child (or group of children) might display phenotypically similar behaviors—in this case, violence or sexual violence—it would be erroneous to assume that they constitute a homogeneous sample. As explained earlier, much of the research used to inform the content of the available risk assessment protocols comes from the delinquency and criminogenic literatures, and much of the literature on antisocial children is derived from methodologies where there is an a priori assumption of homogeneity, with respect to both outcome and predictor variables. This is unlikely. The diverse motivations and modi operandi used by individuals seeking sexual, or some other form of psychological gratification through offending, provides a compelling illustration of this point. An adolescent with low intelligence and pedophilic proclivities, driven by a sense of emotional congruence with children, is likely to differ from another child who shows a predilection for perpetrating predatory stranger rape characterized by severe physical violence, or in the context of homicidal fantasies that satisfy some intrinsic need for control and dominance. In turn, both will differ from a 13-year-old reenacting his or her own abuse experiences on a four-year-old sibling. The available risk assessment protocols are limited in their explanation of how to make sense of the different risk factors for different outcomes, thus assessors who lack an in-depth knowledge of violence and sexual harm, normal development, abnormal psychology and developmental psychopathology, as well as mental disorders in children are therefore vulnerable to inadvertently misusing and misinterpreting the significance of their risk ratings.

Equifinality and Multifinality   Building on the previous argument, it is essential that the concepts of equifinality and multifinality are understood by assessors. Equifinality refers to the process whereby the same end state—in this instance violence or sexual violence risk—may be achieved via many different paths, processes, and trajectories. There is not one direct cause-and-effect relationship. Different early experiences in life (for example, parental divorce, physical abuse, parental substance abuse, genetic vulnerability, bullying and social exclusion, bereavement, and so on) might lead to antisocial behavior problems.

In contrast, multifinality refers to the situation where a very different overt behavior is attributable to a similar, or the same, underlying phenomena. The relevance of these concepts has been used to explain the development of personality disorders. Taking childhood trauma such as sexual abuse as an example, there is research to suggest this might be relevant to the development of borderline, antisocial, narcissistic, and psychopathic personality disorder in adulthood (Beauchaine et al. 2009). To appraise someone's risk, an in-depth knowledge and understanding of these possible pathways is essential.

In addition, it would be erroneous to assume that a risk factor, even if present at all stages, functions in the same way for all people in all contexts and across time. The lack of predictive utility of sexual abuse as a precursor for sexual pathology in adolescence is a case in point. Research has indicated that, when examined on its own, abuse history is not a useful predictor of juvenile sexual offending (Prentky and Knight 1993; Rasmussen 1999). Early-onset child molesters were more likely to have been sexually abused, whereas neglect was more common in the background of those who perpetrated early-onset rape.

It can be concluded then that the significance of sexual abuse to understanding sexual offending is complex, and likely to be influenced by other life events and experiences. These findings reinforce the point that different psychological processes may underpin different forms of violence, and these processes might be different in children than in adults and across contexts.

Change and Stability Although the notion that past behavior is the best predictor of future behavior is often cited as a psychological truism, the validity of this position is questionable, especially with regard to youth violence. Most of the research on children is concerned with persistence. This means we know far less about children who desist and or why this might be the case. Change and stability are important concepts. When it comes to assessing risk in children, it is important to note that antisocial behaviors are commonplace across the formative years. Indeed, according to scholars, it is statistically aberrant to refrain from antisocial conduct during childhood and adolescence (Elliot et al. 1983; Hirschi 1969) and as many as 50 per cent (Robins 1978) to 85 per cent (White et al. 1990) of antisocial children desist.

It is therefore difficult to assess the likelihood that a child's first offence or cluster of offences—no matter how serious—reflects an established antisocial trajectory. Comparing juveniles who have perpetrated homicide with non-violent youth, those who perpetrated killings were less likely to have a history of prior violence, arrests, placement in a juvenile facility, psychiatric problems or problems with youth adjustment (Cornell et al. 1987). Most young offenders do not become persistent adult offenders. After age 17, violence participation rates drop dramatically with around 80 per cent desisting by age 21 (Elliot et al. 1986). The life-course persistent group is relatively small (approximately five to nine per cent). Similar trends apply to juvenile sex offenders, where rates of recidivism are low (Hagan et al. 2001; Kahn and Chambers 1991; Prentky et al. 2000; Rasmussen 1999). Trivits and Reppucci (2002) cautioned that only around 10 per cent reoffend, which means that the false positive rate could be as high as 90 per cent.

Transient Developmental Phenomena Related to the previous point, when it comes to rating risk factors per se, transient developmental phenomena (Seagrave and Grisso 2002) might lead assessors astray. The term refers to the process whereby transient features of the child's presentation could mistakenly be interpreted as evidence to suggest that a risk factor is present. For example, children show an immature theory of mind, are egocentric, and can be oppositional (Piaget 1972; 1973). It is easy to see how this problem could influence risk ratings on the available protocols. Furthermore, impulsivity, sensation seeking and risk taking are more characteristic (and according to some theorists normal) in youth (Baumrind 1991; Peterson 1988; Shedler and Block 1990; Zuckerman et al. 1978). In addition, consequential abstract thinking, which allows one to weigh up the pros and cons of a certain course of action, is dependent on cognitive abilities (Keating 1990), which are far less developed in children than adults.

Opinions that rely on a cross-sectional analysis of a young person's interpersonal, affective, or behavioral functioning may not be an accurate reflection of their typical pattern of relating, feeling, or behaving nor necessarily prognostic of their long-term adjustment. Grisso (1998) aptly characterized youth in the developmental period as moving targets, where it is common for children to try on different identities, beliefs, values, personas, and so on. As a result, a greater range of variability in styles and behaviors will be apparent across a greater range of contexts. Change in all domains is not linear. Cognition, emotion, and physical development does not occur in one unified harmonious process; change emerges at different rates.

Heterotypic and Homotypic Continuity   Notwithstanding all of the aforementioned points, even if an underlying process is present, that is, a risk factor that is present across time, the concepts of heterotypic and homotypic continuity are relevant to understanding its expression. Homotypic continuity refers to the process whereby there is identical expression of an underlying process across developmental stages. Heterotypic continuity refers to the changing behavioral manifestations of the same developmental process.

Homotypic continuity is rare (Kagan 1971). Behavioral expressions of personality, cognitive functioning, social skills, and behavioral functioning are transformed across development. The cognitive, physical, emotional, and interpersonal capacities of a 6-year-old are distinctly different from a post-pubescent 12-year-old; similarly, there are considerable differences between a pre-pubescent 12-year-old and a post-pubescent 15-year-old. The extent to which these risk factors explain the phenotypically similar pattern of overt functioning—in this case violence or sexual violence risk—is highly questionable. Heterotypic continuity, that is, where there is a changing behavioral manifestation of the same development process, is more likely (Caspi 2000; Cicchetti and Rogosch 2002).

Direction of Effects   Finally, when it comes to understanding risk, assessors will need to be aware of the issues associated with the wide range of influences on outcome. The direction of effects may be transactional, interactional, unidirectional, or bidirectional (for example, Sanson and Prior 1999; Rothbart and Bates 1998; Thomas and Chess 1977). Explanatory paradigms for risk need to be complex and need to take account of these influences and their varying levels of importance across time. Research suggests that during early childhood, biological processes and early parent/caregiver factors might be most important. As children mature and become increasingly independent, parental influence declines so that by adolescence, peers become a far more important influence (Augmeri et al. 2001; Lipsey and Derzon 1998; Steinberg and Schwartz 2000). Therefore, the nature of the relationships may follow different pathways and processes, and there is a need for assessors (and researchers) to take account of these complex explanatory paradigms.

In sum, it would be foolhardy for any practitioner or policymaker to proceed with confidence in the uncritical application of any of the available risk assessment protocols to youth. Key concerns remain to be researched and resolved. Obviously this has important implications for the use of dangerous offender provisions (and indeed the use of any legal provision used for children). Some pertinent issues and implications for practitioners and policymakers are summarized next.

Implications for Sentencing

First and foremost, the preceding discussion raises serious questions concerning the assumption that it is possible, with any degree of certainty, to distinguish children who do from children who do not pose an ongoing risk of perpetrating acts of serious harm. This challenges the core philosophy underpinning many of the sentencing policies affecting young people. The implications are far reaching, and traverse the legal, ethical, moral, and scientific domains.

Critics have argued that with public protection and deterrence occupying center stage, the child's interests have become secondary, incidental, or, as in the case of those sentenced to life without parole, entirely absent (see, for example, Parker 2005). The issues highlighted also suggest that there is a very real possibility that children could be unlawfully detained because the integrity of the assessment is poor (Millington 2010). Those required to provide opinions may be relying on flawed protocols.

It is important to highlight that assessors must have highly specialist skills and knowledge. Those who rely on delinquency models may lack the requisite competencies and expertise that would allow for a comprehensive and integrative analysis of the diverse literatures necessary to reach a comprehensive formulation appropriate for children. The appropriateness, legality, constitutionality, fairness, and effectiveness of laws, which depend so heavily on a practice that, like the population itself, is very much in its infancy, makes for a controversial topic. (See Parker 2005, van Zyl Smit 2006, and Zimring 2004 for discussions.) Continued debate and discussion are to be encouraged.

It would appear that some jurisdictions have begun to recognize and respond to some of these concerns. Australia, for example, is considering introducing provisional sentencing for youth (Beckett et al. 2009), and other countries including Norway and Japan respond differently to young offenders.

In the meantime there is a pressing need to develop more sophisticated, developmentally informed and psychometrically sound models of risk assessment. This will not be straightforward or achieved in short timescales. For example, on discussing the concept of psychopathy in children—just one risk factor that might be relevant to risk—there is a need for a strong measurement model (Johnstone and Cooke 2004). The same principles apply to most of the risk factors that have already been identified in relation to youth risk assessment, and indeed risk factors that are yet to be identified.

In terms of research methodologies, it might be helpful to use narrower outcome and predictor variables in research. As well as finding correlates, it will be important to conduct research that sheds light on the processes of risk. This has been a neglected area of study, and if we are to achieve comprehensive, individualized, and configurative explanations of risk, it is essential that this work be done. Case-study methodology might be appropriate for identifying these pathways (Yin 2009) before larger-scale validation research, and important, it is incumbent on researchers to declare without any ambiguity the limitations of their findings.

What Do We Do Meantime?

While we await tomorrow's world of conceptual clarity and psychometric sophistication, today's world is characterized by the very real concerns that relate to the level and type of youth violence being observed in society, as well as the existence of legislative procedures that demand opinions on risk to aid decisions regarding disposal. There is a need to ensure defensible decision-making for those cases already showing worrying behaviors and engaged in the legal system. The question is how.

In terms of achieving defensible decisions in the field of youth violence, the standards and guidelines for assessing risk of violence, articulated in Hart et al. (2003), and the Risk Management Authority Scotland practice documents (2006a), might be helpful. The Risk for Sexual Violence Protocol (RSVP; Hart et al. 2003) and the guidelines by the Risk Management Authority (2006a; see also the chapter by Innes Fyfe and Yvonne Gailey in this volume) build upon the previously published risk assessment guides and give explicit guidance as to how to move beyond a simple listing of risk factors to providing a case-specific, individualized formulation.

The RSVP and Risk Management Authority guidelines accept the premise that it is not possible to predict, with any degree of certainty, what any one person might do at any one point in time and so present a framework for practice that allows for, and to some extent contains, uncertainties and possibilities. The emphasis is on providing theoretically sophisticated and informed risk formulations, scenario planning, and risk management interventions. The assessor is required to refer to, but not be curtailed by, the available risk assessment protocols. The SPJ paradigm allows for, and indeed expects, assessors to refer to any other relevant literatures or findings, so that case-specific or idiopathic variables are identified. In the case of young people, assessors should ensure that risk opinions are individualized and based on theoretically guided speculations (or formulations) about the range of risk processes that might occur. In terms of providing opinions on young people, it would appear essential for evaluators to have a thorough knowledge of several relevant literatures (forensic, developmental, developmental psychopathology, risk assessment, delinquency, mental health, trauma, and so on). When it comes to assessing youth, Hoge argued that "any psychologist engaged in assessing adolescents needs to have a solid background in developmental psychology and a sensitivity to the needs of youth in this age period" (Hoge 2008: 60). This would seem a minimum standard. Thus practitioners (and decisionmakers) must ensure that they have adequate competencies to conduct these assessments.

An example drawn from the United Kingdom is the introduction of the Health Professions Council, a regulatory body set up to ensure professional standards among psychologists and other health care professionals. On reviewing their guidelines, it would seem evident that competencies defined by this body as both clinical and forensic would be essential for starters. Assessors will also need to be fully aware of the limitations of the methodological procedures used to develop, test, and validate risk assessment. Thus a sophisticated knowledge of the methodological underpinnings and weaknesses of the approaches used is essential. These competencies will need to be acquired by the usual routes of demonstrating ability in both the academic and clinical arenas. Because opinions must focus on risk management and prevention, not prediction, assessors will require a thorough knowledge of the various psychosocial treatments for children (offending, trauma, family systems, mental health, etc.) as well as the various supervision, monitoring, educational, and social supports that might be helpful. This also demands high-level skills and knowledge of the treatment and risk management literatures.

It is possible that adhering to the aforementioned standards will go some way toward reducing the likelihood that children will be unlawfully detained or, conversely, that high-risk youth will be left without adequate supports and go on to commit serious harm. Adherence to these standards should increase the likelihood, and indeed the confidence, in which both assessors and decisionmakers may place upon risk assessment opinions. However, it is not a panacea. A range of issues are required to be addressed in the future.

Conclusions and Future Directions

The use of dangerous offender provisions for youth is predicated on the belief that it is possible to identify those children who do from those children who do not pose a risk of serious harm. The extant literature falls short of providing compelling evidence that this is so. Although progress has been made, practitioners and legal decisionmakers do not have access to a fully validated test or instrument that can reliably determine whether a young person will commit a future act of serious harm. There is a pressing need to advance knowledge in this area if developmentally sensitive risk assessments are to be forthcoming. While we await these protocols, practitioners assisting the court, or indeed any decisionmakers, have a duty to ensure that they have the requisite expertise and breadth of knowledge to provide a fully informed developmental and forensic analysis of the young person's specific circumstances. Any opinions about risk should be couched within the considerable caveats that currently pervade this practice.

12
Violence Risk Assessment
Challenging the Illusion of Certainty

DAVID J. COOKE and CHRISTINE MICHIE

Doubt is not a pleasant condition, but certainty is absurd.

François Marie Arouet Voltaire (1768)

Risk Management: The Management of Uncertainty

Risk by definition is about uncertainty, thus risk management should be the management of uncertainty. Uncertainty about violence engenders anxiety in professionals and the public alike. This is not a new idea. Referring to the then in vogue term *dangerousness*, Scott (1977: 127) indicated that "it is a term which raises anxiety and which is therefore peculiarly open to abuse, especially to over-response of a punitive, restrictive or dissociative nature." The same is currently true for the term risk. Although the period since Scott wrote his seminal primer on the assessment of potentially violent individuals has witnessed dramatic improvements in violence risk assessment, anxieties are still prevalent among professionals and the public. Scott's diagnosis of the problem still applies:

> We strive after accurate prediction of dangerousness because this would quell our anxieties, enable us to draw clear lines between the dangerous and non-dangerous, and avoid the necessity of continuing contact and concern for them. But no such magical process will be possible. (1977: 140)

Violence risk assessment is at the center of forensic practice and this is increasingly so as society becomes more risk averse. The focus of this chapter is on the individual offender—whether mentally disordered or not—and decisions about how he or she should be managed. The focus is on the provision of useful, valid, ethically sound information that is probative and not prejudicial. The focus is on how forensic practitioners can assist the decisionmakers—judges, parole board members, and members of other tribunals—to make principled and informed decisions. This focus on the individual is key; we will argue that there is fundamental confusion in the literature regarding what information about groups can tell us about an individual.

Despite Scott's analysis, the belief in magical (statistical) processes is widespread—and spreading. Three eras can be discerned in the evolution of approaches to the assessment of violence risk. Since Scott (1977) three approaches have evolved; from the era of unstructured—and opaque—clinical judgment, through the era of prediction to the era of structured clinical judgment founded on best empirical knowledge and best professional practice (Cooke 2010a).

We should celebrate the achievements made so far, but we must also be conscious of the blind alleys we have driven down and the limitations—indeed—the danger of some of the approaches developed that have become institutionalized to the detriment of individuals and society more broadly.

On the Misapplication of Statistics in Forensic Practice

There is always an easy solution to every human problem—neat, plausible and wrong.

Henry Menken (1917)

Statistical arguments and reasoning are becoming more frequent in court settings (Lucy 2005). Unfortunately, statistical evidence can seriously mislead decisionmakers. As Monahan (2008: i) noted "statistical illiteracy is endemic in the courtrooms." There are notorious cases that highlight the misleading power of statistics, some of which are briefly outlined here.

The English case of Sally Clark is a vivid and heart-rending illustration of this point. Clark was a solicitor whose two baby sons died within a few weeks of their birth. She was wrongfully convicted of murder primarily on the basis of expert evidence given by Sir Roy Meadow, a British pediatrician. He stated at Clark's trial that the chances of her having two natural cot deaths were one in 73 million. This figure suggested that such deaths were beyond coincidence (see Hill 2004 for a detailed analysis of the statistical arguments). Only after a second appeal to the Court of Appeal, was the fallacious reasoning underpinning Meadow's testimony accepted by the Court. Clark was released but died not long after at the age of 42.

In the United States, in the case of O.J. Simpson, Alan Dershowitz argued for the exclusion of evidence about domestic abuse and battering on the grounds that only one in 2,500 of men who assault their partners go on to murder them. Further essential information was omitted. Knowing that murder has taken place, the relevant statistic is that the chances of the batterer being the murderer are approximately 90 per cent (Gigerenzer 2002). Parenthetically, it is perhaps noteworthy that in his account of the Simpson trial, Dershowitz stated that "to tell the truth, the whole truth and nothing but the truth—is applicable only to witnesses. Defense attorneys, prosecutors, and judges don't take this oath—they couldn't" (cited in Gigerenzer 2002: 141).

In Scotland, the case of police officer Shirley McKie, who was accused of perjury in a murder case on the basis of misinterpreted fingerprint evidence, led to a crisis in confidence in fingerprint evidence, a public judicial inquiry, and an award of £750,000 compensation to her. At the heart of this complex case was a failure to properly appreciate probabilities when evaluating points of similarity during fingerprint matching.

These are all dramatic cases where statistical evidence has been at best misunderstood. However, we believe that there is a more pervasive and more insidious misuse of what appears to be statistical evidence in the area of violence risk assessment through the application of actuarial risk assessment instruments (ARAIs).

In this chapter we consider three issues. First, a summary of the misuse of so-called actuarial models will be provided. In our view, the field has become overconfident in the ability of actuarial procedures to make reliable predictions about whether individuals will be violent. This misplaced confidence is founded on a failure to recognize the problems of making predictions for individuals based on aggregate statistics, and important, a misunderstanding of the logic of actuarial approaches (see Cooke 2010a).

Second, it will be argued that there is a growing awareness in psychology that dominant empirical paradigms such as between-subject models (for example, measures of individual differences) cannot test or support causal accounts (for example, pertaining to violence) that are valid at the individual level. This is because there is an unspoken—and unmerited—assumption that the mechanisms that operate to explain variations among individuals also explain the mechanisms that operate at the level of the individual. Individuals are violent for different reasons. Any one individual may be violent for different reasons on different occasions.

Third, it will be argued that for the field to progress toward effective risk management, it is necessary to develop both a taxonomy of risk processes and a systematic approach to risk formulation. The development of criteria to validate individual risk formulations is an important—and pressing challenge for the field.

The Promise and the Peril of the Actuarial Approach

In reaction to the lack of transparency, replicability, and utility of the unstructured clinical approaches, attempts were made from the mid-1980s to adopt empirical methods and to impose structure on the decision-making of clinicians (see Bernadette McSherry and Patrick Keyzer's introductory chapter and the chapter by Lorraine Johnstone in this volume). An increasing number of ARAIs have been developed (see, for example, Hanson and Thornton 1999; Quinsey et al. 1998). These instruments have proved popular. Some commentators such as Craig and Beech (2009) have argued that the superiority of actuarial scales is widely accepted. However, other commentators have been less sanguine (Hart et al. 2003). It is perhaps regrettable that proponents of the actuarial approaches have derided clinicians' understanding of research methods and statistics (Harris 2003). As we will see, the true position is far from obvious.

Proponents have argued for the wholesale adoption of actuarial methods:

> What we are advising is not the addition of actuarial methods to existing practice, but rather the complete replacement of existing practice with actuarial methods ... actuarial methods are too good and clinical judgment too poor to risk contaminating the former with the latter. (Quinsey et al. 1998: 171)

In our view this is both a dangerous and an untenable position (see also Allport 1940; Harcourt 2006).

The adoption of ARAI techniques has become widespread. Craig and Beech (2009: 197) state that "in North America and the United Kingdom, actuarial risk assessment has permeated the entire criminal-justice system." Khiroya, Weaver, and Maden (2009) recently reported that the Risk Matrix 2000 (RM2000) (see Thornton 2007 for a description of the origins of this tool) and the Static-99 (Hanson and Thornton 1999) were the most commonly used sex offender assessments in English medium secure forensic units.

The actuarial paradigm is apparently straightforward. A group of offenders, usually prisoners, is assessed—often in terms of characteristics that are easy to measure, for example age, marital status, history of offending, and type of victims. Sometimes the cohort of prisoners is followed up and new criminal convictions are identified from criminal records. More commonly the cohort is followed back, that is, the files of prisoners who have been released and whose convictions status have been monitored, are reviewed and key characteristics that discriminate between those who offend and those who do not are identified. Statistical methods are then applied to link the assessed characteristics to the observed likelihood of reconviction for this new individual.

This information about group relationships is used to make a prognostication about a new individual. Guidance is then given to decisionmakers about this individual's likelihood of reoffending using a process of analogy such as "this man resembles offenders who are likely to recidivate, therefore, he *is* likely to recidivate" (Hart 2003: 385). Craig and Beech (2009: 205) have recommended the following method of communication:

> Actuarial risk assessment of Mr. X using Risk Matrix/Sexual indicates that his score falls within the "medium" risk category, such a score is associated with a 13 per cent likelihood over five years, 16 per cent over 10 years, and 19 per cent over 15 years, of being

reconvicted for a sexual offence (for known and convicted sexual offenders) in a group of sexual offenders with the same score.

Note this is a form of inductive logic where, in essence, it is argued that because Mr. X belongs to a group, then his level of reoffending is most likely to be the average for the group. This is technically correct but fundamentally misleading. It is misleading because it fails to inform the decisionmaker about the large—extremely large—degree of uncertainty that is associated with this estimate.

Talking about prognostications about individuals, two statisticians observed that "we believe that the distinction between what is achievable at the group and individual level is not well understood" (Altman and Royston 2000: 454). We will examine this distinction in more detail below.

As noted at the start of the chapter, Voltaire remarked that doubt is not a pleasant condition. Indeed, Gigerenzer (2002) has indicated that the removal of doubt and the thirst for certainty is a basic human desire; he argued that such certainty is an illusion. This illusion is central to the problem of risk assessment; evaluating the uncertainty associated with prognostications about violence is essential. This is clear if we consider Gigerenzer's definition of risk. He wrote that "uncertainty associated with an event that can be quantified on the basis of empirical observations or causal knowledge" (Gigerenzer 2002: 256).

In other fields such as weather forecasting and hydrology, the quantification of uncertainty has long been seen as a key process that will lead to rational decision-making (for example, see Cooke 1906). Krzysztofowwicz (2001: 4) indicated such an approach has the advantage of being "scientifically more 'honest.'" Krzyszofowwicz (2001: 3) further stated that:

> A deterministic format forces the forecaster to suppress information and judgment about uncertainty. A deterministic forecast may create the illusion of certainty in a user's mind, which can easily lead to the user to sub-optimal action.

The uncertainty associated with violence risk prediction is at best unstated, at worst it is unrecognized.

A Salient Case

The consideration of an individual case was the stimulus that triggered our interest in the evaluation and quantification of uncertainty in relation to violence risk assessment. The first author was contacted by a Scottish sheriff—a judge—who had received a report by a social worker who used an actuarial tool, the Risk Matrix 2000 (Thornton 2003), and had concluded that the offender was at high risk of reoffending; a psychologist using a structured clinical judgment approach—the Sexual Violence Risk-20 (SVR-20; Boer et al. 1997)—concluded the offender was low risk.

It is disquieting to note that, in essence, the actuarial judgment of high risk was founded on three pieces of information, the offender was 18 years of age, he had not lived in an intimate relationship with someone for two years of more, and he had not met his victim face-to-face before (he and the victim had been in regular contact by phone for five weeks prior to the offence). The offender was convicted of a statutory offence of having sexual intercourse with a minor (see Cooke 2010a for a fuller account). Three pieces of information formed the assessment of high risk—people are generally more complex than that.

This case triggered a process of analysis that led to the publication of Hart et al. (2007), a paper that has been regarded by some as controversial (for example, see Craig and Beech 2009: 203). In the following, we consider and clarify some of the issues raised in response to previous papers (Cooke and Michie 2010; Cooke et al. 2010; Hart et al. 2007 for more technical accounts). The key question is how can the quantification of uncertainty be achieved.

Quantifying Uncertainty

The core purpose of statistical methods is the estimation, description, and quantification of uncertainty. Authors and advocates of ARAIs explicitly state that their purpose is prediction. Take, for example, the following statements: "[the] RM2000/S is a prediction tool for sexual violence" (Thornton 2007: 3) and "[the] Static-2002 predicts sexual, violent and any recidivism as well as other actuarial risk tools" (Static 2002: 1).

How certain or uncertain are these predictions? Statistical methods enable the quantification of uncertainty. All estimates are subject to error: the precision of a parameter estimate (for example, the mean rate of sexual recidivism of a group) is specified by a confidence interval; a confidence interval demarks the range of values within which an unknown population parameter is likely to fall. The width of this interval provides a measure of the precision—or certainty—associated with the estimate of the population parameter.

The width of a confidence interval of a population parameter is linked, in part, to the sample size used to estimate the population parameter. Psychologists are generally familiar with confidence intervals, and practitioners are used to expressing their degree of confidence in a test result, for example, estimating IQ by stating the confidence interval within which the estimated IQ falls. Indeed, in the United Kingdom it is a professional requirement to state confidence intervals (Professional Affairs Board 1991).

Assessing the uncertainty associated with predictions about an individual offender is rather more complex and the methods are less familiar to psychologists (but see Cohen and Cohen 1983; Psychological Corporation 1999). There are two stages where uncertainty can be manifest. In the first stage, the parameters (mean, slope, and variance) of the regression model specifying the association between the independent variable (for example, RM2000 scores) and the dependent variable (for example, the likelihood of reconviction) are estimated.

Uncertainty is associated with each of these parameters. This uncertainty can be expressed by a confidence interval about the regression line. Essentially, data from the group upon which the ARAI was developed is used to assess uncertainty.

In the second stage—the critical stage—a new case for which a decision is to be made is identified, a score calculated, and the likelihood of his reconviction is estimated. This estimate of the likelihood of reconviction for the individual also has a confidence interval—known more specifically as a prediction interval—that expresses the precision, or uncertainty, that should be associated with the prediction made about the new case.

The confidence interval for the group and prediction interval for the individual are very different both conceptually and in terms of magnitude; the latter always being much wider than the former. This is not new; it is standard and established statistical theory (Anderson and Bancroft 1952; Cooke and Michie 2010 for formal definitions).

Concern over the case referred to earlier led us to consider how to quantify the degree of uncertainty associated with the claim that the offender was high risk, that is, that he had a 36 per cent chance of recidivating in a sexual manner during the next 15 years. We have been unable to access the raw data on the RM2000, although access to raw data is normally a requirement for the computation of confidence intervals. It is concerning that access to raw data appears to be a problem in this field (for example, see Waggoner, Wollert, and Cramer 2008). In essence the methods remain unclear and are not available for proper scientific scrutiny.

Fortunately, confidence intervals can be estimated from categorical data by applying a procedure first developed by Wilson (1927). This method is preferred over other possible methods because it is not strongly influenced by extreme values of sample size or the proportion of recidivists, and it does not yield impossible values, such as negative values (Agresti and Coull 1998). We have demonstrated this approach elsewhere (Cooke et al. 2010; Hart, Michie, et al.

2007). In essence we demonstated that prediction intervals associated with ARAIs are so wide that no confidence can be had in these estimates. Our analyses were subject to critiscism (for example, see Mossman and Selke 2007; Hanson and Howard 2010) but this appears to be based, in part, on a misunderstanding of situation when dealing with the prediction of binary events. Statisticians recognize that while the outcome may be binary, the predictions in any statistical model are probabilities (for example, see Altman and Royston 2000).

We have argued elsewhere (Cooke and Michie 2010; Cooke et al. 2010) that logistic regression is the appropriate method for modeling the prediction of a binary outcome (for example, reconviction). It is important that there are established formal methods for estimating both confidence intervals and prediction intervals when logistic regression is applied (Steel et al. 1997).

Using data from the Static-2002 (Hanson and Thornton 2003), we are able to demonstrate that the prediction intervals derived using Wilson's method were narrower than those obtained using logistic regression. In other words, the situation is worse than Wilson's method would imply. Thus, in the highest risk group the point estimate prediction for recidivism—for the group—over five years is 38 per cent; Wilson's method calculates the prediction interval as three per cent to 92 per cent; the logistic method calculates the prediction interval as two per cent to 99 per cent.

Whatever method is used to calculate the prediction interval, it is clear that there is vast uncertainty associated with a point prediction for any individual. This is the case with all ARAIs because the width of prediction intervals reflect the inherent variablity in probablities of reoffending even among offenders with identical characteristics (Henderson and Keiding 2005). Roth (2009: 182) expanded on this point:

> The [prediction interval] will generally be wider than the [confidence interval] since there is usually more uncertainty in predicting the behavior of one randomly selected future measurement from a distribution of values than in estimating a current or past population characteristic. With an increasing sample size, the [prediction interval], unlike the [confidence interval], will narrow to a finite range and no further because there is an inherent patient-to-patient variability (i.e., the distribution of expected future values).

The Illusion of Certainty

Numerical statements—such as, there is an 18 per cent likelihood that this individual will reoffend sexually in the next five years are powerful. It is difficult for decision makers to disregard numbers and alter their evaluation even if presented with detailed, credible, and contradictory information. Judges and other decisionmakers are not immune from this. The anchoring bias is a well-established cognitive bias that influences all human judgment (Englich and Mussweiler 2001). This problem is compounded by the tendency to predict rather than forecast, that is, to provide a single value of the likelihood that someone will offend without any indication of confidence that should be placed on that single value; that is, without an indication such as the range of possible values which that likelihood may take. Is the range narrow or wide?

It is possible to illustrate the degree of uncertainty associated with an estimated likelihood of reoffending by plotting the probability density function. The probability density function can be viewed as a smoothed version of a histogram depicting relative frequencies of the range of probabilities of reoffending consequent on the variability in the original sample. An examination of Static-2002 (Routine sample) data indicates that only two distinct risk groups can be discerned, a low-risk and a high-risk group (Cooke et al. 2010). The low-risk group has a mean of four and the high-risk group has a mean of eight. The point estimated likelihood for the individual in the low group was 14 per cent and the point estimated likelihood for the individual in the high group was 30 per cent. Focusing on these mean values can be misleading.

In Figure 12.1 we plot the probability density functions for the Static-2002. Three observations can be made about these probability density functions. First, the distributions both range from zero to one. Second, the distributions are relatively flat which means that the likelihood of reconviction can take on many values with similar levels of likelihood. Indeed, the most likely value is not at all likely. Third, and perhaps critically, the probability density functions overlap to a considerable extent, which indicates that knowledge of group membership does little to reduce the uncertainty of the estimate of the likelihood of recidivism. One way to clarify this overlap is to think in terms of frequencies. For example, suppose it can be demonstrated that out of 100 offenders in the low group, 36 will have a probability of recidivism greater than 30 per cent (that is, the mean probability of the high group), and, similarly, of 100 offenders in the high group 36 will have a probability of recidivism, which is less than 14 per cent (that is, the mean probability of the low group). In our view, a statement such as "actuarial risk assessment of Mr. X using Risk Matrix/Sexual indicates that his score falls within the 'medium' risk category, such a score is associated with a 13 per cent likelihood over five years, 16 per cent over 10 years, and 19 per cent over 15 years, of being reconvicted for a sexual offence (for known and convicted sexual offenders) in a group of sexual offenders with the same score" as recommended by Craig and Beech (2009: 205) is fundamentally misleading. This is because such a statement fails to communicate to the decisionmaker the true nature of the uncertainty associated with the headline figure of 19 per cent over 15 years.

The problem of making predictions for *individuals* using statistical models is now recognized in other disciplines; it is not merely a function of the complexity of assessing the psychological characteristics of individuals. For example, in relation to medical risks, Rose (1992: 48) indicated that "unfortunately the ability to estimate the average risk for a group, which may be good, is not matched by any corresponding ability to predict which individuals are going to fall ill soon" (see also Altman and Royston 2000; Henderson and Keiding 2005; Roth 2009; Vardeman 1992). Individual cases demonstrate this vividly. Stephen Hawking wryly observed in a BBC interview on 18 February 1996 that "thirty years ago I was diagnosed with motor neurone disease, and given two and a half years to live. I have always wondered how they could be so precise about the half."

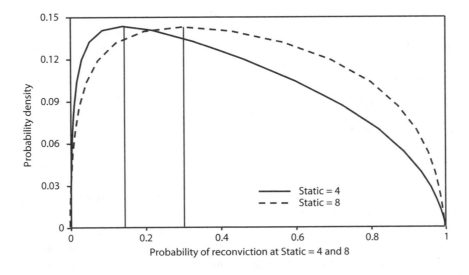

Figure 12.1 Probability density functions for the mean values of the high- and low-risk groups Static-2002 non-routine sample.

It remains worrying that the significance of uncertainty in violence risk assessment based on ARAIs is not widely understood (for example, see Hanson and Howard 2010). The illusion of certainty engendered by the presentation of a single estimate can have profound effects in everyday practice. If a judge is persuaded by such figures it may lead to suboptimal action such as a lenient sentence when more control is required, or equally, a disproportionate sentence when such is not required.

Life Insurance as a False Analogue for Violence Risk Assessment

A common defense of ARAIs is that they are modeled on the practices of life insurance companies. One of the authors has been told this by judges (see also Hanson and Howard 2010). This analogue is false. The life insurance actuary achieves a profit by predicting the *proportion* of insured lives that will end within a particular time period. The actuary has no interest in predicting the deaths of particular individuals and recognizes the impossibility of doing so. By way of contrast, the decisionmaker in court is only interested in the accused in front of him or her, not the properties of any statistical group from which the accused may be derived. This has long been recognized. Conan-Doyle's Sherlock Holmes stated:

> While the individual man is an insoluble puzzle, in the aggregate he becomes a mathematical certainty. You can, for example, never foretell what any one man will do, but you can say with precision what an average number will be up to. Individuals vary, but percentages remain constant. (Conan-Doyle 1890: 86)

Sherlock Holmes clearly understood the logical fallacy of division (Rorer 1990). This fallacy rests on drawing a conclusion about an individual member of a group based on the collective properties of that group. For example, it is self-evidently fallacious to argue that if, in general, intelligent people earn more than less intelligent people then Jules, with an IQ of 120, will earn more than Jim with an IQ of 100. Equally, it is fallacious to argue that although people who score highly on an actuarial risk scale generally reoffend more than people who do not score highly, Bill in the high-risk group will reoffend more often – or more quickly – than Brian in the low-risk group.

ARAIs as Screening Instruments for Violence Risk Assessment

If ARAIs should not be used in risk prediction, do they have a role as screening tools? Interestingly, there appears to be a tendency among some researchers and practitioners to use ARAIs to screen offenders (for example, see Grubin 2008: 29). At first blush this might sound efficient, effective, and reasonable. Unfortunately neither the rationale nor the evidence to support such a use is compelling. There appears to be a fundamental misunderstanding regarding both the effectiveness of screens and the proper tests that need to be carried out to evaluate their effectiveness. Dangerous policies and practices are being promulgated and we remain surprised that they are not subject to more rigorous legal challenge.

Screens are used in medicine in asymptomatic individuals to identify the risk of future disease; those identified as being at risk using a screen are then subject to a more detailed and rigorous "gold standard" test (Greenhaigh 1997). Moderate voices such as Grubin (2008: 28) make their position clear that the "Risk Matrix 2000 ... should be seen as the first step in an assessment process, not a substitute for the assessment process itself."

However, there are two problems with applying this approach to the field of violence risk assessment. First, in practice, screening in the generally accepted sense rarely happens. The practitioners given the task of assessment generally do not have the time nor the training to provide the systematic risk assessment necessary using a comprehensive test (gold standard) for those deemed risky by the screen. In practice, at least in the United Kingdom, the decisionmaker is provided with the results of the actuarial scale with no additional assessment being provided.

Risk assessments based upon ARAIs have been regarded as adequate at the highest level. In the appeal case of *Her Majesty's Advocate v Thomas Russell Currie* (2008: para. 9) a ground of appeal was that the learned trial judge erred in failing to obtain a full risk assessment. In their decision their lordships concluded (2008: para. 11):

> The Risk Matrix 2000 Assessment Tool is regularly and widely used for the purposes of assessing the risk presented by an offender to the public. ... In our view she (the trial judge) was entitled to proceed upon the basis of the outcome of the risk assessment carried out using Risk Matrix 2000.

Second, what is the scientific credibility of this position? Has it been demonstrated that these instruments are effective screens? We believe that it has not (Cooke et al. 2010).

It is not generally appreciated that to be effective as a screen, risk factors—or sets of risk factors—must be very strongly associated with the disorder being screened for (Wald et al. 1999). Within epidemiology, it is conventional to assess the strength of this association using an odds ratio: for example, the risk of developing the disease for those with the highest 20 per cent of scores on a risk factor compared with those with the lowest 20 per cent of scores. Wald et al. (1999) argued that even an odds ratio of 200 will only yield a detection rate (the proportion of affected individuals with a positive result on the screen) of 56 per cent for a false-positive rate of five per cent. It is widely recognized in medicine that established risk factors may make poor screening tests. Wald et al. (1999: 1564) have noted, for example, that "because serum cholesterol is an established risk factor for ischaemic heart disease, it was believed that it would be a useful screening test ... this belief was unfounded."

How does the performance of ARAIs compare to the examples from medicine? To generate comparable plots it is necessary to have access to raw data. This is often difficult to obtain. However, we have plotted the data for the Static-2002; the relative odds of reoffending for the top 20 per cent as compared to the bottom 20 per cent is 6.8; the detection rate is 14 per cent for a false-positive rate of five per cent. A false positive rate of five per cent is a convention in medicine; the idea being to limit the alarm experienced by those misidentified. Within criminal justice settings considerations of policy relating to the protection of the public versus a concern for the human rights of an offender might, in the minds of some, justify higher false-positive rates.

We plotted the detection rate against the false-positive rate. This produces a receiver operator characteristic (ROC) curve, a commonly used process to assess accuracy in violence risk assessment. The area under the curve (AUC) achieved was 0.68; this is comparable with many actuarial scales used in violence risk. How good is this? Fischer, Bachmann, and Jaeschke (2003) offered the following interpretative guidelines: an AUC of 0.9 or higher has high accuracy, 0.7–0.9 moderate, and 0.5–0.7 low accuracy. By these criteria the STATIC-2002 has low accuracy. When procedures are applied to new populations, AUCs tend to be reduced further.

In our view the notion that ARAIs can be used as screening tools is fundamentally flawed. As Scott (1977: 140) observed it is not possible to "draw clear lines between the dangerous and non-dangerous." Attempts to use ARAIs for such a purpose are more likely than not to mislead and the public is poorly served by suboptimal decisions.

From What to Why

The field of violence risk assessment has become mired in a fundamental epistemological quagmire. Some authors have suggested that our critique of ARAIs based on their lack of precision is tantamount to promoting the abandonment of evidence-based risk assessment (Harris et al. 2008). Nothing could be further from the truth. The authors confuse evidence-based with statistically-based. There are various forms of legitimate knowledge—with psychological meaning—other than those based merely upon statistical methods.

As we noted at the outset of this chapter, the focus of the chapter is on the use of ARIAs for courts, parole boards, or other tribunals to make decisions on the risk of violence in the individual case. Historically, the individual was regarded as the proper focus of psychological endeavor. However, Allport (1940) recorded the decline of the idiographic perspective and the ascendancy of the nomothetic perspective in psychology. He illustrated the imbalance created by the emphasis on intersubject nomothetic designs by describing the problem of predicting whether an individual will reoffend using actuarial prediction. Allport (1940: 16–17) noted:

> We find that 72 per cent of the men with John's antecedents make good, and many of us conclude that John, therefore, has a *72 per cent* chance of making good. There is an obvious error here. The fact that *72 per cent* of the men having the same antecedent record as John will make good is merely an actuarial statement. It tells us nothing about John.

Wittgenstein (1958: 243) famously remarked that in psychology "the existence of the experimental method makes us think we have the means of solving the problems which trouble us; though problem and method pass one another by." The actuarial approach to violence risk seems to be a case in point: it cannot answer the question at the level of the individual. Different approaches may be merited.

Recent years have witnessed a growing awareness—perhaps a rediscovery—within psychology that the dominant empirical paradigms such as between-subject models (for example, measures of individual differences) cannot test or support causal accounts (for example, pertaining to violence) that are valid at the individual level (Borsboom et al. 2003; Cooke and Michie 2010; Molenaar 2004; Molenaar and Campbell 2009; Richters 1997).

With a between-subjects design it is possible to argue legitimately that within population differences in the prevalence of personality disorder, or the mean level of psychopathy as measured by, for example, the Psychopathy Check List Revised (PCL-R; Hare 2003), can account for population variations in violent reoffending. However, this position cannot be defended at the level of the individual. It is unmerited to assume that the mechanisms that operate at the level of the individual also explain variations *among* individuals. The fact that the PCL-R frequently shows moderate relationships with future violence at the group level is founded on the fact that it is a complex measure that is underpinned by multifarious processes that increase the likelihood that someone with a high score will offend violently (Cooke 2010b; Hart 1998). Knowing about the structure of the PCL-R (Cooke and Michie 2001; Cooke et al. 2007) might provide information about processes that might distinguish among people. However, it says little about what specific processes operate at the level of the individual.

This may seem surprising. Molenaar and Campbell (2009) summarized the problem, arguing that because the application of findings obtained by pooling results across individuals in a population to a single individual in that population entails a shift in level from interindividual variation to intraindividual variation, it is frequently invalid. Such an inference only applies under very restricted conditions. Classic ergodic theorems demonstrate that for the analysis of interindividual variation to yield the same results as analysis of intraindividual variation, two conditions must apply: First, there must be homogeneity of the population, that is, the same statistical model should apply to the data of all the subjects in that population. Second, the data must be stationary: that is, they must not change over time (Molenaar and Campbell 2009).

Actuarial procedures do not meet these requirements. The populations are inherently heterogeneous. That is, the risk of reoffending will vary with a large number of variables such as substance misuse, personality disorder, supervision, and age. Similarly, the data are unlikely to be stationary varying over time due to a large number of variables including the opportunity to offend, supervision, possible types of offences (for example, Internet crime), decline in sexual drive, changes in the ease of detection of crime, and changes in those criminal-justice processes that influence conviction rates.

At the heart of the matter is the fact that simple linear models cannot explain complex behavior. Richters (1997: 206–207) clarified the fundamental nature of this problem as follows:

> The extraordinary human capacity for equifinal and multifinal functioning, however, render the structural homogeneity assumption untenable. Very similar patterns of overt functioning may be caused by qualitatively differing underlying structures both within the same individual at different points in time, and across different individuals at the same time (equifinality).

Individuals are violent for different reasons: any one individual may be violent for different reasons on different occasions. This inherent complexity dooms simple-minded statistical prediction.

Let us consider the complexity of meaning inherent in one apparently simple variable in the RM2000, namely, single (never married). At the group level, this risk factor is associated with reoffending. The reason why will vary from case to case and the significance for understanding and for risk management will thus also vary by case.

With the case of the 18-year-old student alluded to earlier, it would have been culturally unusual for him to be in a marital type relationship. Other individuals may not have the social skills to achieve an intimate relationship, whereas others—offenders diagnosed with psychopathy for example—may well have the skills to achieve a relationship but have neither the capacity nor the inclination to maintain it. Still others, while achieving an intimate relationship, only achieve a conflictual relationship. A positive score on this individual RM2000 items thus fails to inform an assessor why—in any individual case—the absence of a marital-type relationship might lead to sexual reoffending.

Molenaar and Campbell (2009: 112) have argued that "this reality has wide-ranging consequences for psychological methodologies and statistical analyses that are intended to inform individual treatment and policy." They go on to suggest that a Kuhnian paradigm shift (named after the physicist Thomas Samuel Kuhn) may be required within psychological science. Forensic practice is not immune from this challenge. The following sections consider the implications for effective practice.

From Individual Differences to Different Individuals

Lindley (2006: 7) has remarked that "everything in the future is uncertain, as is most of the past; even the present contains a lot of uncertainty."

Perhaps Lindley's statement should be on the desk of all forensic practitioners. If our task as forensic practitioners is to provide courts, parole boards and other tribunals with considered, reliable, and evidence-based opinions to assist in their deliberations about individual offenders, it is essential that we take on the challenge of moving from group-level information to the ideographic level. From his legal perspective, Faigman (2007) noted this process of applying nomothetic findings to the individual has not been studied with any rigor and this fact may limit the utility of psychological evidence in tribunals. From his clinical perspective Beck (1999: 125) noted that "understanding the workings of the mind of the specific offender is crucial for appropriate intervention as well as prevention."

How can we move from the level of the group to the level of the individual? Current route maps may be inadequate but they can provide some sense of direction.

The Importance of Risk Processes: From What to Why

Monahan (1984) argued persuasively that for violence assessment to progress, the field needed to identify what risk factors were associated with violence. His call was answered and the field has a much clearer vision of what risk factors are important—in general. To move from assessment to intervention, and effective change, it is necessary to move from answering the what questions to answering the why questions. Why, for example, might a high score on the PCL-R (Hare 2003), or a substance misuse problem, or poor intimate relationships lead to an increased risk of violence? Take something as apparently simple as the moderate association between substance misuse and violence (Webster et al. 1997). This association could be underpinned by a myriad of distinct processes; there could be many answers to the why question. Substance misuse may be relevant to future risk because the chemical effect disinhibits aggressive impulses, because it impairs evaluation of relevant social cues (for example, danger or frustration), it may facilitate the justification of aggressive behavior (for example, "I need a fix so I will rob"), it increases interpersonal conflict and the loss of important supports, it impairs consideration of long-term consequences, the need for illicit drugs may expose the user to violent environments and peers, substance abuse may interact with psychotic symptoms to potentiate violence, and so on.

At the individual level, therefore, substance abuse may be relevant for one or more reasons. These reasons will vary from individual to individual. Note also that the effect may be contingent. For example, it may be contingent on the presence of psychotic symptoms, contingent on the presence of antisocial peers or a myriad of other circumstances. This is true for substance abuse: it is also true of the other risk factors commonly considered by structured professional judgment approaches (Cooke 2010b). The only way to deal with this complexity is to think psychologically, not statistically. One approach might be to consider the underlying risk processes (Cooke and Wozniak 2010).

Risk processes are theoretical constructs that can be identified by the systematic and rational consideration of the relevant risk factors that operate in the individual case. They can be thought of as embodying the broad why questions. They are the mechanism whereby the risk factors lead to violence.

Three types of broad mechanism may be relevant; *drivers* (for example, pervasive and persistent thoughts about violence), *disinhibitors* (for example, the chemical effect of alcohol), and *destabilizers* (for example, the loss of a key figure in a social support network). How can risk processes be identified? Risk factors, or elements of risk factors, may be construed as markers of these underlying risk processes. Once individual risk factors have been identified, it is important to deconstruct each risk factor to ask what are the key elements of that risk factor that are relevant to future violence; relevant in the sense that they may drive, disinhibit, or destabilize individuals and, thereby, increase the likelihood of future violence. Asking why a risk factor may be relevant allows an understanding of the underlying distinct but related risk processes that— individually and together—can increase the likelihood of violence and shape its topography. This process not only assists in providing a clearer understanding of the relevant mechanism but it should also guide interventions. Figure 12.2 illustrates a hypothetical case in which several HCR-20 risk factors are considered.

How do we reduce the inherent complexity and impose understanding? An analogue may assist. Risk factors (or elements of risk factors) can be regarded as markers of underlying risk processes in the same way as observable variables are regarded as markers of latent variables in certain forms of factor analysis. In a sense, risk assessors have to engage in a form of conceptual factor analysis guided by their understanding, based both on research and clinical knowledge, of the processes that underpin violence. In this simplified example we are positing only two underlying risk processes: acting without forethought and hypersensitivity to threat to self.

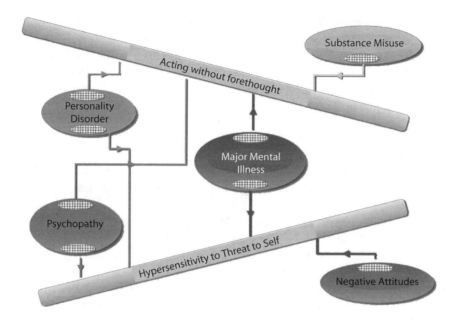

Figure 12.2 HCR-20 risk factors.

In this case we identify that substance misuse, personality disorder, psychopathy, major mental illness, and negative attitudes are present. All of these risk factors are multidimensional in nature. If we consider a putative risk process, acting without forethought, on a rational basis it can be seen that dimensions of each of four risk factors, but not all aspects of the risk factors may contribute to acting without forethought. The chemical disinhibiting effect of some forms of substance misuse, such as alcohol misuse, may contribute to acting without forethought. The impulsivity inherent in some forms of personality disorder, major mental illness, and in psychopathy could also contribute. But other aspects of the latter three risk factors may contribute to another risk process, for example, hypersensitivity to threat to self. The perception of malevolent intent in others is often associated with psychopathy (Kernberg 1990). The paranoid ideation of certain personality disorders and mental disorders, together with certain forms of negative attitudes, may be parsimoniously captured by this second risk process.

The identification of these risk processes allows those engaging in risk management to manage the complexity of risk factors—and their mutual interplays—in such a way that the key risk processes can be identified. Once risk processes are identified they can be managed. Efforts need to be directed toward developing rational and defensible approaches to identifying risk processes.

Some progress has been made. There are at least three sources of direction available. First, there is a long tradition of clinical formulation (for example, see Butler 1998; Logan and Johnstone 2008; Tarrier 2006). Second, there is the application of systematic case-study methods (Yin 2003). Third, there is the development of specialized guidelines to facilitate structured professional judgment (Hart et al. 2003).

Progress is discernable. At the outset, early forms of structured professional judgment gave little or no guidance on how to move from the assessment of risk factors to rather simplistic summary risk ratings of low, moderate, or high (Kropp et al. 1994). Rather more guidance was provided in the HCR-20 manual (Webster et al. 1997), but it was not until the publication of the RSVP (Hart et al. 2003) that a structured process—scenario planning—was described that allowed the assessor to move from an assessment of risk factors to a formulation of the nature of the risk posed by an individual. Gradually the inferential leap from the assessment through understanding and on toward effective risk management has been made. The field is in a state of creative flux. Different complementary methods are evolving and being tested (for example, see Hart et al. 2003; Logan and Johnstone 2010). However, clear—and readily applicable—validity criteria await development.

The Danger of Unstructured Speculation

An obvious challenge to all three approaches—clinical formulation, structured professional judgment, and case study methods—is how the validity of any putative causal association at the individual level can be assessed and how the worst excesses of unstructured speculation can be guarded against.

From past experience, we are afraid that we are likely to be accused of advocating the return to unstructured clinical judgment. This is not the case. We support evidence-based, transparent, multi-informant, multimodal comprehensive assessments of individuals, but we recognize the complexity and inherent uncertainty in the enterprise.

Usefully, all three approaches—formulation, case study, and structured professional judgment methods—have evolved criteria for evaluating validity. Unsurprisingly, these criteria show a great deal of commonality (for example, see Butler 1998; Miller and Waller 2003; Yin 2003). Richters (1997: 224–5) has observed that "in general, judgments made at the individual level must be evaluated by qualitative criteria such as coherence, explanatory power and the ability to account for facts that are otherwise difficult to explain." This position is clearly echoed by Hart (2009: 170) who has pointed out:

> A causal nexus does not exist physically, and cannot be proved or disproved through physical evidence. Rather, it is an explanation, interpretation, or account of evidence whose plausibility is judged according to the extent it coheres with the fact of the case, common sense views of the world, and (where applicable) scientific research and theory.

Criteria for evaluating validity are perhaps most clearly articulated in the case study literature. Yin (2003) provides a systematic account of how to maximize the validity of the interpretation of a case study from the design stage (for example, employing a theory-driven approach, documenting the approach adopted with a predetermined protocol) through the evidence collection phase (for example, seeking multiple sources of evidence, establishing the chain of evidence), to finally, the evaluation stage (for example, pattern matching, explanation building, consideration of rival explanations, and the application of logic models).

Modern structured professional judgment approaches, being based on scenario planning principles (for example, see Hart et al. 2003), apply many of Yin's principles and have the advantage that they can lead to thoughtful interventions. An integration of clinical formulation, systematic case study, and structured professional judgment procedures should improve violence risk assessment. Nonetheless, the development of a comprehensive and comprehensible validation strategy for individual risk assessments remains a pressing need for the field.

Conclusion

We began this chapter highlighting the dangers inherent in the misuse of statistical evidence in courts. We outlined some egregious examples. With the rise of ARAIs and their increasing pervasiveness with regard to decisions about individuals within the criminal justice system, comes the danger of more widespread misuse of apparently statistical evidence.

As a psychologist (DJC) with a long-standing interest in statistics and a professional statistician (CM), we have sympathy with the position statement issued by the Royal Statistical Society (2010) in response to the Sally Clark case:

> Although many scientists have some familiarity with statistical methods, statistics remains a specialised area. The Society urges the Courts to ensure that statistical evidence is presented only by appropriately qualified statistical experts, as would be the case for any other form of expert evidence.

Clearly, forensic practitioners should remain within their realm of expertise, but perhaps even more important, we believe that it behooves public bodies that set standards of practice to ensure that they obtain appropriate statistical advice and do not depend upon scientists and practitioners (for example, psychologists and psychiatrists) who are not qualified statistical experts.

IV
Practice

13

The Role of Forensic Mental Health Services in Managing High-Risk Offenders

Functioning or Failing?

LINDSAY THOMSON

Introduction

This chapter reviews, in an international context, the Scottish approach to the management of high-risk offenders considering in turn the options available for all offenders, those with personality disorders, and those with mental illnesses.

The most recent changes in the management of high-risk offenders have been the establishment of the Risk Management Authority; the development of the risk assessment order and the order for lifelong restriction (OLR); and the introduction of Multi-Agency Public Protection Arrangements (MAPPA; see Caroline Logan's chapter in this volume in relation to MAPPA in England and Wales). To date there have been 41 OLRs applied after a very rigorous risk assessment process compared with over 5,000 indeterminate sentences for public protection awarded in England and Wales. MAPPA was established under the Management of Offenders etc. (Scotland) Act 2005 and provides a framework for multiagency communication, risk assessment, and management of violent and sexual offenders. These arrangements were introduced initially for sex offenders in 2007 and for restricted patients (serious offenders whose mental illness was related to their offending behavior) in 2008.

Many high-risk offenders have a personality disorder. In Scotland mental health services generally, and forensic mental health services specifically, have been reluctant to offer services to individuals with a primary diagnosis of personality disorder. Offenders with personality disorders are therefore dealt with by the criminal justice agencies (prison, police, and probation). The *Forensic Mental Health Services Managed Care Network* (2005) recommended that forensic mental health services should develop services offering assessment and treatment for offenders with personality disorders and this should be done in tandem with criminal justice agencies. To date within the Forensic Network there has been an emphasis on the assessment and treatment of sex offenders, and prescribing for sex offenders; and the development of health practice in MAPPA. The Scottish approach is markedly different from that developed in England and Wales with their specialized units for people with dangerous and severe personality disorder (see Caroline Logan's chapter in this volume).

Offenders in Scotland with major mental illness are diverted to the mental health system. The systems for this are briefly described and evidence presented that these services function well, especially the transfer of psychotic patients from prison to hospital. In particular, the introduction of a human-rights-based approach, a formal system of risk management, and an appeal against excessive security have led to improvements in individual patient care and the development of a wider range of facilities. There is a failure, however, to engage in any systematic way with offenders with primarily personality and behavioral problems and with criminal justice colleagues. Such joint working has the potential to stabilize an individual's behavior, to reduce recidivism, and to improve public safety. There are however, encouraging signs of development within this area particularly in the work with MAPPA and with sex offenders.

Management of High-Risk Offenders

Internationally there is variation in the management of high-risk offenders (Scottish Executive 2000b). For example, Australia, Canada, and New Zealand have discretionary life sentences for serious violent and sexual offenders imposed at the time of sentencing, whereas within the United States, many states have an automatic life sentence for a third conviction for a serious violent and sexual offence and many have sexual predator laws that permit the civil detention of a sex offender at the end of his or her prison sentence (see the chapters by Eric Janus, Chris Slobogin, John La Fond, and John Petrila in this volume). Within Europe, this variation in practice continues with a greater emphasis on treatment and use of psychiatric facilities, and indeed this variation can be found within the countries that make up the United Kingdom (Thomson 2008).

One of the most contentious issues in England and Wales during the debate on new mental health legislation was preventive detention. This was taken into the Criminal Justice Act 2003, which introduced new indeterminate sentences for dangerous offenders whose eligibility for release was dependent on the level of risk they pose in terms of sexual and violent reoffending. Under section 225 of the Criminal Justice Act 2003, the courts will impose an indeterminate sentence for public protection when the offender is aged 18 or over; is convicted of a serious specified violent or sexual offence, for which the maximum penalty is 10 years or more; and who in the court's opinion, poses a significant risk of harm to the public. In Scotland a different approach was taken by the MacLean Committee in dealing with serious violent and sexual offenders including those with personality disorders (Scottish Executive 2000a) with an emphasis on the offence and a formal assessment of risk, and the introduction of the order of lifelong restriction (see the chapters by Innes Fyfe and Yvonne Gailey, and by Rajan Darjee and Katharine Russell in this volume).

Sentencing Options for the Management of Risk in Offenders

In understanding the place of an OLR it is important to understand the wider sentencing options open to the Scottish courts for the management of risk (see Table 13.1). In all but a conviction for murder, the judge has discretion as to the sentence imposed. Decisions on this are based in part on the important underlying principle of proportionality, that is, any restriction of liberty must fit with (be proportionate) to the type of offence committed and to the offender's history. Legislation for automatic life sentences for those committing two qualifying offences, such as attempted murder, rape, or aggravated assault, was passed in the Crime and Punishment (Scotland) Act 1997 but has never been enacted.

Order of Lifelong Restriction

The MacLean recommendations were largely enacted in the Criminal Justice (Scotland) Act 2003 as amendments to the Criminal Procedure (Scotland) Act 1995 and became operational in early 2006. The principal developments were:

1. The creation of the Risk Management Authority (RMA) as an independent public body focused on the effective assessment and minimization of risk of serious violent and sexual offending in Scotland with responsibility for setting standards, guidelines and guidance for offender risk assessment and risk management, training and accreditation

Table 13.1 Sentencing Options for the Management of Risk in Offenders

Sentence	Purpose	Note
Mandatory life sentence • Must be applied if convicted of murder	Punishment period for deterrence and life license to manage risk in the community post-release with option of recall to prison for breach of license conditions	Given a punishment period to serve in prison and then two yearly parole board reviews to make compliant with European Court of Human Rights
Discretionary life sentence • An option available to the judge in serious cases	Used to protect public in cases of serious violent or sexual offending	Limited use following introduction of OLR
Order of lifelong restriction	Indeterminate sentence and lifelong risk management	Imposed at time of sentencing
Extended sentence	In community under parole license conditions and subject to recall to prison	Extension period of up to 10 years for sex offenders and 5 years for violent offenders
Supervised release order	Supervision in the community post-release	For a sentence of less than 4 years
Restriction of liberty order	Electronic monitoring of offenders in the community	Can specify place of residence and prohibited places
Probation order	Community sentence to rehabilitate	Lasts between 6 months to 3 years and can include a condition for psychiatric or psychological treatment
Parole	For release on license with agreed conditions into the community under the supervision of a criminal justice social worker with option of recall to prison for breach of license conditions	For life sentence and long-term (4-plus years) prisoners; former eligible after punishment period and latter after completing half their sentence but will be automatically released after two-thirds
Sex offender registration	Notification requirement for a specified period following conviction for a sexual offence on release into the community	Non-compliance is a criminal offence Applies to mentally disordered offenders as well
Notification order	As for sex offender registration	Applies to those convicted of sexual offences abroad
Foreign travel orders	To prevent convicted sex offenders from travelling abroad	
Sexual offence prevention orders	Applies conditions in the community on a convicted sex offender	Can be imposed at time of sentencing or applied for later by the police
Risk of sexual harm orders	Applies conditions in the community on an individual considered to pose a risk of sexual harm to children	No conviction for sex offending is required
Compulsion order and restriction order	To manage risk of serious harm to others in mentally disordered offenders (MDOs)	For full range of provisions for MDOs

of risk assessors, policy advice to ministers, appraising risk management plans for those on OLR, monitoring of research, and promotion of evidence-based practice.

2. The introduction of a risk assessment order (RAO) which is a 90 (maximum 180) day period of assessment to allow the preparation of a risk assessment report to assist the court in determining if "the nature of, or the circumstances of the commission of, the offence of which the convicted person has been found guilty either in themselves or as part of a pattern of behaviour are such as to demonstrate that there is a likelihood that he, if at liberty, will seriously endanger the lives, or physical or psychological well-being, of members of the public at large." An RAO can be applied by the court to an offender convicted of a serious violent or sexual offence, or an offence that endangers life. The emphasis is on clinical risk assessment.

   The court appoints a risk assessor who must review the appropriate documentation, utilize the structured professional judgment, rather than actuarial, approach to risk including the use of one or more recognized risk assessment tools, interview the offender, liaise with the relevant multidisciplinary team, and report using the approved RMA structure. The offender cannot object to the making of an RAO but may challenge the risk assessment report and commission a separate risk report.

3. The introduction of an Order for Life Long Restriction (OLR). This provides indeterminate detention and life-long risk management of serious violent and sexual offenders assessed as posing an ongoing high risk of serious harm if the court believes on a balance of probabilities that the risk criteria outlined above are met. An OLR is an indeterminate prison sentence although a punishment period, or tariff, is set by the court.

   A risk management plan must be prepared and submitted to the RMA within 9 months of the imposition of an OLR. Responsibility for preparation of this report rests with Scottish ministers while the individual is in prison and is exercised by Scottish Prison Service staff, by hospital managers if the individual is in hospital, and by the local authority in a community setting. The plan must set out an assessment of risk, methods applied to minimize the assessed risks, and the means of coordination of these methods.

   The RMA in its document on standards and guidelines on risk management of offenders subject to an order of lifelong restriction (RMA 2007) sets out fundamental principles for such practice: namely, the importance of public protection, that risk of serious harm can be managed but not eliminated and that risk management practice should be measured against the concept of "the defensible decision." An action or decision is considered to be defensible if a group of professional peers would consider that: all reasonable steps had been taken; that the methods of assessment were reliable; that information had been collated and thoroughly evaluated; that decisions were recorded, communicated, and followed through; that policies and procedures had been followed; and that an investigative and proactive approach had been applied to the management of risk. Release following the set prison period is dependent on an updated risk assessment and a proposed management plan as approved by the RMA, and is considered by the parole board. Victims who wish to be informed of their offender's progress under the victim notification scheme may contribute their views to the parole board tribunal.

   An OLR can be applied to an offender given a hospital direction (an initial period in hospital combined with a prison sentence) who fulfils the risk criteria outlined earlier. This is not the case for patients given a compulsion order with or without restrictions on discharge. Decisions on recommendations of these various psychiatric disposals are based on the strength of the association between an individual's mental disorder, his index offence, and future risk because of that mental disorder.

Multi-Agency Public Protection Arrangements   The newest systematic development for the management of risk in offenders in the United Kingdom is that of Multi-Agency Public Protection Arrangements (MAPPA). These were created in England and Wales under the Criminal Justice and Court Services Act 2000 and require police and probation to work together to manage the risks posed by dangerous offenders in the community. This was extended to include the prison service and there is a statutory duty for health, housing, social services, education, social security and employment services, youth offending teams and electronic monitoring providers to cooperate with multiagency public protection panels. These have four core functions:

- identification of MAPPA offenders;
- sharing of relevant information;
- assessment of risk of serious harm; and
- management of risk of serious harm.

Four features of MAPPA good practice have been identified:

- defensible decisions;
- rigorous risk assessment;
- delivery of risk management plans that match identified public protection need; and
- evaluation of performance to improve delivery.

The guidance clearly recognizes that risk can be reduced and managed but not eliminated. MAPPA offers three levels of input depending on the complexity of multi-agency involvement, media profile, and level of risk: (1) advice; (2) multiple agency involvement in the coordination of an individual's care; and (3), for high risk cases, intensive management and shared responsibility.

A Multi-Agency Sex Offender Risk Assessment and Management (MASRAM) strategy is in place in Northern Ireland using voluntary agreements between agencies. The need to make this statutory and to extend the scheme to all violent and sexual offenders is currently under review.

In Scotland, the Management of Offenders etc. (Scotland) Act 2005 established Community Justice Authorities and MAPPA. Under these, the police, local authorities, and Scottish Prison Service must establish joint arrangements to assess and manage the risk posed by sexual and violent offenders. This includes the NHS where the sexual and violent offenders are also offenders with mental disorders. The principles and aims of MAPPA are precisely the same as in England and Wales. MAPPA was introduced for registered sex offenders in April 2007 and for restricted offenders with mental disorders in April 2008. The plan to include all violent offenders is likely to come to fruition in 2011. Each offender is assigned a MAPPA level based on their risk assessment, complexity of management, and press profile. Level One represents the normal inter-agency management of the offender in the community by one agency, with some liaison. Level Two means that multi-agency public protection meetings will be held where the offender's management will be discussed between various parties involved in the case. Level Three also has MAPPA meetings but these are likely to involve senior management representatives who are able to commit greater resources expected to be used in the management of the offender. The management of MAPPA cases at Levels Two and Three is reviewed at MAPPA meetings. Risk assessment and management is central to the MAPPA. Reoffending rates by offenders managed within MAPPA are very low in comparison with other crime types, and zero for restricted patient to date. Sexual offending has a very low reoffending rate anyway, however, early research indicates that less than two per cent of sex offenders managed within MAPPA in Scotland are convicted of another sexual offence within two years of the index offence (Manson, personal communication 2010).

The National Health Service in Scotland has taken a proactive role in MAPPA through an information-sharing concordat, the establishment of a Forensic Network MAPPA Health Group and by training through the School of Forensic Mental Health.

Management of High-Risk Offenders with Personality Disorders

Personality disorders are common: six to 15 per cent of the general population (Royal College of Psychiatrists 1999); 60 to 80 per cent of male prisoners (50 per cent female prisoners) (Singleton et al. 1998); 82 per cent of a Scottish male prison special program attendees (Bartlett et al 2001); five per cent of the Scottish special security psychiatric population with a primary diagnosis of antisocial personality disorder and 27 to 42 per cent with a secondary diagnosis of antisocial personality disorder (Thomson et al. 1997), and 15 per cent with psychopathy (PCL-R ≥25; Blackburn et al. 2003).

Many high-risk offenders have a personality disorder. In theory, a diagnosis of personality disorder should no longer be a label of exclusion from psychiatric services (Centre for Change and Innovation 2005; National Institute for Mental Health in England 2003b). Efforts have been made throughout the United Kingdom to integrate assessment and management of people with personality disorders into services regardless of their offending history. These initiatives include:

1. The inclusion of personality disorder within the definition of mental disorder in the new mental health legislation for England and Wales (Mental Health Act 1983 as amended by the Mental Health Act 2007), and for Scotland Mental Health (Care and Treatment) (Scotland) Act 2003. The legislation for Northern Ireland excludes detention of those with a primary diagnosis of personality disorder (Mental Health (Northern Ireland) Order 1986) although this legislation is under review.
2. The development of MAPPA as described earlier.
3. The creation of new services and facilities for people with personality disorders. Here, there is a natural effect of devolution with different options being pursued in varying parts of the United Kingdom. In England and Wales there has been considerable investment by the Home Office and Department of Health in establishing pilot services for people with personality disorders in a range of settings and levels of security, the birth of the concept of dangerous and severe personality disorder (DSPD) and the opening of four DSPD units with 300 beds in total, two in high-security psychiatric hospitals, and two in prisons. It is currently proposed that the hospital DSPD units will shut with their patients being integrated into the mainstream high secure personality disorder units or returned to prison. The prison units will reduce their places and be known as psychologically informed protective environments over a timescale of 3 to 5 years. No decision has been made about the medium secure forensic units. In Northern Ireland, the Review of Mental Health and Disability Report on Forensic Services (The Bamford Review 2006) has proposed that specific units should be developed for offenders with personality disorders in spite of their current legislative position. In Scotland, the Scottish Government has established a personality disorder network (http://www.scottishpersonalitydisorder.org/), although resources have not been targeted for the development of specific services.

At the present time it is routine psychiatric practice in Scotland not to admit individuals with a primary diagnosis of personality disorder to forensic psychiatric units. The history of this can be found in Darjee and Crichton (2003). Although community forensic mental health service provision in many parts of Scotland is rudimentary, most forensic psychiatrists and psychologists do have a small cohort of outpatients with a primary diagnosis of personality disorder. The majority of individuals with a primary diagnosis of personality disorder who offend in a manner that merits a custodial disposal will be sent to prison or to a young offenders' institution. The Scottish Prison Service strategy for the management of prisoners is based on the identification of problem behaviors and needs. It does not focus its management of prisoners on the concept of personality disorder, nor is the majority of its staff qualified to assess and diagnose this condition. There are three principal structures that allow for the identification and management of prisoners with behavioral problems and needs: offender case management, risk management groups, and mental health teams. The focus of the latter is mainly on people suffering major mental illnesses rather than personality disorders. A variety of cognitive-behavioral-therapy-based interventions with a focus on violent behavior and sexual offending behavior are delivered by prison staff, including officers, psychologists, and social workers.

A survey of services and treatment strategies in use in Scotland for individuals with a personality disorder who had offended was carried out by the working group (Thomson 2005b). It found that of 10 (of 11) forensic mental health services:

- Seven implicitly excluded people with a primary diagnosis of personality disorder from admission;
- Seven assessed people with a primary diagnosis of personality disorder;
- Eight used multidisciplinary and 10 comprehensive methods of assessment but only four used structured clinical tools for the assessment of personality disorder; and
- Six services did not accept people with a primary diagnosis of personality disorder for specific intervention, treatment, or management, and four services did not accept people with a secondary diagnosis.

No reliable figures on the assessment or management of people with a primary or secondary diagnosis of personality disorder could be supplied. Those that were supplied suggested major unmet need when compared to known prevalence figures. Access to services appropriate to people with personality disorders was variable:

- drug and alcohol services, ten
- cognitive behavioral therapy, nine
- individual psychotherapy, six
- dialectical behavior therapy, two
- specialist interventions (such as relapse prevention, sex offending, problem solving) four.

Training requirements were identified in particular for developing case formulations and employing evidence-based interventions.

Given the findings in this survey the report on services for offenders with personality disorders made a series of recommendations (Thomson 2005b). In particular, it was recommended that:

- Personality disorder should not be a diagnosis of exclusion from forensic mental health services in Scotland;
- Forensic Mental Health Services should develop a philosophy of care or stated service principles for people with personality disorders who offend;
- Services for people with personality disorders be developed given the frequency with which they are found in the criminal justice and mental health systems in Scotland;
- A risk-sharing mechanism should be developed for the management of these offenders;
- A diagnosis of personality disorder (primary or secondary) should be considered during all forensic mental health consultations; and
- The assessment of personality disorder should ideally be multidisciplinary and include:
  - an emphasis on third party information;
  - assessment for the presence of axis I disorders;
  - use of standardized measures of personality disorder;
  - assessment of risk of harm to others using standardized measures; and
- A formulation of symptoms and behaviors associated with the personality disorder.

Services developed for people with personality disorders should adopt a problem behavior focus arising from a case formulation and address a range of interventions that target the factors that underlie risk related behavior. These services need to be developed within a range of environments including the community, hospital, and prison.

In particular, a formal system for criminal justice social workers (probation officers) to request forensic mental health assessments should be established. This should be offered as a pilot service in one or more areas to assess workload and resource requirements.

The Working Group on Services for People with Personality Disorder (Thomson 2005b) identified a need to strengthen mental health teams within prisons. No change was recommended to the current clinical practice in Scotland of offenders with a primary diagnosis of personality disorder being dealt with by the criminal justice, rather than mental health system. All prisons should have a multidisciplinary health team of a standard set out in the policy document *Positive Mental Health* (Scottish Prison Service 2002). At the present time these are focused entirely on the identification and treatment of those with mental illnesses, and struggle to fulfill this role. In addition, they are rarely truly multidisciplinary. The working group identified a need for visiting mental health professionals to engage more widely with the therapeutic work of the prison service, including offender-based programs. One or more pilot prison and mental health teams should be identified to carry out detailed assessments of problematic prisoners, and to develop management plans in conjunction with the prison's Risk Management Group.

Management of High-Risk Offenders with Mental Illnesses

Cultural and Political Influence

Decisions by a society as to how offenders with mental illnesses should be managed are to a degree dependent on cultural and social values as well as socioeconomic, political, and legal frameworks. International comparisons have indicated that the practice of forensic psychiatry is not purely about laws and services but about the relationship between society and the individual (Lindqvist et al. 2009). Mental health practitioners may face ethical issues, such as the application of the death penalty, in some jurisdictions but not others. Although systems may vary, each system should be consistent with human rights principles. Within countries, variations also occur dependent on devolvement of powers. For example, the United Kingdom is made up of four countries (see Table 13.2). Each country has components of a forensic mental health system: varying levels of secure care (low, medium, and high); community services; in-reach services to the criminal justice system; and links with other psychiatric services such as general adult, learning disability, and child and adolescent services. Comparative research suggests that forensic inpatients are similar throughout the developed world with the exception of the existence or not, of specialist units to assess and treat offenders with a primary diagnosis of personality disorder (Lindqvist et al. 2009: Taylor et al. 2008).

Criminal Justice and Mental Health Services

All systems in the United Kingdom have diversion pathways at each stage of the criminal justice process to allow for the assessment and, if necessary, treatment of an individual within a health setting. This does not prevent the justice process from progressing either at the same time or at a later stage. Figure 13.1 illustrates the potential diversion pathways. There is a plethora of legislation (see Table 13.3 for Scottish examples) that allows for the transfer and treatment of offenders with mental illnesses in hospital or in the community. (For comparative legislation both civil and criminal for all countries in the United Kingdom, see Thomson 2008).

Table 13.2 The United Kingdom: Sociodemographic, Policy, and Legal Frameworks

Country	England	Wales	Northern Ireland	Scotland
Geographical area	130,395 km²	20,600 km²	14,139 km²	49,000 km²
Population[a] (2009)	51,446,200	2,993,400	1,775,000	5,168,500
Unemployment rates[b] (2010)	7.8 per cent	9.2 per cent	6.3 per cent	7.6 per cent
Political system	Westminster Parliament	Westminster Parliament & National Assembly for Wales	Westminster Parliament & Northern Irish Assembly	Westminster Parliament & Scottish Parliament
Mental Health Policy Framework for MDOs	Department of Health published the Review of Health and Social Services for Mentally Disordered Offenders and others requiring similar services in 1992 (Department of Health 1992, Reed Report).	The Welsh Revised National Service Framework for Adult Mental Health Services (Welsh Assembly Government 2005)	Bamford Review of Mental Health and Disability Report on Forensic Services (Bamford Review 2006)	Scottish Executive's Health, Social Work and related services for Mentally Disordered Offenders in Scotland (Scottish Office 1999 NHS MEL (1999) 5)
Legal System	Common Law	Common Law	Common Law	Common and Civil Law
Mental Health Legislation	Mental Health Act 1983 as amended by the Mental Health Act 2007	Mental Health Act 1983 as amended by the Mental Health Act 2007	Mental Health (NI) Order 1986	Mental Health (Care and Treatment) (Scotland) Act 2003
Age of Criminal Responsibility (years)	10	10	10	8
Recorded Crime Rates/100,000 (2008–09)	8633[c]	8633[c]	6202[d]	7303[e]
Prison Population/ 100,000 (2010)	156 with Wales[f]	156 with England[f]	81[g]	152[h]

[a] Office for National Statistics (2009) Population Statistics
[b] Office for National Statistics (2010) Employment Statistics
[c] Home Office Research Development Statistics Police Recorded Crime 2008–09
[d] Police Service of Northern Ireland Recorded Crime Central Statistics Branch, Operational Support Department, Belfast 2008–09
[e] Statistical Bulletin Crime and Justice Series: Recorded Crime in Scotland 2008–09
[f] Ministry of Justice National Offender Management Service (2010)
[g] Northern Ireland Prison Service (2010)
[h] Scottish Prison Service (2010)

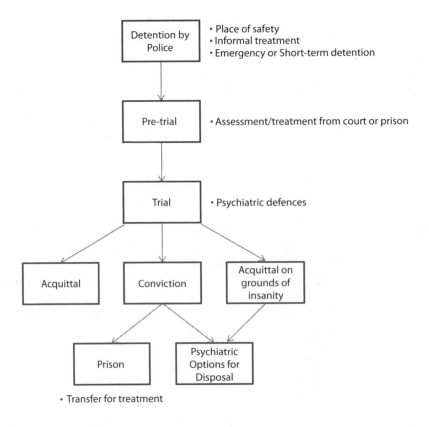

Figure 13.1 Criminal justice and mental health systems: diversion pathways.

Table 13.3 Legislation for Offenders with Mental Disorders in Scotland

Power	Act
Removal to a place of safety from a public place	S.297 MH(C&T)(S)A 2003*
Removal to a place of safety from private premises	S.293 MH(C&T)(S)A 2003
Removal to hospital for assessment	S.52D MH(C&T)(S)A 2003
Removal to hospital for treatment	S.52M MH(C&T)(S)A 2003
Transfer of remand prisoner to hospital	S.52D MH(C&T)(S)A 2003
Interim compulsion order	S.53 CP(S)A 1995**
Compulsion Order	S.57A CP(S)A 1995
Compulsion Order and Restriction Order	S.57A and S.59 CP(S)A 1995
Hospital Direction	S.59A CP(S)A 1995
Transfer of sentenced prisoner to hospital	S.136 MH(C&T)(S)A 2003
Guardianship	S.58(1A) CP(S)A 1995
Intervention Order	S.60B CP(S)A 1995
Compulsory Treatment in Community	S.57A CP(S)A 1995
Probation Order	S.230 CP(S)A 1995

* Mental Health (Care and Treatment) (Scotland) Act 2003 [MH(C&T)(S)A 2003]
**Criminal Procedure (Scotland) Act 1995 CP(S)A 1995

Management of Risk in Serious Violent or Sexual Offenders with Mental Disorders

As with any offender, risk of harm to others is a major concern in the assessment and management of offenders with mental disorders. This risk is defined as "the nature, likelihood, frequency, duration, seriousness and imminence of an offence" (Risk Management Authority 2006b: 17). The major mechanism for the management of risk in serious violent or sexual mentally disorder offenders in Scotland is via a compulsion order or a compulsion order and restriction order (CORO). A compulsion order can be applied following conviction for an offence punishable by imprisonment where the offender has a mental disorder and available treatment is likely to prevent the mental disorder from worsening or alleviate symptoms or effects; and there is a risk to his or her health, safety, or welfare, or the safety of others. A compulsion order can be community-or hospital-based but it is only the latter that is relevant to a restriction order. A restriction order is made having regard to the nature of the offence, the antecedents of the person, and the risk of him or her committing further offences if set at large and where it is necessary for the protection of the public from serious harm to impose special restrictions on the patient. A CORO is applied without limit of time and a patient subject to a CORO may only be transferred to a less secure hospital or granted leave out of hospital with the permission of the Scottish government. Discharge (whether conditional or absolute) may only be granted by the Mental Health Tribunal for Scotland. Risk assessment and management is central to the management of restricted patients, and their management is kept under review using the care program approach. Restricted patients are all notified to MAPPA and must be reviewed at MAPPA Level Two meetings at key stages in their rehabilitation, such as getting unescorted leave or before discharge into the community. Most cases proceed to the community via conditional discharge, with strict conditions in relation to monitoring, supervision, and treatment. COROs are reviewed at least every two years by the Mental Health Tribunal Scotland or on appeal by the patient or his or her representatives. If the responsible medical officer no longer believes that the patient is detainable, he or she must inform the Scottish Government, which has a duty to inform the tribunal. A hearing will then be arranged.

Working with the risk of harm to others is divided into four stages:

- risk assessment utilizing structured professional judgment to identify risk and protective factors;
- risk formulation to analyze comprehensively violent behavior, and to identify predisposing, precipitating, and perpetuating factors;
- scenario planning to consider potential future events; and
- risk management to reduce the likelihood of an adverse event occurring and to minimize the severity of any such event.

Risk management involves monitoring (surveillance techniques), supervision (direct control over an individual's choices and activities), treatment, and victim safety planning. Studies of risk assessment tools used with offenders with mental disorders in a Scottish context have found such tools to be of moderate to good predictive validity, but symptom severity and persistence have been found to be better predictors of violence in inpatient settings rather than historical or criminogenic factors (Ho et al. 2009; Thomson et al. 2008). A tool designed to highlight the risk of aggression in an inpatient setting, the Dynamic Appraisal of Situational Aggression–Inpatient Version (DASA-IV) was found to be of moderate to good predictive power (Vojt et al. 2010).

Contingency plans should be made for any adverse events. A simple contingency planning system uses a traffic lights approach (Scottish Government Mental Health Division 2007). This identifies specific risk factors, and describes early warning signs and an action plan if present.

For example, in a patient with a history of alcohol abuse, the contingency plan may read:

- green—no evidence of alcohol misuse continues to take antabuse—no action required;
- amber—empty cans found in kitchen and intermittently refusing antabuse—inform responsible medical officer and use alcometer; or
- red—found intoxicated—inform duty consultant and recall to hospital.

For further information see the chapter by Alex Quinn and John Crichton in this volume.

Staff training is essential for the safe management of offenders with mental disorders. In Scotland, the New to Forensic Programme has been developed to provide basic knowledge for all staff (Thomson et al. 2008). It gives staff a working knowledge of mental disorders and the complexity of diagnoses in forensic patients; definitions, principles and policy for offenders with mental disorders; mental health legislation; forensic mental health services; attitudes toward offenders with mental disorders; relationship between forensic mental health services and the criminal justice system; psychiatric defenses and legislation for offenders with mental disorders; multidisciplinary working; assessment, treatment, management, and support of offenders with mental disorders; risk assessment and management; and the participation of users and carers. The program is designed to promote self-directed learning and is multidisciplinary and multiagency in approach. A mentor supports each student and each chapter includes clinical scenarios, multiple-choice questions, and a reflective diary.

Current Issues in the Management of Offenders with Mental Disorders

Human Rights   The Human Rights Act 1998 was introduced into Scotland 12 years ago. The high-security hospital for Scotland and Northern Ireland (the State Hospital) adopted a human-rights-based approach (HRBA). In practice, this means placing considerations about human rights at the center of all policies and practices. HRBA generated simple tests to apply to considerations of policy and procedures: Is it legal? Is it necessary? Is it proportionate? This approach removed many blanket security policies and allowed greater consideration of each individual by clinical teams. This approach has been independently evaluated positively by both staff and patients, and found to reduce organizational risks such as adverse media comment and legal proceedings (Scottish Human Rights Commission 2009). For a wider consideration of human rights, see the chapter by Ronli Sifris in this volume.

Excessive Security   Use of the least restrictive alternative for any psychiatric care is a basic principle of the Mental Health (Care and Treatment) (Scotland) Act 2003. It was known that patients in a high-security setting in Scotland are frequently subject to a level of security in excess of their needs (Thomson et al. 1997). Under the 2003 Act, appeals against excessive security were introduced for the first time.

Patients subject to a compulsory treatment order, compulsion order, hospital direction, or a transfer for treatment direction may appeal against their detention in conditions of excessive security Mental Health (Care and Treatment) (Scotland) Act (2003, sec. 264–273). The patient, his or her named person, his or her guardian or welfare attorney, or the Mental Welfare Commission may apply. Any of these people can apply in the first six months of an order and thereafter once per 12-month period. Patients resident in a state hospital must be thought to require conditions of special security and that such conditions can only be provided in a state hospital. In addition, a state hospital patient must have "dangerous, violent or criminal propensities" (National Health Service (Scotland) Act (1978, sec. 102).

The appeal is made to the Mental Health Tribunal for Scotland and the tribunal can agree with the existing order or give up to three months for a Health Board to identify a lower secure hospital. Scottish ministers must agree on any proposed setting for restricted patients. If the patient has not moved by the end of the delineated period there are further hearings and the act specifies up to three hearings in total. As long as the tribunal continues to give extensions no appeal can be made to the Court of Session. At the end of the process, the Mental Welfare Commission or the patient can make an application under section 45(b) of the Court of Session Act 1988. This allows for fines and imprisonment in the event of an order not being implemented (Thomson 2006). At the present time the Scottish government has not taken a decision on the possible extension of appeals against excessive security to medium or low security settings.

To date 177 appeals have been lodged: 59 (49) have been approved, 38 (12) declined, 10 (8) adjourned, 53 (17) canceled or withdrawn, 15 (nine) to be heard, and two (one) incomplete. The numbers in parentheses indicate those who have been transferred. In total, 96 patients have been transferred and two have died (Forensic Network, personal communication 2010). In only one case has a patient been successful in his appeal against excessive security without the support of his responsible medical officer.

A study of 154 patients who have appealed against excessive security found that 51 (44) appeals were approved, 29 (eight) were declined, 13 (nine) adjourned, 46 (14) withdrawn, 12 (eight) were still to be heard, and 3 (1) were incomplete (Skilling and Thomson 2010). The number in brackets indicates those who have already been transferred. The only statistically significant factor found in predicting a successful appeal was whether it was supported by the patient's responsible medical officer. This was the case for 36 (94.7 per cent) of those approved but only one (7.1 per cent) of those declined. Two (5.3 per cent) patients won their appeal although it was not supported by their responsible medical officer.

Transfer from Prison

Prisons are the unfortunate and involuntary receiving unit for people with mental and many other health problems. In a recent audit of prisoners who were transferred under the new Mental Health (Care and Treatment) (Scotland) Act 2003 over a seven-month period to secure psychiatric care, over half of those on remand were recognizably ill on reception into prison. Nurses and prison officers were the first to notice and refer the patient for expert assessment. Practice varies extensively around the world with some jurisdictions operating prison mental health inpatient units. Scottish prisons in the public sector have no in-patient accommodation. Such prison hospitals as there were could only act as clearing stations and intermediate primary care units, and they were closed in the last decade. Recent improvements in the prison service offer limited day care but do not provide intensive mental health care. Nor should they. The hospital is the correct place for very sick patients. The audit showed that, with few exceptions, people who came to the notice of mental health services in prison transferred promptly—16 out of 22 had complete documentation in 3 days or less, with a further 3 within 1 week. Sixteen out of 22 then waited three days or less to transfer to the hospital. Considerable differences have been found in the United Kingdom with major delays in transferring prisoners with recognized need to a psychiatric hospital in England and Wales (Sales and McKenzie 2007). So what are the possible differences between Scotland and England that may account for such a difference in waiting times before transfer to a hospital. We offer four possible explanations:

1. The prison population in England (156/100,000 population) is greater than in Scotland (152/100,000 population) although it is only in this decade that this has occurred (Ministry of Justice National Offender Management Service 2010; Scottish Prison Service 2010). This may result in proportionately more prisoners in England requiring placement in psychiatric hospital.
2. The prevalence of major mental illnesses likely to require transfer of an individual to psychiatric hospital may be greater in the English prison population. Some evidence for

this can be found in prevalence studies of remand prisoners in Scotland and England where rates of psychosis were found to be 2.3 per cent and 10 per cent, respectively (Davidson et al. 1995; Singleton, Meltzer, and Gatward 1998). The recorded crime rates are higher in England (8633/100,000 population; Home Office Research Development Statistics Police Recorded Crime 2008–09) than in Scotland (7303/100,000 population; Statistical Bulletin Crime and Justice Series 2009), but given that there is no difference in the general prevalence rates of major mental disorders throughout the United Kingdom. It may be that more offenders are diverted from the criminal justice system at an earlier stage. Some evidence for this can be found in the percentage of sentenced prisoners transferred from the English (404, 0.46 per cent) and Scottish (29, 0.37 per cent) prisons in 2008 (Mental Welfare Commission 2009; Ministry of Justice 2010).

3. The number of psychiatric beds (general adult psychiatry and secure care) per 100,000 population was greater in Scotland (55; Information and Statistics Division 2009) than in England (30; Department of Health 2010a) in 2007–08.

4. The configuration of secure psychiatric services is different north and south of the border. There is a strong tradition of local prisons being served by local mental health services with access to secure beds in Scotland. Prisons with a national role are often served by forensic psychiatrists from the national high-secure facility at the State Hospital, and this again provides access to beds in an appropriate level of security. It is likely that the scale of both prison and psychiatric services in Scotland, and the personal contacts that this promotes, will ease the path to transfer.

There is undoubted pressure on secure mental health facilities. Diluting the effort by dividing care between prisons and secure hospitals is no solution for people with serious and treatable disorders. Building the capacity of good community alternatives for custody or care, with mental health at the core, will serve much better the community that such institutions are there to protect as well as protecting the human rights of offenders with mental disorders. Legal duties can assist, but there is no substitute for clear purpose and good understanding between prisons and secure hospitals, and adequate services in the correct places for the most vulnerable patients.

Management of High-Risk Offenders: Functioning or Failing?

High-Risk Offenders

It is too early to say if the MacLean Committee proposals have been successful in reducing violent and sexual recidivism in Scotland. The scheme has provided the courts with a more structured approach to high-risk offenders and the creation of the Risk Management Authority has led to greater clarity of thought and more consistent practice by mental health and criminal justice professionals on the assessment and management of risk. The OLR is markedly different in approach from the imprisonment (or detention if under 21 years of age) for public protection applied by the courts in England and Wales without any formal assessment of risk. To date there have been over 5,000 of these orders applied, whereas there have been 41 OLRs. There has still to be a formal study of these cases although an outline description is available in the chapter by Rajan Darjee and Katharine Russell in this volume. Many OLR cases are reported in the media and a decision to apply an OLR has been unsurprising. The OLR numbers are slightly higher than those predicted by the Maclean Committee at 10 rather than five cases per year; this does not present an alarming trend although it emphasizes the need for study in this area. Likewise there is a need to examine the court process, and the nature and the quality of evidence presented to the court in considering a risk assessment report and an OLR. The risk assessor is appointed by the court. This is normal practice within inquisitorial legal systems but unusual in Scotland with its adversarial system in which experts are appointed independently by both the prosecution and the defense. It is perfectly possible within the current set up for the defense to appoint its own expert, but the established detailed RMA practices with an average of 60 to 80 hours required per report may be a deterrent and it may be that the defense expert would struggle to access all the potential material and experts involved in a case. This is an issue in need of study.

The OLR is part of a range of measures open to the Scottish courts that assist in the management of risk of harm to others. Although control of the high-risk offender is a major factor in these measures, the control and treatment debate should not be dichotomized. The risk management plans required for offenders with OLRs emphasize the need for treatment to reduce the risks of these individuals. Again, it will be important while maintaining anonymity to study the content and quality of these plans.

Similarly, there has been no formal study to date of the effects of MAPPA in Scotland but these arrangements have undoubtedly assisted in information sharing and risk management, and have provided health professionals with a forum within which to participate in the shared management of sex offenders and offenders with complex needs including those with personality disorders.

Offenders with Personality Disorders

In Scotland, there was no major change in the use of short-term detention orders (28 days) following the inclusion of personality disorder into the Mental Health (Public Safety and Appeals) (Scotland) Act 1999 with 1,575 orders in 1997–98 and 1,579 in 2000–01. Only three per cent of patients (111) detained under a short-term detention certificate and seven patients placed on a new compulsory treatment order in 2008–09 had a primary diagnosis of personality disorder (Mental Welfare Commission 2009). Although no direct comparison can be made with the previous legislation as information on primary diagnosis of personality disorder was not recorded, the small numbers suggest that the new legislation alone has not made a large difference to psychiatric practice. It is service development, research, and changing attitudes, rather than legislation, that is more likely to drive this forward.

There has not been a wholesale move of forensic mental health services in Scotland to engage with offenders with personality disorders and this is not surprising given the current service structure and resources. Disappointingly, in Scotland there has not been the same considerable level of resources given to this area as has occurred in England and Wales.

Mental health professionals have however seen the beginnings of joint working with criminal justice colleagues in the area of sex offending and in complex cases often involving offenders with personality disorders. An overarching risk-sharing structure has been obtained through MAPPA, which encourages such joint work and a problem behavior approach, is being developed for example with sex offending. This is not, however, being developed throughout the country and has not extended in any systematic way to other commonly recognized problem behaviors such as stalking, threatening, fire setting, violent offending, persistent complaining, morbid jealousy, or problem gambling. The mechanism to encourage such development of practice is there through the Forensic Network and the School of Forensic Mental Health. The Forensic Network was established by the Scottish government in 2003 to provide a pan-Scotland approach to strategic planning; to review the process for the right care for mentally disordered offenders (MDOs); and to develop information systems, education and training. The School of Forensic Mental Health was established in 2007 to meet educational, training, and research needs across the network.

Offenders with Mental Disorders

There is no shortage of principles, policy, and legislation to assess and treat offenders with mental disorders as required. Diversion systems appear to function well for those with major mental illnesses and there is evidence to show that offenders with mental disorders do not wait a prolonged period for transfer from prison to a psychiatric hospital. There is also, however, evidence to show considerable psychiatric morbidity at a level not generally requiring hospital care within prisons.

There has been some debate in Scottish forensic psychiatry concerning the appropriate disposals of offenders with major mental illnesses. In a homicide report (National Confidential Inquiry into Suicide and Homicide 2008) the issue of the disposal of people with major mental disorders who had committed a homicide was highlighted. Six of the 12 individuals with known schizophrenia over a five-year period were sent to prison rather than to mental health services in Scotland. It is not clear whether the diagnosis changed before the final disposal was made by the court or if in the view of the assessing psychiatrists that the individual was stable although suffering from schizophrenia and the homicide was unrelated to the mental illness. In either case, this was a surprising finding.

The major change in the last decade to the management of offenders with mental disorders and of high-risk offenders generally has been the introduction of systematic risk assessment and management processes. The major mistake in the early years of this development was to send staff on costly risk-assessment courses for specific tools. These were ultimately ineffectual because the processes to implement risk assessment across the relevant organization had not been established. This required not only specific training of some staff but awareness training of multidisciplinary teams, standardized paperwork and processes for completion of risk assessment and management plans, and major management support to implement change. Haque et al. (2008) have summarized the following requirements for successful implementation of risk assessment and management:

- key personnel with a good understanding of approaches to the implementation of evidence-based strategies;
- managers with clinical and financial responsibility to give regular contact and support;
- responsibilities and job descriptions to be clear for individuals with key roles in clinical risk management and training;
- early and regular consultation with staff to understand reasons for resistance;
- discussion and sharing of risk assessments among the different disciplines;
- collaboration with service users, service providers, and families; and
- ongoing research.

The successful implementation of a risk management strategy is still an ongoing issue in many services and its efficacy requires further study.

Statistics indicate that serious violent (including homicide) or sexual offences constitute roughly five per cent of all crimes and offences (approximately 5,000 incidents) known to the police each year (National Statistics Publication for Scotland 2009). Those serving sentences of more than four years have a recidivism rate of 27 per cent over two years, whereas those serving a short sentence of less than six months have a recidivism rate of 74 per cent. Sexual crime has the lowest recidivism rate of 17 per cent over a two-year period, whereas crimes of dishonesty have the highest at 58 per cent. The overall reconviction rate in the two-year follow-up period is usually just under 45 per cent, but this falls to 13 per cent for sexual assault perpetrators and 33 per cent for serious assault and homicide. For offenders with mental disorders transferred from a special security hospital, the recidivism rate over a two-year follow-up period was 20 per cent for all types of offending and 12 per cent for violent offending. However, the recall rate for patients on restriction orders over a 4-year period was 0.75 per cent, whereas recall from life license was 16 per cent per year.

Outcome studies of patients transferred from high security have found recidivism rates of 34 per cent and 31 per cent in England and Scotland, respectively, and a violent recidivism rate of

15 per cent and 19 per cent after 10 years (Buchanan 1998; Thomson 2005a). General recidivism rates for a 12-month discharge cohort from medium secure units in England and Wales were 16 per cent for men and nine per cent for women over a two-year period (Maden et al. 2006). The evidence suggests that our risk management of offenders with mental disorders from secure units is reasonable.

The introduction of the appeal against excessive security has had a profound effect on the development of the forensic estate in Scotland, and therefore on the movement of individuals to a level of security appropriate to their needs that allows testing in the community from a secure environment.

Conclusions

It would appear that there has been much progress in a Scottish context for the management of high-risk offenders in the last decade although the short timescale of some of these developments means that the evidence to examine their impact is not yet available. The systems appear to be functioning well in terms of multiagency risk review and sharing arrangements, and for diversion and management of offenders with major mental illnesses. The introduction of a human-rights-based approach into forensic mental health has allowed a focus on the individual and not a blanket application of security policies. A systematic approach to risk management has been developed, but there continues to be problems in its daily implementation in forensic mental health services. Major mental illnesses in prisons are well dealt with, but further development of prison mental health teams is required to manage the high rates of depression and anxiety. Mental health professionals have so far failed to systematically engage with criminal justice colleagues in the assessment and management of offenders with complex needs, problem behaviors, and personality disorders. There are, however, encouraging signs of development within this area particularly in the work with MAPPA and with sex offenders.

14

Case Managing High-Risk Offenders With Mental Disorders in Scotland

ALEX QUINN and JOHN CRICHTON

Introduction

This chapter provides an overview of how high-risk offenders with mental disorders are managed in Scotland via the Care Programme Approach (CPA) and assesses some of the challenges that have occurred in putting this approach into practice. Parts of this chapter have appeared in the Forensic Network Expert Group report (Forensic Network 2007) and although many sections originally authored by John Crichton are drawn upon, they were honed by the other members of the group and by consultation. A full acknowledgment of everyone involved and access to all the reports of the Forensic Network can be found at www.forensicnetwork.scot.nhs.uk.

The CPA was developed to help manage the personal risks posed by offenders with complex clinical features. It was introduced as mandatory in England in 1992 and was recommended for use in Scotland in 1996, but has been mandatory for "restricted patients" (explained later) from 2002.

The CPA was endorsed by the Scottish government as it

- formalized communication between agencies and multidisciplinary colleagues;
- was explicit about the roles of each professional;
- gave clarity to service user and carer;
- did not need to be bureaucratic;
- avoided duplication in services when working properly; and
- could be used to manage risk.

Scottish law is distinct from other jurisdictions in the United Kingdom. When an offender with a mental disorder is sentenced for a criminal offence, is found unfit to plead, or is found not guilty by reason of insanity, a court, having considered oral psychiatric evidence may, in order to protect the public from serious harm, place special restrictions on the offender. A restricted patient cannot be transferred or have time outside hospital without the permission of Scottish ministers. Restricted patient cases are reviewed by a tribunal that is chaired by a judge (termed in Scotland a sheriff). The tribunal has the power to discharge the order, lift restrictions, or conditionally discharge the patient to live in the community. Scottish ministers can vary the conditions of discharge and recall patients to hospital. Currently there are 300 restricted patients, 47 of whom are on conditional discharge in the community.

New CPA Guidance for Restricted Patients in Scotland

Following a homicide perpetrated by a restricted patient supervised in the community, there was a review of CPA guidance for restricted patients in Scotland in 2007 (Forensic Network 2007). In particular the review introduced a novel risk management contingency system: risk management traffic lights (Forensic Network 2007). This translates complex risk assessments into concise directions for clinical teams in various scenarios. They are designed to aid clinicians asked to intervene in urgent high-risk cases when they may not be familiar with the case in hand.

As risk assessment becomes evermore sophisticated, a mismatch can be created between lengthy reports, which are often primarily intended to aid a legal process, and their clinical utility. There is a clinical need to communicate the essence of risk assessment and risk management plans in summary form, especially for untrained, temporary, or on-call clinicians.

For instance, consider the scenario where the weekend on-call clinician is confronted with a phone call to the hospital from a mother worried about her son relapsing into a psychotic illness. The clinician may choose to manage the situation in a variety of ways. Could the son be brought up to an assessment facility? Is a home visit required? Can assessment wait until after the weekend? Even if a risk assessment is available, the time required to digest the resulting information may not be. To manage this scenario a summary document is required. If in a page or two it confirms that the son had previously stabbed the mother while psychotic, and the usual clinical team considers in this scenario an immediate return to hospital is indicated, then the emergency management task is clear.

In another scenario, imagine that the untrained support worker arrives to find her client scrubbing away at dried vomit on the living room carpet. Her client explains that she is very embarrassed to have drunk too much the previous night and been sick. She pleads to the support worker, as a friend, not to tell anyone else. Although desirable, it is unlikely the support worker is familiar with all the background information regarding all her clients. She can empathize with her client's situation and does not want to undermine their relationship. To guide her, a summary document is required that tells her what to do. Even better is a document to which the client has contributed. More important than knowing that alcohol use is identified as an important risk factor is knowing that the wider clinical team is required to be informed the next working day about alcohol use. Apologetically, the support worker can turn to the summary document and let the client know she will be calling other members of the team.

The Development of Forensic Psychiatry in Scotland

The Policy for Offenders with Mental Disorders

The first attempt to introduce a comprehensive policy for offenders with mental disorders in Scotland was in 1968. The Harper Report (Scottish Home and Health Department 1969) advocated the development of regional step-down services to complement Scotland's only secure hospital, the State Hospital at Carstairs. Looking back over 40 years, the impact of the Harper Report is hard to judge.

In England, the scandal of Graham Young, the murderer who killed again after his release from prison, led to the Aarvold and Butler Inquiries (Aarvold 1973; Committee on Mentally Abnormal Offenders 1975) and subsequently the building of medium secure units. In contrast, in Scotland an equally scandalous homicide inquiry (Reid et al. 1977) was not associated with service developments of the therapeutic kind. This was the inquiry into the escape from the State Hospital of two patients with antisocial personality disorder, who killed three others in the course of their escape.

Finally, after many years of campaigning by the Royal College of Psychiatrists and others, on 28 January 1999 the Minister for Health in Scotland launched the policy document *Health, Social Work and Related Services for Mentally Disordered Offenders in Scotland* (Scottish Office 1999). The policy statement examined the provision of mental health and social work services for offenders with mental disorders (and others requiring similar services) in the care of the police, prisons, courts, social work departments, the State Hospital, other psychiatric hospitals, and community services. The Scottish policy endorsed certain recommendations made, in the English context, by the *Review of Health and Social Services for Mentally Disordered Offenders and Others Requiring Similar Services* (the Reed Report; Department of Health 1994). The same set of guiding principles was adopted; namely, that offenders with mental disorders should be cared for

- with regard to quality of care and proper attention to the needs of individuals;
- as far as possible in the community rather than institutional settings;
- under conditions of no greater security than is justified by the degree of danger they present to themselves or to others; and
- in such a way as to maximize rehabilitation and their chances of sustaining an independent life as near as possible to their own homes or families if they have them (Scottish Office 1999).

The Scottish Policy has subsequently been adopted by the devolved administration (now known as the Scottish government), and continues to guide services for offenders with mental disorders. The principle of "least restriction" was endorsed by the Mental Health (Care and Treatment) (Scotland) Act 2003.

Creation of the Forensic Network

The Scottish policy was complementary to the *Framework for Mental Health Services in Scotland* (Scottish Office 1997). Priority in the provision of care and support was to be given to those with severe or enduring mental health problems. A central principle of the framework was that no patient should have a planned discharged from hospital unless services and accommodation were in place and available. It was also anticipated that there exist a "managed clinical network" as described by the *Acute Services Review* report (Scottish Office 1998). This report highlighted the need for a formal relationship between components of a service, based on standards of service, quality assurance, and seamless provision of care.

In the autumn of 2001 a review group was set up to consider the governance and accountability of the State Hospital's Board for Scotland. A consultation paper resulted from that review: *The Right Place—The Right Time* (Scottish Executive 2001c). Following consultation, the Forensic Mental Health Services Managed Care Network (the Forensic Network) was created in 2003. The Forensic Network has the task of overseeing the development of services for offenders with mental disorders across Scotland. It provides a strategic overview and direction for the planning and development of forensic services.

The Memorandum of Procedure on Restricted Patients

After several years of consultation, the revised *Memorandum of Procedure on Restricted Patients* (the memorandum) was published by the Scottish government in 2010 (Scottish Government Health Department 2010). The memorandum sets out the formal responsibilities of professionals within health and social work services in relation to those offenders who have been subject to special restrictions. In Scotland, restricted patients are those subject to special restrictions because of the risk posed because of mental disorder. Restrictions are applied by the court following conviction, a finding of insanity in bar of trial, or acquittal on the grounds of insanity, by the making of a compulsion order and restriction order (CORO) or a hospital direction. These are also applied following transfer of a sentenced prisoner on a transfer for treatment direction, and to remand patients (Thomson and Cherry 2010). Restricted patients on a CORO are detained without limit of time.

The effect of the CORO is that a department of Scottish government oversees the management of patients. Scottish ministers must approve any time spent outside of a hospital and any transfers to lesser security. Mental health tribunals for restricted patients are convened by a judge. As of 30 March 2010, 300 restricted patients (including 23 remand patients) were in a hospital, and 47 were on conditional discharge in the community. Of the inpatients, 94 (37 per cent of the total) were at the State Hospital, making up 67 per cent of the population in high security. The two Scottish medium secure units had 23 per cent of the total restricted inpatient population (making up 52 per cent of the medium secure population), with the remaining 31 per cent of inpatient restricted offenders in low-security settings across Scotland. Since 2002 earlier editions of the memorandum have endorsed the use of the Care Programme Approach.

Origins of the Care Programme Approach

The Care Programme Approach (CPA) is a system of case management for those with severe mental illnesses and was first introduced in England in 1990 (Department of Health 1990). Its introduction has its origins in case management strategies used in the United States in the 1970s, which were intended to improve efficiency and coordination of mental health services. In essence there is emphasis on a clinical case manager who assesses a patient's needs and arranges a plan to meet those needs with a variety of service providers. Various types of case management were in use in the United Kingdom following the American experience prior to the introduction of the CPA (Mueser et al. 1998). In most models of case management the assessment is individualized, drawing on a patient's strengths, but the process can also be assertive when needed to prevent harm (Ford et al. 1993, 2001; Stein and Test 1980).

The CPA originally included an assessment of health and social needs, the appointment of a key worker to coordinate care, a written care plan, regular review, interprofessional collaboration, and consultation with users and carers. Its introduction in England was precipitated by the Spokes inquiry into the care of Sharon Campbell (Spokes et al. 1988). The inquiry concluded there had been a breakdown in the delivery of services, which contributed to the homicide of Campbell's social worker, Isabel Schwarz. Recommendations were made to improve the system of discharge from hospital and aftercare, with improvements to the delivery and organization of services. A particular concern was for patients who fell away from follow-up.

Inquiries into psychiatric care are not new in the United Kingdom (Crichton and Sheppard 1996), but their number since 1990 dwarf what went before. Rose (1986: 206) suggested that "yesterday's 'scandals' of the institution have already been replaced by todays [sic] 'scandals' of the community." That statement was written in the context of increasing criticism of psychiatric care in the community, and had followed an earlier series of inquiries into restrictive and abusive practices in psychiatric institutions, mostly during the 1970s (Martin 1984). During the accelerated hospital closure program of the 1980s (Jones 1993) such scandals became a focus of concern about the whole policy of care in the community. By the early 1990s there were already several external homicide inquiries about patients in the community either underway or planned.

In 1993 the United Kingdom government announced a 10-point plan to meet concerns about community psychiatric care, which included an announcement that whenever a psychiatric patient committed a homicide, an independent inquiry should be held. This policy, Health Service Guidance 27 (HSG(94)27) (National Health Service Executive 1994), which applies only to England, includes the requirement for a particular scrutiny of the CPA in all cases. There have been approximately 200 independent homicide inquiries set up under this guidance to date.

However, despite the recommendations of Spokes, an analysis of subsequent such inquiries by Crichton (2006) has supported earlier research (Crichton and Sheppard 1996), which concluded that care coordination and communication is often inadequate in providing good quality of care in the community to people suffering from a mental illness who are at risk of committing violent acts. In their inquiry into the care and treatment of Christopher Clunis, Ritchie and colleague (1994) exposed a catalog of lost opportunities and poor communications reflecting a failure of interprofessional working.

The CPA's introduction was initially patchy and there was wide variation in practice leading to criticism by the Audit Commission for Local Authorities in England and Wales (1994) and further government guidance, *Building Bridges*, in 1995 (Department of Health 1995). There was a further revision in 1999 (National Health Service Executive and Social Services Inspectorate 1999), which led to the development of two tiers of CPA, standard and enhanced, and the replacement of the term *key-worker* with *care coordinator*. Standard CPA was intended for those whose needs could be met by a single agency and posed low risk to themselves or others. In contrast, enhanced CPA was intended for those supported by multiple agencies whose risks were assessed as greater. Standard 4 of the National Service Framework for Mental Health (Department of Health 1999) required patients to have a copy of their CPA Care Plan, which should include a crisis plan and clear actions to be taken by all involved in case of recurrence of illness.

The CPA was introduced in Wales in 2004 (Welsh Assembly Government 2002) and Scotland in 1996 (Scottish Office 1996). To support professionals and organizations in running CPA, the Care Programme Approach Association (CPAA 2003a, 2003b, 2003c) formed in 1996. The Sainsbury Centre for Mental Health (2005) comprehensively reviews the CPA in England and critically appraises its contribution to mental healthcare.

The Care Programme Approach and Restricted Patients in Scotland

In Scotland the CPA was developed to help manage the personal risks posed in complex cases. It was recommended for use in Scotland in 1996 (Scottish Office 1996). Given its non-mandatory status, the use of the CPA in Scotland has been variable except in the case of restricted patients for whom it was mandatory by virtue of the memorandum.

In 2006 the Scottish Government set up an expert group to review the use of the CPA for restricted patients in Scotland. Chaired by George Hunter, the *Review of Care Programme Approach Guidance for Restricted Patients in Scotland* (2006) was endorsed as government policy in 2007 (Scottish Government 2007). Drivers for the review were

- new legislation, particularly sections 10 and 11 of the Management of Offenders etc. (Scotland) Act 2005; and
- new multiagency public protection arrangements (MAPPA; see Lindsay Thomson's chapter in this volume).

Subsequently, the Mental Welfare Commission's *Report of the Inquiry into the Care and Treatment of Mr L and Mr M*, published in March 2006, further reinforced the need for revised guidance on these matters. This case involved a conditionally discharged restricted patient in the community who committed a homicide.

The Mental Welfare Commission report (2006) identified weaknesses in the management of risk and the systems of clinical governance in local services. The requirements of the memorandum were found to be ineffective in addressing these weaknesses. The report drew a number of conclusions associated with the management of Mr. L, which are of particular significance to the application of CPA, in particular for those patients on conditional discharge. It noted that there was no plan adequately to identify and to respond to the relapse of active psychotic symptoms. This should have been part of a risk management plan. There had not been a systematic approach to risk assessment and management or the development of a contingency plan, to enable those involved in his care to identify risk indicators and respond to them appropriately. The report also noted inadequate intra- and interagency communication and liaison with the case management branch of the Scottish government.

The Hunter Report (2006) carried out a study of the use of CPA across forensic services in Scotland. It was clear that practice varied considerably between different teams. Some areas had a specific policy relating to the use of CPA for the forensic client group. Other areas have included the use of CPA within service operational policies. Others again have used CPA in line with local area policy with no specific forensic consideration. In in-patient services, it was common practice for CPA to only be implemented at point of transfer or discharge. In other areas the process was closely linked with patient review. Paperwork used for CPA varied considerably throughout Scotland, ranging from the comprehensive to very basic.

The Scottish Executive Restricted Patient team carried out an audit of CPA for conditionally discharged patients in 2006 (Hunter 2006). There were 50 cases of restricted patients living in the community in Scotland at that time. In only 28 of the cases was specific CPA paperwork present. In the remaining 22, information had to be gleaned from a variety of other paperwork. The results were very disappointing. In the majority of cases there was no clear recording of even basic information as to the name of the consultant in charge, the name of the social worker, date of conviction/insanity acquittal, or date of next CPA review. The significant majority of cases had no recorded statement regarding risk present, no clear identification of risk factors and no contingency plan. There was no clear list of those in attendance and participation of the police seemed to be exceptionally rare.

From this examination of the CPA it was clear that arrangements were unsatisfactory and although there were pockets of good practice, often at specific forensic centers, overall CPA was not implemented fully. Even where it was operational, essential information, especially regarding risk management, was often absent.

New Guidance for the Use of CPA for Restricted Patients in Scotland

The CPA continues to be adopted as the mechanism of regular review for all restricted patients in Scotland, with the exception of remand patients (Hunter 2006). The CPA is clearly not limited to those patients approaching transfer or those patients in the community. An initial CPA meeting is held approximately four to 10 weeks after admission to hospital and review meetings at a minimum of every six months.

The psychiatrist in charge of the case, the responsible medical officer, continues to have overall responsibility for the care of the patient, but to facilitate the CPA there needs, for each patient, to be a care coordinator. The key function of the care coordinator is to organize meetings in a timely fashion, and be responsible for proper invitation to those involved in the meeting and distribution of CPA documentation. The care coordinator will not assume responsibility for other professionals—all the professionals involved will retain accountability for their own practice. Box 14.1 summarizes the responsibilities of the care coordinator (Hunter 2006).

The CPA meeting itself has two stages (Hunter 2006):

- the pre-CPA meeting, which is primarily focused on third-party information or sensitive information at which the patient is not present; and
- the CPA meeting at which at which the patient is present.

The principle is that whenever information can appropriately be shared with the patient, then that information should be shared. Exceptions to this are primarily third-party information or information that is likely to cause the patient distress. It is the responsibility of the chair of the meeting to decide if information in this part of the meeting should be more

BOX 14.1: RESPONSIBILITIES OF THE CARE COORDINATOR

It is important that the care coordinator:

- Has a key role in the clinical care of the patient (often they will be the patient's key-worker)
- Provides continuity of care coordination
- Maintains regular contact with the patient
- Ensures members of the relevant clinical team have access to relevant documentation
- Ensures that the patient's named person and relevant others have access to relevant information about the patient's care and are appropriately invited to meetings
- Alerts clinical team members with any difficulties in fulfillment of the care plan
- Advises colleagues of any changes of circumstances or any matters that may require modification to the care plan between CPA meetings
- Ensures that appropriate agencies involved in the patient's care have appropriate access to the CPA care plan and are invited to reviews
- Reviews are arranged
- Actively participates in reviews
- Ensures that every effort is made to facilitate patient involvement and access to independent advocacy
- Ensures that requisite documentation is updated within specified timescales and distributed accordingly
- Has a clear understanding of professional boundaries, roles, and responsibilities of each team member
- Maintains contact with the general practitioner advising of all the relevant circumstances
- Provides clear instruction on who should provide cover in the absence of the care coordinator either for planned annual leave or unexpected absences

appropriately dealt with in the main meeting involving the patient. The pre-CPA meeting will give rise to a brief minute, which would normally be considered third-party information and not shared with the patient along with the rest of the CPA documentation. In many cases where there is police involvement, they take part or contribute information in the pre-CPA meeting.

The CPA meeting should involve the patient, their named person (an individual, often a relative or carer nominated by the patient), and/or lay advocate. There is discretion on who chairs the meeting. Box 14.2 offers suggested competencies for an effective chair (Hunter 2006).

In this model of case management, it is not envisaged that there needs to be a full repetition of the patient's past history at every CPA. The CPA document in itself should state where a historical summary can be found. It is assumed that members of the multidisciplinary team will be familiar with that summary.

The first part of the CPA meeting begins with feedback from the various professionals who have had contact with the patient. This feedback is a verbal summary of written submissions prepared in advance of the meeting, and presented by those involved in the meeting. Then there is the opportunity for the patient, or named person (the patient's representative), to state his or her hopes for the next stage of his or her journey. There should then be a review and updating

---

BOX 14.2: COMPETENCIES FOR CHAIRING A CPA MEETING

- Familiar with the clinical case
- Able to ensure that objectives of the meeting and details of the care plan are set and agreed by members
- Able to identify, coordinate, and steer the meeting
- Able to ensure that all members of the team fully participate in the meeting
- Able to ensure that team members remain focused on the meeting and present information on their objectives in respect of the process
- Has the skills and attributes to lead a large meeting, keeping focus and timekeeping
- Able to adopt a facilitative style when chairing meetings to encourage full and frank discussion
- Knows when to be decisive
- Able to tackle conflict at an early stage
- Able to communicate effectively orally
- Able to negotiate and influence others to review and set objectives
- Able to make sound decisions
- Has both analytic and strategic ability
- Sensitive to the needs of the patients and carers

---

of care plan objectives. The care plan states various treatment objectives and specifies who is responsible within the team for meeting those objectives.

During the CPA meeting there should be clear reference to whatever risk management document has been produced. The risk assessment identifies the risk factors relevant to the patient. Scenario planning informs what risk management contingencies are required. As part of the risk assessment/management process, the clinical team will have considered what practical contingencies are indicated in various basic relevant risk scenarios. In many cases this includes what to do if there is a relapse of symptoms of mental disorder or the use of illicit drugs or alcohol.

The risk contingency traffic lights, an innovation introduced first to this area by one of the authors, John Crichton, translate the findings from complex risk assessments to practical actions, intended especially for people who, for whatever reason, are not fully familiar with a case. For each risk indicator a green light signals continuance with the agreed care plan. For example, if the risk factor is recurrence of psychotic symptoms, a green light would be identified where there is no evidence of relapse and the routine monitoring identified in the care plan would continue. If substance misuse is identified as a risk factor, a green light may indicate no positive results despite the regular testing identified in the care plan.

An amber light indicates a divergence from a settled presentation and would precipitate an early clinical review—usually the next working day. For example, if psychotic symptoms are identified as a risk factor, an amber alert may be triggered if the patient's relative was concerned about paranoid sensitivity. The risk assessment informs the urgency of response in individual cases. As a whole, a next day review in response to paranoid sensitivity would be appropriate, but the risk assessment may identify individuals where a more urgent response is required. A red light contingency would be the presence of a major risk factor and would trigger emergency action such as urgent recall to hospital for conditionally discharged patients. An example of such a trigger would be command hallucinations to harm others.

Many patients may have very similar looking risk contingency traffic lights: psychotic symptoms, substance misuse, and non-engagement with the clinical team are common risk factors. The important point is that the risk assessment in some specific cases will identify more assertive action than is normally warranted. For certain patients, occasionally missed appointments may give rise only to an amber alert; in others. the risk assessment might indicate an emergency recall is necessary.

There are a number of core documents that support the CPA document. These will include a past historical summary, a risk assessment document, recent reports by those members of the multidisciplinary team regularly involved in the case, detailed multiprofessional care plan, minutes of third-party discussions held in the pre-CPA meeting, and minutes of discussions at the CPA meeting. The main document produced specifically from the CPA meeting however is the CPA document, and a fictionalized CPA document is included as the Appendix at the end of this chapter.

The CPA document is intended to be updated as circumstances change. It is also intended to be distributed to all those involved in the care of the patient, including the patient. The first part of the document clearly identifies key demographic information of relevance to the patient. There is a statement about the index offence or index offending. There is clarity about the patient's current legal status, the date of the conviction or insanity acquittal, and clarity regarding whether the patient is subject to any other offender registration, for example, the sex offenders register.

The next section of the CPA includes all those individuals involved in the CPA process and whether they have attended the most recent meeting. There follows the care plan, which precedes the risk management traffic lights and a risk summary. Finally there is an opportunity to note comments from the patient and arrangements for the next CPA meeting.

Response to the New Guidance

The Forensic Network and the Scottish government arranged a number of meetings to publicize the new arrangements, and a reaudit was carried out by one of the authors, Alex Quinn, in November 2009 on conditionally discharged restricted patients. The results across Scotland showed much improvement. The majority of conditionally discharged patients had appropriate CPA paperwork (92 per cent), although a number of regions used an altered format, which made accessing the information more difficult to those unfamiliar with regional variations.

The recording of contact details had much improved, with 98 per cent of cases having a recorded social worker and care coordinator. Only one patient had no recorded psychiatrist in charge. Two areas of deficit were noted. Only 78 per cent of cases had a recorded community psychiatric nurse, and 61 per cent a named police contact.

Involvement in MAPPA has been a recent development in the management of Scottish restricted patients. MAPPA was implemented to manage sex offenders in April 2007 and restricted patients were included from April 2008. According to the available CPA paperwork, nine cases were not subject to these arrangements. The relative youth of these developments may reflect these anomalies.

A concern in the initial audit had been that of risk assessment. This was probably the most significant area of improvement. Only one case did not have a recorded statement regarding risk, with risk factors and contingency plans identified.

The majority of cases (94 per cent) used the traffic light system. This has proved easy to use.

In summary, there was a significant improvement in both documentation of risk and contingency plans, and the identification of key members of the multidisciplinary team. Services had largely adhered to the approved format but not without a degree of local adaptation.

Appendix: Example of a CPA Document

Care Plan — dated 08.02.10
John Smith DOB — 08.09.1966
Care Programme Approach DOCUMENT

Patient Details	
Name	John Smith
Date of Birth	08.09.66
Permanent Address	12/8 Hope Crescent
CHI	1404007790
Unit Number	0400767
Sex	Male
Occupation	Unemployed
Marital Status	Single
Ethnic Origin (standard codes)	White Scottish
First Language	English
Communication Assistance Required (Yes/No)	No
Religion	Roman Catholic

Service Details	
Hospital	Royal Edinburgh Hospital
Ward	Cedar ward (Orchard Clinic)
Phone No	0131 537 6000
Responsible Local Authority	City of Edinburgh
Responsible Health Board	Lothian
Clinical Team	Dr John Crichton

Relationship Details	
Named Person	Mrs Doreen Smith
Relationship to Patient	Mother
Address	57 Potter's Way, Edinburgh, EH4 2NR
Phone Number	
Primary Carer (if different)	
Relationship to Patient	
Address	
Phone Number	
Next of Kin	As above
Relationship to Patient	
Address	
Phone Number	

Useful Contacts:				
	Name	**Address & Email**	**Office Hours Contact No**	**Out of Hours Contact Name and No**
CPA Co-Coordinator/ Key Worker	Hugh McDiarmid	Cedar Ward, Orchard Clinic, REH	0131 537 5802	
RMO	Dr John Crichton	Orchard Clinic, REH j.crichton@nhs.net	0131 537 5858	
MHO	Amy Dorrit	Orchard Clinic, REH	0131 537 5823	
GP		Dr Davies GroupPractice, Armadale Terrace		

Legal Details	
Legal Status and Section	Compulsion Order with Restriction Order
Date of Conviction/Insanity Acquittal*	21/12/02
Date Order Began*	21/12/02
Date of Previous Annual Review*	20/02/10
Date of Next Annual Review*	20/02/11
RMO Details*	Dr John Crichton Orchard Clinic Royal Edinburgh Hospital Morningside Terrace Edinburgh EH10 5HF
MHO Details*	Amy Dorrit Orchard Clinic (address above)
For Determinate Sentences Earliest Liberation Date/Parole Qualifying Date (for HD/TTD)	
For Life Sentences Punishment Part	

Index Offence	
Details of Index Offence	Attempted murder of Mother
Brief Statement	Whilst acutely psychotic and intoxicated with alcohol stabbed mother with a knife in response to command hallucinations.

Subject to Requirements of Other Legislation	
Notifiable Under Part 2 Sexual Offences Act 2003 (2) Yes/No*	No
If yes to above detail offence(s) and period of order*	
Schedule 1 Notification (offences against children) Yes/No*	No

MAPPA Status		
Is patient subject to MAPPA (Yes/No)	Yes	
Local Office	Edinburgh	
Co-ordinator	Name	Roger Blake
	Contact Number	0131 222 444
Level	One (lowest)	

Compulsory Treatment Details	
Compulsory Measures authorised under Mental Health (Care and Treatment) (Scotland) Act 2003	
Date of T2/T3 Certificate	17.03.08
Description of Treatments authorised by T2 or T3 certificates	• Clozapine or one other antipsychotic drug given orally and regularly (BNF Section 4.2.1) • Clozapine monitoring as guided by latest pharmaceutical company protocol
Conditions Set for Conditional Discharge	The Tribunal, having resumed consideration of the cause, and being satisfied that conditional discharge should take place forthwith, orders that the patient be conditionally discharged subject to the following conditions: • He shall reside at such address as The Scottish Ministers may approve. • He shall be under the psychiatric supervision of his Responsible Medical Officer, Dr John Crichton, or his successor or nominee, and should be seen at regular intervals of not more than eight weeks. • He shall subject himself to social work supervision and should be seen once monthly. • He shall subject himself to Forensic Community Psychiatric Nurse supervision and should be seen fortnightly. • He must abstain from alcohol or using illicit drugs and shall be subject to routine and reactive testing for both. • He shall participate in a programme of activities agreed by his Responsible Medical Officer and Social Work Supervisor, Monday to Friday. The programme of activities will be subject to regular Review by the Care Programme Approach and the Scottish Ministers.

Record of Those Involved in CPA					
	Name	Address	Contact No.	Invited to Meeting	Attended
Patient	John Smith	12/8 Hope Crescent	0131 007 5858	Yes	Yes
Responsible Medical Officer	Dr John Crichton	The Orchard Clinic	0131 537 5858	Yes	Yes
Mental Health Officer	Amy Dorrit	The Orchard Clinic	0131 537 5823	Yes	Yes
Care Co-ordinator	Hugh McDiarmid	Cedar Ward The Orchard Clinic	0131 537 5802	Yes	No
CPN	Sandy McCall	The Orchard Clinic	0131 537 5849	Yes	Yes
Other Professional	Henry James	Advocacy REH		Yes	No

Review of Previous Objectives

This section sets out the objectives from the previous CPA documentation and should be reviewed as part of the meeting.

Review of Previous Objectives

Need*	Objective*	Action Plan	By Whom	Review Points
Address Mental Health Issues	Monitoring of mental state and ongoing Treatment of mental illness	• Monitor conversation and behaviour, review daily. Record observations. • Drug screens to be taken twice weekly.	Multi-professional team	Ongoing
Address Physical Health Issues		• Monthly weights to be taken and recorded. • Annual physical examination • Encourage Healthy diet choices. — cholesterol • 6/12 blood tests/opiates/glucose • Referral to dentist for tongue ulcer	• Nursing staff • Medical staff • Nursing staff • Primary Care Doctor	Ongoing
Address Occupational and Recreational Issues	• Support and encourage John to maintain a balanced routine	a) Sandy McCall will meet with John regularly to ensure his routine is maintained (with support from the rest of the team). b) Support John to identify and engage in leisure/social occupations in community to help reduce feelings of boredom or loneliness.	Sandy McCall	John now attending Rook Walled Garden Project 3 days a week and is doing very well. He is shortly to complete Ballenden House computing course.
	• Support to develop worker role.	John will attend 3 sessions of work training per week. The length of sessions will be gradually increased to prepare John for potential move Rook Walled Gardens.		
Family Liaison	To complete brief family therapy course with Mum	For John to understand and attend sessions — compliant and attending	BFT trained staff	Now Complete
Address Smoking	Support John to stop smoking	Encourage attendance at smoking cessation group — prepare to stop in the community	• Nurse Pharmacist • Psychology	Currently, down to smoking 15/day (used to smoke up to 40/day).

(Continued)

Review of Previous Objectives (Continued)

Need*	Objective*	Action Plan	By Whom	Review Points
Address Self Care Issues	Monitor John's female friends	• Stress to John the importance of safe sex and appropriate relationships. • Encourage John to not allow people to take advantage of him.	Multi professional team	Ongoing
Assess Self Control and Acceptance of Personal Responsibility	Prevent use of drugs and alcohol	For John to attend next drugs and alcohol group — not attending due to clash with work. Support and encourage by all staff.	• Psychology • All Staff	One to one drugs and alcohol work with psychologist.
Risk Assessment	Ongoing risk assessment	HCR20 review — July 2010	• Multi-Professional Team • Nursing staff	Review July

Contingency Plan		
Issue	Early Warning Signs (Relapse Indicators)	Contingency Actions
Symptoms of Mental Illness	**Green**: Symptoms	Continue routine monitoring and visits.
	Amber: Early signs of psychosis Attempting to negotiate level of medication and have this reduced. Increase in level of aggression or hostility towards family. Poor sleep and appetite, tendency to chain-smoke, grow hair longer and become unshaven. Presence of speech and feelings of paranoia.	Contact all involved and Clinical Team next working day review.
	Red: Clear psychotic symptoms Paranoia and thoughts of acting out on these feelings. Active threats towards family (in particular, mother).	Emergency recall to hospital via the on-call team if out of hours.
Substance misuse	**Green**: No evidence	Continue twice weekly urine drug screens
	Amber: Single unconfirmed test result or concerns about drug or alcohol misuse	Contact all involved and Clinical Team next working day review
	Red: Clear evidence of substance misuse and deterioration in mental state Smelling of alcohol, evidence of alcohol in flat, positive breathalyser.	Emergency recall to hospital via the on-call team if out of hours.
Engagement with treatment	**Green**: Attends all appointments and taking medication	Continue with Care Plan regular appointments
	Amber: Beginning to miss placements	Contact all involved and Clinical Team next working day review
	Red: Not taking medication, refusing access to Clinical Team	Emergency recall to hospital via the on-call team if out of hours.

Risk Summary

Offending History	
Index offence	Attempted murder
Other offences	Assault, misuse of drugs

History of ...	Yes/No	Brief Details
Violence	Yes	Physical assaults
Sexual aggression	Yes	Historical disinhibited behaviour
Fire raising	No	—
Hostage taking	No	—
Use of weapons	Yes	Kitchen knife
Alcohol or substance misuse	Yes	Alcohol
	Yes	Various illicit drugs
Absconding/escape	Yes	Historical absconding from leave
Self-harm	Unknown	
Other factors of relevance		

Current Risk Status	
Setting	Likelihood, imminence, frequency and severity of harmful behaviour towards whom under what circumstances
In hospital	Low
In community escorted	Low
In community unescorted	Low
Other	Low

Victim Considerations	Yes/No	Details
Is/are there specific person(s) that patients poses a risk to		Mother
Does the patient pose a potential risk to certain types of people (e.g., children, women, vulnerable adults)	No	

Monitoring and Supervision Requirements		
In Hospital	Nursing observation level	General
	Restrictions regarding contact with staff	Nil
	Restrictions regarding access to indoor areas	As per policy
	Restrictions regarding access to outside areas	As per policy
	Restrictions on telephone use and letters	n/a
	Room searches	Weekly
	Personal searches	Random
	Alcohol/drug testing	Weekly
	Access to sharps and other utensils	Yes
	Visitors	
	Other hospital requirements	Nil
In Community (on pass)	Escort requirements	
	Special considerations for staff visiting patient	
	Special considerations for out-patient appointments	
	Alcohol/drug testing	
	Other community requirements	

Patient/Carer Views	
Patient Comments	"I don't want back in hospital and I'll comply with your requests."
Carer Comments	"John this is your last chance, but John's done much after this time."

Arrangements Next CPA	
Date	Monday 19th April 2010
Time	14.30
	15.00
Place	Rook Garden project

The Care Programme has been agreed by those concerned.

Patient: John Smith

Carer: Mrs Smith (verbally agreed)

RMO: Dr John Crichton

Care Co-ordinator: Hugh McDiarmid
(verbally agreed)
(on behalf of all consulted)

MHO: Amy Dorrit

15
The Scottish Approach to High-Risk Offenders
Early Answers or Further Questions

INNES FYFE and YVONNE GAILEY

Introduction

In this chapter we will describe the policy underpinning the introduction of a new sentence for the long-term risk management of serious violent and sexual offenders in Scotland called the order for lifelong restriction. We will explore some of the distinctive features of the sentence and we will then examine emerging practice since its introduction in 2006. We will conclude with some questions and suggestions for future research.

The introduction of the order for lifelong restriction was recommended by the Committee on Serious Violent and Sexual Offenders chaired by Lord MacLean (hereafter referred to as the MacLean Committee; Scottish Executive 2000a). The MacLean Committee's remit was

> to consider experience in Scotland and elsewhere and to make proposals for the sentencing disposals for, and the future management and treatment of serious sexual and violent offenders who may present a continuing danger to the public. (Scottish Executive 2000a: 1)

The sentence was proposed in the context of an international trend toward preventive detention and indeterminate sentences (McSherry et al. 2006). This trend has been observed by many as moving toward a paradigm based upon risk that emphasizes punishment and control in order to respond to both economic conditions and public scrutiny (Power 2003: 72). In the United Kingdom, a rights-based discourse that emphasizes the balancing of competing rights and supports a principle of proportionality was also evident as the Human Rights Act 1998 (UK) was brought into force.

In addition to international influence, Scottish criminal justice policy, like that of many of its neighbors, has a tendency to evolve in response to tragic incidents where individual or system error has been identified or suspected. Notwithstanding a genuine desire among the agencies to learn and improve practice, there is also a political challenge in perceived public anxiety about the "dangerous offender" (Kemshall 2009).

The MacLean Committee was established in March 1999 and reported in June 2000. This was contemporaneous with the Expert Panel on Sex Offending chaired by Lady Cosgrove (March 1998, reported June 2001, Scottish Executive 2001b) and the Review of the Mental Health (Scotland) Act 1984 chaired by the Right Honourable Bruce Millan (February 1999, reported January 2001, Scottish Executive 2001d) who were concerned with sexual offenders and mental health legislation, respectively. This allowed the MacLean Committee to focus on its remitted group of serious violent and sexual offenders who may present a continuing danger to the public, without being drawn into the wider issues of management of sexual offenders, and to focus on personality disordered offenders without being drawn into wider issues of mental health legislation. There is also discernible cross-fertilization of ideas between the groups of experts; all three were concerned with risk assessment and management in a human rights context or "meet[ing] the requirements of public safety, while respecting human rights" (Scottish Executive 2000a: 2).

The MacLean Committee considered several options when deciding upon the need for a new sentence in Scotland. It considered existing Scottish sentencing options such as the increased use of mandatory life sentences and extended sentences (custodial sentences with up to 10 years statutory supervision in the community); longer determinate sentences; and altering legislation regarding sexual offenders, stalking and harassment, and supervised release orders.

The committee also considered approaches to the management of similar groups of offenders in other jurisdictions. It identified a clinical or therapeutic model adopted in many European countries and a community protection model used in common law countries such as Australia and the United States of America (Scottish Executive 2000a).

The order for lifelong restriction provides for a level of treatment and community management that have been recognized as unique in the international context (McSherry and Keyzer 2009). In addition to these features, the sentence also has some others, which, if not unique, are unusual among preventive detention policies. The order

- is made at the point of sentencing rather than after a custodial sentence as a civil measure;
- is only made following a risk assessment that is undertaken by persons and in manners that have been accredited by an independent body;
- provides for a community part of the sentence, which is as important as the custodial part;
- provides for mechanisms to evaluate the planning for and implementation of the management of the offender against standards; and
- is available for a range of crimes including violent and sexual offences.

The order for lifelong restriction became available to the High Court in June 2006 and by 31 March 2010, 60 risk assessment orders had been concluded. A risk assessor accredited by the Scottish Risk Management Authority (RMA) conducts these assessments when the court decides that the risk criteria may be met and makes a risk assessment order (see further the chapter by Raj Darjee and Katharine Russell in this volume). The assessor must conduct such assessments in a manner that is consistent with standards set by the RMA. For the purpose of examining the use of the sentence, assessors provide information regarding the characteristics of the convicted person's offending history that led the court to consider the order for lifelong restriction. In addition, links can be made between the risk assessment and the court decision that, on the balance of probabilities, the risk criteria are met, or alternatively, that a sentence other than the order for lifelong restriction is appropriate. The risk criteria used by the court are

> that the nature of, or the circumstances of the commission of, the offence of which the convicted person has been found guilty either in themselves or as part of a pattern of behaviour are such as to demonstrate that there is a likelihood that he, if at liberty, will seriously endanger the lives, or physical or psychological well-being, of members of the public at large. (Criminal Procedure (Scotland) Act 1995, sec. 210E)

The RMA approves and reviews risk management plans throughout the sentence to ensure that proportionate, relevant, and evidence-based risk management strategies are put in place, implemented, and maintained. However, it is too early in the implementation of the sentence to draw many conclusions regarding this distinctive feature of the sentence. Nevertheless, to date, risk management plans have been submitted and approved in respect of all individuals subject to an order for lifelong restriction.

The Scottish Risk Management Approach

The MacLean Committee recommended that rather than the seriousness of the index offence, pathology or concepts such as "dangerousness" (for a discussion of this concept see Eastman 1999 and the introductory chapter by Bernadette McSherry and Patrick Keyzer in this volume), the identification of a pattern of behavior that indicates continuing risk to the public should be the cornerstone of the order for lifelong restriction. While some have seen this as a more ethical position than the concept of dangerousness (Darjee and Crichton 2002), indeterminate sentences raise profound human rights concerns and the MacLean Committee recognized that the integrity of its risk rationale would rely on sound risk assessment and management practice. It also recognized that there were a number of challenges to be overcome to achieve the required standard of practice.

Risk is not a homogeneous concept; the range of different types of uncertainty expressed by the word *risk* can make one wish that, like the apocryphal Inuit vocabulary for *snow*, that we had hundreds of terms to differentiate between the different kinds of risk. Garland's observation is of several different risk literatures, "all linked tenuously together by a tantalizing four letter word" (Garland 2003: 49).

Even within the offender risk discourse, there is a range of ideas, ranging from the uncertainty and unpredictability of the post-modern society (Brown and Pratt 2000a) to the argument that the study of risk is associated with the view that what we fear tells us more about ourselves than the source of our fears (Bell 2002).

Murphy and Whitty (2007) have highlighted the lack of a risk and human rights discourse and the separation of these concepts between disciplines: criminologists with risk and lawyers with human rights. They suggest that there have been two parallel arguments, particularly with regard to sexual and violent offenders, that have highlighted tensions between a risk management paradigm that emphasizes control and a human rights ethos (for examples, see Akuffo 2004; Henham 1998; McHarg 1999; Royal College of Psychiatrists 2004). However, we propose that there is a different risk management approach emerging in Scotland: one that embraces a rights-based approach.

There is also evidence of an unresolved pursuit of conflicting goals in the criminal justice arena. It has been suggested that there is a fundamental contradiction between conceptualizations of the offender as, on the one hand, a threat to be isolated through punishment, corrected through treatment, and controlled through management, and on the other, someone who is in possession of human rights (Houchin 2003).

In contrast, the approach that has been promoted in Scotland is that sound risk management is the means by which to ensure that restriction of liberty upholds the human rights ideal of proportionality. Nevertheless, preventive detention sits uncomfortably with the concept of proportionality as the anticipated event may not occur, and so such measures should always be considered as extraordinary measures (Keyzer and Blay 2006). For this reason, risk management in this context promotes use of the least restrictive measures, rehabilitation and reintegration (Kemshall 2009).

The MacLean Committee envisaged a possible solution to the conflicting goals of punishment and treatment in the strengthening of risk management practice and the harnessing of risk assessment as a means to ensure transparency, balance, and fairness.

However, recognizing that practice did not consistently meet this standard, a further recommendation of the MacLean Committee was the creation of a Risk Management Authority (RMA). This non-departmental public body was established in 2004 to set standards for risk assessment and management, accredit persons to undertake such assessments and methods by which assessment should be conducted, and scrutinize and oversee risk management plans.

Replacing the Discretionary Life Sentence

The MacLean Committee perceived a need to replace the discretionary life sentence and to introduce a "structured and systematic way" (Scottish Executive 2000b: 1) for judges to consider the sentencing of serious violent and sexual offenders. In addition, the proposal was for risk management throughout the sentence, and for the period spent in the community to be an integral part of the sentence. The MacLean Committee proposed that "community services for offenders serving this sentence would involve a greater degree of intensive supervision than is the current norm" (Scottish Executive 2000b: 2).

A discretionary life sentence may be imposed on the basis of the risk posed by the offender, in contrast to a mandatory life sentence that may be imposed on the basis of the nature of the crime of which the offender has been convicted (that is, murder). The Home Secretary explained the significance of this distinction during the debates on the Criminal Justice Bill for England and Wales:

> In a discretionary case, the decision on release is based purely on whether the offender continues to be a risk to the public … The nature of the mandatory sentence is different … According to the judicial process, the offender has committed a crime of such gravity that he forfeits his liberty to the State for the rest of his days. (Parliamentary Debates, House of Commons 16 July 1991)

The European Court of Human Rights case law has reflected the view that there is a justifiable difference between mandatory and discretionary life sentences. In the case of *Thynne, Wilson and Gunnell v United Kingdom* (1990) the Court held that, unlike mandatory life sentences, a discretionary life sentence is imposed not only because the offence committed is a serious one, but because the accused is considered to be a danger to the public.

A life sentence continues to be mandatory for those convicted of murder and the discretionary life sentence is still an available sentence in Scotland. However, the intention is that for violent and sexual offenders who pose a risk to the public, the order for lifelong restriction should be considered. At the point that the court considers that the risk criteria may be met and the risk assessment order is made, a discretionary life sentence is no longer an available sentence for the case. Since the order for lifelong restriction legislation came into force, four discretionary life sentences have been made. All these cases involved sexual offences committed prior to the legislation coming into force and the order for lifelong restriction was not available to the court. Article 7(1) of the European Convention on Human Rights and Fundamental Freedoms precludes retrospective application of the order for lifelong restriction legislation.

An Extraordinary Sentence

Since the order for lifelong restriction replaces the discretionary life sentence, the expectation is that it will be used rarely. The founding report by the MacLean Committee, the policy statement in it, and the resulting legislation are clear that this is an extraordinary sentence intended to deal with the extraordinary offender. Equally evident is the aim of identifying, assessing, and managing those critical few, not by clinical definitions or categorizations but by risk. The Criminal Justice (Scotland) Act 2003 inserted risk criteria into the Criminal Procedure (Scotland) Act 1995. The risk assessment report must include the assessor's opinion as to whether the individual risk is low, medium, or high.

In application, the RMA sought to further guide the evaluation of risk by setting definitions of low, medium, and high risk (RMA 2006), while recognizing the inherent flaws in any such set of definitions. These were designed to promote proportionality and consistency, and minimize net widening.

At the outset of the policy, it was estimated that by largely replacing the discretionary life sentence, the order for lifelong restriction would be imposed in approximately 15 cases a year. This would represent judicial restraint in comparison to similar measures in other jurisdictions (see, for example, the later discussion of the indeterminate public protection sentence). At 31 March 2010 less than 50 orders for lifelong restriction had been made, within the initial estimate, and providing a broad indication that the targeting of the order may have been effective.

Expectations may have been met regarding the overall number, but further research is warranted to gauge whether these sentences have been well targeted. The Scottish Government and the RMA share the concern that the numbers of orders for lifelong restriction should not exceed the anticipated level without good cause. The outcome of the monitoring activities of the RMA reported in this chapter is shared with stakeholders to promote learning and propose changes in practice where necessary.

Indeterminate Sentence for Public Protection

A comparable policy development in England and Wales is the indeterminate sentence for public protection that was introduced by the Criminal Justice Act 2003 (see the chapter by Lindsay Thomson in this volume). Prior to 2005, the life sentence was the only indeterminate sentence available in England and Wales. In common with the order for lifelong restriction, the indeterminate sentence for public protection has a minimum term to be served in custody; thereafter release can only be authorized by the parole board. It differs from the order for lifelong restriction in that it does not necessarily entail a lifelong license period, it is available for specified offences, and there are no statutory risk assessment and management mechanisms.

Implemented in April 2005, by 31 December 2009, 5,788 individuals had been made subject to one of these sentences, 99 had been released, 24 of whom had been recalled (HMI Probation and HMI Prisons 2010).

Concern over the unprecedented growth in the number of individuals subject to an indeterminate sentence for public protection is well documented (see Jacobson and Hough 2010, and the chapter by Lindsay Thomson in this volume) and led in 2008 to the amendment of the legislation in an effort to target the sentence more effectively. Criminal justice inspections have identified scope for improvement of the assessment process prior to imposition of the sentence (HMI Probation and HMI Prisons 2010).

Features of the Order for Lifelong Restriction

In this section we consider several aspects of the order for lifelong restriction:

- the broad range of offences for which it may be considered;
- the explicit consideration of whether the offence is part of a pattern of behavior;
- the inclusion of allegation information in the risk assessment report;
- the relationship between risk assessment and the court's decision; and
- the position of prolific offenders.

And finally, we compare its risk management provisions with a similar sentence in England and Wales, the indeterminate sentence for public protection.

Broad Range of Offences

The circumstances in which the High Court in Scotland may consider making a risk assessment order in respect of a convicted person are broad. Other than murder (when there is a mandatory life sentence) there are no exclusions to the offences that may be considered. However, three specific categories of crime are mentioned:

- sexual offences;
- violent offences; and
- offences that endanger life.

In addition, there is a category of offences where "the nature of which, or circumstances of the commission of which, is such that it appears to the court that the person has a propensity to commit any such offence" as given in the three other specific categories (Criminal Procedure (Scotland) Act 1995, sec. 210B). Of the 60 reports examined, over half concerned sexual offences as the current offence. Of the remainder, three quarters concerned violent offences, with small numbers coming from the offences that endanger life, and the nature or circumstances of commission categories. It may be noted in passing that offenders who have been assessed as a medium-level risk are currently overrepresented in this small group.

The range of offences that have in practice led to the court considering that the risk criteria may be met is broad. They range from culpable homicide and attempted murder to breach of civil orders. However, the current offence is only one part of the early consideration; it may be part of a pattern of behavior.

The sentence provides for a punishment commensurate with the index offences, while allowing for lifelong management due to a pattern of behavior, which forms part of the risk criteria.

Pattern of Behavior

The risk assessment order provides for a risk assessor accredited by the RMA to carry out a risk assessment and to prepare a risk assessment report, the purpose of which is to assist the court in making a decision about the level of risk an offender poses to the community. A unique aspect of this assessment is that the identification of the necessary pattern of behavior may include information about allegations in addition to convictions. If on the basis of this report and other evidence, the court is satisfied on the balance of probabilities that the risk criteria are met, it must impose an order for lifelong restriction (Criminal Procedure (Scotland) Act 1995, sec. 210F).

Consider this hypothetical case. An individual is before the court for a breach of the peace and assault during a drunken fight with his wife that was broken up by the police. His wife suffered only minor injuries and he pleads guilty and expresses his remorse. On this evidence alone, he might not be considered a candidate for the order for lifelong restriction.

However, imagine that this man has several convictions and allegations of violence and sexual violence against partners, some of which have put previous partners in the hospital. Further, there are two convictions for stabbing men against whom he had a vendetta. Previous court orders have ranged from an early probation order to a prison career of several lengthy sentences with extended periods of post-release supervision. When his behavior in prison and on supervision in the community is considered, there is evidence of discipline problems in prison, not engaging with professionals, not participating in programs, and further offences resulting in recall to prison. These additional factors may be given weight by the sentencing judge.

Of the 60 reports in our cohort, less than a third of the offenders have five or fewer previous convictions, with very few offenders where the current offence is their first conviction. This indicates that the court gives consideration to the pattern of offending. This is different from that of other sentencing, where most weight is given to the current offence, and then previous convictions are taken into account. Allegation information is only considered at the point that it is included in the risk assessment report, where the extent of its influence on conclusions is set out by the assessor.

Allegation Information

Allegation information can be defined as any information about offending behavior that has not been proven in court. On examination of the reports for 60 concluded cases, allegation information was indicated by assessors to have been a factor in over two thirds of the cases. Of those, almost half stated that the information did not alter their assessment of the risk posed. A majority stated that they used the allegation information purely to inform recommendations for risk management. Less than a quarter of reports stated that the allegation information supported the assertion that, taken with conviction information, there is a pattern of behavior.

Risk Criteria and Risk Level

In balancing the rights of dangerous offenders with consideration of public safety, a number of principles are involved:

- The rights of the offender in regard to Article 5 of the European Convention on Human Rights and Fundamental Freedoms (ECHR) "right to liberty and security," balanced with the positive obligation of the state to protect the right of future victims, whether they are identifiable members of the public or not, to Article 2(1) "right to life" of the ECHR.
- The rights of the offender with regard to ECHR Article 7 "no punishment without law" and Article 6 "right to a fair trial" balanced with the public interest in the fair administration of justice (see also the chapters by Patrick Keyzer and Ronli Sifris in this volume).

Risk assessment can help with regard to the first balancing exercise but should be separated from the second consideration. This is in order to avoid some of the negative effects that have been seen in some jurisdictions when risk assessment has been used to redress a perceived imbalance between the offender's right to a fair trial and the public interest, for example:

- assumptions that allegations and original charges commuted to lower charges are true;
- punishment for crimes for which the offender has already been sentenced;
- proliferation of civil orders which lead to criminal offences when breached; and
- detention under mental health legislation without the expectation of treatment benefit.

What is important is the type of risk assessment undertaken. Some risk assessments give a score or result without a description of the nature, pattern likelihood, and severity of the risk, or suggestions for the management of the risk posed. Risk management is a primary aim of the order for lifelong restriction, and so RMA Standards and Guidelines (2006a) set out a model that fulfills the requirements of the court for expert opinion and conclusions and has the additional benefit of informing future risk management.

As stated earlier, if the court considers that the risk criteria are met, then an order for lifelong restriction is made. Examining the risk criteria a number of dimensions of risk are indicated: the likelihood of reoffending, seriousness, nature, and the capacity of the individual to cause such harm if at liberty. The criteria are sufficiently broad that they do not in themselves identify the exceptional offender for which the order is intended.

Notwithstanding the court's decision on the balance of probabilities that the risk criteria are met, the likelihood dimension of risk is not further described. However, impact or severity of the future offending is expected to be physical or psychological endangerment.

A consideration of the phrase "if at liberty" implies that the assessor must consider what risk would exist if there were no restrictions in place or treatment benefits in evidence. However, as the court has decided that the risk criteria may be met in ordering a risk assessment, there is also an implied need for measures to mitigate the likelihood and impact of future offending. As the risk criteria are a test only for the appropriateness of the order for lifelong restriction, the extent of those measures is not quantified. However, this is an important consideration for the assessor.

Risk assessment reports include a description of the person's risk factors; the scenarios in which they might offend; along with an analysis of his or her offending behavior and the management strategies required to curtail it (RMA 2006a). The phrase "if at liberty" would seem to preclude the consideration of scenarios where measures short of the order for lifelong restriction were in place. However, the risk criteria are for the court to consider and the question for the assessor is different: whether the risk posed is high, medium, or low. The RMA has defined these terms in order that the assessor may use them to describe the risk posed, rather than reduce it to a one-word term (RMA 2006a). These terms are defined as follows (RMA 2006a):

High

- This offender presents an ongoing risk of committing an offence causing serious harm.
- The identified scenarios involve pervasive risk and there are few if any protective factors to mitigate that risk.
- The offender requires long-term risk management, including supervision and where the offender has the capacity to respond, ongoing treatment.

Medium

- This offender is capable of causing serious harm, but in the most probable future scenarios there are sufficient protective factors to moderate that risk.
- The offender evidences the capacity to engage with risk management strategies and may respond to treatment.
- This offender may become a high risk in the absence of the protective factors identified in this report.

Low

- This offender may have caused serious harm in the past, but a repeat of such behavior is not probable.
- The offender is likely to cooperate well with risk management strategies and they may respond to treatment.
- All probable future scenarios for this offender have sufficient protective factors to minimize risk of offending.

The connection between these determinations is subtle. It could be assumed that any case assessed as low by such definitions would not be determined to meet the risk criteria. However, those assessed as medium may; and indeed a case may be classified as high risk against the above definitions but the need for long-term risk management does not necessarily equate to concerted lifelong efforts. Nevertheless, in the majority of cases where the assessor has rated the risk as high, an order for lifelong restriction was made. The high definition is most closely related to the risk criteria and refers to the enduring nature of the risk, its pervasiveness, and the need for long-term risk management. However, it stops short of including the identified need for concerted lifelong efforts, and as such there is cause to question whether this criterion imposes an unnecessary layer of complication.

Conversely, in cases where the assessor has rated the risk as medium, the court tends to make a different disposal. There is no case where the assessor has rated the risk as low. This could mean that there is already a filtering process undertaken by the court before a risk assessment order is made. Alternatively, it could mean that the high and medium risk definitions cover too many offenders: that is, the low risk definition may be too low.

In this examination of the risk criteria and the risk level definitions it appears that an aspect of the policy that may be lacking sufficient articulation in practice is the need for concerted lifelong efforts. This criterion echoes, and may be enhanced by attention to the concept of unde-terrability (Slobogin 2003) or manageability (Rajan Darjee and Katharine Russell's chapter in this volume).

An examination of the court reports allows for a more detailed analysis of the cases in terms of the extent to which offenders meet the risk criteria. We compared a number of key areas of the offenders' criminal histories, for example, what types of offences they had convictions for, what sentences had been used by the courts and indications of compliance (or non-compliance) with previous remediation attempts.

From this analysis it is evident that there are clear distinctions between those who receive the order for lifelong restriction as opposed to an alternative sentence. Reminiscent of the categories put forward by Rajan Darjee and Katharine Russell elsewhere in this volume, it is evident that the majority of individuals who become subject to an order for lifelong restriction demonstrate a clear pattern of seriously harmful offending to which they are predisposed by a number of long-standing risk factors that have not been (and are unlikely to become) amenable to change. Typically they have been undeterred by previous sentencing and intervention options, and present complex management challenges in prison.

On the other hand, those who do not receive the order for lifelong restriction may well be considered for the sentence when convicted of an offence that is of a serious nature, but examination of their previous history reveals that this is not part of a pattern of behavior. For these cases, less restrictive sanctions are applied, generally an extended sentence.

However, it is also evident that a small group of offenders given orders for lifelong restriction has more in common with the latter group. Typically they are prolific offenders but have not been subject to substantial periods of incarceration and post-release supervision. However, they may have enduring vulnerability factors such as social skills deficits and cognitive impairment that will necessitate long-term management. This raises the question of the appropriateness of the order in those cases, as the long-term management that they require relates more to their needs than their risk to others. This could arguably be met more appropriately through a joint social services/health and criminal justice partnership. In some cases, the individual is presenting with an index offence of a serious nature, but amid a pattern of less harmful behavior; in others there is a persistent pattern of offending that causes a lesser degree of personal injury. For this reason we are cautious about the fourth category in Darjee and Russell's hypothetical typology: that it is, we argue that it not an appropriate use of the order for lifelong restriction that it is used to prevent an individual becoming a suitable candidate by accessing otherwise unavailable resources.

In its early days the order for lifelong restriction may have been restrained in its application and largely met the initial targeting expectations. However, two concerns are raised:

- a human concern regarding each unnecessary application of this sentence; and
- over time should this pattern continue, a systemic and political concern regarding the use of the order for lifelong restriction.

Individuals subject to this order are afforded a particular level of risk management that is resource intensive and in keeping with evidence-based, ethical practice; this degree of management should be based on the risk posed rather than the sentence being served. Failure to adhere to those principles may result not only in interference with human rights but system pressure and failure.

Indeterminate Sentence for Public Protection

Both the indeterminate sentence for public protection and the order for lifelong restriction provide for explicit planning of the interventions to be undertaken with the offender. However in the case of the order for lifelong restriction, the lead authority (prison service; hospital; or in the community, the local authority) must prepare a risk management plan within nine months of the order being made. This must follow guidelines issued by the RMA and be submitted for approval to the RMA. An annual report on implementation and further plans must then be produced throughout the sentence.

This is not the case for indeterminate sentence for public protection prisoners. In a recent joint inspection, the problem of dealing with so many prisoners was highlighted:

> The wide scope of these sentences means that there will continue to be a huge number of such prisoners that neither the probation service nor the prison system currently have the capacity to handle effectively. (HMI Probation and HMI Prisons 2010: 1)

The order for lifelong restriction has many features in common with the indeterminate sentence for public protection and notwithstanding the former's more limited use, it is important that Scottish authorities remain aware that

- offenders will not necessarily jump the queue for programs because they are subject to the order rather than a determinate sentence;
- the Parole Board for Scotland will use a separate assessment of risk from the courts; and
- review by the Parole Board for Scotland will not be synchronized with completion of interventions or treatments.

All of these issues could feasibly constitute barriers to the release of offenders into the community, thus raising the possibility of legal challenge. However, the risk management plan provisions employed within the context of orders for lifelong restriction may limit concerns. Lack of these provisions has been highlighted as an issue with the indeterminate sentence for public protection:

> Without a secure framework provided by good sentence planning, it was difficult to ensure that effective work with IPP [indeterminate sentence for public protection] prisoners was undertaken. Shortfalls in the initial plans led to uncertainty and difficulty at the review stage. (HMI Probation and HMI Prisons 2010: 28)

The Parole Board for Scotland has considered no offenders for release at the time of writing, although there are a few cases where the punishment part is short and the offender will be eligible for consideration soon. It remains to be seen if the order for lifelong restriction will come under legal challenges similar to the indeterminate sentence for public protection (see for example *Secretary of State for Justice v David Walker and Brett James* 2008). However it is to be hoped that the much lower numbers of offenders and the external scrutiny of the development and implementation of risk management plans will avoid some of the same problems.

Risk Assessment: Identifying the Target Group

The communication of risk based on shared understanding and definitions has been a perennial challenge (Breakwell 2007). Further, the MacLean Committee recognized that risk assessment practices are often found to be inadequate and inconsistent (Scottish Executive 2000a).

However, as discussed earlier, the risk assessment report is a key information source when the court is considering whether the risk criteria are met and the order for lifelong restriction is appropriate.

Experience of over three years of the new sentence now allows for reflection on the initial assumptions about the target group, examination of the profile of the actual group, and exploration of the influence of the risk assessment.

Younger Offenders

Amid general endorsement of the Scottish approach, McSherry and Keyzer (2009) raise a concern that the order for lifelong restriction may target young offenders. In 2001 the Scottish Executive considered

> given the nature of the offending which will attract an Order for Lifelong Restriction that it is extremely unlikely that offenders under the age of 21 will be considered for an Order for Lifelong Restriction. However, in the interests of public safety, we consider that it is desirable to make the disposal available for any high risk offender regardless of age (Scottish Executive 2001a: 25)

The rationale for the latter statement is not made clear. However, the MacLean Committee made a similar earlier assumption:

> The majority of the offenders with whom we are concerned will be adult, but the principles behind our recommendations apply irrespective of the age or gender of the offender. (Scottish Executive 2000b: 38)

Therefore, while the policy did not intend to explicitly target young people, there was an assumption that the sentence and the principles underpinning it were applicable to all. However, the proposal that the sentence should be "available for any high-risk offender regardless of age" disguises an array of complex professional and ethical issues. A high-risk offender in the context of those policy documents is an individual with a pattern of behavior that suggests the need for concerted lifelong efforts to manage the risk of serious harm posed to the public at large.

Elsewhere in this volume, Lorraine Johnstone presents a review of the profound challenges associated with accurately distinguishing between young people who do and do not pose such a level of risk, and argues that practitioners should adhere to a set of standards of risk assessment practice that echo those set by the RMA.

The RMA's Standards and Guidelines for Risk Assessment (2006a) require a highly individualized, risk-management-focused assessment, based on information collated from extensive file review, interviews, and multiagency working, but there is little reference to age-specific assessment, over and above the requirement to select appropriate risk instruments.

On 31 March 2010, 12 (20 per cent) of the individuals considered under the auspices of the risk assessment order have been between 15 and 21 years of age, and in 10 of those cases an order for lifelong restriction was made. Four of the young offenders considered were under 18 years of age at the commission of the offence; two became subject to the order for lifelong restriction. While the MacLean Committee's projection that the majority of individuals of concern would be adults has been borne out to date, consideration of young people has occurred more frequently than anticipated, and resulted in the imposition of orders for lifelong restriction.

Of the 10 young people subject to the sentence, nine cases show an index offence that was of a serious sexual or violent nature. The young people's history of sentences varies considerably from more than one previous custodial sentence to community disposals. The majority was known to child care or youth justice services with the interventions ranging from secure care to foster care, and five were reported to have been victims of sexual or physical abuse.

There is growing recognition (Dunkel and Pruin 2009) of the United Nations Convention on the Rights of the Child (1991), the principles of which require that the best interests of the child must be a primary consideration in any relevant regulatory context. Those principles have been elaborated by the Council of Europe (2009) and applied to the administration and delivery of sanctions and measures in a publication that reinforces the fundamental principle that deprivation of liberty should be avoided wherever possible, be employed as a last resort, and for the minimum time feasible (Hammarberg 2008). The activities of risk assessment, evidence-based intervention and evaluations are identified as examples of means by which those principles are promoted (Dunkel 2009).

The order for lifelong restriction is an exceptional deprivation of liberty involving the potential for indeterminate and repeated incarceration, without provision for review. Therefore, it is suggested here that, in order to embrace the principles of the Convention on the Rights of the Child, the assessment of young people being considered for the order for lifelong restriction should ensure that due consideration is given to the individual's status as a child or young person. This would involve

- the application of age-appropriate risk assessment instruments;
- evidence of attention to the age and stage of development of the individual;
- the implications for future risk; and
- ensuring that the best interests of the child remain a primary consideration.

Prolific Offenders

A small number of offenders have an offending profile that, although extensive, does not include behavior that has caused serious harm in the past. They tend to have served repeated short terms in custody or have been subject to several other non-custodial sentences. These offenders personify what has been referred to as the revolving door phenomenon (Scottish Prisons Commission 2008). They can meet the definition of high risk, but they do not seem similar to other offenders who are subject to an order for lifelong restriction. They represent a group that may be managed in the community. However, ongoing monitoring of the implementation of the order for lifelong restriction for this group is required.

Consider this hypothetical case: an individual who is before the court deliberately pushed a friend down a flight of concrete steps and ran after him, not to help but to repeatedly jump on the victim's head. The victim suffers a head injury, broken leg, and some internal bleeding. The offender pleads guilty explaining that his friend had stolen his MP3 player. We may reasonably think that such an offence warrants consideration of an order for lifelong restriction.

Looking at this individual's history imagine that he has learning difficulties and has had a childhood in care, with several moves and school exclusions due to behavioral problems. He has a criminal history featuring many low-level antisocial offences that have resulted in fines, statutory supervision, and very short custodial sentences. There is a social work report that he is difficult to manage and although he can benefit from support and structure he often "goes off the rails" when things are not going right for him.

An order for lifelong restriction may be an appropriate option for such an offender. Then again, it may not: there are alternatives and in Scotland the closest alternative disposal for this group may be the extended sentence (Crime and Disorder Act 1998, sec. 86) that allows a period of detention and subsequent supervision in the community to a maximum of 10 years. In cases where an order for lifelong restriction was not made, an extended sentence was the most popular disposal. However, the decision that the risk assessment seeks to inform is binary in nature: to make the order for lifelong restriction or not.

Assessors must be concerned with the risk as it presents now, and from this make judgments about the measures required to manage that risk in the future. A concept that emerges in the

White Paper (Scottish Executive 2001a) that is important to the discipline of proportionality, but is absent from the risk criteria, and the RMA's current definition of high risk is that of the need for "concerted lifelong efforts to minimize or manage risk." It is approximated in the RMA definition of high risk—"requires long-term risk management"—but not in such strict terms. Identifying the need for such lifelong strategies would require the satisfaction of at least one of two of the following elements:

1. Evidence that lesser efforts such as determinate sentences have been tried and have failed to manage the risk in the past; and/or
2. Evidence that in the absence of the first element, the most probable risk scenarios based on the pattern of behavior are opined to be such that an order for lifelong restriction is required to protect the public, without recourse to a less serious sentence.

There is an implicit ethical professional challenge for the author of a risk assessment report to provide evidence that an order for lifelong restriction is justified on the basis of the assessment of risk without earlier recourse to a less restrictive disposal. Therefore, although the assessor does not explicitly recommend a sentence, it may be helpful to the court for them to consider when proffering an opinion that a person is high risk, the reasons why an extended sentence would be insufficient.

Risk Management: Addressing the Risk Posed

In relation to the order for lifelong restriction, the term *risk management* is used to mean a set of coordinated activities including measures taken to restrict the offender, to engage and treat the offender, to monitor behavior, and to protect potential victims. The RMA has recognized that:

> Violent and sexual offending are complex phenomena and so require individualised responses that are dynamic and derived from multi-faceted risk assessment. In turn this requires multi-layered and multi-modal risk management plans delivered through multi-agency and multi-disciplinary collaboration. (RMA 2007a: 4)

This is an important point, because risk management has been used to describe a purely restrictive regime, in identifying those who pose a risk and restricting them or separating them from the public. While the MacLean Committee recognized that "some offenders will not improve" (Scottish Executive 2000b: 26), it also recognized that there is a spectrum of offending behavior and therefore a need for a spectrum of measures to reduce it:

> Since it is impossible to predict the outcome of treatment in advance, the principles of rehabilitation should mainly inform the way a sentence is served, rather than the overall length of the sentence. (Scottish Executive 2000b: 26)

To this end, the RMA standards and guidelines governing the preparation of risk management plans set out seven areas of risk management practice (RMA 2007a):

1. collaborative working (among partners, with a victim focus, with offenders);
2. risk assessment;
3. risk formulation—linking risk assessment to risk management;
4. risk management strategies;
5. accommodation;
6. responding to change; and
7. organizational support.

Specifically, in terms of linking risk assessment with risk management, the standards and guidelines set out that in response to the risk assessment, the Lead Authority will document preventive actions and contingency actions in the RMP [risk management plan]. The plan will outline clear lines of accountability and responsibility and timeframes for delivery.

The preventive action section of the RMP will set out risk management strategies to:

- address the identified risk factors; and
- support and enhance protective factors.

The contingency action section will set out planned responses to:

- the appearance of early warning signs;
- the weakening or breakdown of protective factors; and
- the weakening or breakdown of the risk management strategies set out in the preventive action section.

The action plans will be designed to both minimise critical risk factors and maximise protective factors in order to prevent harmful outcomes. (RMA 2007a: 6)

The form set by the RMA for risk management plans presents the possible risk management strategies under four categories:

- Supervision—Defined as having "a dual focus of promoting rehabilitation and reducing harm, through restricting liberty as necessary, and engaging an offender in the process of change" (RMA 2007a: 48).
- Monitoring—Which "should identify changes in individual and situational factors which could increase [or reduce] the likelihood of risk of harm to others so that management strategies can be revised as appropriate" (RMA 2007a: 52).
- Treatment/intervention—Which "may involve a combination of group, individual and family work. The appropriateness of each will be determined by the factors which are identified as being related to the offending, the offender's circumstances, and the objectives of the risk management plan" (RMA 2007a: 56).
- Victim safety planning—"To reduce the likelihood of future harm, including the effects of further violence, serious injury and homicide on *known* adult and child victims and *potential* future victims" (RMA 2007a: 56; emphasis added).

Of the cohort of 60 concluded court reports available for analysis at this point, 48 offenders were made subject to an order for lifelong restriction. Of these, 29 had approved plans in place in accordance with the statutory nine-month timescale. In turn, slightly less than a quarter of these plans had been in place long enough to have implementation reports associated with them. Therefore, we are limited in what we can say about the risk management of offenders subject to the order.

The risk management plans submitted for approval to the RMA thus far have been characterized primarily by monitoring and supervision strategies, as may be expected in the early years of what may be a long custodial sentence.

As all of the plans for the cohort have been for a custodial setting, the establishment's regime has been the most common strategy for potential victim safety planning, and further information was sought in this regard by the RMA, particularly for early plans. In some cases, where for example there was a recognized risk to an identifiable group of staff or prisoners, specific measures regarding victim safety planning were described.

Interventions, which include treatments, group work or change programs, have been undertaken by few of the cohort at this stage in the implementation of the sentences. Few annual implementation reports state that interventions have been completed; more commonly assessments for group work entry have been completed or motivational work is being undertaken.

The risk management plan approval process does not preclude risk management strategies being implemented before the risk management plan has been approved at the nine-month stage. In addition to victim safety measures and monitoring, there is evidence of motivational work or group work taking place, particularly if the offender has a particularly short punishment component of the sentence and if the offender has shown readiness to begin interventions.

Although there could be a tendency to prioritize such offenders to undertake interventions, some of these offenders are not ready to participate in group-work programs, or have significant stability or motivation issues that must be addressed first.

Conclusions

In this early review of the implementation of the new sentencing regime, a number of issues have emerged that may lead to the refinement of its operation in Scotland, and which may also be informative to other jurisdictions.

The order for lifelong restriction is intended to be an extraordinary measure and has a number of distinctive features, designed to produce a proportionate response to risk. Practice since its introduction in 2006 seems to have met expectations in terms of replacing the discretionary life sentence in Scotland, while avoiding the net-widening effect that has resulted from similar legislation in England and Wales. However, as the number of offenders considered by the courts for the order for lifelong restriction increases, the opportunity to examine its application reveals areas that warrant attention. There is strong commitment in Scotland, as evidenced in the contributions of others in this volume, to ensure that the sentence is applied with due attention to proportionality, and that practitioners with the necessary competencies prepare reports that provide an individualized and comprehensive risk assessment with the objective of holistic and balanced risk management.

The nature of the risk assessment report has, as intended by the MacLean Committee, served an important purpose, of informing highly tailored risk management plans which focus on risk reduction, treatment, and rehabilitation. The challenges associated with the preparation and implementation of those plans have to date been met by the Scottish Prison Service, which, despite the considerable resource implications, has submitted plans and annual implementation reports that have been evaluated and approved by the RMA. It is through the implementation of such risk management plans that the success of the ultimate objective of the policy will be judged. It is only as offenders are released in the community that we can really test the effectiveness of the disposal in this regard. This presents a further set of challenges that the Scottish agencies have yet to meet, and they will require early attention in those cases where short punishment parts have been set.

In addition, future research is required regarding the influence of the risk assessment and the question of the gatekeeping role of the risk criteria. In addition, formulation-based risk assessment has the power to inform an individual risk management plan, which can in turn encourage the outward-facing role of prison and promote human rights principles of transparency and proportionality. This has provided an opportunity for Scotland to keep focus on the critical few.

Although a review of the numbers of orders for lifelong restriction, as opposed to discretionary life sentences, gives a broad picture of effective targeting, there is scope for further refinement. The need to ensure that human rights principles are honored requires that all involved in policy and practice avoid complacency.

In the current redrafting of standards and guidelines, the RMA should emphasize that the order for lifelong restriction is intended to provide for *concerted lifelong efforts* in cases where alternative measures would be inadequate. Assessors should be guided, in every case, to identify and analyze the extent of and response to alternative previous measures. This is of particular importance in regard to young people where explicit attention should be paid to the implications of lifelong restriction when it is imposed at an early age.

The initial assumption of the policy that the order for lifelong restriction would be an unlikely sentence for those under 21 years of age has proven to be unfounded. While in this examination it is evident that the majority of young people made subject to an order for lifelong restriction were demonstrated to have strong indications of future risk of serious harm, it is less clear that all other measures had been employed in advance of such a lifelong measure of restriction. In those cases the argument could have been stronger to justify the categorization of high risk. In the forthcoming revision of its standards and guidelines for risk assessment and management, the RMA should ensure that practitioners are guided to adopt the general human-rights-based principles that underpin the standards set, and pay explicit attention to the implications of life-long restriction when it is imposed at an early age.

Other chapters in this volume propose the risk management approach adopted in Scotland as an alternative to the argued counterproductive, economically and ethically questionable alternatives. Scotland offers a very tentative and preliminary example of an alternative in practice. With those caveats it is suggested that the alternative merits consideration from other jurisdictions. The early experience in Scotland suggests that this alternative needs to be

- founded in a strong political intent;
- supported by the commitment of the professional groups and agencies;
- grounded in standards of collaborative, evidence-based, and rights conscious practice; and
- subject to oversight, scrutiny, and the aim of continuous improvement.

A rights-based risk management approach is indisputably resource intensive. However, it is an alternative to the more commonly adopted option that is founded primarily on indeterminate detention. That approach, discussed extensively by Eric Janus, John La Fond, John Petrila, and Patrick Keyzer in this volume, has proven costly, and breaches traditional principles of justice and human rights.

Scotland's policy offers an alternative to preventive detention regimes. It is an alternative that is relatively new; but while improvements can be made, it shows promise.

16

The Assessment and Sentencing of High-Risk Offenders in Scotland

A Forensic Clinical Perspective

RAJAN DARJEE and KATHARINE RUSSELL

Introduction

In 2006 Scotland introduced a new system for the assessment and sentencing of violent and sexual offenders considered to pose an ongoing risk of serious harm to others (see also the chapters by Lindsay Thomson, and by Innes Fyfe and Yvonne Gailey in this volume). Following conviction, such offenders are placed on a risk assessment order (RAO), and are assessed by an accredited expert while in custody on remand awaiting sentence. The expert's role is to assess the ongoing risk of serious harm using an assessment method that follows national standards and guidance. The risk assessment report produced through this process is submitted to the High Court, which then decides whether the legal criteria are met for the imposition of an order for lifelong restriction (OLR). An offender given an OLR will be subject to risk management, both in institutional and community settings, indefinitely.

In this chapter we give a forensic clinical perspective on the RAO–OLR process based on our direct experience of undertaking these assessments as accredited assessors, our awareness of the experiences of other accredited assessors, and a brief survey of RAO cases. As will be highlighted in this chapter, the Scottish approach is unique in many ways. Although other countries have indeterminate sentencing for dangerous offenders, none have a national body to oversee and prescribe the process, none have accreditation of experts for the specific task, none have detailed national standards and guidance on risk assessment, and none have a sentencing option so specifically focused on risk management in the institutional setting and the community.

In Scotland, incarceration at the end of a determinate prison sentence, which occurs in jurisdictions such as the United States, Australia, and England and Wales, has never been seen as an appropriate way to deal with such cases. Rather the emphasis is on assessment prior to sentencing, and applying a sentence that allows appropriate risk management for the small number of individuals who pose an ongoing risk of serious harm to others and who may be difficult to manage. For those in other countries, it may be instructive to compare what happens in their jurisdiction to Scotland, to consider the practical realities of the Scottish approach, and to highlight the advantages and disadvantages of the Scottish approach.

An Overview of the Process

The background to the RAO and OLR in terms of policy developments (Darjee 2003; Darjee and Crichton 2002) and legislation (Darjee 2005) have been described elsewhere. Part 1 of the Criminal Justice (Scotland) Act 2003 introduced provisions for the assessment and sentencing of high-risk offenders and established the Risk Management Authority (RMA). A detailed overview of the process and related policy is given in Innes Fyfe and Yvonne Gailey's chapter in this volume.

When a person is convicted of a sexual offence, a violent offence, an offence that endangers life, or an offence the nature or circumstances of which indicate a propensity to commit such offences, and it appears that the risk criteria for an OLR may be met, then the court may make an RAO. The RAO allows for a pre-sentence remand of 90 days (which may be extended by a further 90 days) so that a risk assessment report may be prepared. This report must be prepared by an assessor who is accredited by the RMA, and must follow standards and guidance produced by the RMA. The legislation stipulates that the assessor must categorize the offender as low, medium, or high risk, and guidance from the RMA operationalizes these three categories based on the assessment of ongoing risk of serious harm and the manageability of that risk. Having received the assessor's report, the court must then determine if the risk criteria are met. These criteria are set out under section 210E of the Criminal Procedure (Scotland) Act 1995 as amended by the Criminal Justice (Scotland) Act 2003 (see Box 16.1).

BOX 16.1   "RISK CRITERIA" UNDER SECTION 210E CRIMINAL PROCEDURE (SCOTLAND) ACT 1995

"[T]he risk criteria are that the nature of, or the circumstances of the commission of, the offence of which the convicted person has been found guilty either in themselves or as part of a pattern of behaviour are such as to demonstrate that there is a likelihood that he, if at liberty, will seriously endanger the lives, or physical or psychological well-being, of members of public at large."

A motion for the consideration of an RAO may be made by the prosecutor or an RAO may be initiated by the judge. In many cases the police will make a case for an RAO to the prosecutor. However the issue of risk leading to the consideration of an RAO may be raised by various professionals: criminal justice social workers; psychologists or psychiatrists preparing pre-sentence reports; and multiagency public protection panels when an offender has previously been managed in the community. The decision as to whether an individual is placed on an RAO will depend on the offence he or she has committed; the pattern of previous offending behavior; and, crucially, opinions and decisions made by police, prosecutors, and judges, influenced in some cases by other professionals. There may be an argument that this could lead to inconsistency and arbitrariness; and there does appear to be geographical variation in the use of RAOs in Scotland, but that issue is not discussed in this chapter.

If the court is satisfied, on a balance of probabilities, that the Section 210E risk criteria are met, then the court will make an OLR, which is an indeterminate prison sentence. A punishment part or tariff will be imposed by the court, based on the court's determination of the minimum length of imprisonment that must be served to satisfy the need for punishment in the particular case. After this term has been served, release will depend on the risk the offender poses as determined by the parole board. When released, the offender will be subject to conditions and ongoing management, with the potential for recall to prison indefinitely. Assessment and management of risk of harm to others are central to the OLR, and both in prison and in the community, a risk management plan, approved by the RMA, must be put in place.

The OLR needs to be considered in the context of other sentences and measures available for serious violent and sexual offenders in Scotland (see Lindsay Thomson's chapter in this volume). There are automatic life-sentences for those convicted of murder. Discretionary life-sentences, although still available, have been replaced by the OLR. Before the OLR these sentences were used rather arbitrarily about five times per year (McCallum 2000). A discretionary life sentence has been used in Scotland only once since the introduction of the OLR. Extended sentences allow for a prolonged period of community supervision subject to recall to prison, but are finite. A range of civil orders may be used to place restrictions on sexual offenders in the community, for example the sexual offences prevention order (SOPO). An OLR should only be used where less restrictive alternatives would be insufficient to manage the long-term risk of serious violent or sexual offending.

When offenders suffer from mental disorders such that fitness to plead, insanity at the time of the offence, or detention in a secure hospital are relevant, then the risk assessment will be undertaken while the offender is on remand in a secure hospital, and a mental health disposal may be used either alongside or instead of an OLR if the risk criteria are met (see Darjee 2005 for further details).

Accredited Assessors

Experts who undertake risk assessments on offenders subject to an OLR must be accredited by the RMA. To become accredited the practitioner makes an application to the RMA including copies of two risk assessments they have completed. The application, an interview, and references are used by the RMA to decide whether the candidate has the appropriate competencies to be an accredited assessor. The areas of competence include standing and character, qualifications and experience, the commitment to maintaining and improving professional standards, and the ability to deliver risk assessment reports. The latter competency covers understanding, knowledge of, or ability in the following areas:

- criminal justice;
- risk assessment tools;
- report writing;
- risk formulation;
- information management;
- communication skills;
- multiagency working;
- risk management of offenders; and
- risk assessment processes.

Accredited assessors have to comply with a code of conduct. Unsuccessful applicants may appeal. Accreditation is for one year initially, and then must be renewed every three years. Assessors can specify particular areas of expertise. All will have expertise in assessing male violent and sexual offenders, but specified areas may include women, young offenders, and mentally disordered offenders. Accreditation was set up so as to be non-discipline specific, and it was envisaged that assessors would come from psychology, psychiatry, and social work backgrounds.

At the time of writing there are 15 accredited risk assessors in Scotland. Seven are clinical psychologists, six are forensic psychologists, and two are forensic psychiatrists. Seven work in mental health services, two in prisons, one in a children's secure unit, three in independent practice, and two are retired (although both the retirees worked in mental health services until very recently). Geographically, six are based in southeast Scotland, one in the north of Scotland, seven in the west of Scotland, and one in England. The current number of assessors is adequate to provide the assessments requested by courts. Most assessors work full time for public sector employers (the health service and prison service). Work as an accredited assessor is done outside of these full-time commitments. Risk assessments are commissioned by the High Court and assessors are paid a fee to undertake them.

Initially it was envisaged that assessors would also come from a social work background, but none have materialized as yet. Factors that may have mitigated against social workers applying include, limited involvement in independent/private work, problems being released from work commitments, the perception that this is an area requiring psychological expertise, and a lack of perceived expertise in the structured professional judgment approach. It is important to note that in day-to-day practice in the work we undertake with sex offenders in the community in southeast Scotland, where cases arise similar to RAO–OLR cases, social workers usually invite psychologists or psychiatrists to make assessments. The key issues in determining whether practitioners do or do not apply for accreditation have been the time commitment, the perception that the application process is particularly arduous, and fitting in the work alongside other commitments.

It has become apparent that the types of individuals referred for assessment have clinically complex features where there is a need to assess personality disorder, psychopathy, paraphilias, cognitive deficits, and mental illness. The assessment and understanding of such conditions and their relevance to risk assessment and management requires appropriate experience and expertise. Such experience and expertise is unlikely outside of psychology and psychiatry. The most important area of competence and expertise in such cases is the assessment of personality and personality dysfunction, as personality disorder is often present in the offenders referred for assessment. Assessors therefore require a high level of appropriate forensic and clinical skills.

Although most jurisdictions have legal criteria for the admissibility of expert evidence in court and professional standards for psychologists and psychiatrists, none has specific accreditation linked to risk assessment for sentencing as we have in Scotland. In no other area of forensic work are we subject to the level of scrutiny and examination as when undertaking these assessments. These other areas of work include

- pre-trial criminal cases where issues of fitness to plead and criminal responsibility arise;
- post-conviction criminal cases where issues of risk and appropriate disposal arise;
- mental health tribunals considering ongoing compulsory measures for people with mental disorders; and
- civil court cases (for example, applications for sexual offences prevention orders).

In legal settings in Scotland, the expert credentials of psychologists and psychiatrists are rarely scrutinized or rigorously challenged. It is against the backdrop of this generally laissez-faire attitude to the qualifications and capacities of experts in such cases that this new accreditation needs to be seen. It has been said that the accreditation process is too arduous and exacting. Our view is that it is not, and such statements are a sad reflection on the lack of rigor displayed in other areas of practice in Scotland.

Conducting Risk Assessments for Sentencing

Standards and Guidance

When conducting risk assessments, assessors have to follow the standards and guidelines for such assessments issued by the RMA (Risk Management Authority 2006b). Scotland has detailed mandatory standards and guidance. In Chapter 5 of this volume, John La Fond raises the issue of the importance of developing such an approach in the United States context.

The five mandatory standards are:

- Document review—The assessor must review a range of relevant documents.
- Professional judgment—The assessor must use a structured professional judgment approach and use at least one risk assessment tool approved by the RMA. If an actuarial tool is used this must be alongside a structured professional judgment tool.

- Offender contact—A minimum of 6 hours face-to-face contact on at least three occasions spanning several weeks. In addition there must be an offender feedback session.
- Multidisciplinary working—Must meet with a range of professionals from varying disciplines involved with the case.
- Report structure—Must use RMA Risk Assessment Report Structure.

This report structure has the following sections:

1. Front sheet with identifying information
2. Table of contents
3. Executive summary
4. Opinion on risk level, specifying whether the person poses a low, medium, or high risk to the safety of the public at large
5. Risk assessment report body:
   a. Offender background information
   b. Analysis of past and current offending
   c. Risk and protective factors
   d. Opinion on future risk
   e. To whom does this offender present the greatest risk?
   f. What is the likely impact and severity of harm associated with this offender?
   g. Describe the most probable future risk scenarios for this offender
6. Conclusions
   a. Overall conclusions
   b. What should be the main objectives of risk management?
7. Report evidence base
   a. Documents regarding convictions
   b. Allegation information
   c. Interviews with offender
   d. Reports from third parties
   e. Other interviews
   f. Other evidence including risk assessment tools
8. Appendices

In practice this has involved between 50 and 120 hours work in the cases we have assessed. The process involves a substantial amount of time and work, and the guidance is quite prescriptive. Is this really necessary? When we conduct risk assessments outside of this context we do not follow the structure for RAO reports, and the amount of time and work on an assessment will rarely be as much as when conducting one of these assessments. Although the stakes are high in these assessments (that is, potential life-long deprivation of liberty), the stakes are equally high in other evaluation settings (for example, should this man be allowed back into the community where he may rape or otherwise seriously harm another victim?). Our view is that the principles for these assessments are sound, but the guidance is overly prescriptive and the report structure is too rigid. If experts are accredited, then they should have to follow certain principles, but they should be able to exercise their expertise and judgment as to exactly how they conduct their assessment. There should be a report structure, but it should have broad headings rather than the current, very tight boxes. The current structure has not been adopted by assessors in other areas of practice and leads to reports that may repeat the same material three or four times. However, a broad structure for reports that provides some consistency for sentencing judges is required.

In Scotland it has traditionally been very difficult to gain access to all the documents and records necessary to complete a comprehensive assessment. This new process has made such information available, but the process of getting access to this information is far from smooth. Assessors may spend weeks and months trying to gain access to records from various agencies and trying to view information regarding previous offences. Courts and prosecutors still seem reluctant to send detailed information about previous offences, which is usually crucial to the assessment of risk. In some cases getting access to information has depended on who the assessor knows in relevant agencies, rather than on any uniform understanding and approach to access to information by agencies across Scotland. The general ethos of increased sharing of information between agencies in relation to risk posed by violent and sexual offenders following the introduction of Multi-Agency Public Protection Arrangements (MAPPA) (Scottish Government 2010) has helped to some extent.

The RMA requires the use of a structured professional judgment approach when undertaking these risk assessments. This will involve the use of appropriate tools and instruments to inform the assessment of risk. The standards and guidance state that at least one risk assessment tool approved by the RMA should be used in such cases. The RMA has produced a Risk Assessment Tools Evaluation Directory (RATED; Risk Management Authority 2007b), which sets out a number of actuarial and structured professional judgment instruments and assesses their reliability, validity, utility, and applicability to offenders in Scotland. When an assessor uses only one tool, this must be a structured professional judgment tool, such as the HCR-20 (Webster et al. 1997), the SVR-20 (Boer et al. 1997), or the RSVP (Hart et al. 2003). The structured professional judgment approach is discussed in the chapter by Lorraine Johnstone in this volume. In reality assessors use a variety of instruments in each case.

In some jurisdictions an actuarial tool alone is used to determine risk when consideration is being given to special measures, for example, adjudication as a sexually violent predator in some states of the United States (Grudzinskas et al. 2009). In Scotland, although assessors sometimes use actuarial tools alongside structured professional judgment tools and assessments of psychopathy, they are never used on their own. Although actuarial approaches may give a nomothetic anchor to help with an examination of the long-term likelihood of reoffending, they do not address issues such as the risk of serious harm or the manageability of that risk and therefore have limited utility in such evaluations. They also have limited, if any, utility in unusual or complex cases, and if used as screening measures in Scotland would not capture sexual offenders who go on to commit life-threatening offences (Grubin 2008). There are arguments that actuarial tools have no utility in the assessment of risk in individual cases (see, for example, David Cooke and Christine Michie's chapter in this volume), although these arguments have been countered (Harris and Rice 2007). The use of actuarial instruments within a structured professional judgment framework has been recommended by some authors (Boer 2006; Craig et al. 2008), and is the approach we take to assessing sex offenders in our clinical practice working with sex offenders in the community (Russell and Darjee, in press).

In most sexual offence cases in Scotland, the Risk Matrix 2000 (Thornton 2007) and the Stable and Acute 2007 (Hanson et al. 2007) will have already been used in a pre-sentence report by a social worker. The assessor will need to consider and explain whether an assessment using those tools is valid or helpful, particularly if his or her assessment reaches a different conclusion. If different tools lead to different conclusions, then the assessor should have the expertise and ability to explain this with reference to the psychometric properties of the tool, the applicability of the tool to the specific case, and the risk question being addressed.

An individualized formulation of risk is required to address the two crucial questions: (1) Does the offender pose an ongoing risk of serious harm? (2) What will be required to manage that risk? Such a formulation requires expert knowledge of violent and sexual offending applied within a structured framework. In some cases there may be no specific tool of relevance. For example, consider the case of a potential spree murderer with no previous convictions and no history of violence. In such a case, the principles of the structured professional judgment approach can be applied within the framework set out by the RMA. The assessor would have to review the scientific and clinical literature to ascertain which factors need to be assessed, before coming to a reasoned judgment, based on an explicit and transparent process and formulation, setting out the limitations of the assessment.

The key issue in determining whether a case deserves a categorization of high risk is in most cases the manageability of the risk of serious harm. Most cases referred for assessment clearly pose an ongoing risk of serious violent or sexual offending, but how does that risk need to be managed? What is the least restrictive approach that will enable others to be protected? The expertise required to make a judgment on this issue includes knowledge not only of risk assessment (including the application of appropriate tools) but also, and crucially, the application of risk management interventions in criminal justice and forensic mental health settings. Although the legal criteria include the phrase "at liberty" in the assessments, we do not envisage that the case will be unmanaged if the offender does not receive an OLR. If the expert is simply determining what the risk would be if the person was set free with no input or restrictions, then far fewer cases would be judged medium or low risk. The OLR is meant to be used where other less restrictive approaches would not sufficiently reduce risk. This may make it seem like the assessor is overstepping the mark in relation to the ultimate legal issue, but given the close correlation between risk level and judges' sentences, it is incumbent on assessors to take this approach to prevent the unnecessary use of OLRs. The assessor must be an expert in both risk assessment and risk management of offenders.

Allegations about sexual or violent behavior, which have not led to criminal convictions in the past, may be used by assessors when conducting risk assessments. This is made explicit in the legislation. Such allegations include a range of incidents and information: briefly alluded to incidents in case files, incidents that are documented in detail, incidents that have received non-criminal sanctions (for example, revocation of conditional release or sanctions in prison), incidents that have been prosecuted but have not led to conviction, incidents that have satisfied civil but not criminal courts (for example, children's hearings in child protection cases or the sheriff court in considering a sexual offences prevention order), and incidents that have led to criminal conviction but have been pleaded down (for example, a rape allegation that results in a conviction for assault). Assessors must use their judgment in considering such allegations and in weighing how much emphasis to place on them in their assessment of risk. Assessors need to consider how their opinion would be different with and without the allegation information. This may be straightforward when there is one allegation, but when there are many this can become complex. It is also difficult to pretend not to know something when considering how an allegation may change the formulation of a case. A concern that has been raised by prosecutors and the police, although it has not come to pass, is that the victim of a previous allegation cited in a report may be called to give oral evidence for sentencing. This has led to cautious approaches to information sharing with assessors by these agencies in some cases. The structured professional judgment approach can be particularly helpful when considering allegation information, as it gives a structure within which an assessor can at each stage consider the difference that allegations would make (identifying present and relevant risk factors, formulating the case, considering plausible risk scenarios, and making risk management recommendations). Setting out different future risk scenarios based on whether allegations are true or false can help clarify the relevance of allegations when considering the case at hand. Then if the court decides that a particular allegation is or is not to be taken into account they can proceed on the basis of the relevant future risk scenarios.

Ethical Issues

To date, only two offenders have refused to be assessed. If assessors are unable to access all relevant information, this will limit confidence in their conclusions. Further, if crucial information is missing then the outcome of the assessment will need to be so couched that its utility would be questionable. One crucial source of information is the offender, and the RMA standards place emphasis on spending substantial time with the offender when conducting assessments. However, if comprehensive case information is available (perhaps including videos of police interviews) then there may be enough information to complete an assessment without needing to interview the offender. There is an argument that it is unethical to assess a person without his or her consent. However if such assessments could not be undertaken when the offender refuses, then the whole system would collapse very quickly. In our view an ethical approach includes the following steps:

- attempt to see the offender (repeatedly if necessary);
- make sure the offender is informed about the nature and purpose of the assessment and that the assessment will go ahead with or without his or her cooperation;
- gather as much information as is possible;
- gauge if any helpful conclusion can be reached; and
- make sure the limitations of the assessment are made explicit.

We are not aware of cases when defense lawyers have encouraged their clients to be uncooperative. In the few cases where lack of cooperation has been an issue, its roots have been in the personality pathology of the offender.

There has been some debate, particularly in psychiatry, as to whether conducting risk assessments for sentencing is unethical (Miller 2008; see also McSherry and Keyzer 2009 for an overview of ethical arguments). Some argue that because the duty of doctors is to the individual (their patient), they must act in their best interests and must do them no harm. In undertaking this work the assessor acts for the court—primarily in the interests of society rather than the individual—and may come to a conclusion that leads to the loss of liberty. The counterargument is that in forensic work, the first duty of doctors is to the court, and in this work they must be objective and truthful, so traditional medical ethics do not apply. Our view is that the latter approach is the correct one in any forensic work. An expert who acts only in the individual's best interests could be biased and lack objectivity. It is important to be aware of the ethical tensions, and to be explicit with the offender about the nature of the assessment. Although death penalty evaluations are often cited in the ethical debate, it is important to note the difference between the following: a one-off assessment of risk leading to an irreversible and, in our view, immoral and ineffective practice (that is, execution); and an assessment primarily aimed at addressing the manageability of risk of serious harm, which may potentially lead to an intrusive set of interventions indefinitely, but within the context of a risk management plan that is based on principles including least restrictive intervention and proportionality. If the primary question was whether these individuals should be locked away forever, then a different approach may be required.

There is discomfort when experts appear to be deciding the ultimate legal issue. Whether an offender meets the legal criteria for an OLR and whether they receive such a sentence is for the court, not the assessor, to decide. The assessor has to place the offender into one of three risk categories (see Table 16.1).

These criteria are operationalized to emphasize the risk of very serious harm to potential victims, the extent to which the risk will be manageable, and how that risk will need to be managed in the future. As mentioned earlier, the legal criteria in section 210E (Box 16.1) are broad and would potentially capture every offender referred for assessment on an RAO along with many

Table 16.1 Definition of Risk Categories to be Used by Assessors in RAO Cases

Risk Level	RMA Definition
High	This offender presents an ongoing risk of committing an offence causing serious harm.
	The identified scenarios involve pervasive risk and there are few if any protective factors to mitigate that risk.
	The offender requires long-term risk management, including supervision and where the offender has the capacity to respond, ongoing treatment.
Medium	This offender is capable of causing serious harm, but in the most probable future scenarios there are sufficient protective factors to moderate that risk.
	The offender evidences the capacity to engage with risk management strategies and may respond to treatment.
	This offender may become a high risk in the absence of the protective factors identified in this report.
Low	This offender may have caused serious harm in the past, but a repeat of such behavior is not probable.
	They are likely to cooperate well with risk management strategies and they may respond to treatment.
	All probable future scenarios for this offender have sufficient protective factors to support ongoing desistance from offending.

who are not referred for assessment. This reflects the difficulty of setting out legal criteria to define such a complex group, as has been the case with similar legislation in other jurisdictions. In theory the assessor considers the RMA criteria in Table 16.1 and then the judge will consider Section 210E (Box 16.1). In practice an assessment of high risk invariably leads to an OLR. In cases where it has not, the assessor had made it explicit that the individual did not seem to need lifelong risk management. Similarly an assessment of low risk (which has not occurred so far) or medium risk invariably leads to a non-OLR disposal. In the vast majority of cases the level of risk as determined by the assessor is determining the sentence.

It is important that assessors make the limits of their expertise explicit. Risk assessment is about making reasoned judgments rather than infallible predictions. The RMA standards and guidance fall down in not requiring an explicit statement about the limitations of risk assessment generally and the specific limitations in a particular case (for example, where information is missing or the case is highly unusual). In communicating the outcome of the assessment it is important to use probabilistic language (likely, very likely, unlikely, possible, may) and conditional language (if … then …, under the following circumstances …), rather than absolute and definitive language. Making definitive statements is virtually impossible when assessing risk, and reports that exude certainty and predictive confidence should be viewed with legal and scientific skepticism. Producing reports like that is unethical.

To be working ethically, it is important that assessors undertake assessments in keeping with the latest evidence base. Having up-to-date knowledge and expertise is a requirement of the structured professional judgment approach and a requirement for accreditation by the RMA. So the dubious and unethical practice of experts putting themselves forward on the basis of titles (for example, professor) or experience (for example, "I've worked in the field for 30 years"), without having competence in violence risk assessment can be avoided. It is interesting to note that some of the defense assessments that have been put forward in cases have been conducted by individuals who would not meet basic criteria for competence let alone the criteria if they were to apply to be accredited assessors. The question is do the courts realize this.

The Characteristics of Cases

We have undertaken 13 RAO assessments, we have directly assessed another seven RAO cases (although we did not undertake the assessment for the RAO), and we have provided consultation/supervision in another nine cases. We have also put together some basic data that we gathered from accredited assessors on the characteristics of individuals assessed (see Table 16.2). The data in Table 16.2 cover 63 cases and were collected from a brief survey sent to accredited assessors. All but one assessor (who had assessed one case) provided data.

Only one woman has been put forward, and she did not receive an OLR. Most offenders were aged 18–49, with two being children (17 or under), and four aged 50 or over. Most index offences were serious violent or sexual offences, although in at least five cases, index offences were relatively minor (for example, a breach of the peace or a breach of sexual offences prevention order). Only two did not have previous convictions, and many had convictions for serious violent or sexual offending previously. As mentioned earlier, assessments of psychopathy using the Psychopathy Check List Revised (PCL-R; Hare 1991) or a related instrument were undertaken in all cases. The International Personality Disorder Examination (IPDE; Loranger 1999) was used in almost 60 per cent of cases. Structured professional judgment instruments were used in all cases. The favored violence instrument was HCR-20 (Webster et al. 1997) and the favored sexual offending instrument was the RSVP (Hart et al. 2003). Actuarial assessments were used in few cases. The tools used reflect the RMA guidance, but the use of the IPDE highlights concerns about broader aspects of personality pathology than those covered by psychopathy.

Over a third of cases scored 25 or over on the PCL-R (Hare 1991) and 14 per cent scored 30 or over. A half of all cases were assessed as having a definite personality disorder. This may be an underestimate. The vast majority of cases we have had some involvement with personality dysfunction, which was integral to understanding the risk posed. Paraphilias were indicated in almost half of the cases. Learning disabilities and mental illness were issues in fewer cases. These limited data confirm our clinical impression that the majority of individuals put forward for RAOs have clinically complex features, particularly in the domains of personality and sexual psychopathology.

Over three quarters of cases, 49 out of 63, received an OLR, and the sentence imposed closely matched the assessors' conclusion about risk level. There were few cases, five, where there were discrepancies. Defense reports were prepared in a small number of cases, and these rarely followed the standards and guidance set by the RMA, despite a legislative requirement that defense reports should be undertaken in this way. In seven cases, oral evidence was heard before sentencing. These were usually cases where the defense was challenging a report concluding that the offender posed a high risk. Two offenders refused to participate in the assessment. None of the individuals were assessed while detained in a secure hospital, although one such case has arisen since the survey was undertaken.

The number of RAO and OLR cases is tiny when compared to the equivalent sentence in England and Wales—the indeterminate public protection (IPP) sentence. This has been imposed over 6,000 times since it was introduced in 2005, but less than 100 of these individuals have been released (Jacobson and Hough 2010; see also the chapter by Lindsay Thomson in this volume). Not one of the 47 individuals who received an OLR has been released yet, although a small number have completed their tariffs and have applied for release on parole license. Even taking into account that the OLR was introduced in 2006 rather than 2005, and Scotland has a tenth of the population of England and Wales, there is still a huge discrepancy. Why is this? This has not been systematically studied, but we would suggest the following.

Table 16.2 Summary of Risk Assessment Order (RAO) Cases Over the First 4 Years

	Number	Percentage
Total number of cases	63	100.0
Gender		
Male	62	98.4
Female	1	1.6
Age ($n = 57$)		
17 or under	2	3.5
18–21	9	15.8
22–29	15	26.3
30–39	16	28.1
40–49	11	19.3
50–59	4	7.0
Index offences (not mutually exclusive)		
Homicide/attempted homicide	13	20.6
Other non-sexual violence	20	31.7
Sexual offending	41	65.1
Fire-raising	2	3.2
Other offences	4	1.6
Previous convictions		
Any	61	96.8
Non-sexual violence	48	76.2
Sexual offending	31	49.2
Assessment instruments used		
PCL-R, PCL:SV or PCL:YV	63	100.0
IPDE	37	58.7
HCR-20	42	66.7
RSVP	42	66.7
SVR-20	3	4.8
RM 2000	9	14.3
Static 99	2	3.2
SARA	1	1.6
SAM	1	1.6
VRAG	0	0.0
SORAG	0	0.0
Other assessment instruments used	Risk assessment tools for juveniles: ERASOR, AIM2, SAVRY	
	Assessments of sexual behavior: MSI II, SSS, attitude questionnaires	
	Personality assessments: MCMI-III, DSM-IV criteria, Jesness Inventory, Impulsive-Nonconformity Scale	
	Neuropsychological assessments: WASI, WTAR, WAIS-III, D-KEFS	
	Various self-report questionnaires for mental health symptoms	

(Continued)

Table 16.2 Summary of Risk Assessment Order (RAO) Cases Over the First 4 Years (Continued)

	Number	Percentage
Clinical conditions (n = 57)		
Psychopathy (PCL-R 30 or over)	8	14.0
Psychopathy (PCL-R 25 or over)	20	35.1
Personality disorder (any including psychopathy)	29	50.9
Learning disability	7	12.3
Paraphilia	27	47.4
Severe mental illness	2	3.5
Risk conclusion		
High	49	77.8
Medium	14	22.2
Low	0	0.0
Received OLR	49	77.8
Discrepancy between risk conclusion and sentencing	5	7.9
High risk but no OLR	2	3.2
Medium risk but given OLR	3	4.8
Defense reports commissioned	12	19.0
Oral evidence given in court	7	11.1
Subject refused to be interviewed	2	3.2

Notes: AIM2 = Assessment, Intervention and Moving on Project, 2nd edition
D-KEFS = Delis-Kaplan Executive Function System
DSM-IV = Diagnostic and Statistical Manual, 4th edition
ERASOR = Estimate of Risk of Adolescent Sexual Offence Recidivism
HCR-20 = Historical Clinical Risk management – 20
IPDE = International Personality Disorder Examination
MCMI-III = Millon Clinical Multiaxial Inventory, 3rd edition
MSI II = Multiphasic Sex Inventory, 2nd edition
PCL:SV = Psychopathy Check List Screening Version
PCL:YV = Psychopathy Check List Youth Version
PCL-R = Psychopathy Check List – Revised
RM 2000 = Risk Matrix 2000
RSVP = Risk for Sexual Violence Protocol
SAM = Stalking Assessment and Management
SARA = Spousal Assault Risk Assessment
SAVRY = Structured Assessment of Violence Risk in Youth
SORAG = Sex Offence Risk Appraisal Guide
SSS = Sexual Sadism Scale
SVR-20 = Sexual Violence Risk – 20
VRAG = Violence Risk Appraisal Guide
WAIS-III = Wechsler Adult Intelligence Scale, 3rd edition
WASI = Wechsler Abbreviated Scale of Intelligence
WTAR = Wechsler Test of Adult Reading

In England and Wales there is no standardized process for the assessment of risk; in fact the sentence can be imposed by a judge without a risk assessment. The law in England includes over 150 offences as qualifying, and if an offender has a previous conviction for one of these offences, then an IPP sentence will usually be imposed. The system in England is not set around managing risk of serious harm in a practical way that links assessment and management of risk of serious harm. It could be argued that Scotland has been cautious, and not used the OLR enough, although the rate of cases coming forward for OLRs now (about 30 a year) is similar to that initially estimated before the introduction of the legislation. However, it is clear that in England and Wales the sentence is being used far too often for many individuals who do not pose an ongoing risk of serious harm to others. This illustrates that using a blunt approach, which relies primarily on the nature of current and previous convictions and the interpretation of prescriptive legal criteria by judges, is inferior to a system that relies on a thorough, structured, and evidence-based expert assessment of manageability of risk of serious harm to inform judges using less prescriptive legal criteria. However, it should also be noted that the judiciary in Scotland has always been fiercely independent of the legislature and also reluctant to use indeterminate sentences.

From Risk Opinion to Sentence

As previously mentioned, there is a close correlation between the risk assessor's risk categorization and the imposition of an OLR. The legal criteria are so broad as to potentially capture a large number of cases (although not as many as are "netted" in England and Wales). The risk categorization criteria (Table 16.1) add a practical nuance to these legal criteria and incorporate the notion of manageability above. Although some would wish to dislocate the legal criteria from the risk categories, the practical reality is that the two are intimately linked. Although it may seem that the assessor is making the final legal decision, in reality this is not the case. They are providing expert advice to judges, who are experts on sentencing, but not on assessing and managing risk of serious harm.

Oral evidence for sentencing in these cases is unique in Scotland. There is no other criminal sentence that allows for oral evidence to be heard in this way. The expert's assessment may be challenged and counterevidence, including evidence from other experts, may be heard. There have been seven cases where oral evidence has been given so far. All have been cases where experts opined that the individual posed a high risk, and in all cases the final outcome has been the imposition of an OLR. One of us has given oral evidence in such a case (*Her Majesty's Advocate v Johnstone* 2009). The case was not clear-cut and was contentious for a number of reasons. The issues were given a full airing with skilled leading of evidence by the Crown and skilled cross-examination by the defense. The issues of assessment of risk of serious harm and the manageability of risk were scrutinized in detail, and appropriately. There were no apparent problems with translating these complex forensic clinical issues into issues of legal relevance to sentencing.

Post-Sentencing

The risk assessor's task ends at sentencing. But if the offender receives an OLR this is the start of a lifelong process of risk management for the offender, initially in prison and eventually in the community. Within a month of receiving an OLR, the institution where the offender is held, a prison or young offenders' institution, must prepare a risk management plan that has to be submitted to the RMA for approval (Risk Management Authority 2007a). The assessor's report plays a crucial role in this process. Although the report was produced for the purpose of sentencing, arguably it has more utility in relation to subsequent risk management planning, as it comprises a detailed and comprehensive synthesis of all the information relevant to the risk the offender poses. Assessors' reports are used in risk management planning and assessors are usually invited to the risk management planning meeting. Legal purists may question this and assessors are not paid by the courts, or anyone else, to do this. But as mentioned earlier, the key issue is manageability of risk and risk management planning. The assessor, having produced a comprehensive piece of work, is in a position to play a useful role in this process. Although this is not technically part of the assessor's role, would it be ethical to put so much effort (and public money) into producing such an assessment and then not using it fully in planning intervention? On the other hand, is it necessary to get the court (as the commissioner) and the offender (as the subject of the report) to consent to such ongoing work? In the cases we have been involved in so far, the offenders have been happy for this extended involvement to occur.

A further issue arises regarding interventions and treatment. As noted, most OLR cases are clinically complex, with personality disorders (including psychopathy) and paraphilias featuring prominently. The treatment required by such individuals is not straightforward, and programs available in prisons in Scotland at present may not meet the criminogenic needs or attend to the responsivity issues in such cases. There is emerging evidence that properly delivered treatment programs for personality disordered offenders (Dowsett and Craissati 2008), psychopathic offenders (Skeem et al. 2009), and paraphilic offenders (Hanson et al. 2009) can reduce recidivism rates. Staff working with such cases need to be highly skilled, well trained, properly supported, well supervised, and have the right aptitude. Although other jurisdictions have developed specific innovative programs for such offenders, no such programs exist in prisons, secure hospitals, or the community in Scotland. There is only one program for sex offenders with complex clinical features in prison in Scotland, the extended sex offender program, which incorporates work on schema. Programs for sex offenders in the community and prisons in Scotland are being redesigned, and there has been some initial interest in looking at the needs and responsivity issues that arise with such cases. But as things are, there is a serious question mark over whether Scotland can meet the treatment needs of offenders who receive OLRs.

Given that the RAO–OLR process in Scotland is new and unique, it should be subject to evaluation. Are the right offenders being placed on RAOs? Is the assessment identifying individuals who require an OLR? Are the reports useful to sentencers? What are the outcomes of OLR cases in the long term? These questions should be addressed through ongoing research, evaluation, and feedback from sentencing judges.

Pros and Cons of the Scottish Approach

The approach in Scotland has many advantages over approaches adopted elsewhere:

- Assessment of risk is upfront at sentencing and not undertaken at the end of a sentence (unlike sexually violent predator laws in the United States; see the chapters by Eric Janus, John La Fond, and John Petrila in this volume) and the approach in Australia (see the chapters by Patrick Keyzer and Ronli Sifris in this volume).
- There is no overreliance on a particular risk assessment tool or diagnostic assessment (unlike other areas of risk assessment, for example, in relation to sexually violent predators in the United States and individuals with dangerous and severe personality disorder in England and Wales).
- There is a focus on serious harm and manageability following a comprehensive individual assessment, rather than broader criteria based on offences committed (two strikes and you're out) or overreliance on non-practical legal criteria (as is the case with IPPs).
- There is a standardized national approach embedded in legislation and linked to other areas of risk assessment and management through the overarching role of the RMA.
- The complexity of such cases is recognized, thus and correspondingly, the necessity of complex expert assessments.
- Accreditation of experts is competence and evidence-based, rather than based on charismatic authority, status, or experience alone.

Some potential difficulties with the Scottish approach are:

- Assessments are time consuming and expensive. Such resources are not put into assessing similar cases in different contexts—for example, where serious violent and sexual offenders (who were sentenced to determinate sentences before the introduction of the OLR) are released from prison to the community where potential victims will be available. Is it appropriate to put such resources into so few cases? With time will there be enough resources available for the assessment and management of these cases? Or with the limited number of cases, compared to other jurisdictions, is this an efficient way to target resources to the most high-risk offenders?
- The expert could be seen to play the determining role in the sentence imposed. This may be seen as overstepping the mark into ultimate issue testimony, although we have argued earlier that the assessor is the expert in risk management so it is not surprising or inappropriate that judges follow the risk judgments. A close correlation between opinion and outcome is found in other psycholegal and medicolegal contexts.
- Forensic clinical resources for risk management do not match the amount of time and effort put into assessments for sentencing. There is a lack of appropriate treatment programs for offenders with clinically complex features in prisons and community settings.

The clinical complexity of the cases is the elephant in the room. Personality disorder and sexual pathology is very common in this group. It is helpful that the legal criteria and process do not rely on any diagnosis. But the management of such individuals requires sophisticated approaches to management and treatment, which are not well developed in Scotland. To address the needs of such cases the development of programs and approaches requiring specialist psychological, and perhaps psychiatric, input will be required. This will require the development of models where forensic mental health clinicians work alongside psychologists, social workers, and other staff in prisons and the community to develop interventions and programs. Unfortunately in Scotland many forensic mental health clinicians believe their only role is to detain people in hospitals—treating and managing offenders with major mental illness. This has led to the neglect of clinical work with personality-disordered and paraphilic offenders within a criminal justice context, in prison and the community. We would argue that forensic mental health is not just about assessing and treating people with mental health problems who offend, but about understanding, assessing, and treating the psychopathology found in sexual and violent offenders. Individuals who fall within the RAO/OLR group require such input from competent clinicians and practitioners. Such input is not widely available in Scotland.

Conclusions

In Scotland the response to the problem of protecting the public from serious violent and sexual offenders has been to introduce a sentence at conviction that allows for the lifelong risk management of individuals who pose an ongoing risk of serious harm and are unmanageable using less restrictive interventions. A further response has been the introduction of Multi-Agency Public Protection Arrangements (MAPPA) to coordinate the interagency management of the highest risk offenders in the community (Scottish Government 2010), but space does not allow for a description of MAPPA here (these are considered in the chapters by Lindsay Thomson, and by Alex Quinn and John Crichton in this volume). The OLR can only be imposed after a comprehensive structured risk assessment undertaken by an accredited expert following national standards and guidance, which are required by legislation. Although there are some problems and areas for improvement with the RAO/OLR, the approach in Scotland is more ethical (from a legal, human rights, and mental health perspective) than approaches in other jurisdictions, including the approach taken under sexual violent predator laws in the United States, post-sentence imprisonment in Australia, and the IPP sentences ordered in England and Wales.

Based on our experience of assessments, thinking about RAO/OLR cases and discussing these cases with people from various agencies in Scotland, we would suggest that the OLR is appropriate for, and can be used for, the following three types of cases:

1. Extremely dangerous individuals where it is impossible to envisage release to the community ever being safe. Such individuals have repeatedly committed very harmful or escalating offences (for example, sadistic rapes or sexually motivated attempted homicides) despite receiving long prison sentences in the past and despite being subject to robust multiagency risk management in the community.

2. Individuals who pose a risk of serious harm that could not be managed in the community unless they respond to treatment. Such individuals have committed serious sexual and violent offences and as they are at sentencing, could not be managed in the community, even with very robust legally enforceable risk management plans. However, they have the potential to respond to treatment so that indefinite robust risk management in the community could be feasible in the future. Examples are sexually deviant and personality disordered sex offenders who may respond to intensive and long-term programs in prison, who will then require very gradual release with intensive monitoring and supervision in the community.

3. Individuals who could be managed in the community at the point of sentencing, but when alternative sentences do not allow for supervision, monitoring, support, and treatment of sufficient duration or intensity to manage the long-term risk of serious harm. Such offenders may have responded to previous attempts at risk management, but failed very soon after legally enforceable management was withdrawn.

Some assume that it is only the first group that require measures like an OLR. This misses the point that the OLR is about long-term risk management, not just indefinite confinement. If only the first group required such measures, then the assessments would be easy, and not require prolonged expert assessment, as the first group is the no-brainer cases. In fact, there is an argument that for such cases, an RAO should not be required, and the judge should be able to impose an indeterminate sentence without needing such a detailed and thorough assessment. The expertise of assessors really comes into play with groups two and three. To reemphasize, this whole process is about risk management in institutions and the community, not just identifying dangerous people and sequestrating them from society. Risk is dynamic and responds to interventions, but sometimes those interventions require a robust framework.

17
Managing High-Risk Personality Disordered Offenders
Lessons Learned to Date

CAROLINE LOGAN

Introduction

In England and Wales, mental health services for clients with personality disorder diagnoses are being improved and coordinated. There is increasing awareness of the relevance of comorbid personality disorder diagnoses in the identification and treatment of primary mental health problems, such as depression (Newton-Howes et al. 2006), and drug and alcohol abuse and dependence (Coid et al. 2006b). In addition, there is an increasing willingness to identify personality disorder as a main diagnosis in mental health care settings (Department of Health 2009a), because there is growing capacity to engage clients in evidence-based interventions for personality disorder (Davidson 2007) and with some expectation of success (Linehan et al. 2006).

In England and Wales, a number of national policy initiatives have given structure, breadth, validity, and impetus to these developments. In 2003, the National Institute for Mental Health in England (NIMHE) published *Personality Disorder: No Longer a Diagnosis of Exclusion* (NIMHE 2003b), which set out proposals for the development of personality disorder services within general mental health and forensic settings. Prior to the publication of this guidance, those with a diagnosis of personality disorder were routinely unable to access mainstream mental health services. Instead, the burden of their care and support fell upon services dedicated to other conditions (for example, drug and alcohol services) or other agencies such as social work, housing authorities, agencies across the voluntary sector, and the probation and prison services, all of which were ill-equipped to cope (Snowden and Kane 2003). Change was necessary—both to relieve the burden on unprepared services and to improve the expectations of clients leading troubled and problematic lives—and *No Longer a Diagnosis of Exclusion* was the first government commitment to such change at a national level.

In support of the implementation of this proposal, NIMHE also published *Breaking the Cycle of Rejection: The Personality Disorder Capabilities Framework* (NIMHE 2003a). This paper aimed to describe the knowledge and skills required in the mental health and social care systems—statutory and voluntary—to support effective and safe working with clients with personality disorders. *Breaking the Cycle of Rejection* led eventually to the knowledge and understanding framework, a joint Department of Health and Ministry of Justice undertaking with key health and educational providers to establish a national education and training resource for practitioners working directly or indirectly with those with a personality disorder (Institute of Mental Health 2008). For the first time, the prospects of those with personality disorder may improve as services and practitioners prepare themselves to address the unavoidable challenge of their care.

More recent government publications have continued to prioritize mental health care in England and Wales (Department of Health 2010b) and personality disorder remains a priority (Department of Health 2009a) because of the scale of the challenge facing services obliged to work with those with this diagnosis. The management of offenders with a personality disorder is a particular concern because it is in this sector that a substantial amount of work remains to be done (Department of Health 2009b). This is urgent because of the association—real and imagined—between personality disorder and violence (McMurran and Howard 2009). However, in early 2010, it was announced that government funding will be substantially reduced to a program dedicated to providing treatment and intensive risk management to a small group of dangerous and severely personality disordered men (less than 300) in two high secure prisons, and five high and medium secure forensic psychiatric hospitals. Funding is to be reduced because research describes only modest treatment outcomes in the 10 years the program has been running, which do not measure up to the size of the investment made (Tyrer et al. 2010). Instead, money will be diverted to the implementation of a new national strategy for the treatment and management of a much larger number of personality disordered offenders across a wider range of services.

With these developments in mind, this chapter examines current policy and practice in England and Wales in relation to the institutional and community treatment and management of personality disordered offenders and, in particular, those at high risk of harm. The chapter is divided into four parts. In the first part, there is a brief overview of research on the relevance of personality disorder to violence, which will address the issue of why attention to the treatment and management of personality disordered offenders is warranted. In the second part of the chapter, current service provision in England and Wales for high-risk personality disordered offenders is described. This is followed by the description of a novel intensive community risk management service for personality disordered offenders in Merseyside in the northwest of England. In the fourth part of the chapter, there is a review of the challenges involved in establishing and running services for personality disordered offenders that endeavor to balance the support their clients require with the expectation of public protection. The chapter concludes with a summary of what is now known about providing for high-risk personality disordered offenders and a set of recommendations for future developments in this area.

What Is the Link Between Personality Disorder and Risk?

Multiple studies indicate a high prevalence of personality disorder in offenders in general, a high prevalence of personality disorder diagnoses, including psychopathy, in individuals with convictions for violent offences in particular, and an association between personality pathology and violent reoffending, both in terms of the greater likelihood of violent reoffending in those with a diagnosis and more rapid reoffending after release. Each of these areas will be considered briefly, followed by an examination of how and why personality disorder may be linked to violence.

Personality Disorder Is Common Among Offenders

Research indicates a higher prevalence of *Diagnostic and Statistical Manual (DSM-IV-TR;* American Psychiatric Association 2000) personality disorder diagnoses in prison and forensic psychiatric samples compared to samples from community settings (British Psychological Society 2006). Personality disorder diagnoses made using validated assessment tools have been detected in between 42 and 78 per cent of adult male and female prisoners (for example, Fazel and Danesh 2002; Singleton et al. 1998). Also using validated methods, research into mentally disordered offenders suggests that approximately two thirds of males (Blackburn et al. 2003) and over three quarters of females (Logan and Blackburn 2009) have one or more *DSM-IV-TR* personality disorder diagnoses.

Psychopathy, a particular form of severe personality disorder usually measured by the Psychopathy Checklist–Revised (PCL-R; Hare 2003), has been detected (using a 30-plus diagnostic threshold score) in 16 per cent of a sample of over 5,000 North American male prisoners, in 10 per cent of 1,200 North American male forensic psychiatric patients, and in seven per cent of over 1,200 North American female offenders (Hare 2003). The prevalence of psychopathy is lower in some other geographical areas, such as Britain. This appears to be for important cultural reasons relating to the expression of emotions (for example, Cooke 1998); psychopathy has been detected in a little over four per cent of approximately 1,100 British male offenders using the same 30-plus diagnostic cut-off score (Hare 2003). However, the prevalence of this severe personality disorder is higher in studies of men and women in maximum secure settings (Nicholls et al. 2005; Warren et al. 2003), even in Britain (Blackburn and Coid 1998).

Personality Disorder Is Common Among Violent Offenders

In studies of men and women who are violent, personality disorders are diagnosed at an elevated rate (Watzke et al. 2006), especially the *DSM-IV-TR* cluster B disorders, antisocial and borderline in particular. In studies of personality disordered men and women, violence is detected at a higher than expected rate; individuals with diagnoses of cluster B personality disorders have been found to be 10 times more likely to have a criminal conviction than those without, whereas individuals with cluster A and cluster C personality disorders showed no increased risk of violent offending (Coid et al. 2006a).

In a Finnish study, a diagnosis of antisocial personality disorder increased the odds ratio of homicidal violence by 10-fold in men and by 50-fold in women (Eronen et al. 1996). Borderline personality disorder is associated with a more general range of criminal activities (Reid 2009) but with domestic violence in particular (Dutton 2002). Psychopathy has also been linked to the seriousness of violent and sexually violent offending (Porter and Woodworth 2006). Unfortunately, other personality disorders have been subject to less research scrutiny, despite their potential clinical relevance in the individual case (McMurran and Howard 2009).

Reoffending Is Common Among Offenders with Personality Pathology

Antisocial and borderline personality disorders as well as psychopathy have been strongly linked to general and violent recidivism in men (for example, Hare et al. 2000; Hemphill et al. 1998) and women (Nicholls et al. 2005). Hiscoke et al. (2003) noted an association between violent recidivism and schizoid personality disorder also. Jamieson and Taylor (2004), in a 12-year follow-up of 204 patients discharged from high secure forensic psychiatric facilities, reported that the odds of committing a serious reoffence were seven times higher for those with a personality disorder diagnosis compared to those with a mental illness diagnosis; 38 per cent of discharged personality disordered patients were reconvicted, 26 per cent for a serious offence. A meta-analysis of studies using the PCL-R showed that offenders diagnosed as psychopathic were three times more likely than nonpsychopaths to commit further offences and about four times more likely to commit further violent offences (Hemphill et al. 1998). In a two-year follow-up study of 278 English and Welsh offenders, Hare et al. (2000) noted that the reconviction rate among those scoring 25 or more on the PCL-R was 82 per cent for general offences and 38 per cent for violent offences; the reoffending rate for those scoring below 25 on the PCL-R was 40 per cent for general offences and three per cent for violent offences. However, while individuals with personality disorder are more likely than those with mental illness to reoffend after discharge from hospital, the comorbid presentation of personality disorder and mental illness appears more predictive of future violence than personality disorder alone (Dean et al. 2006).

The Functional Link Between Personality Disorder and Violence

Although correlations clearly exist between personality disorder and violence, the nature of that association is not clear: Does a history of violence make a personality disorder diagnosis more likely, does personality disorder cause individuals to be violent, or are personality disorder and violence linked through a third unknown variable? Duggan and Howard (2009) suggest four reasons that may account for why a functional link between personality disorder and violence has been difficult to establish (see also Haynes 1992).

First, evidence for the covariation of personality disorder and violence exists for some presentations (for example, antisocial personality disorder) but not others (for example, avoidant or obsessive-compulsive personality disorders). Therefore, the currently available research is too narrow to support a general conclusion about the nature of the link. Second, determining functional, even causal, links between personality pathology and violence requires evidence that the pathology preceded the violence. The absence of sufficient longitudinal studies of personality and violence limits this specific line of investigation. Third, it is difficult to exclude alternative causes of violence apart from personality disorder; establishing a causal link between personality pathology and violence in studies to date has been complicated by noise, which has not been effectively defined or controlled in research. Finally, causal links may be verified if there is a logical connection—an understandable mechanism by which the personality disorder might generate violence—which thus far, has been given only some consideration (for a review, see McMurran and Howard 2009).

Further research is required to address the first three of the aforementioned points, but the final point about the logical connection between personality disorder and violence is worthy of some further consideration here. Why? The key to effective risk management is an understanding of the link between the risk factors identified as relevant in the individual case and violence—the critical task of risk formulation. (Logan and Johnstone 2010). We do not understand. A poor understanding of the links between risk factors and violence can lead to unduly restrictive risk management strategies are likely (Reid and Thorne 2007). Therefore, what hypotheses exist about the logical connection between personality disorder and violence?

Logan and Johnstone (2010) suggest that hypotheses can be generated about the connection between personality pathology and violence based on an understanding of how the different pathologies render an individual vulnerable to psychological hurt or emotional injury by another person, creating an impetus for violence. Using the personality disorder types proposed for the *DSM-5* (American Psychiatric Association 2010), the authors plot possible explanatory links between disorder and violence. For example, the antisocial/psychopathic individual is rendered vulnerable to injury because of a fragile and inflated self-regard, a difficulty in regulating strong emotions such as anger and guilt, and interpersonal relationships that are dominated by the fear of experiences such as envy and shame (Kernberg 1998). Injury, in the form of actual or perceived criticism—threatened egotism (Baumeister et al. 1996)—creates intolerable emotions (such as shame, envy, and humiliation) that have the capacity to destroy the fragile ego. In a self-righteous response, the individual punishes the perceived aggressor in a way that is proportionate in nature and scale to the injury perceived. The success of this usually excessive retaliatory response repairs the injured self-regard, restoring the individual to a position of precarious domination.

In contrast, the borderline or emotionally dysregulated individual is made vulnerable by an incomplete or poorly integrated sense of self, by labile and poorly controlled affect, and by a high level of social anxiety (Livesley 2003). Injury, in the form of actual or perceived rejection or abandonment, creates intolerable emotions such as distress, emptiness, loss of identity, or fear of annihilation. Efforts to cope with these intolerable feelings (such as through self-harm, drug or alcohol abuse) offer only short-term relief and usually compound rather than resolve the underlying difficulty. When the injury is extreme or the individual especially vulnerable, impulsive, emotionally reactive rage against the perpetrator of the threatened loss may occur, either to prevent the loss or punish the attempt. However, feelings of helplessness are compounded not resolved by such action—nothing has substantially changed as a consequence of violence—and so the cycle of vulnerability continues.

Logan and Johnstone (2010) elaborate on these and other possible associations between personality pathology and violence, in the context of a discussion about risk formulation—the process of understanding the underlying mechanism of a presenting problem (violence) in order to create hypotheses for change (risk management plans). However, although the underlying mechanism is still the subject of speculation, without any effort at understanding, risk management may be insensitive to the particular needs of the individual and therefore unresponsive to the circumstances that might trigger a recurrence of violence (Dowsett and Craissati 2008). Further, offenders are prone to disengagement from risk management that they perceive to be insensitive and disproportionate to their risks, needs, and circumstances (Kemshall 2008). Therefore, attention to this issue is warranted; risk management with personality disordered offenders has to be underpinned by an understanding of the person with the potential for harm and of the ways in which critical risk factors, like personality pathology, influence that potential.

Concluding Comments

This section has outlined the literature indicating that personality disorder is common among offenders and more common still among offenders who are violent. On the basis of the evidence provided, the management of personality disordered offenders is already a core task of professionals working in criminal justice and mental health settings, even if those professionals are unaware of the extent to which this is the case. This section has also proposed that the link between personality disorder and violence may be understood by considering the particular vulnerabilities underlying each of the disorders.

It is suggested that it is only through such an understanding that sensitivity and proportionality can be achieved in the risk management plans made for these offenders. However, an understanding of the relevance and role of personality disorder in risk of violence has not been a priority in research to date and the quality and efficacy of risk management may be undermined as a result. The following section examines current service provision for high-risk offenders, and high-risk personality disordered offenders in particular.

Existing Services for High-Risk Personality Disordered Offenders

The challenge of risk management with personality disordered offenders is preventing or limiting future harm by better managing the risk; reducing the influence of risk factors on behavior while increasing the role played by protective factors (de Vogel et al. 2009). However, this challenge needs to be faced in a criminal justice system that appears increasingly intent on incarcerating or otherwise incapacitating those at risk of harming others, regardless of the consequences for the offender. What services currently exist for the management of high-risk personality disordered offenders? This section will begin with a very general overview of services for high-risk offenders as a whole.

High-Risk Offenders

The level of risk posed by a convicted offender has a bearing on the sentence imposed on him or her by the courts (see Rajan Darjee and Katharine Russell's chapter in this volume). High-risk offenders are broadly defined as those who have committed a violent or sexual offence and who are assessed as more likely than not to do so again. Thus, past behavior influences judgments about the individual's propensity to act in a similar way in the future (Monahan 1981). However, the determination of risk in an individual is at best an inconsistent and haphazard affair involving a judgment based on his or her characteristics, the nature of the offences before the courts, the seriousness of these offences, and the likelihood of reoffending (Kemshall 2008).

In the main, the courts rely on probation reports to inform decision-making about risk-based sentencing, that is, sentences passed on individuals with the express purpose of restricting their movements and limiting their opportunity to exercise the harm it is thought they have the potential to demonstrate. Probation services in England and Wales utilize the Offender Assessment System (OASys) of risk assessment (Howard et al. 2006), plus the Risk Matrix 2000 (Kingston et al. 2008) for sexual offenders and the Spousal Assault Risk Assessment Guide (Kropp et al. 1999) for domestic violence perpetrators, to try to encapsulate these variables. However, restricted time and resources and experience can limit the quality of the assessments undertaken (Kemshall 2008), increasing the risk of poor decision-making. Also the Criminal Justice Act 2003, which underpins sentencing in this jurisdiction, fails to define key terms such as *significant risk, serious harm,* and *dangerousness* (Kemshall 2008). In addition, the assessment of individual risk is fraught with significant statistical, ethical, and legal concerns (see David Cooke and Christine Michie's chapter in this volume) largely unappreciated by those who use such tools and make decisions based on the findings reported. Psychiatric or psychological opinion is sought in a small number of cases, usually where future risk is unclear due to mental health factors. Consequently, risk-based sentencing may be inadequately grounded in what might be regarded as best practice in risk assessment. This raises questions about what a high-risk offender actually is and whether more offenders are rated as high risk than actually are as a precaution against the consequences of getting it wrong (Kemshall 2008).

Two sentences are available to the courts in England and Wales for those judged to pose a high risk of serious reoffending but who are not eligible for a mandatory life sentence. The first is an indefinite sentence of imprisonment where the parole board on the basis of evidence of reduced risk and an effective risk management plan determine eventual release into the community on long-term license (for at least 10 years). Such sentences are called indeterminate public protection sentences (IPPS; see the chapter by Lindsay Thomson in this volume). They amount to discretionary life sentences for those whose index offence could warrant a determinate sentence of 10 years or more. IPPS have been available to the courts in England and Wales since 2003. The Scottish courts have a different sentence, an order for lifelong restriction, which has been available since 2005 and serves essentially the same function except that risk management is lifelong (see the chapters by Innes Fyfe and Yvonne Gailey, and by Rajan Darjee and Katharine Russell in this volume). At the end of July 2010, the prison population in England and Wales was 85,009 (Howard League for Penal Reform 2010), around 6,000 of whom are men serving IPPS.

The second option available to the courts is a finite or determinate sentence followed by a comprehensive range of supervision requirements including license conditions, tagging, exclusions, and registers. Violent offenders can be supervised after release from custody for up to five years and sexual offenders for up to eight years. The objective of supervision is to reduce the opportunities for high-risk offenders to reoffend by restricting and controlling their activities and creating legitimate options for surveillance, monitoring, and, if required, compulsory treatment.

Prior to 2000, the community management of high-risk offenders was plagued by the difficulty of creating effective cooperation and information sharing between different agencies (for example, prison, probation, police, also mental health services, housing, and social services). In 2000, Multi-Agency Public Protection Arrangements (MAPPA) were created to support the community-based supervision of offenders (Criminal Justice and Court Services Act 2000) thought to be high risk even after punishment by a custodial sentence. On the establishment of MAPPA, the probation, police, and prison services were identified as the lead agencies in managing the cross-service collaboration in each of the administrative police and probation areas across England and Wales. Subsequently, the Criminal Justice Act 2003 imposed a duty upon health care services and other agencies that were not part of the formal criminal justice system to cooperate with MAPPA. This system of multiagency cooperation in the risk management of high-risk offenders continues to this day.

The aim of the MAPPA is public protection—to reduce serious offending by convicted sexual and violent offenders after their release into the community by multiagency collaboration in their control and rehabilitation. The extent of an offender's involvement with MAPPA is dependent on the outcome of assessments of his risk of harm to others and the complexity of the risk management plans that are required to contain the risks identified. There are three levels of risk management, Level 1 to Level 3, and offenders will be moved up and down levels as appropriate.

Offenders allocated to Level 1 MAPPA are subject to ordinary management arrangements applied by whichever single agency is tasked with supervising him or her. Information sharing may take place between relevant agencies but the expectation is that these individuals, generally assessed as presenting a low or moderate level of risk, can be managed by a single agency. Offenders allocated to Level 2 MAPPA are subject to multiagency management. The risk management plans for these offenders require the active involvement of several agencies through regular multi-agency public protection panel (MAPPP) meetings whose purpose is to ensure such plans are implemented and reviewed regularly. Offenders are of concern but the complexity of their risk management requirements is less than that of Level 3 offenders. Therefore, offenders subject to Level 3 MAPPA are high (or very high) risk, their risks to others are regarded as potentially imminent, and they are difficult and complex cases, either because of their resistance to supervision and interventions or because of the high profile nature of their past offences. Consequently, senior criminal justice personnel are required to attend panel meetings to make decisions about management, including the allocation of costly resources (for example, police surveillance, specialized accommodation, specialist interventions). Level 3 MAPPA endeavors both to prevent reoffending and to ensure that public confidence in the criminal justice system is maintained. In 2008–09, two per cent ($n = 924$) of all offenders in England and Wales subject to MAPPA were Level 3—the "critical few"—and 22 per cent ($n = 10,000$) to Level 2 arrangements.

Therefore, Level 3 MAPPA constitutes the primary approach to the management of high-risk offenders. Does it work? Evaluations of the effectiveness of MAPPA have been undertaken (for example, Wood and Kemshall 2010), but they are imperfect for a number of reasons. An important problem in determining effectiveness is differences of opinion about what constitutes a good outcome. For example, a recall to prison in response to a judgment of increasing or imminent risk may be viewed as a negative outcome: supervision has failed, the offender has not succeeded in the community, a costly custodial place will now be required. However, recall may also be regarded as a positive outcome: supervision and monitoring have resulted in action that has prevented a serious further offence (Wood and Kemshall 2010).

An additional problem is that evaluation may be affected by disagreement about what is the primary purpose of MAPPA. For example, to the police, the primary purpose of MAPPA is public protection through control and monitoring. Probation and mental health services, on the other hand, are more likely to place the highest value on rehabilitation and positive risk management through treatment and support (Wood and Kemshall 2010).

In general, despite its imperfections, MAPPA is regarded as effective and valuable in the management of high-risk offenders (Wood et al. 2007). However, those limitations are easily exposed when media and public expectations about risk management arise following serious further offences. One recent example illustrates the point.

In June 2008, Dano Sonnex and an accomplice broke into a London flat looking for money for drugs. The flat was occupied by two young male French students, who were horrifically murdered in the course of the robbery. Sonnex was 23 at the time and had only recently been released from prison following convictions when he was 17 years of age for multiple offences of violence and robbery. Due to failures in communication, Sonnex was regarded as a medium-risk offender toward the end of his sentence and therefore was not subject to MAPPA on his release. Consequently, he returned to the community without safeguards and he began offending almost immediately. A number of arrests for minor offences led to an order for his recall to prison two weeks before the murders. The recall was not followed up with any urgency because he was not thought to be high risk of harm, and the murders were committed while he was at large.

The public, media, and political response to this case was highly critical: the murders should not have happened because Sonnex should have been in prison (Worrall 2009). The public protection system faltered, subjected itself to extensive review, changed and disciplined key personnel, and carried on with renewed dedication to public protection in a society increasingly intolerant of what was seen as the failure of agencies to keep this promise (Ministry of Justice 2009).

This case and others like it raise questions about how realistic it is to expect that the management of high-risk offenders can be achieved without failure. First, how feasible is it to expect full and prompt communication about complex offenders among multiple agencies with different agendas in the control and resettlement of offenders? Second, how can public protection be achieved by chronically underresourced services? (For example, Sonnex's probation officer had a caseload that was over four times the recommended size.) Third, how can public protection from high-risk offenders be achieved in an environment where public, media, and politicians have unrealistic expectations of what the critical task of risk assessment can really achieve? These questions have yet to be answered but the public protection system as described carries on anyway. Is it any better prepared to manage the risks posed by personality disordered offenders?

High-Risk Personality Disordered Offenders

In July 1996 in Kent, Lin Russell, aged 45, her two daughters, six-year-old Megan and nine-year-old Josie and their dog Lucy, were tied up and beaten with a hammer during an attempted robbery. Lin, Megan, and Lucy died but, despite serious head injuries, Josie survived. In 1998, Michael Stone was convicted of murdering Lin and Megan, and of attempting to murder Josie.

Stone had a complicated mental health history and was in contact with a number of services among which communication was poor. His history was complicated by the fact that his principle diagnosis was antisocial personality disorder, which was thought not to be amenable to treatment. Treatment was offered for other conditions (for example, drug and alcohol problems, symptoms of psychosis) but not for what was thought to be the underlying problem. The treatability of his antisocial personality disorder was a critical requirement for detention under the then Mental Health Act (South East Coast Strategic Health Authority et al. 2006). Its untreatable nature meant that Stone could not be detained against his will, he was not provided with treatment for his main presenting problem and, critically, he was at liberty to offend despite evidence of what appeared to be escalating risk.

The government's precipitate response to this event was the publication in 1999 of *Managing Dangerous People with Severe Personality Disorder: Proposals for Policy Development* (Home Office 1999). In this document, proposals were made for the detention and intensive treatment of a small number of individuals with severe personality disorder who pose significant risks of harm to others as a direct result of personality pathology, regardless of their desire to receive treatment and despite only modest evidence of the potential treatability of their conditions. This paper eventually led to the formation of the Dangerous People with Severe Personality Disorder (DSPD) Programme, a joint undertaking by the Department of Health, the Ministry of Justice, and the National Offender Management Service. Subsequently, a number of treatment facilities in high and medium secure prison and psychiatric settings were established across England. Eventually, in 2007, the Mental Health Act was amended to include provision for care under the act regardless of whether treatment was likely to be successful or not. Therefore, concerns about treatability can no longer exclude any person—not just personality disordered offenders—from care in a mental health facility in England and Wales. This package of measures is intended to address the risk-related needs of personality disordered offenders, specifically, those thought to be most at risk of harming others.

DSPD units were established in two category A prisons (Whitemoor and Frankland) and two high secure psychiatric hospitals (Rampton and Broadmoor). More recently, DSPD-funded beds were opened in three medium secure units and a 12-bedded unit for women was opened in HMP Low Newton. In total, approximately 450 men and women have experienced DSPD Programme treatment over the last 10 years, involving a comprehensive range of structured interventions, mainly cognitive-behavioral in orientation, designed to treat and manage personality disorder and related problems linked to risk of harm.

The criteria for entry to one of the DSPD Programme units are:

1. that offenders are more likely than not to commit a violent or sexual offence within five years, which might lead to serious physical or psychological harm from which the victim would find it difficult if not impossible to recover;
2. that offenders have a significant or severe disorder of personality as defined by a high PCL-R score or a number of different personality disorder diagnoses; and
3. that the risk of harm presented appears to be functionally linked to the significant personality disorder (Duggan and Howard 2009). This functional link is not clearly specified but is taken to mean that the disorder of personality is the likely main cause of the harmful behavior (Duggan and Howard 2009). Prisoners eligible for a DSPD Programme facility may be transferred to Whitemoor or Frankland prisons if they meet these admission criteria. Alternatively, if near the end of their prison sentence, consideration may be given to transfer under the Mental Health Act 2007 to one of the hospital DSPD Programme sites for treatment there, a controversial option akin to preventive detention. Mentally disordered offenders already in secure forensic facilities may be transferred to a hospital DSPD site if specialist treatment for severe personality disorder is thought necessary to reduce risk.

The DSPD Programme sites have been subject to various forms of evaluation since their inception. However, evaluation has been problematic because of the comprehensive nature of the interventions on offer, the wide range of outcomes that could indicate positive change, the different treatments available at the different DSPD sites, and the very long-term nature of the treatment on offer.

Overall, the program has not been regarded as a success (Tyrer et al. 2010). The considerable costs involved in providing treatment to such a small group of men appear not to have been justified by the modest gains made from treatment so far. In March 2010, the government announced that funding for the seven sites for men would be scaled back to pay for initiatives for personality disordered offenders in other areas. The DSPD services are in the process of reconfiguring and reducing their capacity, becoming smaller but more efficient, to treat a reduced population of men. So where can high-risk personality disordered offenders go now for specialized treatment?

There are a small number of prison-based therapeutic communities for men (and women) with personality disorders. HMP Grendon, for example, which has approximately 225 places, has been treating male offenders with complex personality disorders and serious offending histories for over 40 years and has been an accredited therapeutic community prison treatment program since 2003. The model of treatment is based on that which was used at the London Henderson Hospital, incorporating key elements of positive, supportive, and honest relationships; responsibility for behavior and offending; and the importance of trust and openness. There are just over 500 places in prison-based therapeutic communities in England and Wales, including HMP Grendon. Therapeutic communities are seen as both progression services for those who have completed treatment in a DSPD unit and as treatment facilities in their own right for high-risk personality disordered offenders (Joseph 2008).

There are also a small number of NHS forensic mental health facilities that offer care for offenders with a primary diagnosis of personality disorder. Each of the high secure hospitals in England admits mentally disordered offenders with personality disorder (not including those into DSPD-funded beds). In addition, there is some provision in medium and low secure forensic psychiatric care for personality disordered offenders. For example, the East Midlands Centre for Forensic Mental Health based at Arnold Lodge in Leicester has 22 beds dedicated to the care of personality disordered offenders and an extremely experienced staff group. There are, in addition, a small number of private forensic mental health facilities that offer beds for offenders with severe personality disorder. However, inpatient beds for personality disordered offenders in mental health facilities outside of high secure hospitals are very limited. Further, research into and evaluations of the efficacy of secure forensic care are limited and, where research exists, not strongly supportive of the treatment gains possible with this group (for example, Davies et al. 2007). Specialist provision for the support of personality disordered offenders in the community, the subject of the following section, is more limited still (Dowsett and Craissati 2008).

Concluding Comments

Dowsett and Craissati (2008) urge services to acknowledge and try to understand the importance of personality disorder in the assessment and management of the risks posed by some offenders. To fail to do so, they argue, creates the significant possibility that assessments will highlight a too-narrow range of risks and needs, and consequently, that interventions—treatment, supervision, monitoring, and victim safety plans—may be redundant, ineffective, destabilizing, and risk increasing rather than risk reducing. Yet the capacity to take personality disorder into account in already overstretched criminal justice services is limited.

Further, the certainty of what action to take once personality disorder is recognized is limited by an inadequate evidence base on which to plan and evaluate provision. Therefore, significant gaps exist in the care of high-risk personality disordered offenders despite improvements to the legal framework (such as in the amended Mental Health Act 2007) allowing intervention without the consent of the client and without the expectation of change in accordance with traditional notions of treatment. So, where to from here? In the following sections, an innovative and intensive risk management service for personality disordered offenders released from prison will be described, followed by a summary of the challenges of undertaking rehabilitation and public protection with this group.

A Study in Community Risk Management of Personality Disordered Offenders

Best practice in the management of high-risk offenders involves a range of variously controlling, restrictive, intensive/intrusive treatment, supervision, and monitoring techniques (Kemshall 2008). Examples of such techniques include proactive pre-release planning, supervised accommodation, accredited programs addressing criminogenic and welfare needs, police intelligence, targeted surveillance, victim protection, clearly specified boundaries, and swift enforcement in the event of indications of failure. Best practice in the management of personality disordered offenders involves (a) an understanding of the potential role of personality disorder in the risk-related needs of the offender, (b) effective assessment in order that the right people are identified for specialist risk management techniques, and (c) a coordinated range of interventions targeting offending behavior, mental health problems, and social functioning (Dowsett and Craissati 2008). In addition, Dowsett and Craissati (2008) emphasize that, as it is unlikely that any one agency could appropriately or adequately address the range of needs of personality disordered offenders, multiagency working with this group is essential. If a service was to incorporate all of these best practice features, what might it look like?

Resettle

Resettle is a prototype community risk assessment and intensive case management service based in Merseyside in the northwest of England; it promotes the enhanced risk management of high risk personality disordered offenders subject to MAPPA. Resettle aims to enhance the life opportunities of these offenders and aid their successful integration into the community. This service is for male offenders who have been released from prison following convictions for serious violent or sexual offences, who have one or more personality disorder diagnoses, and whose high risk of harming others is believed to be linked to their personality pathology. Resettle is managed by a board consisting of representatives from local probation and mental health services, police and housing agencies, Her Majesty's Prison Service, and the service user and carer community, and it implements and supports the work of the MAPPPs that oversee the risk management of all Resettle clients. The Criminal Justice and Courts Services Act 2000 and the Criminal Justice Act 2003 underpin the work of Resettle, as does the Department of Health guidance *Personality Disorder: No Longer a Diagnosis of Exclusion* (Department of Health 2003). Therefore, a comprehensive legal and policy governance framework guides Resettle and, using existing evidence, it aspires to provide a restrictive but effective service that will reduce the offending of its clients and protect the public. In this respect, Resettle mirrors the objectives of the DSPD Programme.

However, Resettle deals with offenders who have to be released from prison into the community because their determinate sentences have expired as opposed to those still incarcerated. In addition, while the future of the residential DSPD units is now in question, the future of Resettle is safe until the end of an agreed four-year evaluation period when Resettle clients will be compared with a treatment-as-usual control group on a variety of indicators of possible change. Thereafter, on the basis of whatever evidence exists on the success or otherwise of this prototype service, the decision will be made on whether to replicate it elsewhere.

Referrals for Resettle are taken directly from Merseyside MAPPA. The service works intensively with men subject to Level 2 and 3 MAPPA. Clients are housed in approved probation premises while their work with Resettle is ongoing and until they are safe to move on to more appropriate accommodations. They are transported from their accommodations into the Resettle center each day to undergo a range of relevant group and individual therapies, education, and training work related to the acquisition of basic life skills (such as employment), as well as treatment, victim- and offence-focused work, support, and guidance.

All work with Resettle clients is based on a social therapy model, borrowing heavily from the Dutch *terbeschikkingstelling* (or TBS) model of intervention with offenders (de Boer and Gerrits 2007). A range of interventions is available, predominantly cognitive-behavior therapy based, and its focus is on recovery and "good lives" (Prochaska et al. 1992; Ward et al. 2006). Practitioners in Resettle come from a range of backgrounds including probation, psychology, mental health nursing, and social therapy, and have been chosen because of both their individual skills and experiences. and their own personality characteristics.

How Resettle Tries to Work

Resettle works by ensuring that what underpins engagement with individual clients and specific interventions is a sound understanding of the nature of the personality pathology of the individual and its possible links to his offending—violent or sexually violent—behavior. This understanding is used to inform the choice of techniques used to engage the client in the service as well as the nature, range, and timing of the different interventions required during the course of the first two years of contact. A range of assessment techniques are used to gather the information needed to generate this formulation and to keep it up to date.

First, the client is a critical source of information and as such, considerable efforts are made to engage with him and to maintain his engagement within a collaborative working relationship. Second, a range of structured and validated tools are used as a framework for information gathering, including semistructured interviews, self-report questionnaires, and structured observations. Third, interventions on offer are evidence-based and intended to manage personality disorder symptoms directly (for example, cognitive analytic therapy) or to address some of its most negative consequences (for example, interventions on thinking skills work or drug and alcohol abuse), delivered in a setting in which interactions are governed by the principles of social therapy. Finally, practitioners deliver interventions with the clients and support one another through regular team meetings, reflective practice, and clinical supervision. The supervision of clients when not at the Resettle center involves a range of supportive and controlling techniques, which are managed by multiple agencies—police, housing, mental health services, employment agencies, voluntary groups (for example, Circles of Support and Accountability) in addition to Resettle—all coordinated by MAPPA.

Observations

Resettle is an example of a well-resourced, community-based, intensive risk management service for high-risk personality disordered offenders who would otherwise have routine MAPPA Level 3 supervision, which is intensive but not specific to the demands posed and experienced by severely personality disordered offenders. Resettle is still in the pilot phase—its evaluation is ongoing. Clients in Resettle were randomly selected to participate from all those eligible to do so in the Merseyside area. Evaluation is therefore by a randomized controlled trial and this thorough form of testing is the raison d'être of the project: without such comprehensive testing, in the absence of evidence that the Resettle approach works, it is not worthwhile financially, clinically, and even ethically.

Whether and how Resettle works to maximize both public protection and the rehabilitation of this category of offender awaits description. However, its work is underpinned by the principles of best practice in managing high-risk personality disordered offenders (Dowsett and Craissati 2008; Kemshall 2008), embodying the most up-to-date literature on what works or could work with this group. Resettle is a positive development in offender management. However, the following section examines why well-founded and resourced services like Resettle could still fail to deliver the outcomes desired.

The Challenge of Managing High-Risk Personality Disordered Offenders

This chapter has examined the management of high-risk personality disordered offenders in England and Wales at the current time. Existing services for this group have been described briefly and the paucity of empirical evidence identifying what works has been highlighted. Yet personality disordered offenders exist in the criminal justice system in very high numbers and the existence of a direct association between violence and personality disorder is widely acknowledged, even if the nature of the association remains poorly understood. Why is more not known about how to treat and manage this group of individuals? The following section identifies a number of the challenges facing current and future services trying to manage high-risk personality disordered offenders.

Resisting the Possibility of Change

For a substantial period, clients with personality disorder were thought to have lifelong conditions that defied effective treatment. Slowly, this view has been challenged and *Personality*

Disorder: No Longer a Diagnosis of Exclusion (NIMHE 2003b) was a national response intended to consolidate a change in attitude towards this client group. Increasingly, research supports the view that clients with personality disorder can change in response to a variety of coordinated and psychologically informed interventions (Livesley 2003). However, the link between offending behavior and complex clinical presentations featuring personality pathology has resisted this increasing optimism about the possibility of change (McMurran and Howard 2009) and the treatment of offenders with psychopathic personality disorder has probably been most resistant of all (Wong 2000). Therefore, one quite basic challenge to the establishment of specialist provision for offenders with personality disorder has been the lack of empirical evidence about the possibility of meaningful change through intervention. Why identify personality disorder when the evidence base supports treatment interventions for more understandable problems like thinking skills (Friendship et al. 2002) or sexual offending (Hanson et al. 2002)? The therapeutic pessimism engendered by such a poor evidence base may be responsible for the relative unwillingness of practitioners to identify personality disorder in their clients and address the special needs these clients have (Dowsett and Craissati 2008). The prospect of turning personality disordered offenders into the new social pariahs after sex offenders may be a further discouragement. Services that highlight the special needs of personality disordered offenders risk identifying, isolating, and shaming these clients the way severe restrictions on the activities of sexual offenders have limited their access to the kinds of support and contacts with others that might in fact act to limit their risks (Farmer and Mann 2010).

The Empty Promise of Public Protection

Dowsett and Craissati (2008: 194) observe that the probation service has only been subject to intense public scrutiny and criticism "since it explicitly reframed itself as a public protection service rather than as an offender welfare service." The authors do not regard this attention as coincidental, suggesting instead that when agencies make unrealistic promises about outcomes they cannot deliver, the public and others are bound to feel betrayed when offenders supervised in the community commit serious further offences. Dowsett and Craissati (2008) ponder whether the development of treatment and risk management services for high-risk personality disordered offenders, which promise better than average public protection, will also experience the same effect. The promise of so much sets the service up to fail in a society increasingly intolerant of risk (Garland 2001). A well-resourced service, with good and effective partnership working may be able to contain such anxieties. However, less well-resourced and functioning services may use more control and restraint techniques for risk management than treatment and support, a precautionary move against the fear of failure, which might paradoxically increase rather than decrease risk as offenders rail against restraints disproportionate to the risks they actually pose (Kemshall 2008).

Risk Assessment: The Achilles Heel of Public Protection

The risk assessment industry has established itself on the premise that risky individuals can be identified and prevented from exercising their harmful potential. However, Hart et al. (2007) and David Cooke and Christine Michie's chapter in this volume highlight the problems of predicting risk in the individual case; risk assessment tools cannot be used to identify individuals who are at risk of harming others. Consequently, tools used by practitioners not confident about their clinical judgment about such a contentious subject as risk of violence or practitioners discouraged by their managers from exercising such judgment, may either fail to identify the risks of some people (like Dano Sonnex) or overestimate the risks posed by others in exercise of the precautionary principle (Hood and Jones 1996, and see Bernadette McSherry and Patrick Keyzer's introductory chapter to this volume). This is a problem because, however good the system of multiagency cooperation in risk management might be on paper, if the wrong people are in the system and if the system is informed by practitioners who have no confidence in their own judgments or the judgments of others, it cannot possibly be effective.

The Rhetoric of Partnership (Kemshall 2008: 85)

Partnership underpins multi-agency cooperation in the management of high-risk offenders. Dowsett and Craissati (2008) suggest that multiagency cooperation is particularly important in the management of personality disordered offenders because no single agency can manage the myriad of problems they experience and present. Yet, the agencies among which partnership working is expected have very different aims and objectives in the management of high-risk offenders (Kemshall 2008). Disagreements and fuzzy boundaries between responsible and relevant authorities create the potential for distracting disagreements and missed opportunities to cooperate, joined-up worrying (Lieb 2003) rather than joined-up working.

Managing High-Risk Personality Disordered Offenders on a Shoestring

A last and perennial challenge to the development of public services is accessing adequate resources. The chief inspector of probation in England noted the chronic underfunding of offender management services, which is becoming increasingly out of step with public and political expectations of what can and should be delivered in terms of public protection (Her Majesty's Inspectorate of Probation 2007). Chronic underfunding is a threat to the management of high-risk offenders who require extra resources and additional vigilance; practitioners with inadequate time to do the job well are at increased risk of errors, inflated levels of sickness absence, and not having the time to work proactively with this group (Kemshall 2008). The current economic climate, where tens of thousands of public sector jobs are expected to be lost while the country seeks economic recovery from the recession, does not engender any hope that resources for high-risk offenders will improve soon.

Conclusions

Services for clients with personality disorder is a government commitment in England and Wales (for example, Department of Health 2010b), promising a cross-departmental strategy that will ensure improvements in recognition, access, and intervention to enhance health and social outcomes, public protection, and the social inclusion of those diagnosed with this condition. Such a strategy will be based on the best available evidence of treatment efficacy—such as it is—in order to ensure early intervention and ongoing risk management for offenders, whether in custody or the community. Given the challenges identified earlier, not least that of inadequate resources, how can such provision be achieved?

At the core of work with personality disordered offenders has to be partnership working—multiagency collaboration enshrined and required by law. The reality of partnership working is that it is far from perfect; MAPPA works well but mistakes are still made. However, multiagency cooperation offers the best possible chance of having the most relevant people around the table, applying their skills to the care and management of a highly complex group of individuals who are a challenge to provide for. More research and published service evaluation is essential to inform the working practices recommended. It is only through knowing what works—and critically, what does not work—that effective interventions and services will be designed and critical formats like MAPPA will improve. The future of Resettle is unclear, but its commitment to comprehensive evaluation in the form of a randomized controlled trial is an investment in the future of services for personality disordered offenders worldwide.

Services for high-risk offenders would do well to promise slightly less. Services that promise public protection set themselves up to fail because no system can prevent every negative outcome. Of course, they must aspire to the prevention of all violence, and adherence to local and national policies and procedures that promote this outcome is critical, and a robust system for learning from adverse events is necessary. Also, as serious further offences are likely in a very small number of cases, services should develop strategies for handling negative publicity and limiting its impact on the nature of the service being offered to clients. However, promising total safety nurtures zero tolerance, making the task of public protection harder rather than more possible.

A further essential requirement for future services for personality disordered offenders is more realistic use of risk assessment tools. More discussion about challenging papers like David Cooke and Christine Michie's chapter in this volume is called for as well as more education for practitioners tasked with interpreting the findings of the assessments they undertake in terms of their relevance to the individual case. Keeping personality disordered offenders and the risks they pose to others at the forefront of the minds of practitioners, as well as politicians and policymakers with resources to give to starved public services, is a final wish.

V
Conclusions

18

"Dangerous" People

The Road Ahead for Policy, Prediction, and Practice

BERNADETTE McSHERRY and PATRICK KEYZER

Arie Freiberg (2000: 52) has observed that "like the poor, the dangerous have always been with us" and governments will continue to battle with the perennial issue of what to do with those considered dangerous. What is clear from many of the chapters in this book is that schemes for imprisoning or detaining people for what they might do are costly, likely to contravene international human rights obligations, and have not proven to be effective in reducing crime, particularly sex offences. Detaining more and more people gives rise to the risk that detention regimes will collapse under the weight of numbers.

There is no doubt that some people present a risk to society or sections of it, and there is an obvious need for further research on risk management strategies and measures, particularly in the community, so that responses to risk are nuanced and flexible: there is no one-size-fits-all answer. In particular, further research is needed on how methods of supervision and management in the community can be proportionate and individualized. Some of the chapters have outlined evidence-based, therapeutic schemes for high-risk offenders and there is obviously a need to carry this research further.

Of the regimes outlined that deal with those considered dangerous, the Scottish approach (outlined in the chapters in this volume by Innes Fyfe and Yvonne Gailey, Lorraine Johnstone, Lindsay Thomson, and Rajan Darjee and Katharine Russell) has certain advantages. It avoids the human rights objections that have been made to the Australian regimes for the reimprisonment of sex offenders. The order for lifelong restriction is made at the time of sentencing, so there is no retrospectivity issue, and no double punishment is inflicted (see the chapter by Patrick Keyzer in this volume, and the discussion in McSherry and Keyzer 2009). There is no evidence to suggest that the restrictions imposed under this regime are arbitrary (McSherry and Keyzer 2009).

Should litigation arise in respect of the Scottish regime, the European Convention on Human Rights, which contains an identical guarantee against arbitrary arrest or detention to the International Covenant on Civil and Political Rights (see the chapter by Ronli Sifris in this volume) would provide a normative reference point for review. Lindsay Thomson in her chapter in this volume reports that human rights principles are central to the consideration of detention and supervision options in this area, and that new rules have been developed to enable offenders with mental disorders to appeal against excessive security arrangements (to ensure the least restrictive alternative to psychiatric care).

The Scottish system seems best to settle a balance between punishment for offences, the rehabilitation of offenders, the protection of the community, together with the realization of civil and human rights. However, Lindsay Thomson points out in her chapter in this volume that it is too early to say if the Scottish system has been successful in reducing violent and sexual recidivism.

New concerns have also emerged, warranting further research. Lindsay Thomson has noted that the transition of offenders with mental disorders from prison to hospital has been slower than is necessary. The daily implementation of detailed assessment recommendations within forensic mental health systems remains a challenge. Concerns remain about the use of orders for lifelong restriction for juveniles (McSherry and Keyzer 2009; and see the chapters by Innes Fyfe and Yvonne Gailey, and by Lorraine Johnstone in this volume). Rajan Darjee and Katharine Russell in their chapter in this volume note that assessments are time consuming and expensive, and the time and effort invested in assessments is not matched by the application of forensic clinical resources in offender management contexts. These are all concerns that will need to be addressed as the scheme continues to be developed in Scotland and if it is considered for implementation elsewhere.

As well as the Scottish scheme of orders for lifelong restriction for high-risk offenders, there are other policies that have indicated some positive results in reducing reoffending. The Multi-Agency Public Protection Arrangements (MAPPA) that exist in Scotland, England, and Wales are statutorily-based and provide a framework for the police, local authorities, prison services, and health care agencies to establish joint arrangements to assess and manage the risk posed by sexual and violent offenders. The focus is on supervision and rehabilitation of offenders through multiagency collaboration after the release into the community of certain offenders.

There have been criticisms of these arrangements in terms of differing perspectives about what is the main purpose of MAPPA—control or rehabilitation—and in terms of presumed ineffectiveness when a further crime is committed (see the chapter by Caroline Logan in this volume). However, Caroline Logan writes that "despite its imperfections, MAPPA is regarded as effective and valuable in the management of high-risk offenders." Lindsay Thomson points out in her chapter that reoffending rates by offenders managed within these arrangements in Scotland are "very low in comparison with other crime types, and zero for restricted patients to date." This indicates that such arrangements may be worth exploring in other jurisdictions.

The Issue of Risk Assessment

The current structured professional judgment (SPJ) model of risk assessment is far more sophisticated than early attempts to identify dangerous people. As outlined by Lorraine Johnstone in her chapter in this volume, it involves assessing personal history and psychosocial functioning, rating certain risk factors, and developing risk management interventions among other matters. Risk management is thus far more capable of being individualized using the SPJ approach than using actuarial tools alone. Johnstone points out that the "SPJ model is well established and a burgeoning literature attests to its utility in terms of its reliability, validity, and clinical utility." When used in conjunction with schemes such as the Scottish scheme of orders for lifelong restriction or via MAPPA, then the risk of future harm may well be diminished.

Risk assessment techniques may be useful for management and treatment purposes, but, as the chapters by David Cooke and Christine Michie and by Lorraine Johnstone in this volume point out, such techniques are highly questionable in relation to the detention of certain groups in order to prevent future harm. Cooke and Michie have raised a number of issues with the use of risk assessment tools in predicting harm for the purpose of the deprivation of liberty of individual offenders. It could be argued, however, that at least risk assessment techniques offer some guidance for treatment-focused practice; it is much worse to fall back on the concept of reasonable suspicion or belief about the propensities of certain individuals as is the case with suspected terrorists (see the chapter by Bernadette McSherry in this volume).

Shoba Sreenivasan, Allen Frances, and Linda Weinberger (2010: 390) point out in the context of sexually violent predator laws that risk assessment is left "to be determined in a possibly arbitrary, case-by-case manner by the individual … evaluator." Instead:

> An ethical approach [to risk assessment] calls for building into the system as much quality control standardization and procedural safeguards to protect against incomplete analysis, arbitrariness, and individual bias.

One of the advantages of the Scottish scheme is that it has provided the courts with a more structured approach to high-risk offenders than existed in the past. The creation of the Risk Management Authority to accredit risk assessors and to provide guidelines has led to more consistent practice by mental health and criminal justice professionals on the assessment and management of risk. This may not answer all the criticisms of risk assessment in the forensic context, but it does go some way toward alleviating the problem of inconsistent approaches.

Conclusion: The Road Ahead

If detaining and managing those considered dangerous is viewed in terms of a balance simply between individual rights and community protection, then governments will inevitably tip the scales in favor of community protection, particularly in the forms of continued detention and supervision orders. Sreenivasan et al. (2010: 387) state that "there is no universal right way to balance the important normative ethic of protecting individual rights with the equally important normative ethic of protecting public safety." Similarly, Simon Bronitt (2008) has pointed out in the context of antiterrorism laws that state powers will continue to expand if the defining framework is seen simply as a balance between security and liberty.

Preventive detention regimes have proved popular with both policymakers and the community. A number of the authors in this volume have recognized this, and proposed methods of minimizing the expansion of state powers and potential abuses through ensuring periodic review, moving beyond concepts of reasonable suspicion or belief to providing consistent and workable guidelines for risk assessment, requiring treatment and detention in the least restrictive manner possible and exploring options for supervision and treatment in the community. International human rights principles provide a normative framework for the development of domestic laws and risk management systems: they remind us that the least restrictive alternative and the preservation of individual liberty must be given due weight in constructing the balance between individual rights and community protection. Patrick Keyzer and Sam Blay (2006: 409) have observed that

> preventive detention sits uncomfortably with the notions that the punishment must be proportionate to the crime and that the liberty of the individual is sacrosanct. Imprisonment for what a person *is likely to do* is, by its very essence, predictive of what may or *may not* occur in the future. Since there exists the possibility that a predicted offence may never occur, which renders any consideration of the proportionality of the response meaningless, preventive detention is always an extraordinary step to take. Furthermore, since the logic of preventive detention is that a detainee has the potential to offend if released, the concept permits indefinite detention so long as the detainer is able to "prove" that the detainee has the potential to meet the detainer's predictions of what the detainee will do. But what constitutes acceptable, cogent evidence of "dangerousness"? By its very nature, preventive detention allows for imprisonment of "criminal types," rather than imprisonment for criminal conduct.

In addition, as noted earlier, there are real questions as to whether the social sciences can actually deliver what governments want in relation to identifying dangerous or high-risk individuals. The law requires black-and-white answers—is this person dangerous or not?—in comparison to the treatment and rehabilitation focus of mental health professionals.

A further important barrier is that the reactions of the public to high-profile violent events put pressure on governments to respond immediately through legal strategies that are more and more draconian. It is worthwhile exploring why this is the case. Arie Freiberg and WG Carson (2010: 156) have pointed out that "the role of emotion or affect in the shaping of governmental decision must be taken into account." Preventive detention schemes can thus be seen as manifestations of the emotions of fear and anger rather than harm reduction measures. It is difficult to influence policy enabling preventive detention in the face of strong public support "unless the underlying causes of the public's emotional discomfort are addressed" (Freiberg and Carson 2010: 158).

Ken Young et al. (2002) have outlined a number of models used to explain evidence-based policy making and have argued that the enlightenment model provides a useful way forward for the social sciences. This model aims at understanding and explaining the context of policy making rather than providing policy solutions. It sees researchers as contributors to an informed discourse about an issue so that decision-makers have a better idea of the context for their decisions. This approach may serve as a model for future research in this field, with the focus on contributing to an informed discourse rather than simply telling policymakers that preventive detention is ineffective. It is to be hoped that the chapters in this volume can serve as a starting point in this context.

Appendix A: Table of Cases

*These cases are marked 'R' because they have restricted access available

European Commission of Human Rights

Scotland

United Kingdom

United States of America

United Nations Human Rights Committee

Appendix B: Table of Statutes

References

Aarvold, C. (1973) *Report on the Review of Procedures for the Discharge and Supervision of Psychiatric Patients Subject to Special Restrictions*, London: Department of Health and Social Security.

Abram, K. and Teplin, L. (1991) Co-Occurring Disorders among Mentally Ill Jail Detainees: Implications for Public Policy, *American Psychologist*, 46(10): 1036–45.

Abram, K., Teplin, L. and McClelland, G. (2003) 'Co-Morbidity of Severe Psychiatric Disorders and Substance Use Disorders among Women in Jail', *American Journal of Psychiatry*, 160(12): 1007–10.

Agamben, G. (2005) *State of Exception*, trans. K. Attell, Chicago: University of Chicago Press.

Agresti, A. and Coull, B.A. (1998) Approximate is Better than "Exact" for Interval Estimation of Binomial Proportions, *American Statistician*, 52(2): 119–26.

Akuffo, K. (2004) The Involuntary Detention of Persons with Mental Disorder in England and Wales— A Human Rights Critique, *International Journal of Law and Psychiatry*, 27(2): 109–33.

Allen, G. (2009) Sex Offenders Forced to Live Under Miami Bridge, National Public Radio, May 20. Available http://www.npr.org/templates/story/story.php?storyId=104150499 (accessed 23 November 2010).

Alpert, G.P. and Smith, W.C. (1994) How Reasonable is the Reasonable Man? Police and Excessive Force, *Journal of Criminal Law and Criminology*, 85(2): 481–501.

Allport, G. (1940) The Psychologist's Frame of Reference, *Psychological Bulletin*, 37(1): 1–28.

Altman, D.G. and Royston, P. (2000) What Do We Mean by Validating a Prognostic Model?, *Statistics in Medicine*, 19(4): 453–73.

Amador, X.F. and David, A.S. (eds) (1998) *Insight and Psychosis*, New York: Oxford University Press.

American Bar Association (1989) *Criminal Justice Mental Health Standards: Standard 7-8.1: Repeal of Psychopath Statutes*, Washington: American Bar Association. Available http://www.abanet.org/crimjust/standards/mentalhealth_toc.html (accessed 23 November 2010).

American Psychiatric Association (2000) *Diagnostic and Statistical Manual of Mental Disorders*, 4th edn text rev version, Washington: American Psychiatric Association.

_____ (2010) *Personality and Personality Disorders*, Washington: American Psychiatric Association. Available http://www.dsm5.org/PROPOSEDREVISIONS/Pages/PersonalityandPersonalityDisorders.aspx (accessed 23 November 2010).

Anderson, R.L. and Bancroft, T.A. (1952) *Statistical Theory in Research*, New York: McGraw-Hill.

Andrews, D.A. and Bonta, J. (2006) *The Psychology of Criminal Conduct*, 4th edn, Newark: Anderson.

Andrews, D., Bonta, J. and Wormith, S. (2004) *The Level of Service/Case Management Inventory (LS/CMI)*, Toronto: Multi-Health Systems.

_____ (2006) The Recent Past and Near Future of Risk and/or Need Assessment, *Crime and Delinquency*, 52(1): 7–27.

Antonowicz, D.H. (2005) The Reasoning and Rehabilitation Programme: Outcome Evaluations with Offenders, in M. McMurran and J. McGuire (eds) *Social Problem Solving and Offending: Evidence, Evaluation and Evolution*, Chichester: Wiley, p. 163–82.

Aos, S., Miller, M. and Drake, E. (2006) *Evidence-Based Adult Corrections Programs: What Works and What Does Not*, Olympia: Washington State Institute for Public Policy. Online. Available http://www.wsipp.wa.gov/rptfiles/06-01-1201.pdf (accessed 23 November 2010).

Appelbaum, P. (2005) Law and Psychiatry: Dangerous Severe Personality Disorders: England's Experiment in Using Psychiatry for Public Protection, *Psychiatric Services*, 56(4): 397–9.

Aradau, C. and Van Munster, R. (2007) Governing Terrorism through Risk: Taking Precautions, (un) Knowing the Future, *European Journal of International Relations*, 13(1): 89–115.

Associated Press (2005) Sex Offenders Kept From Storm Shelters, *New York Times*, August 8. Available http://www.nytimes.com/2005/08/08/national/08florida.html?scp=18sq=&st=nyt (accessed 23 November 2010).

_____ (2009a) Sex Offenders Illegally Get Public Housing, *CBS News*, 20 August. Available http://www.cbsnews.com/stories/2009/08/20/national/main5256158.shtml (accessed 23 November 2010).

_____ (2009b) Sex Offenders Ordered Out of Tent City, *Boston Globe*, 30 September. Available http://www.boston.com/news/nation/articles/2009/09/30/homeless_ga_sex_offenders_ordered_to_move_from_tent_city/ (accessed 23 November 2010).

Audit Commission (1994) *Finding a Place: A Review of Mental Health Services for Adults*, London: HMSO.

Augmeri, L.K., Koegl, C.J., Webster, C.D. and Levine, K.S. (2001) *Early Assessment Risk List for Boys (EARL-20B), Version 2*, Toronto: Earlscourt Child Family Centre.

Bachman, R. and Paternoster, R. (1993) A Contemporary Look at the Effects of Rape Law Reform: How Far Have We Really Come?, *Journal of Criminal Law and Criminology*, 84(3): 554–74.

Backus, N. (2010) Violence Spike Draws Eye of Local Prosecutors, *Quad Community Press*, 16 February. Available http://www.presspubs.com/articles/2010/02/16/quad_community_press/news/doc4b7af9eed8bfa902922548.txt (accessed 23 November 2010).

Bamford Review of Mental Health and Learning Disability (2006) *Forensic Services*. Available http://www.rmhldni.gov.uk/forensic_services_report.pdf (accessed 23 November 2010).

Barbaree, H.E. and Marshall, W.L. (2006) *The Juvenile Sex Offenders*, 2nd edn, New York: Guilford Press.

Bartlett, K.L.H., Thomson, L.D.G. and Johnstone, E.C. (2001) *Mentally Disordered Offenders: An Evaluation of the "Open Doors" Programme at H.M. Prison, Barlinnie*, Edinburgh: Scottish Prison Service.

Baumeister, R.F., Smart, L. and Boden, J.M. (1996) Relation of Threatened Egotism to Violence and Aggression: The Dark Side of High Self-Esteem, *Psychological Review*, 103(1): 5–33.

Baumrind, D. (1991) The Influence of Parenting Style on Adolescent Competency and Substance Use, *Journal of Early Adolescence*, 11(1): 56–95.

Beauchaine, T.P., Klein, D.N., Crowell, S.E., Derbidge, C. and Gatzke-Kopp, L. (2009) Multifinality in the Development of Personality Disorders: A Biology × Sex × Environment Model of Antisocial and Borderline Traits, *Developmental Psychopathology*, 21(3): 735–70.

Beck, A.T. (1999) *Prisoners of Hate: The Cognitive Basis of Anger, Hostility, and Violence*, New York: Harper Collins.

Beckett, S., Fernandez, L. and McFarlane, K. (2009) *Provisional Sentencing for Children: A Report for New South Wales Sentencing Council*, Sydney: New South Wales Sentencing Council.

Bell, V. (2002) The Vigilant(e) Parent and the Paedophile: The *News of the World* Campaign 2000 and the Contemporary Governmentality of Child Sexual Abuse, *Feminist Theory*, 3(1): 83–102.

Beyond Bars Alliance (2007) *Mental Illness and the Criminal Justice System*. Available http://www.beyond-bars.org.au/facts.htm (accessed 23 November 2010).

Blackburn, R. and Coid, J. (1998) Psychopathy and the Dimensions of Personality Disorder in Violent Offenders, *Personality and Individual Differences*, 25(1): 129–45.

Blackburn, R., Logan, C., Donnelly, J.P. and Renwick, S. (2003) Personality Disorders, Psychopathy, and other Mental Disorders: Co-Morbidity among Patients at English and Scottish High Security Hospitals, *Journal of Forensic Psychiatry and Psychology*, 14(1): 111–37.

Blay, S., Burn, J. and Keyzer, P. (2007) *Offshore Processing of Asylum Seekers: The Search for Legitimate Parameters*, Ultimo, New South Wales: Halstead Press.

Blay, S. and Piotrowicz, R. (2000) The Awfulness of Lawfulness: Some Reflections on the Tension between International and Domestic Law, *Australian Yearbook of International Law*, 21: 1–19.

Boer, D.P. (2006) Sexual Offender Risk Assessment Strategies: Is There a Convergence of Opinion Yet? *Sexual Offender Treatment*, 1(2): 1–4. Available http://sexual-offender-treatment.org/38.html (accessed 23 November 2010).

Boer, D.P., Wilson, R.J., Gauthier, C.M. and Hart, S.D. (1997) Assessing Risk of Sexual Violence: Guidelines for Clinical Practice, in C.D. Webster and M.A. Jackson (eds) *Impulsivity: Theory, Assessment and Treatment*, New York: Guilford Press, 362–42.

Boerner, D. (1992) Confronting Violence: In the Act and in the Word, *University of Puget Sound Law Review*, 15(3): 525–77.

Bonta, J., Law, M. and Hanson, C. (1998) The Prediction of Criminal and Violent Recidivism among Mentally Disordered Offenders: A Meta-Analysis, *Psychological Bulletin*, 123(2): 123–42.

Bonta, J., Rugge, T., Scott, T.L., Bourgon, G. and Yessine, A.K. (2008) Exploring the Black Box of Community Supervision, *Journal of Offender Rehabilitation*, 47(3): 248–70.

Borg, M. and Kristiansen, K. (2004) Recovery-Oriented Professionals: Helping Relationships in Mental Health Services, *Journal of Mental Health*, 13(5): 493–505.

Borsboom, D., Mellenbergh, G.J. and van Heerden, J. (2003) The Theoretical Status of Latent Variables, *Psychological Review*, 110(2): 203–19.

Borum, R. (1996) Improving the Clinical Practice of Violence Risk Assessment: Technology, Guidelines, and Training, *American Psychologist*, 51(9): 954–56.

Borum, R., Bartel, P., and Forth, A. (2003) *Manual for the Structured Assessment of Violence Risk in Youth (SAVRY): Version 1.1*, Tampa: University of South Florida, Louis de la Parte Florida Mental Health Institute.

_____ (2006) *Manual for the Structured Assessment of Violence Risk in Youth (SAVRY): Professional Manual*, Odessa, FL: Psychological Assessment Resources.

Borum, R. and Verhaagen, D. (2006) *Assessing and Managing Violence Risk in Juveniles*, New York: Guilford Press.

Bouhours, B. and Daly, K. (2007) Youth Sex Offenders in Court: An Analysis of Judicial Sentencing Remarks, *Punishment and Society*, 9(4): 371–94.

Brakel, S.J. and Cavenaugh, J.L. (2000) Of Psychopaths and Pendulums: Legal and Psychiatric Treatment of Sex Offenders in the United States, *New Mexico Law Review*, 30(1): 69–94.

Breakwell, G.M. (2007) *The Psychology of Risk*, Cambridge: Cambridge University Press.

British Psychological Society (2006) *Understanding Personality Disorder: A Report by the British Psychological Society*, Leicester: British Psychological Society.

Bronitt, S. (2008) Balancing Security and Liberty: Critical Perspectives on Terrorism and law reform, in M. Gani and P. Mathew (eds) *Fresh Perspectives on the "War on Terror,"* Canberra: ANU E Press, 65–83.

Brooks, A. (1974) *Law, Psychiatry and the Mental Health Systems,* New York: Aspen.

Brown, M. and Pratt, J. (2000a) *Dangerous Offenders: Punishment and Social Order*, London: Routledge.

Brown, M. and Pratt, J. (2000b) Introduction, in M. Brown and J. Pratt (eds) *Dangerous Offenders: Punishment and Social Order*, London: Routledge, 1–13.

Brownlie, I. (1998) *Principles of Public International Law*, 5th edn, Oxford: Clarendon Press, 1–13.

Buchanan, A. (1998) Criminal Conviction after Discharge from Special (High Security) Hospital: Incidence in the First 10 Years, *British Journal of Psychiatry*, 172(6): 472–6.

_____ (2008) Risk of Violence by Psychiatric Patients: Beyond the 'Actuarial versus Clinical' Assessment Debate, *Psychiatric Services*, 59(2): 184–90.

Bureau of Justice Assistance (2009) *Improving Responses to People with Mental Illness: The Essentials of a Mental Health Court*. Available http://www.ojp.usdoj.gov/BJA/grant/mentalhealth.html (accessed 23 November 2009).

Burman, M., Armstrong, S., Batchelor, S., McNeil, F. and Nicholson, J. (2007) *Research and Practice in Risk Assessment and Risk Management of Children and Young People Engaging in Offending Behaviours: A Literature Review*, Paisley: Risk Management Review Authority. Available http://www.rmascotland.gov.uk/try/research-papers/ (accessed 23 November 2010).

Butler, G. (1998) Clinical Formulation, in A.S. Bellack and M.E. Hersen (eds) *Comprehensive Clinical Psychology*, New York: Pergammon Press, 1–23.

California Department of Mental Health (2010) *Sex Offender Commitment Program*, Sacramento: California Department of Mental Health. Available http://www.dmh.ca.gov/Services_and_Programs/Forensic_Services/Sex_Offender_Commitment_Program (accessed 23 November 2010).

California Sex Offender Management Board (2008) An Assessment of Current Management Practices of Adult Sex Offenders in California, Sacramento: California Sex Offender Management Board. Available www.casomb.org/docs/SOMBReport1.pdf (accessed 23 November 2010).

Calsyn, R., Yonker, R., Lemming, M., Morse, G. and Klinkenberg, D. (2005) Impact of Assertive Community Treatment and Client Characteristics on Criminal Justice Outcomes in Dual Disorder Homeless Individuals, *Criminal Behaviour and Mental Health*, 15(4): 236–48.

Cantone, J.A. (2009) Rational Enough to Punish, But Too Irrational to Release: The Integrity of Sex Offender Civil Commitment, *Drake Law Review*, 57(3): 693–727.

Care Programme Approach Association (2003a) *Audit Tool for the Monitoring of the Care Programme Approach*, Chesterfield: Care Programme Approach Association.

_____ (2003b) *National Standards*, Chesterfield: Care Programme Approach Association.

_____ (2003c) *The CPA Handbook*, Chesterfield: Care Programme Approach Association.

Carlsmith, K.M., Monahan, J., and Evans, A. (2007) The Function of Punishment in the 'Civil' Commitment of Sexually Violent Predators, *Behavioral Sciences and the Law*, 25(4): 437–48.

Carlson, S.N. and Gisvold, G. (2003) *Practical Guide to the International Covenant on Civil and Political Rights*, New York: Transnational.

Carpenter, C.L. (2010) Legislative Epidemics: A Cautionary Tale of Criminal Laws that Have Swept the Country, *Buffalo Law Review*, 58(1): 1–67.

Caspi, A. (2000) The Child is Father of the Man: Personality Continuities from Childhood to Adulthood, *Journal of Personality and Social Psychology*, 78(1): 158–72.

Center on Budget and Policy Priorities (2010a) *Policy Basics: Where Do Our State Tax Dollars Go?* March 19. Available http://www.cbpp.org/files/policybasics-statetaxdollars.pdf (accessed 23 November 2010).

_____ (2010b) *Policy Points: Recession Still Causing Trouble for States: Federal Economic Recovery Funds Providing Some Relief*. Available www.cbpp.org/cms/index.cfm?fa=view&id=1283 (23 accessed November 2010).

Centre for Change and Innovation (2005) *Personality Disorder in Scotland: Demanding Patients or Deserving People?*, Edinburgh: Scottish Executive.

Chaffin, M., Levenson, J., Letourneau, E. and Stern, P. (2009) How Safe are Trick-or-Treaters?: An Analysis of Child Sex Crime Rates on Halloween, *Sexual Abuse: A Journal of Research and Treatment*, 21(3): 363–74.

Chairpersons of the Human Rights Treaty Bodies (2006) *Concept Paper on the High Commissioner's Proposal for a Unified Standing Treaty Body*, UN Doc HRI/MC/2006/2 (22 March 2006).

Chandler, D. and Spicer, G. (2006) Integrated Treatment for Jail Recidivists with Co-Occurring Psychiatric and Substance Use Disorders, *Community Mental Health Journal*, 42(4): 405–25.

Cicchetti, D. and Rogosch, F. (2002) A Developmental Psychopathology Perspective on Adolescence, *Journal of Consulting and Clinical Psychology*, 70(1): 6–20.

Clark, R., Ricketts, S. and McHugo, G. (1999) Legal System Involvement and Costs for Persons in Treatment for Severe Mental Illness and Substance Use Disorders, *Psychiatric Services*, 50(5): 641–47.

Clarke, J. (2008) *Report of the Inquiry into the Case of Mohamed Haneef*, Caberra: Commonwealth of Australia. Available http://www.haneefcaseinquiry.gov.au/www/inquiry/rwpattach.nsf/VAP/(3A679 0B96C927794AF1031D9395C5C20)~Volume+1+FINAL.pdf/$file/Volume+1+FINAL.pdf (accessed 23 November 2010).

Cohen, J. and Cohen, P. (1983) *Applied Multiple Regression/Correlation Analysis for the Behavioural Sciences*, 2nd edn, London: Lawrence Erlbaum Associates.

Coid, J., Yang, M., Roberts, A., Ullrich S., Moran, P., Bebbington, P., Brugha, T., Jenkins, R., Farrell, M., Lewis, G. and Singleton, N. (2006a) Violence and Psychiatric Morbidity in a National Household Population: A Report from the British Household Survey, *American Journal of Epidemiology*, 164(12): 1199–1208.

Coid, J., Yang, M., Tyrer, P., Roberts, A. and Ullrich, S. (2006b) Prevalence and Correlates of Personality Disorder in Great Britain, *British Journal of Psychiatry*, 188(5): 423–31.

Committee on Mentally Abnormal Offenders (1975) *Report of the Committee on Mentally Abnormal Offenders* (Butler Report), London: Home Office and Department of Health and Social Services.

Conan Doyle, A. (1890) *The Sign of the Four*, 1994 edn, Oxford: Oxford University Press.

Cooke, D.J. (1998) Psychopathy Across Cultures, in D.J. Cooke, A.E. Forth and R.D. Hare (eds) *Psychopathy: Theory, Research and Implications for Society*, Dordrecht: Kluwer, 13–45.

———— (2010a) More Prejudicial than Probative, *Journal of the Law Society of Scotland*, 55(1): 20–23.

———— (2010b) Personality Disorder and Violence: Understand Violence Risk and Risk Processes, *Journal of Personality Disorders*, 24(5): 539–50.

Cooke, D.J. and Michie, C. (2001) Refining the Construct of Psychopathy: Towards a Hierarchical Model, *Psychological Assessment*, 13(2): 171–88.

———— (2010) Limitations of Diagnostic Precision and Predictive Utility in the Individual Case: A Challenge for Forensic Practice, *Law and Human Behavior*, 34(4): 259–74.

Cooke, D.J., Michie, C., and Hart, S.D. (2010) (forthcoming) *Screening for Sex Offender Risk: A Dangerous Clinical Practice*.

Cooke, D.J., Michie, C., and Skeem, J.L. (2007) Understanding the Structure of the Psychopathy Checklist Revised: An Exploration of Methodological Confusion, *British Journal of Psychiatry*, 190(49): 39–50.

Cooke, D.J. and Wozniak, E. (2010) (in press) Hell in Paradise: Using PRISM to Critically Review the Glendairy Prison Riot and its Aftermath in Barbados, *International Journal of Forensic Mental Health*.

Cooke, W.E. (1906) Forecasts and Verifications in Western Australia, *Monthly Weather Review*, 34(1): 23–24.

Cooper, V.G. and Zapf, P.A. (2003) Predictor Variables in Competency to Stand Trial Decisions, *Law and Human Behavior*, 27(4): 423–36.

Cornell, D., Benedek, E. and Benedek, D. (1987) Juvenile Homicide: Prior Adjustment and a Proposed Typology, *American Journal of Orthopsychiatry*, 57: 383–93.

Cornwell, J.P. (2004) The Right to Community Treatment for Mentally Disordered Sex Offenders, *Seton Hall Law Review*, 34(4): 1213–32.

Council of State Governments (2002) *Criminal Justice/Mental Health Consensus Project*. Available http://www.consensusproject.org (accessed 23 November 2008).

Craig, L. and Beech, A.R. (2009) Best Practice in Conducting Actuarial Risk Assessments with Adult Sexual Offenders, *Journal of Sexual Aggression*, 15(2): 193–211.

Craig, L.A., Browne, K.D. and Beech, A.R. (2008) *Assessing Risk in Sex Offenders: A Practitioner's Guide*, Chichester: Wiley.

Crais, L.E. (2005) Domestic Violence and the Federal Government, *Georgetown Journal of Gender and the Law*, 6(3): 405–30.

Crichton, J. (2006) *A Review of Critical Incident Review Guidance*, Lanark, Scotland: Forensic Network.

_____ (2010) (Chair) *Report of the Care Programme Review Group*, Lanark, Scotland: Forensic Network.

Crichton, J. and Sheppard, D. (1996) Psychiatric Inquiries: Learning the Lessons, in J. Peay (ed.) *Inquiries after Homicide*, London: Duckworths, 75–78.

Darjee, R. (2003) The Reports of the MacLean and Millan Committees: New Proposals for Mental Health Legislation and for High Risk Offenders in Scotland, *Journal of Forensic Psychiatry and Psychology*, 14(1): 7–25.

_____ (2005) Legislation for Mentally Disordered Offenders, in L. Thomson and J. McManus (eds) *Mental Health and Scots Law in Practice*, Edinburgh: Greens.

Darjee, R. and Crichton, J. (2002) The MacLean Committee: Scotland's Answer to the Dangerous People with Severe Personality Disorder Proposals?, *Psychiatric Bulletin*, 26: 6–8.

_____ (2003) Personality Disorder and the Law in Scotland: A Historical Perspective, *Journal of Forensic Psychiatry and Psychology*, 14(2): 394–425.

Davey, M. and Goodnough, A. (2007) Doubts Rise as States Hold Sex Offenders After Prison, *New York Times*. 4 March. Available http://www.nytimes.com/2007/03/04/us/04civil.html (accessed 23 November 2010).

Davidson, K. (2007) *Cognitive Therapy for Personality Disorders: A Guide for Clinicians*, London: Routledge.

Davidson, M., Humphreys, M.S., Johnstone, E.C. and Owens, D.G.C. (1995) Prevalence of Psychiatric Morbidity among Remand Prisoners in Scotland, *British Journal of Psychiatry*, 167(4): 545–8.

Davies, S., Clarke, M., Hollin, C. and Duggan, C. (2007) Long-Term Outcomes after Discharge from Medium Secure Care: A Cause for Concern, *British Journal of Psychiatry*, 191(1): 70–74.

Dawson, J. and Mullen, R. (2008) Insight and the Use of Community Treatment Orders, *Journal of Mental Health*, 17(3): 269–80.

de Boer, J and Gerrits, J. (2007) Learning from Holland: The TBS System, *Psychiatry*, 6: 459–61.

deFiebre, C. (2004) Life and Death: Getting Tough on Sex Offenders, *Minneapolis Star Tribune*, April 19, A6.

de Vogel, V., de Ruiter, C., Bouman, Y. and de Vries Robbé, M. (2009) *SAPROF: Structured Assessment of PROtective Factors for Violence Risk*, Utrecht, Netherlands: Forum Educatief.

Dean, K., Walsh, E., Moran, P., Tyrer, P., Creed, F., Byford, S., Burns, T., Murray, R. and Fahy, T. (2006) Violence in Women with Psychosis in the Community: Prospective Study, *British Journal of Psychiatry*, 188(3): 264–70.

Delaney, S. (1998) Controlling the Governor's Pleasure—Some Gain, Some Pain, *Law Institute Journal*, 72(1): 46–47.

Demko, P. (2009) MN Sex Offender Program Costs $70 Million a Year But Rehabilitates No One, *Minnesota Independent*, 13 November. Available http://minnesotaindependent.com/48675/minnesota-sex-offender-program-costs-70-million-a-year-but-rehabilitates-no-one (accessed 23 November 2010).

_____ (2010a) Pawlenty Seeks Longer Sentences for Sex Offenders, *Politics in Minnesota*, 9 February.

_____ (2010b) Legal Scholar Warns about Minnesota Sex Offender Program's Failures, *Politics in Minnesota*, March 3.

Department of Health (1990) *Caring for People: The Care Programme Approach for People with a Mental Illness Referred to Specialist Mental Health Services,* Joint Health/Social Services Circular C(90)23/LASSL(90)11.

_____ (1995) *Building Bridges: A Guide to Arrangements for Interagency Working for the Care and Protection of Severely Mentally Ill People*, London: Department of Health.

_____ (1999) *A National Service Framework for Mental Health: Modern Standards and Service Models for Mental Health*, London: Department of Health.

_____ (2003) *Personality Disorder: No Longer a Diagnosis of Exclusion*, London: Department of Health.

_____ (2009a) *Recognising Complexity: Commissioning Guidance for Personality Disorder Services*, London: Department of Health.

_____ (2009b) *The Bradley Report*, London: Department of Health.

_____ (2010a) *Bed Statistics 2007–08*, London: Department of Health. Available http://www.performance.doh.gov.uk/hospitalactivity/data_requests/download/beds_open_overnight/bed_08_summary.xls (accessed 23 November 2010).

_____ (2010b) *New Horizons: A Shared Vision for Mental Health*, London: Department of Health.

Dernevik, M., Beck, A., Grann, M., Hogue, T. and McGuire, J. (2009) The Use of Psychiatric and Psychological Evidence in the Assessment of Terrorist Offenders, *Journal of Forensic Psychiatry and Psychology*, 20(4): 508–15.

Diamond, S.D. (1996) Juror Reactions to Attorneys at Trial, *Journal of Criminal Law and Criminology*, 87(1): 17–47.

Dickinger, E., Eno Louden, J., Robinson, J., Troshynski, E. and Skeem, J. (2008) The Effect of Individual- and Neighborhood-Level Characteristics on Recidivism for Parolees with Mental Disorder, in S. Manchak (chair) *Offenders with Mental Illness in Community Corrections.* Symposium conducted at the annual meeting of the American Psychology-Law Society, Jacksonville, FL. Available https://webfiles.uci. edu:443/skeem/Downloads.html (accessed 23 November 2010).

Diesfeld, K. (2003) Insights on "Insight": The Impact of Extra-Legislative Factors in Decisions to Discharge Detained Patients, in K. Diesfeld and I. Freckelton (eds) *Involuntary Detention and Therapeutic Jurisprudence: International Perspectives on Civil Commitment,* Aldershot: Ashgate, 359–82.

DiIuilo, J. (1995) The Coming of the Super-Predators, *The Weekly Standard,* September 16, 30–35.

Dinstein, Y. (1981) The Right to Life, Physical Integrity, and Liberty, in L. Henkin (ed.) *The International Bill of Rights: The Covenant on Civil and Political Rights,* New York: Columbia University Press, 114–37.

Douglas, K., Guy, L. and Hart, S. (2009) Psychosis as a Risk Factor for Violence to Others: A Meta-Analysis, *Psychology Bulletin,* 135(5): 679–706.

Douglas, K.S. and Kropp, R. (2002) A Prevention-Based Paradigm for Violence Risk Assessment: Clinical and Research Application, *Criminal Justice and Behavior,* 29(5): 617–58.

Dowden, C. and Andrews, D.A. (2004) The Importance of Staff Practice in Delivering Effective Correctional Treatment: A Meta-Analytic Review of Core Correctional Practice, *International Journal of Offender Therapy and Comparative Criminology,* 48(2): 203–14.

Dowsett, J. and Craissati, J. (2008) *Managing Personality Disordered Offenders in the Community: A Psychological Approach,* London: Routledge.

Draine, J., Wilson, A. and Pogorzelski, W. (2007) Limitations and Potential in Current Research on Services for People with Mental Illness in the Criminal Justice System, *Journal of Offender Rehabilitation,* 45(3): 159–77.

Duggan, C. and Howard, R. (2009) The 'Functional Link' between Personality Disorder and Violence: A Critical Appraisal, in M. McMurran and R. Howard (eds) *Personality, Personality Disorder and Violence,* Chichester: Wiley-Blackwell, 19–38.

Dunkel, F. (2009) Young People's Rights: The Role of The Council of Europe, in J. Junger-Tas and F. Dunkel (eds) *Reforming Juvenile Justice,* New York: Springer, 33–44.

Dunkel, F. and Pruin, I. (2009) Community Sanctions and the Sanctioning Practice: Juvenile Justice Systems in Europe, in J. Junger-Tas and F. Dunkel (eds) *Reforming Juvenile Justice,* New York: Springer, 183–204.

Dutton, D.G. (2002) Personality Dynamics of Intimate Abusiveness, *Journal of Psychiatric Practice,* 8(4): 216–28.

Duwe, G., Donnay, W. and Tewksbury, R. (2008) Does Residential Proximity Matter?: A Geographic Analysis of Sex Offense Recidivism, *Criminal Justice and Behavior,* 35(4): 484–504.

Dworkin, A. (1993) I Want a Twenty-Four-Hour Truce During Which There is No Rape, in E. Buchwald, P. Fletcher and M. Roth (eds) *Transforming a Rape Culture,* Minneapolis: Milkweed Editions, 11–22.

Eastman, N. (1999) Public Health Psychiatry or Crime Prevention?: Government's Proposals Emphasise Doctors' Role as Public Protectors, *British Medical Journal,* 318(7183): 549–51.

Edney, R. (2000) Overcrowded Prisons, Degraded Prisoners: Res Ipsa Loquitur?, *Deakin Law Review,* 5(1): 81–93.

——— (2002) Hard Time, Less Time: Prison Conditions and the Sentencing Process, *Criminal Law Journal,* 26(3): 139–51.

Elkovitch, N., Viljoen, J.L., Scalora, M.J. and Ullman, D. (2008) Assessing Risk of Reoffending in Adolescents who have Committed a Sexual Offense: The Accuracy of Clinical Judgements after Completion of Risk Assessment Instruments, *Behavioral Sciences and the Law,* 26(4): 511–28.

Elliot, D., Ageton, S., Huizinga, D., Knowles, B. and Canter, R. (1983) *The Prevalence and Incidents of Delinquent Behavior, 1976–1980: National Estimates of Delinquent Behavior by Sex, Race, Social Class, and Other Selected Variables,* Washington: United States Department of Justice/United States Department of Health and Human Services.

Elliot, D., Huzinga, D. and Morse, B. (1986) Self-Reported Violent Offending: A Descriptive Analysis of Juvenile Violent Offenders and their Offending Careers, *Journal of Interpersonal Violence,* 1(4): 472–514.

Englich, B. and Mussweiler, T. (2001) Sentencing under Uncertainty: Anchoring Effects in the Courtroom, *Journal of Applied Social Psychology,* 31(7): 1535–51.

English, K., Jones, L. and Patrick, D. (2003) Community Containment of Sex Offender Risk: A Promising Approach in B. Winick and J. La Fond (eds) *Protecting Society from Sexually Dangerous Offenders: Law, Justice, and Therapy,* Washington: American Psychological Association, 265–80.

Enniss, B. (2008) Quickly Assuaging Public Fear: How the Well-Intended Adam Walsh Act Led To Unintended Consequences, *Utah Law Review*, 2008(2): 697–717.

Eno Louden, J. and Skeem, J. (2011) Parolees with Mental Disorder: Toward Evidence-Based Practice, *Bulletin of the Center for Evidence-Based Corrections*.

Eno Louden, J., Skeem, J., Camp, J., Vidal, S., & Peterson, J. (2010). Supervision Practices in Specialty Mental Health Probation: What Happens in Officer-Probationer Meetings? *Law and Human Behavior*, published online, 23 Dec 2010, DOI 10.1007/s10979-010-9260-2.

Eno Louden, J., Skeem, J.L., Camp, J., Vidal, S. and Peterson, J. (2010) Supervision Practices in Specialty Mental Health Probation: What Happens in Officer-Probationer Meetings?, Law and Human Behaviour, published online 23 Dec. 2010.

Epperson, D.L., Kaul, J.D., Huot, S., Goldman, R. and Alexander, W. (2003) *Minnesota Sex Offender Screening Tool–Revised (MnSOST-R) Technical Paper: Development, Validation, and Recommended Risk Level Cut Scores.* Available http://www.psychology.iastate.edu/~dle/TechUpdatePaper12-03.pdf (accessed 23 November 2010).

Epps, K. and Fisher, D. (2004) A Review of Research Literature on Young People who Sexually Abuse, in G. O'Reilly, W.L., Marshall, R.C., Beckett and A. Carr (eds) *The Handbook of Clinical Intervention with Young People Who Sexually Abuse*, Hove, England: Psychological Press, 62–102.

Ericson, R.V. (2007) *Crime in an Insecure World*, Cambridge: Polity Press.

Eronon, M., Hakola, P. and Tiihonen, J. (1996) Mental Disorders and Homicidal Behavior in Finland, *Archives of General Psychiatry*, 53(6): 497–501.

Evans, S.M. (2003) *Tidal Wave: How Women Changed America at Century's End*, New York: Free Press.

Ewart, J. (2009) *Haneef: A Question of Character*, Ultimo, New South Wales: Halstead Press.

Faigman, D.L. (2007) The Limits of Science in the Courtroom, in E. Borgida and S.T. Fiske (eds) *Beyond Common Sense: Psychological Science in the Courtroom*, Oxford: Blackwells, 303–13.

Farmer, M. and Mann, R. (2010) High-Risk Sex Offenders: Issues of Policy, in K. Harrison (ed.) *Managing High-Risk Sex Offenders in the Community: Risk Management, Treatment and Social Responsibility*, Cullompton, England: Willan, 18–35.

Fazel, S. and Danesh, J. (2002) Serious Mental Disorder in 23000 Prisoners: A Systematic Review of 62 Surveys, *Lancet*, 359(9306): 545–50.

Federal Bureau of Investigation (1999) Juveniles and Violence, in B.C. Feld (ed.) *Readings in Juvenile Justice Administration*, New York: Oxford University Press, 167–72.

Fellner, J. (2006) A Corrections Quandary: Mental Illness and Prison Rules, *Harvard Civil Rights Civil Liberties Law Review*, 41(2): 391–412.

Fennell, P. (1992) The Criminal Procedure (Insanity and Unfitness to Plead) Act 1991, *Modern Law Review*, 55(4): 547–55.

Filler, D.M. (2001) Making the Case for Megan's Law: A Study in Legislative Rhetoric, *Indiana Law Journal*, 76(2): 315–65.

Finkelhor, D. (1994) Current Information on the Scope and Nature of Child Sexual Abuse, *Future Child*, 4(2): 31–53.

Fischer, J.E., Bachman, L.M. and Jaeschke, R. (2003) A Readers' Guide to the Interpretation of Diagnostic Test Properties: Clinical Examples of Sepsis, *Intensive Care Medicine*, 29(7): 1043–51.

Fisher, W. and Drake, R. (2007) Forensic Mental Illness and Other Policy Misadventures: Commentary on "Extending Assertive Community Treatment to Criminal Justice Settings: Origins, Current Evidence, and Future Directions," *Community Mental Health Journal*, 43(5): 545–8.

Fisher, W., Silver, E. and Wolff, N. (2006) Beyond Criminalization: Toward a Criminologically Informed Framework for Mental Health Policy and Services Research, *Administration and Policy in Mental Health*, 33(5): 544–57.

Florida Office of Program Policy Analysis and Government Accountability (2008) *The Delays in Screening Sexually Violent Predators Increase Costs: Treatment Facility Security Enhanced*, Tallahassee, FL: Office of Program Policy Analysis and Government Accountability. Available http://www.oppaga.state.fl.us/MonitorDocs/Reports/pdf/0810rpt.pdf (accessed 23 November 2010).

Forensic Mental Health Services Managed Care Network Working Group (2005) *Report on Services for People with Personality Disorder*, Edinburgh: Forensic Mental Health Services.

Ford, R., Barnes, A., Davies, R., Chalmers, C., Hardy, P. and Muijen, M. (2001) Maintaining Contact with People with Severe Mental Illness: 5 Year Follow-Up of Assertive Outreach, *Social Psychiatry and Psychiatric Epidemiology*, 36(9): 444–7.

Ford, R., Beadsmoore, A., Norton, P., Cooke, A. and Repper, J. (1993) Developing Case Management for the Long Term Mentally Ill, *Psychiatric Bulletin*, 17(7) 409–11.

Forensic Network (2007) *Review of Care Programme Approach: Guidance for Restricted Patients in Scotland*, Lanark, Scotland: Forensic Network.

_____ (2010) Outcome of Appeals against Excessive Security, personal communication, March 2010.

Francis, A. (2009) A Warning Sign on the Road to *DSM-V*: Beware of Its Unintended Consequences, *Psychiatric Times*, 26(8): 1, 4–5, 8–9.

Frank, J. (2010) Five Years after Jessica Lunsford's Killing, Legislators Rethink Sex Offender Laws, *St. Petersburg Times*, 24 February. Available http://www.tampabay.com/news/politics/stateroundup/five-years-after-jessica-lunsfords-killing-legislators-rethink-sex/1075251 (accessed 23 November 2010).

Frank, R. and Glied, S. (2006a) *Better But Not Well: Mental Health Policy in the United States Since 1950*, Baltimore: Johns Hopkins University Press.

_____ (2006b) Changes In Mental Health Financing Since 1971: Implications for Policymakers and Patients, *Health Affairs*, 25(3): 601–13.

Frank, R., Goldman, H. and McGuire, T. (2009) Trends in Mental Health Cost Growth: An Expanded Role for Management?, *Health Affairs*, 28(3): 649–59.

Franklin, K. (2010) *In the News: Forensic Psychology, Criminology, and Psychology-Law*, 16 February. Available http://forensicpsychologist.blogspot.com/2010/02/dsm-paraphilia-controversy-escalating.html (accessed 23 November 2010).

Frankowski, S. and Shelton, D.L. (eds) (1992) *Preventive Detention: A Comparative and International Law Perspective*, Dordrecht, Netherlands: Martinus Nijhoff Publishers.

Frase, R.S. (2005) Excessive Prison Sentences, Punishment Goals, and the Eighth Amendment: "Proportionality" Relative to What?, *Minnesota Law Review*, 89(3): 571–651.

Freckelton, I. (2003) Involuntary Detention of Persons Found Not Guilty of Murder by Reason of Mental Impairment or Found Unfit to Stand Trial: A New Jurisprudence from Victoria, in K. Diesfeld and I. Freckelton (eds) *Involuntary Detention and Therapeutic Jurisprudence*, Aldershot: Ashgate. 383–434.

_____ (2005) Distractors and Distressors in Involuntary Status Decision-Making, *Psychiatry, Psychology and Law*, 12(1): 88–102.

_____ (2010) Extra-Legislative Factors in Involuntary Status Decision-Making, in B. McSherry and P. Weller (eds) *Rethinking Rights-Based Mental Health Laws*, Oxford: Hart, 203–30.

Freiberg, A. (2000) Guerrillas in our Midst?—Judicial Responses to Governing the Dangerous, in M. Brown and J. Pratt (eds) *Dangerous Offenders: Punishment and Social Order*, London: Routledge. 51–70.

_____ (2001) Affective versus Effective Justice: Instrumentation and Emotionalism in Criminal Justice, *Punishment and Society*, 3(2): 265–78.

Freiberg, A. and Carson, W.G. (2010) The Limits of Evidence-Based Policy: Evidence, Emotion and Criminal Justice, *Australian Journal of Public Administration*, 69(2): 152–64.

Frieden, J. (2003) Medicaid Mental Health Bears Brunt of State Cuts, *Clinical Psychiatric News*, 31(6); 6–7.

Friendship, C., Blud, L. and Erikson, M. (2002) *An Evaluation of Cognitive Behavioural Treatment for Prisoners*, London: Home Office.

Fry-Browers, E.K. (2004) Controversy and Consequence in California: Choosing Between Children and the Constitution, *Whittier Law Review*, 25(4): 889–925.

Garcia, D.A. (2010) Breakdown of Michigan Juvenile Sex Offender Cases by Age, *Michigan Messenger*, 2 February. Available http://michiganmessenger.com/34591/breakdown-of-michigan-juvenile-sex-offender-cases-by-age (accessed 23 November 2010).

Gardner, D. (2008) *Risk: The Science and Politics of Fear*, Carlton North, Australia: Scribe Publications.

Garfinkle, E. (2003) Coming of Age in America: The Misapplication of Sex-Offender Registration and Community-Notification Laws to Juveniles, *California Law Review*, 91(1): 163–208.

Garland, D. (2001) *The Culture of Control: Crime and Social Order in Contemporary Society*, Oxford: Oxford University Press.

_____ (2003) The Rise of Risk, in R. Ericson and A. Doyle (eds) *Risk and Morality*, Toronto: University of Toronto Press, 23–48.

Geissenhainer, M.T. (2008) The $62 Million Question: Is Virginia's New Center to House Sexually Violent Predators Money Well Spent? *University of Richmond Law Review*, 42(5): 1301–36.

Gelb, K. (2007) *Recidivism of Sex Offenders: A Research Paper*, Melbourne: Sentencing Advisory Council.

Gendreau, P. and Goggin, C. (1997) Correctional Treatment: Accomplishments and Realities, in P. Van Voorhis, M. Braswell and D. Lester (eds) *Correctional Counseling and Rehabilitation*, 3rd edn, Cincinnati: Anderson.

Gigerenzer, G. (2002) *Reckoning with Risk: Learning to Live with Uncertainty*, London: Penguin.

Girard, L. and Wormith, J. (2004) The Predictive Validity of the Level of Service Inventory—Ontario Revision on General and Violent Recidivism Among Various Offender Groups, *Criminal Justice and Behavior*, 31(2): 150–81.

Gold, S. and Romney, L. (2007) Turmoil Replaces Treatment at Coalinga Hospital, *Los Angeles Times*, 15 November. Available http://www.disabilityrightsca.org/news/LATimes-2007-11-15.htm (accessed 23 November 2010).

Goldsmith, A. (2008) The Governance of Terror: Precautionary Logic and Counterterrorist Law Reform After September 11, *Law and Policy*, 30(2): 141–67.

Goodnough, A. and Davey, M. (2007) A Record of Failure at Center for Sex Offenders, *New York Times*, 5 March. Available http://www.nytimes.com/2007/03/05/us/05civil.html (accessed 23 November 2010).

Gray, A. (2005) Preventive Detention Laws: High Court Validates Queensland's Dangerous Prisoners Act 2003, *Alternative Law Journal*, 30(2): 75–79.

Greenfield, L.A. (1997) *Sex Offenses and Offenders: An Analysis of Data on Rape and Sexual Assault*, Washington: Department of Justice, Bureau of Justice Statistics. Available http://bjs.ojp.usdoj.gov/content/pub/pdf/SOO.PDF (accessed 23 November 2010).

Greenhaigh, T. (1997) How to Read a Paper: Papers that Report Diagnostic or Screening Tests, *British Medical Journal*, 315(7107): 540–3.

Gregg, N. (2010) Mohamed Haneef Sues Kevin Andrews for Defamation, *Courier-Mail*, 1 July. Available http://www.couriermail.com.au/news/queensland/mohamed-haneef-sues-kevin-andrews-for-defamation/story-e6freoof-1225886791072 (accessed 23 November 2010).

Grinberg, E. (2009) Police Try to Monitor Sex Offenders at Halloween, *CNN Justice.com*, 31 October. Available http://www.cnn.com/2009/CRIME/10/31/sex.offenders.halloween/index.html (accessed 23 November 2010).

Grisso, T. (1996) Society's Retributive Response to Juvenile Violence: A Developmental Perspective, *Law and Human Behaviour*, 20(4): 229–47.

_____ (1998) *Forensic Evaluation of Juveniles*, Sarasota, FL: Professional Resource Press.

Grossman, L., Martis, B. and Fichtner, C. (1999) Are Sex Offenders Treatable? A Research Review, *Psychiatric Services*, 50: 349–361.

Grove, W. and Meehl, P. (1996) Comparative Efficiency of Informal (Subjective, Impressionistic) and Formal (Mechanical, Algorithmic) Prediction Procedures: The Clinical-Statistical Controversy, *Psychology, Public Policy and Law*, 2(2): 293–323.

Grubin, D. (2008) *Validation of Risk Matrix 2000 for Use in Scotland*, Paisley, Scotland: Risk Management Authority.

Grudzinskas, A.J., Brodsky, D.J., Zaitchik, M., Federoff, J.P., DiCataldo, F. and Clayfield, J.C. (2009) Sexual Predator Laws and their History, in F.M. Saleh and A.J. Grudzinskas (eds) *Sex Offenders: Identification, Risk Assessment, Treatment, and Legal Issues*, Oxford: Oxford University Press, 386–411.

Gudjonsson, G.H. (2009) The Assessment of Terrorist Offenders: A Commentary on the Dernevik et al. Article and Suggestions for Future Directions, *Journal of Forensic Psychiatry and Psychology*, 20(4): 516–19.

Haaken, J. and Lamb, S. (2000) The Politics of Child Sexual Abuse Research, *Society*, 37(4): 7–14.

Hagan, M., Gust-Brey, K., Cho, M. and Dow, E. (2001) Eight Year Comparative Analysis of Adolescent Rapists, Adolescent Child Molesters, Other Adolescent Delinquents, and the General Population, *International Journal of Offender Therapy and Comparative Criminology*, 45(3): 314–24.

Hammarberg, T. (2008) A Juvenile Justice Approach Built on Human Rights Principles, *Youth Justice*, 8(3): 193–6.

Hammel, A. (2006) Preventive Detention in Comparative Perspective, in R. Miller and P. Zumbansen, *Annual of German & European Law Volume II & III*, Oxford: Berghahn Books, 85–115.

Hancock, N. (2002) *Terrorism: Legislation for Security*, Canberra: Parliament of Australia. Available http://www.aph.gov.au/library/pubs/rn/2001-02/02rn25.htm (accessed 23 November 2010).

Hanson, R.K., Bourgon, G., Helmus, L. and Hodgson, S. (2009) The Principles of Effective Correctional Treatment Also Apply to Sexual Offenders: A Meta-Analysis, *Criminal Justice and Behavior*, 36(9): 865–91.

Hanson, R.K., Gordon, A., Harris, A.J.R., Marques, J.K., Murphy, W., Quinsey, V.L. and Seto, M.C. (2002) First Report of the Collaborative Outcome Data on the Effectiveness of Psychological Treatment of Sex Offenders, *Sexual Abuse: A Journal of Research and Treatment*, 14(2): 169–94.

Hanson, R. K., Harris, A. J. R., Scott, T.-L., & Helmus, L. (2007). *Assessing the Risk of Sexual Offenders on Community supervision: The Dynamic Supervision Project (User Report 2007–05)*, Ottawa, ON: Public Safety Canada.

Hanson, R.K. and Howard, P.D. (2010) Individual Confidence Intervals Do Not Inform Decision Makers about the Accuracy of Risk Assessment Evaluations, *Law and Human Behavior*, 34(4): 275–81.

Hanson, R.K. and Thornton, D.M. (1999) *Static 99: Improving Actuarial Risk Assessments for Sex Offenders (User Report 2000-01)*, Ottawa: Department of the Solicitor General of Canada. Available http://www.static99.org/ (accessed 23 November 2010).

____ (2000) Improving Risk Assessments for Sex Offenders: A Comparison of Three Actuarial Scales, *Law and Human Behavior*, 24(1): 119–36.

____ (2002) *Notes on the Development of Static-2002: Report 2003-01*, Ottawa: Department of the Solicitor General of Canada. Available http://www.publicsafety.gc.ca/res/cor/rep/_fl/2003-01-not-sttc-eng.pdf (accessed 23 November 2010).

Haque, Q., Cree, A., Webster, C. and Hasnie, B. (2008) Best Practice in Managing Violence and Related Risks, *Psychiatrist*, 32: 403–5.

Harcourt, B.E. (2006) *Against Prediction; Profiling, Policing, and Punishing In an Actuarial Age*, Chicago: University of Chicago Press.

Harding, C. (2002) International Terrorism: The British Response, *Singapore Journal of Legal Studies*, 16–29.

Hare, R.D. (2003) *The Hare Psychopathy Checklist-Revised*, 2nd edn, Toronto, Ohio: Multi-Health Systems.

Hare, R.D., Clark, D., Grann, M. and Thornton, D. (2000) Psychopathy and the Predictive Validity of the PCL-R: An International Perspective, *Behavioral Sciences and the Law*, 18(5): 623–45.

Harkins, L. and Beech, A. (2006) Measurement of the Effectiveness of Sex Offender Treatment, *Aggression and Violent Behavior*, 12: 36–44.

Harris, A.J. (2006) Risk Assessment and Sex Offender Community Supervision: A Context-Specific Framework, *Federal Probation*, 70(2): 36–42.

Harris, G. T. (2003) Men In His Category have a 50% Likelihood, But Which Half Is He In? Comments on Berlin, Galbraith, Geary and McClone, *Sexual Abuse: A Journal of Research and Treatment*, 15(4): 389–92.

Harris, G.T. and Rice, M.E. (2007) Characterizing the Value of Actuarial Violence Risk Assessments, *Criminal Justice and Behavior*, 34(12): 1638–58.

Harris, G. T., Rice, M. E., and Quinsey, V. (2008) Shall Evidence-Based Risk Assessment Be Abandoned?, *British Journal of Psychiatry*, 192(2): 154.

Hart, S.D. (1998) The Role of Psychopathy in Assessing Risk for Violence: Conceptual and Methodological Issues, *Legal and Criminological Psychology*, 3(1): 121–37.

____ (2008) Psychopathy, Culpability and Commitment in R.F. Schopp, R.L. Weiner, B.H. Bornstein and S.L. Willborn (eds) *Mental Disorder and Criminal Law: Responsibility, Punishment and Competence*, New York: Springer. 159–78.

Hart, S.D., Kropp, P.R., Laws, D., Logan, C. and Watt, K. (2003) *The Risk for Sexual Violence Protocol (RSVP): Structured Professional Guidelines for Assessing Risk of Sexual Violence*, Vancouver: Simon Fraser University Mental Health, Law and Policy Institute.

Hart, S.D., Michie, C. and Cooke, D.J. (2007) Precision of Actuarial Risk Assessment Instruments: Evaluating the "Margins of Error" of Group versus Individual Predictions of Violence, *British Journal of Psychiatry*, 190(sup. 49): s60–s65.

Hassan, P. (1973) The International Covenant on Civil and Political Rights: Background and Perspective on Article 9(1), *Denver Journal of International Law and Policy*, 3(2): 153–83.

Haynes, S.N. (1992) *Models of Causality in Psychopathology: Toward Dynamic, Synthetic, and Nonlinear Models of Behavior Disorders*, New York: Macmillan.

Head, M. (2004) Another Threat to Democratic Rights: ASIO Detentions Cloaked in Secrecy, *Alternative Law Journal*, 29(3): 127–30.

____ (2005) Detention Without Trial: A Threat to Democratic Rights, *University of Western Sydney Law Review*, 9: 33–51.

Heilbrun, K., Ogloff, J.R.P. and Picarello, K. (1999) Dangerous Offender Statutes in the United States and Canada: Implications for Risk Assessment, *International Journal of Law and Psychiatry*, 22(3–4): 393–415.

Hemphill, J.F., Hare, R.D. and Wong, S. (1998) Psychopathy and Recidivism: A Review, *Legal and Criminological Psychology*, 3: 139–70.

Henderson, R. and Keiding, N. (2005) Individual Survival Time Prediction Using Statistical Models, *Journal of Medical Ethics*, 31(11): 703–6.

Henham, R. (1998) Human Rights, Due Process and Sentencing, *British Journal of Criminology*, 38(4): 592–610.

Henkin, L., Pugh, R.C., Schachter, O. and Smit, H. (1987) *International Law: Cases and Materials*, 2nd edn, St. Paul, MN: West Publishing Company.

Her Majesty's Inspectorate of Probation (2007) *Independent Inspection of Probation and Youth Work: Annual Report 2006–7*, London: Her Majesty's Inspectorate of Probation.

Hill, R. (2004) Multiple Sudden Infant Deaths: Coincidence or Beyond Coincidence, *Paediatrics and Perinatal Epidemiology*, 18: 320–6.

Hillyard, P. (1987) The Normalisation of Special Powers: From Northern Ireland to Britain, in P. Scraton (ed.) *Law, Order and the Authoritarian State: Readings in Critical Criminology*, Milton Keynes: Open University Press, 279–312.

Hirschi, T. (1969) *Causes of Delinquency*, Berkeley: University of California Press.

Hiscoke, U.L., Långström, N., Ottosson, H. and Grann, M. (2003) Self-Reported Personality Traits and Disorders (DSM-IV) and Risk of Criminal Recidivism: A Prospective Study, *Journal of Personality Disorders*, 17(4): 293–305.

HMI Probation and HMI Prisons (2010) *Indeterminate Sentences for Public Protection: A Joint Inspection by HMI Probation and HMI Prisons*. Available http://www.justice.gov.uk/inspectorates/hmi-probation/docs/IPP_report_final_2-rps.pdf (accessed 23 November 2010).

Ho, H., Thomson, L. and Darjee, R., (2009) Violence Risk Assessment: The Use of the PCL-SV, HCR-20, and VRAG to Predict Violence in Mentally Disordered Offenders Discharged from a Medium Secure Unit in Scotland, *Journal of Forensic Psychiatry and Psychology*, 20(4): 523–541.

Hodgins, S. (2000) The Etiology and Development of Offending among Persons with Major Mental Disorders, in S. Hodgins (ed.) *Violence among the Mentally Ill: Effective Treatments and Management Strategies*, Dordrecht: Kluwer, p. 89–116.

_____ (2008) Violent Behaviour Among People with Schizophrenia: A Framework for Investigations of Causes, and Effective Treatment, and Prevention, *Philosophical Transactions of the Royal Society of London*, Series B 363(1503): 2505–18.

Hogan, M.F. (2003) The President's New Freedom Commission: Recommendations to Transform Mental Health Care in America, *Psychiatric Services*, 54(11): 1467–74.

Hoge, R.D. (2008) Assessment in Juvenile Justice Systems, in R.D. Hoge, N.G. Guerra and P. Boxer (eds) *Treating the Juvenile Offender*, New York: Guilford Press, p. 54–75.

Hoge, R. and Andrews, D. (2002) *The Youth Level of Service/Case Management Inventory*, Toronto: Multi-Health Systems.

Home Office (1999*) Managing Dangerous People with Severe Personality Disorder: Proposals for Policy Development*, London: Home Office.

_____ (2004) *Dangerous and Severe Personality Disorder (DSPD) High Secure Services: Planning and Delivery Guide*, London: Home Office, HM Prison Service and Department of Health.

_____ (2009) *Police Recorded Crime 2008–09*, London: Home Office.

Hood, C. and Jones, D.K.C. (eds) (1996) *Accident and Design: Contemporary Debates in Risk Management*, London: UCL Press.

Houchin, R. (2003) Significant Change is Likely in Our Prisons: The Question Is, Change in What Direction?, *Probation Journal*, 50(2): 142–8.

Howard, P., Clark, D. and Garnham, N. (2006) *An Evaluation of the Offender Assessment System (OASys) in Three Pilots 1999–2001*, London: National Offender Management Service.

Howard League for Penal Reform (2010) *Weekly Prison Watch*. Available http://www.howardleague.org/1114/ (accessed 23 November 2010).

Hudson, B. (2009) Justice in a Time of Terror, *British Journal of Criminology*, 49(5): 702–17.

Human Rights Committee (1982) *General Comment No 8: Right to Liberty and Security of Persons (Art 9)*, UN Doc HRI/GEN/1/Rev.1 (30 June 1982).

_____ (2001) *General Comment No 29: States of Emergency (Art 4)*, UN Doc CCPR/C/21/Rev.1/Add.11 (21 August 2001).

Hunter, G. (2006) *Review of Care Programme Approach Guidance for Restricted Patients in Scotland*, Lanark, Scotland: Forensic Network.

Hyun, J.K., Nawka, P., Kang, H., Hu, T. and Bloom, J. (2008). Recovery-and-Community-Based Mental Health Services in the Slovak Republic: A Pilot Study on the Implications for Hospitalization and Inpatient Length-of-Stay for Individuals with Severe and Persistent Mental Illness, *International Journal of Psychosocial Rehabilitation*, 13(1): 67–80.

Information and Statistics Division Scotland (2010) *Bed Statistics: Available Beds by Specialty and NHS Board of Treatment*, Edinburgh: Information and Statistics Division Scotland.

Institute of Mental Health (2008) *Working Effectively with Personality Disorder: The New KUF Framework*, Nottingham: Institute of Mental Health. Available http://www.institutemh.org.uk/images/stories/Personality%20disorder_nov_09.pdf (accessed 23 November 2010).

International Commission of Jurists (2005) *Memorandum on International Legal Framework on Administrative Detention and Counter-Terrorism*. Available http://www.mafhoum.com/press9/278S25.pdf (accessed 23 November 2010).

Jacob Wetterling Resource Center (2010) *Does JWRC Support Laws that Prohibit Sex Offenders from Living Within a Certain Distance from Schools, Parks, or Daycare Centers?* Available http://www.jwrc.org/GetHelpNow/SexualExploitation/ResidencyRestrictions/tabid/84/Default.aspx (accessed 23 November 2010).

Jacobson, J. and Hough, M. (2010) *Unjust Deserts: Imprisonment for Public Protection*, London: Prison Reform Trust.

Jagirdar, S. (2009) Florida Department of Law Enforcement Launches New Halloween-Themed Radio Public Service Announcement, *Florida Department of Law Enforcement*, 12 October. Available http://www.fdle.state.fl.us/Content/News/October-2009/FDLE-Launches-New-Halloween-Themed-Radio-Public-Se.aspx (accessed 23 November 2010).

Jamieson, E. and Taylor, P.J. (2004) A Re-Conviction Study of Special (High Security) Hospital Patients, *British Journal of Criminology*, 44(5): 783–802.

Jamison, K.R. (1993) *Touched with Fire: Manic Depressive Illness and the Artistic Temperament*, New York: Free Press.

____ (1995) *An Unquiet Mind*, New York: A.A. Knopf.

Janus, E.S. (2003) Minnesota's Sex Offender Commitment Program: Would an Empirically-Based Prevention Policy Be More Effective?, *William Mitchell Law Review*, 29(4): 1083–1133.

____ (2004) Closing Pandora's Box: Sexual Predators and the Politics of Sexual Violence, *Seton Hall Law Review*, 34(4): 1233–53.

____ (2006) *Failure to Protect: America's Sexual Predator Laws and the Rise of the Preventive State*, Ithaca: Cornell University Press.

Janus, E.S. and Bolin, B. (2008) An End-Game for Sexually Violent Predator Laws: As-Applied Invalidation, *Ohio State Journal of Criminal Law*, 6(1): 25–49.

Janus, E.S. and Logan, W.A. (2003) Substantive Due Process and the Involuntary Confinement of Sexually Violent Predators, *Connecticut Law Review*, 35(2): 319–84.

Janus, E.S. and Prentky, R.A. (2003) Forensic Use of Actuarial Risk Assessment with Sex Offenders: Accuracy, Admissibility and Accountability, *American Criminal Law Review*, 40(4): 1443–99.

____ (2008) Sexual Predator Laws: A Two-Decade Retrospective, *Federal Sentencing Reporter*, 21(2): 90–97.

Jenkins, P. (2009) Failure to Launch: Why Do Some Social Issues Fail to Detonate Moral Panics?, *British Journal of Criminology*, 49(1): 35–47.

John Howard Society of Alberta (1999) *Dangerous Offender Legislation Around the World*, Edmonton: John Howard Society of Alberta.

Johnstone, L. and Cooke, D.J. (2004) Psychopathic-Like Traits in Childhood: Conceptual and Developmental Concerns, *Behavioral Sciences and the Law*, 22(1): 103–25.

Jones, K (1993) *Asylums and After: A Revised History of the Mental Health Services: From Early Eighteenth Century to 1990s*, London: Athloane Press.

Joseph, N. (2008) *PC21/2008—Managing High Risk of Serious Harm Offenders with Severe Personality Disorder: Probation Circular*. Available www.dspdprogramme.gov.uk/media/pdfs/ProbationCircular_Nov08.pdf (accessed 23 November 2010).

Joseph, S. (2004) Australian Counter-Terrorism Legislation and the International Human Rights Framework, *University of New South Wales Law Journal*, 27(2): 428–53.

Joseph, S., Schultz, J. and Castan, M. (2004) *The International Covenant on Civil and Political Rights: Cases Materials and Commentary*, 2nd edn, Oxford: Oxford University Press.

Junginger, J., Claypoole, K., Laygo, R. and Cristiani, A. (2006) Effects of Serious Mental Illness and Substance Abuse on Criminal Offenses, *Psychiatric Services*, 57(6): 879–82.

Kagan, J. (1971) *Change and Continuity in Infancy*, New York: Wiley.

Kahn, T.J. and Chambers, H.J. (1991) Assessing Reoffense Risk with Juvenile Sex Offenders, *Child Welfare*, 70: 333–45.

Kaszuba, M. (2010) Bill Stuck on Sex Offender Funding, *Minneapolis Star Tribune*, 9 March. Available http://www.highbeam.com/doc/1G1-220803858.html (accessed 23 November 2010).

Kazdin, A.E. (2007) Mediators and Mechanisms of Change in Psychotherapy Research, *Annual Review in Clinical Psychology*, 3: 1–27.

Keating, D. (1990) Adolescent Thinking, in S. Feldman and G. Elliot (eds) *At the Threshold: The Developing Adolescent*, Cambridge: Harvard University Press, p. 54–94.

Keiser, G. (2009) *Program Design Elements and Principles of Effective Community Corrections Responses.* Invited panel presented at the Bureau of Justice Assistance Technical Assistance and Training Event for National Grantees, Washington, July 2009.

Kemshall, H. (2008) *Understanding the Community Management of High Risk Offenders*, Maidenhead, England: Open University Press.

_____ (2009) Understanding the Community Management of High Risk Sex Offenders, *Howard Journal of Criminal Justice*, 48(5): 543–4.

Kernberg, O.F. (1990). Hatred as Pleasure, in R.A. Glick and S. Bone (eds) *Pleasure Beyond the Pleasure Principle*, New Haven, CT: Yale University Press, pp. 177–88.

_____ (1998) Pathological Narcissism and Narcissistic Personality Disorder: Theoretical Background and Diagnostic Classifications, in E.F. Ronningstam (ed.) *Disorders of Narcissism: Diagnostic, Clinical and Empirical Implications*, Washington: American Psychiatric Press, pp. 29–52.

Kerr, D. (2004) Australia's Legislative Response to Terrorism: Strengthening Arbitrary Executive Power at the Expense of the Rule of Law, *Alternative Law Journal*, 29(3): 131–4.

Keyzer, P. (2008) Preserving Due Process or Warehousing the Undesirables: To What End the Separation of Judicial Power of the Commonwealth?, *Sydney Law Review*, 30(1): 101–13.

_____ (2009a) The Dangerous Prisoners (Sexual Offenders) Act: Are the Best Available Rehabilitative Resources Available?, *Criminal Law Journal*, 33(3): 175–9.

_____ (2009b) The "Preventive Detention" of Serious Sex Offenders: Further Consideration of the International Human Rights Dimensions, *Psychiatry, Psychology and Law*, 16(2): 262–70.

Keyzer, P. and Blay, S. (2006) Double Punishment? Preventive Detention Schemes under Australian Legislation and their Consistency with International Law: The Fardon Communication, *Melbourne Journal of International Law*, 7(2): 407–27.

Keyzer, P. and Coyle, I. (2009) Reintegrating Sex Offenders into the Community, *Alternative Law Journal*, 34(1): 27–31.

Keyzer, P., Periera, C. and Southwood, S. (2004) Pre-Emptive Imprisonment for Dangerousness in Queensland under the Dangerous Prisoners (Sexual Offenders) Act 2003: The Constitutional Issues, *Psychiatry, Psychology and Law*, 11: 244–53.

Khiroya, R., Weaver, T. and Maden, A. (2009) Use and Perceived Utility of Structured Violence Risk Assessments in English Medium Secure Forensic Units, *Psychiatrist*, 33: 129–32.

Kingston, D.A., Yates, P.M., Firestone, P., Babchishin, K. and Bradford, J.M. (2008) Long-Term Predictive Validity of the Risk Matrix 2000: A Comparison with the Static-99 and the Sex Offender Risk Appraisal Guide, *Sexual Abuse: A Journal of Research and Treatment*, 20(4): 466–84.

Kirk, S. and Kutchins, H. (1994) The Myth of the Reliability of DSM, *Journal of Mind and Behavior*, 15: 71–86.

Koch, W. (2005) Despite High-Profile Cases, Sex-Offense Crimes Decline, *USA Today*, 24 August. Available http://www.usatoday.com/news/nation/2005-08-24-sex-crimes-cover_x.htm (accessed 23 November 2010).

Kroner, D.G., Mills, J.F. and Reddon, J.R. (2005) A Coffee Can, Factor Analysis, and Prediction of Antisocial Behavior: The Structure of Criminal Risk, *International Journal of Law and Psychiatry*, 28(4): 360–74.

Kropp, P.R., Hart, S.D. and Webster, C.D. (1999) *Spousal Assault Risk Assessment Guide (SARA)*, Toronto: Multi-Health Systems.

Kropp, P.R., Hart, S.D., Webster, C.D., and Eaves, D. (1994) *Manual for the Spousal Assault Risk Assessment Guide*, Vancouver: British Columbia Institute for Family Violence.

Krzysztofowwicz, R. (2001) The Case for Probalistic Forcasting in Hydrology, *Journal of Hydrology*, 249: 2–9.

La Fond, J.Q. (1992a) Washington's Sexually Violent Predator Law: A Deliberate Misuse of the Therapeutic State for Social Control, *University of Puget Sound Law Review*, 15: 655–708.

_____ (1992b) Washington's Violent Predator Statute: Law or Lottery? A Response to Professor Brooks, *University of Puget Sound Law Review*, 15: 755–9.

_____ (1998) The Costs of Enacting a Sexual Predator Law, *Psychology, Public Policy and Law*, 4(1): 468–504.

_____ (2005) *Preventing Sexual Violence: How Society Should Cope with Sex Offenders*, Washington: American Psychological Association.

_____ (2008) Sexually Violent Predator Laws and the Liberal State: An Ominous Threat to Individual Liberty, *International Journal of Law and Psychiatry*, 31(2): 158–71.

La Fond, J.Q. and Durham, M.L. (1992) *Back to the Asylum: The Future of Mental Health Law and Policy in the United States*, New York: Oxford University Press.

La Fond, J.Q. and Winick, B.J. (2003) Sex Offender Reentry Courts: A Cost-Effective Proposal for Managing Sex Offender Risk in the Community, *Annals of New York Academy of Sciences,* 989: 300–23.

_____ (2004) Sex Offender Reentry Courts: A Proposal for Managing the Risk of Returning Sex Offenders to the Community, *Seton Hall Law Review,* 34(4): 1172–1212.

Lamb, H. and Weinberger, L. (1998) Persons with Severe Mental Illness in Jails and Prisons: A Review, *Psychiatric Services,* 49(4): 483–92.

Lanagan, P.A., Schmitt, E.L. and Durose, M.R. (2003) *Recidivism of Sex Offenders Released from Prison in 1994,* Washington: Department of Justice, Bureau of Justice Statistics. Available http://bjs.ojp.usdoj.gov/content/pub/pdf/rsorp94.pdf (accessed 23 November 2010).

Landenberger, N. and Lipsey, M. (2005) The Positive Effects of Cognitive-Behavioral Programs for Offenders: A Meta-Analysis of Factors Associated with Effective Treatment, *Journal of Experimental Criminology,* 1(4): 451–76.

Landers, C. (2008) Exiles on Main Street, *Baltimore City Pages,* 10 December. Available http://www.citypaper.com/news/story.asp?id=17180 (accessed 23 November 2010).

Laney, G.P. (2008) *Residence Restrictions for Released Sex Offenders: CRS Report for Congress: Domestic Social Policy Division.* Available http://www.criminallawlibraryblog.com/CRS_RPT_DomesticViolence_02-05-2008.pdf (accessed 23 November 2010).

Lantigua, J. (2009) Nearly 80 Sex Offenders Scratch out a Life under Miami's Julia Tuttle Causeway, *The Palm Beach Post,* 1 July. Available http://www.palmbeachpost.com/state/content/state/epaper/2009/07/01/sexoffenders.html (accessed 23 November 2010).

Laville, S. (2009) Counter-Terror Police "Failed to Seek Legal Advice Before Arrests," *The Guardian Online,* 24 November. Available http://www.guardian.co.uk/uk/2009/nov/24/counter-terrorism-police-legal-advice (accessed 23 November 2010).

Levene, K.S., Madsen, K.C., Pepler, D., Walsh, M., Webster, C.D. and Koegl, C.J. (2001) *The Early Assessment of Risk for Girls (EARL-21G),* Toronto: Earlscourt Child and Family Centre.

Levenson, J. and Tewksbury, R. (2009) Collateral Damage: Family Members of Registered Sex Offenders, *American Journal of Criminal Justice,* 34(1): 54–68.

Lieb, R. (2003) Joined-Up Worrying: The Multi-Agency Public Protection Panels, in A. Matravers (ed) *Sex Offenders in the Community: Managing and Reducing the Risk,* Cullompton, England: Willan, pp. 207–18.

Lightfoot, J. (1998) Striking the Balance—Abolition of the Governor's Pleasure System, *Psychiatry, Psychology and Law,* 5(2): 265–9.

Lillich, R. and Hannum, H. (1995) *International Human Rights: Problems of Law, Policy and Practice,* 3rd edn, New York: Aspen.

Lindley, D.V. (2006) *Understanding Uncertainty,* Hoboken, NJ: Wiley.

Lindqvist, P., Taylor, P., Kramp, P., Kaliski, S., Yoshikawa, K., Gagné, P. and Thomson, L. (2009) Offenders with Mental Disorder on Five Continents: A Comparison of Approaches to Treatment and Demographic Factors Relevant to Measurement of Outcome, *International Journal of Forensic Mental Health* 8(2): 81–96.

Linehan, M.M., Comtois, K.A., Murray, A.M., Brown, M.Z., Gallop, R.J., Heard, H.L., Korslund, K.E., Tutek, D.A., Reynolds, S.K. and Lindenboim, M. (2006) Two-Year Randomized Controlled Trial and Follow-Up of Dialectical Behavior Therapy vs Therapy by Experts for Suicidal Behaviors and Borderline Personality Disorder, *Archives of General Psychiatry,* 63(7): 757–66.

Lipsey, M. and Derzon, J. (1998) Predictors of Violent or Serious Delinquency in Adolescence and Early Adulthood: A Synthesis of Longitudinal Research, in R. Loeber and D.P. Farrington (eds) *Serious and Violent Juvenile Offenders: Risk Factors and Successful Interventions,* Thousand Oaks, CA: Sage. 86-105.

Lipsey, M.W. and Landenberger, N.A. (2006) Cognitive-Behavioral Interventions, in B.C. Welsh and D.P. Farrington (eds) *Preventing Crime: What Works for Children, Offenders, Victims, and Places,* Dordrecht: Springer, pp. 57–72.

Livesley, J. (2003) *Practical Management of Personality Disorder,* New York: Guilford Press.

Logan, C. and Blackburn, R. (2009) Mental Disorder in Violent Women in Secure Settings: Potential Relevance to Risk for Future Violence, *International Journal of Law and Psychiatry,* 32(1): 31–38.

Logan, C. and Johnstone, L. (2010) Personality Disorder and Violence: Making the Link through Risk Formulation, *Journal of Personality Disorder* 24(5): 610–33.

Logan, W.A. (2009) *Knowledge as Power: Criminal Registration and Community Notification Laws in America,* Stanford, CA: Stanford Law Books.

Loranger, A.W. (1999) *International Personality Disorder Examination Manual*, Odessa: Psychological Assessment Resources.

Lovell, D.L., Johnson, L.C. and Kane, K.C. (2007) Recidivism of Supermax Prisoners in Washington State, *Crime and Delinquency*, 53(4): 633–56.

Lowenkamp, C., Latessa, E. and Holsinger, A. (2006a) The Risk Principle in Action: What Have We Learned from 13,676 Offenders and 97 Correctional Programs?, *Crime and Delinquency*, 52(1): 77–93.

Lowenkamp, C., Pealer, J., Smith, P. and Latessa, E. (2006b) Adhering to the Risk and Need Principles: Does It Matter for Supervision-Based Programs, *Federal Probation*, 70(3): 3–8.

Lucy, D. (2005) *Introduction to Statistics for Forensic Scientists*, Chichester: Wiley.

Lutterman, T. (2007) *Fiscal Year 2005 State Mental Health Agency Revenues and Expenditures: Key Findings*. Washington D.C.: National Association of State Mental Health Program Directors Research Institute. Available http://www.nri-inc.org/projects/Profiles/RevExp2005/keyfinds2005.pdf (accessed 23 November 2010).

Lynch, A., and Williams, G. (2006) *What Price Security?: Taking Stock of Australia's Anti-Terror Laws*, Sydney: University of New South Wales Press.

Macken, C. (2005) Preventive Detention and the Right of Personal Liberty and Security under the International Covenant on Civil and Political Rights, 1966, *Adelaide Law Review*, 26(1): 1–28.

Maden, A., Skapinakis, P., Lewis, G., Scott, F. and Jamieson, E. (2006) Gender Differences in Re-Offending after Discharge from Medium Secure Units: National Cohort Study in England and Wales, *British Journal of Psychiatry*, 189(4): 168–72.

Manson, W. (2010) Outcomes of Offenders within MAPPA in Scotland, personal communication.

Marr, D. (2007) We Got it Wrong on Haneef: DPP Chief, *Sydney Morning Herald*, 13 October 2007. Available http://www.smh.com.au/news/national/we-got-it-wrong-on-haneef/2007/10/12/1191696181083.html (accessed 23 November 2010).

Marshall, D. (2009) *Lambs to the Slaughter: Inside the Depraved Mind of Child Killer Derek Percy*, North Sydney: Random House.

Marton, J. and Wildasin, D.E. (2007) Medicaid Expenditures and State Budgets: Past, Present, and Future, *National Tax Journal*, 60(2): 279–304.

Martin, J. (1984) *Hospitals in Trouble*, Oxford: Basil Blackwell.

McCallum, F. (2000) *Sentencing of Serious Violent and Sexual Offenders. Annex 2: A Report of the Committee on Serious Violent and Sexual Offenders*, Edinburgh: Scottish Executive.

McCauliff, C.M.A. (1982) Burdens of Proof: Degrees of Belief, Quanta of Evidence, or Constitutional Guarantees?, *Vanderbilt Law Review*, 35(6): 1293–1335.

MacDonald, S. (2007) ASBOs and Control Orders: Two Recurring Themes, Two Apparent Contradictions, *Parliamentary Affairs*, 60(4): 601–24.

MacDonald, E. and Williams, G., (2007) Combating Terrorism: Australia's *Criminal Code* since September 11, 2001, *Griffith Law Review*, 16(1): 27–54.

McHarg, A. (1999) Reconciling Human Rights and the Public Interest: Conceptual Problems and Doctrinal Uncertainty in the Jurisprudence of the European Court of Human Rights, *Modern Law Review*, 62: 671–96.

McMurran, M. (2009) Personality, Personality Disorder and Violence: Implications for Future Research and Practice, in M. McMurran and R. Howard (eds) *Personality, Personality Disorder and Violence*, Chichester: Wiley-Blackwell, pp. 3–18.

McMurran, M. and Howard, R. (eds) (2009) *Personality, Personality Disorder and Violence*, Chichester: Wiley-Blackwell.

McSherry, B. (1999) Criminal Detention of Those with Mental Impairment, *Journal of Law and Medicine*, 6(3): 216–21.

____ (2004) Terrorism Offences in the Criminal Code (Cth): Broadening the Boundaries of Australian Criminal Laws, *University of New South Wales Law Journal*, 27(2): 354–72.

____ (2005) Indefinite and Preventive Detention Legislation: From Caution to an Open Door, *Criminal Law Journal*, 29(2): 94–110.

McSherry, B. and Keyzer, P. (2009) *Sex Offenders and Preventive Detention: Politics, Policy and Practice*, Annandale: Federation Press.

McSherry, B., Keyzer, P. and Freiberg, A. (2006) *Preventive Detention for "Dangerous" Offenders in Australia: A Critical Analysis and Proposals for Policy Development: Report to the Criminology Research Council*, Canberra: Criminology Research Council.

Melton, G., Petrila, J., Poythress, N. and Slobogin, C. (2007) *Psychological Evaluations for the Courts: A Handbook for Mental Health Professionals and Lawyers,* 3rd edn, New York: Guilford Press.

Mental Welfare Commission (2006) *Report of the Inquiry into the Care and Treatment of Mr L and Mr M*, Edinburgh: Mental Welfare Commission.

Mental Welfare Commission for Scotland (2009) *Annual Report 2008–09*, Edinburgh: Mental Welfare Commission for Scotland.

Mercado, C.C. (2009) Are Residence Restrictions an Effective Way to Reduce the Risk Posed by Sex Offenders?, *American Psychology Law News*, 29(2): 6–8.

Miccio-Fonseca, L.C. (2006a) *Multiplex Empirically Guided Inventory of Ecological Aggregates for Assessing Sexually Abusive Children and Adolescents (Ages 19 and Under)*, San Diego: MEGA.

_____ (2006b) *Multiplex Empirically Guided Inventory of Ecological Aggregates for Assessing Sexually Abusive Children and Adolescents (Ages 19 and Under)—MEGA Annual and Rating Booklet*, San Diego: MEGA.

_____ (2009) MEGA: A New Paradigm in Protocol Assessing Sexually Abusive Children and Adolescents, *Journal of Child and Adolescent Trauma*, 2:124–41.

Miccio-Fonseca, L.C. and Rasmussen, L.A. (2006) *Implementing MEGA, a New Tool for Assessing Risk of Concern for Sexually Abusive Behavior in Youth Ages 19 and Under: An Empirically Guided Paradigm for Risk Assessment* (rev. version), Orange, CA: California Coalition on Sexual Offending.

Michaelsen, C. (2008) The Proportionality Principle in the Context of Anti-Terrorism Laws: An Inquiry into the Boundaries Between Human Rights Law and Public Policy, in M. Gani and P. Mathew (eds) *Fresh Perspectives on the "War on Terror,"* Canberra: ANU E Press, pp. 109–24.

Mildwurf, B. (2009) Budget Cuts Hitting Mental Health With "Vengeance," *WRAL.com*. October 7. Available http://www.wral.com/news/local/story/6119965/ (accessed 23 November 2010).

Mill, J.S. (1863) *Utilitarianism*, London: Parker, Son and Bourn.

Miller, G.H. (2008) Alan Stone and the Ethics of Forensic Psychiatry: An Overview, *Journal of the American Academy of Psychiatry and Law*, 36(2): 191–194.

Miller, K.D. and Waller, G.H. (2003) Scenarios, Real Options and Integrated Risk Management, *Long Range Planning*, 36(1): 93–107.

Miller, N. (2009) *Sex-Crime Panic: A Journey to the Paranoid Heart of the 1950s*, Los Angeles: Alyson Books.

Miller, T.R., Taylor, D.M. and Sheppard, M.A. (2007) *Costs of Sexual Violence in Minnesota*, St. Paul: Minnesota Department of Health.

Milligton, J. (2010) personal communication.

Miner, M. (2007) Editorial: Is This Any Way to Develop Policy?, *Sexual Offender Treatment.org*, 2(1). Available http://www.sexual-offender-treatment.org/54.html (accessed 23 November 2010).

Ministry of Justice (2009) *Reports into the Management of Dano Sonnex Within the Criminal Justice System*. Available http://www.justice.gov.uk/news/announcement040609a.htm (accessed 23 November 2010).

_____ (2010a) personal communication.

_____ (2010b) *Statistics of Mentally Disordered Offenders 2008 England and Wales*, London: Ministry of Justice. Available http://www.justice.gov.uk/publications/mentally-disordered-offenders.htm (accessed 23 November 2010).

Ministry of Justice and Department of Health (2010) *The DSPD Programme: Dangerous People with Severe Personality Disorder*, London: Ministry of Justice and Department of Health. Online. Available http://www.dspdprogramme.gov.uk/research.html (accessed 23 November 2010).

Ministry of Justice National Offender Management Service (2010) *Population in Custody Statistics*, London: Ministry of Justice. Available http://www.justice.gov.uk/publications/populationincustody.htm (accessed 23 November 2010).

Minnesota Department of Health (2009) *The Promise of Primary Prevention of Sexual Violence: A Five-Year Plan to Prevent Sexual Violence and Exploitation in Minnesota*. Available www.health.state.mn.us/injury/pub/svpplan.pdf (accessed 23 November 2010).

Molenaar, P.C.M. (2004) A Manifesto on Psychology as Idiographic Science: Bringing the Person Back into Scientific Psychology, This Time Forever, *Measurement: Interdisciplinary Research and Perspective*, 2(4): 201–18.

Molenaar, P.C.M. and Campbell, C.G. (2009) The New Person-Specific Paradigm in Psychology, *Current Directions in Psychological Science*, 18(2): 112–17.

Monahan, J. (1981) *Predicting Violent Behavior: An Assessment of Clinical Techniques*, Beverly Hills: Sage.

_____ (1984) The Prediction of Violent Behaviour: Towards a Second Generation of Theory and Policy, *American Journal of Psychiatry*, 141(1): 10–15.

_____ (2006) A Jurisprudence of Risk Assessment: Forecasting Harm among Prisoners, Predators and Patients, *Virginia Law Review*, 92(3): 391–435.

_____ (2008) Statistical Literacy: A Prerequisite for Evidence-Based Medicine, *Psychological Science in the Public Interest*, 8(2): i–ii.

Monahan, J., Steadman, H., Appelbaum, P., Grisso, T., Mulvey, E. and Silver, E. (2001) *Rethinking Risk Assessment: The MacArthur Study of Mental Disorder and Violence*, Oxford: Oxford University Press.

Morgan, F., Morgan, N. and Morgan, I. (1998) *Risk Assessment in Sentencing and Corrections*, Perth: University of Western Australia.

Morgan, R., Fisher, W. and Wolff, N. (2010) *Criminal Thinking: Do People with Mental Illnesses Think Differently? Policy Brief of the Center for Behavioral Health Services and Criminal Justice Research.* Available www.cbhs-cjr.rutgers.edu/pdfs/Policy_Brief_April_2010.pdf (accessed 23 November 2010).

Morrissey, J., Meyer, P. and Cuddeback, G. (2007) Extending Assertive Community Treatment to Criminal Justice Settings: Origins, Current Evidence, and Future Directions, *Community Mental Health Journal*, 43(5): 527–44.

Mossman, D. (1994) Assessing Predictions of Violence: Being Accurate about Accuracy, *Journal of Consulting and Clinical Psychology*, 62(4): 783–92.

_____ (2009) The Imperfection of Protection through Detection and Intervention: Lessons from Three Decades of Research on the Psychiatric Assessment of Violence Risk, *Journal of Legal Medicine*, 30(1): 109–40.

Mossman, D. and Sellke, T. (2007) Avoiding Errors about "Margins of Error," *British Journal of Psychiatry*, 191: 561.

Mueser, K., Bond, G., Drake, R. and Resnick, S. (1998) Models of Community Care for Severe Mental Illness: A Review of Research on Case Management, *Schizophrenia Bulletin*, 24(1): 37–74.

Mullen, P.E. (2001) *Mental Health and Criminal Justice: A Review of the Relationship Between Mental Disorders and Offending Behaviours on the Management of Mentally Abnormal Offenders in the Health and Criminal Justice Services*, Melbourne: Criminology Research Council.

Murphy, T. and Whitty, N. (2007) Risk and Human Rights: Ending Slopping Out in a Scottish Prison, in J. Morison, K. McEvoy and G. Anthony (eds) *Judges, Transition and Human Rights*, Oxford: Oxford University Press, pp. 535–8.

National Center for Missing and Exploited Children (2010) *Map of Registered Sex Offenders in the United States December 8, 2009.* Available http://www.missingkids.com/en_US/documents/sex-offender-map.pdf (accessed 23 November 2010).

National Confidential Inquiry into Suicide and Homicide by People with Mental Illness (2008) *Lessons for Mental Health Care in Scotland*, Manchester: University of Manchester.

National Health Service Executive (1994) *Health Service Guidance 27(HSG(94)27)*, London: NHS Executive.

National Health Service Executive and Social Services Inspectorate (1999) *Effective Care Co-ordination in Mental Health Services: Modernising the Care Programme Approach: A Policy Booklet*, London: NHS Executive.

National Institute for Mental Health in England (2003a) *Breaking the Cycle of Rejection: The Personality Disorder Capabilities Framework*, Leeds: National Institute for Mental Health in England.

_____ (2003b) *Personality Disorder: No Longer a Diagnosis of Exclusion: Policy Implementation Guidance of the Development of Services for People with Personality Disorder,* London: National Institute for Mental Health in England.

National Statistics Publication for Scotland (2009) *Reconviction Rates in Scotland: 2005-06 and 2006-07: Offender Cohorts*, Edinburgh: National Statistics Publication for Scotland.

Neighbour, S. (2007) Charge Suspects to Test Terror Laws, *The Australian*, 13 November. Available http://www.theaustralian.com.au/news/charge-suspects-to-test-terror-laws/story-e6frg6o6-1111114862643 (accessed 23 November 2010).

Newton-Howes, G., Tyrer, P. and Johnson, T. (2006) Personality Disorder and the Outcome of Depression: Meta-Analysis of Published Studies, *British Journal of Psychiatry*, 188(1): 13–20.

Nicholls T., Ogloff J., Brink J. and Spidel, A. (2005) Psychopathy in Women: A Review of its Clinical Usefulness for Assessing Risk for Aggression and Criminality, *Behavioral Sciences and the Law*, 23(6): 779–802.

Northern Ireland Prison Service (2010) *Prison Statistics*, Belfast: Northern Ireland Prison Service. Available http://www.niprisonservice.gov.uk/index.cfm/area/information/page/factandfigures (accessed 23 November 2010).

Nowak, M. (2005) *U.N. Covenant on Civil and Political Rights: CCPR Commentary*, 2nd edn, Kehl, Germany: N.P. Engel.

O'Brien, T. (1998) Would Megan's Law Have Saved Megan?, *New Jersey Law Journal*, 145(2): 1–3.

Office of the High Commissioner for Human Rights in Cooperation with the International Bar Association (2003) *Human Rights in the Administration of Justice: A Manual on Human Rights for Judges, Prosecutors and Lawyers*, New York: United Nations.

Office for National Statistics (2009) *Population Statistics*, Newport: Office for National Statistics.

_____ (2010) *Employment Statistics*, Newport: Office for National Statistics.

Office of the Surgeon-General (2001) *Youth Violence: A Report of the Surgeon-General: Executive Summary*, Rockville, MD: US Department of Health and Human Services.

O'Meara, K. (1999) Innocence Lost?, *Insight Magazine*, 24 May. Available http://www.prevent-abuse-now.com/rebuttal.htm#Lost (accessed 23 November 2010).

O'Neill, N. (1987) Constitutional Human Rights in Australia, *Federal Law Review*, 17(2): 85–131.

Osher, F. and Steadman, H. (2007) Adapting Evidence-Based Practices for Person with Mental Illness Involved with the Criminal Justice System', *Psychiatric Services*, 58(11): 1472–8.

Palmer, A. (2004) Investigating and Prosecuting Terrorism: The Counter-Terrorism Legislation and the Law of Evidence, *University of New South Wales Law Journal*, 27(2): 373–97.

Parker, A. (2005) *The Rest of Their Lives: Life without Parole for Child Offenders in the United States*, New York: Amnesty International/Human Rights Watch.

Parliament of Victoria Community Development Committee (1995) *Report Upon the Review of Legislation Under which Persons are Detained at the Governor's Pleasure in Victoria*, Melbourne: Victorian Government Printer.

Parliamentary Debates (1991) House of Commons, 16 July (Home Secretary on Discretionary Life Sentences).

Pereira, C. (2001) The Tyranny of Distance: Disadvantage in Queensland's Regional Prisons, *Alternative Law Journal*, 26(2): 74–80, 84.

Petersen, A.C. (1988) Adolescent Development, *Annual Review of Psychology*, 39: 583–607.

Peterson, J.K., Skeem, J.L., Hart, E., Vidal, S. and Keith, F. (in press) Comparing the Offense Patterns of Offenders with and without Mental Disorder: Exploring the Criminalization Hypothesis, *Psychiatric Services*.

Petrila, J. (2009) An International Perspective on Juvenile Justice Issues, in B.L. Bottoms and C.J. Najdowski (eds) *Children as Victims, Witnesses and Offenders: Psychological Science and the Law*, New York: Guilford Press, pp. 369–84.

Petrunik, M. (2003) The Hare and the Tortoise: Dangerousness and Sex Offender Policy in the United States and Canada, *Canadian Journal of Criminology and Criminal Justice*, 45(1): 43–72.

Petrunik, M., Murphy, L. and Federoff, J.P. (2008) American and Canadian Approaches to Sex Offenders: A Study of the Politics of Dangerousness, *Federal Sentencing Reporter*, 21(2): 111–23.

Pfaffenroth, P.C. (2003) The Need for Coherence: States' Civil Commitment of Sex Offenders in the Wake of Kansas v. Crane, *Stanford Law Review*, 55(6): 2229–66.

Piaget, J. (1972) Intellectual Evolution from Adolescence to Adulthood, *Human Development*, 15: 1–21.

_____ (1973) *The Child's Conception of the World*, London: Paladin.

Piat, M. Sabetti, J. and Bloom, D. (2010) The Transformation of Mental Health Services to a Recovery-Oriented System of Care: Canadian Decision Maker Perspectives, *International Journal of Social Psychiatry*, 56(2): 168–77.

Piller, C. and Romney, L. (2008a) Jessica's Law May not be Hospitalizing More Post-Prison Sex Offenders, *Los Angeles Times*, 11 August.

_____ (2008b) Jessica's Law Pays Dividend for Some, *Los Angeles Times*, 10 August. Available http://articles.latimes.com/2008/aug/10/local/me-jessica10 (accessed 23 November 2010).

Pinkham, P. (2005) Offender Center Run in Disarray, *Florida Times-Union*, April 25. Available http://jacksonville.com/tu-online/stories/042505/met_debt1.shtml (accessed 23 November 2010).

Police Service of Northern Ireland Recorded Crime Central Statistics Branch (2009), *Recorded Crime and Clearances 1st April 2008 – 31st March 2009*, Belfast: Police Service of Northern Ireland Operational Support Department. Available http://www.psni.police.uk/08_09_recorded_crime.pdf (accessed 23 November 2010).

Porter, S. and Woodworth, M. (2006) Psychopathy and Aggression, in C.J. Patrick (ed) *Handbook of Psychopathy*, New York: Guilford Press, pp. 481–94.

Potter, D. (2010) Sexual-Predator Program Faces $26 Million Shortfall, *Richmond Times-Dispatch*, 10 July. Available http://www2.timesdispatch.com/news/rtd-news/2010/jul/10/pred10-ar-287188/ (accessed 23 November 2010).

Power, H. (2003) Disclosing Information on Sex Offenders: The Human Rights Implication, in A. Matravers (ed) *Sex Offenders in the Community: Managing and Reducing the Risks*, Cullompton, England: Willan, pp. 72–101.

Pratt, J. (1997) *Governing the Dangerous: Dangerousness, Law and Social Change*, Leichhardt, New South Wales: Federation Press.

Predators and Politics (1992) A Symposium on Washington State's Sexually Violent Predators Statute, *University of Puget Sound Law Review*, 15: 507–911.

Prentky, R.A. and Knight, R.A. (1993) Age of Onset of Sexual Assault: Criminal and Life History Correlates, in G.C.N. Hall, R. Hirschman, J.R. Graham and M.S. Zaragoza (eds) *Sexual Aggression: Issues in Etiology, Assessment and Treatment*, Washington: Taylor & Francis, pp. 43–62.

Prentky, R.A., Knight, R.A., Frizzell, K. and Righthand, S. (2000) An Actuarial Procedure for Assessing Risk with Juvenile Sex Offenders, *Sexual Abuse: A Journal of Research and Treatment*, 12(2): 71–93.

Prentky, R.A., Nien-Chen, L., Righthand, S., Schuler, A., Cavanaugh, D. and Lee, A.F. (2010) Assessing Risk of Sexually Abusive Behaviour Among Youth in a Child Welfare Sample, *Behavioral Sciences and the Law* 28(1): 24–45.

Prentky, R. and Righthand, S. (2003) *Juvenile Sex Offender Assessment Protocol-II (J-SOAP-II) Manual*, Rockville: United States Department of Justice, Office of Juvenile Justice and Delinquency Prevention. Available http://www.csom.org/pubs/JSOAP.pdf (accessed 23 November 2010).

Prescott, J.J. and Rockoff, J.E. (2008) Do Sex Offender Registration and Notification Laws Affect Criminal Behavior?, *NBER Working Paper Series* No. 13803.

Press Association (2007) 1,166 Anti-Terror Arrests Net 40 Convictions, *The Guardian Online*, 5 March. Available http://www.guardian.co.uk/uk/2007/mar/05/politics.terrorism (accessed 23 November 2010).

Pressman, D.E. (2009) *Risk Assessment Decisions for Violent Political Extremism*, Ottawa: Public Safety Canada. Available http://www.publicsafety.gc.ca/res/cor/rep/2009-02-rdv-eng.aspx (accessed 23 November 2010).

Prins, S.J. and Draper, L. (2009) *Improving Outcomes for People with Mental Illnesses under Community Corrections Supervision: A Guide to Research-Informed Policy and Practice*, New York: Council of State Governments Justice Center.

Prochaska, J.O., DiClemente, C.C. and Norcross, J.C. (1992) In Search of How People Change: Applications to Addictive Behaviour, *American Psychologist*, 47(9): 1102–14.

Professional Affairs Board (1991) Mental Impairment and Severe Mental Impairment, *Psychologist*, 373–6.

Psychological Corporation (1999) *Wechsler Abbreviated Scale of Intelligence (WASI) Manual*, San Antonio, TX: Psychological Corporation.

Queensland Government (2003) *Parliamentary Debates,* Legislative Assembly, 3 June (Robert Welford).

Quinsey, V.L., Harris, G.T., Rice, M.E. and Cormier, C.A. (1998) *Violent Offenders: Appraising and Managing Risk*, Washington: American Psychological Association.

_____ (2006) *Violent Offenders: Appraising and Managing Risk*, 2nd edn, Washington: American Psychological Association.

Ramon, S., Healy, B. and Renouf, N. (2007) Recovery from Mental Illness as an Emergent Concept and Practice in Australia and the UK, *International Journal of Social Psychiatry*, 53(2): 108–22.

Ramraj, V. (2002) Terrorism, Security and Rights: A New Dialogue, *Singapore Journal of Legal Studies*, 1–15.

Rasmussen, L.A. (1999) Factors Related to Recidivism Among Juvenile Sex Offenders, *Sexual Abuse: A Journal of Research and Treatment*, 11(1): 69–85.

Reid, R., Oliver, J., Scott, P.D. and Lee, A. (1977) *State Hospital, Carstairs: Report of Public Local Inquiry into Circumstances Surrounding the Escape of Two Patients on 30 November 1976 and into Security and other Arrangements at the Hospital*, Edinburgh: HMSO.

Reid, W.H. (2009) Borderline Personality Disorder and Related Traits in Forensic Psychiatry, *Journal of Psychiatric Practice*, 15: 216–20.

Reid, W.H. and Thorne, S.A. (2007) Personality Disorders and Violence Potential, *Journal of Psychiatric Practice*, 13: 261–8.

Rethink and Sainsbury Centre for Mental Health (2010) *The Diversion Dividend: Interim Report*. Available http://www.centreformentalhealth.org.uk/pdfs/Diversion_Dividend.pdf (accessed 23 November 2010).

Retka, A. (2009) Missouri Sex Offenders Remain Locked Up Despite Serving Prison Sentences, *Missouri Lawyers Weekly*, 12 June.

Rice, M.E., Harris G.T. and Hilton, Z. (2010) The Violence Risk Appraisal Guide and Sex Offender Risk Appraisal Guide for Violence Risk Assessment, in R.K. Otto and K. Douglas (eds) *Handbook of Violence Risk Assessment*, New York: Brunner-Routledge, pp. 99–120.

Richards, E.P. (1989) The Jurisprudence of Prevention: The Right of Societal Self-Defense Against Dangerous Individuals, *Hastings Constitutional Law Quarterly*, 16(2): 329–92.

Richardson, E. and McSherry, B. (2010) Diversion Down Under: Programs for Offenders with Mental Illnesses in Australia, *International Journal of Law and Psychiatry*, 33(4): 249–57.

Richardson, G., (unpublished) *The Sexually Harmful Adolescent Risk Protocol (SHARP)*.

_____ (2009) SHARP Practice: The Sexually Harmful Adolescent Risk Protocol, in M.C. Calder (ed) *Sexual Abuse Assessments: Using and Developing Frameworks for Practice*, Lyme Regis: Russell House Publishers, pp. 108–47.

Richters, J.E. (1997) The Hubble Hypothesis and the Developmentalist's Dilemma, *Development and Psychopathology*, 9(2): 193–229.

Risk Management Authority (2006a) *Risk Management Authority Standards and Guidelines for Risk Assessment*, Paisley, Scotland: Risk Management Authority.

_____ (2006b) *Standards and Guidelines for Risk Assessment*, Paisley, Scotland: Risk Management Authority.

_____ (2007a) *Standards and Guidelines: Risk Management of Offenders Subject to an Order for Lifelong Restriction*, Paisley, Scotland: Risk Management Authority.

_____ (2007b) *Risk Assessment Tools Evaluation Directory: RATED Version 2*, Paisley, Scotland: Risk Management Authority.

Ritchie, J., Dick, D. and Lingham, R. (1994) *Report of the Inquiry into the Care and Treatment of Christopher Clunis*, London: HMSO.

Robins, L.N. (1978) Sturdy Predictors of Adult Antisocial Behavior: Replications from Longitudinal Studies, *Psychological Medicine*, 8: 611–22.

Rodley, N. and Pollard, M. (2009) *The Treatment of Prisoners under International Law*, 3rd edn, Oxford: Oxford University Press.

Rorer, L. (1990) Personality Assessment: A Conceptual Survey, in L.A. Pervin (ed.) *Handbook of Personality: Theory and Research*, New York: Guilford Press, pp. 693–720.

Rose, G. (1992) *The Strategy of Preventive Medicine*, Oxford: Oxford University Press.

Rose, N. (1986) Law, Rights and Psychiatry, in P. Miller and N. Rose (eds) *The Power of Psychiatry*, Cambridge: Polity Press, pp. 177–213.

_____ (1998) Governing Risky Individuals: The Role of Psychiatry in New Regimes of Control, *Psychiatry, Psychology and Law*, 5(2): 177–95.

Roth, J.V. (2009) Prediction Interval Analysis is Underutilized and Can Be More Helpful than Just Confidence Interval Analysis, *Journal of Clinical Monitoring and Computing*, 23(3): 181–3.

Roth, L. (1979) A Commitment Law for Patients, Doctors and Lawyers, *American Journal of Psychiatry*, 136: 1121–1127.

Rothbart, M.K. and Bates, J.E. (1998) Temperament, in W. Dammon (ed.) *Handbook of Child Psychology, Vol. 3., Social, Emotional and Personality Development*, 5th edn, New York: Wiley, pp. 105–76.

Rothenberg, B. (2002) The Success of the Battered Woman Syndrome: An Analysis of How Cultural Arguments Succeed, *Sociological Forum*, 17(1): 81–103.

Rothschild, S. (2009) Price High for Sex Offender Treatment Expansion, *Lawrence World Journal*, 20 December.

Royal College of Psychiatrists (1999) *Offenders with Personality Disorder*, London: Gaskell.

_____ (2004) The Psychiatrist, Courts and Sentencing: The Impact of Extended Sentencing on the Ethical Framework of Forensic Psychiatry: Council Report CR129, *Psychiatric Bulletin*, 29: 73–77.

Royal Statistical Society (2010) Royal Statistical Society Concerning the Issues Raised in the Sally Clark Case, Internet communication.

Ruffles, J. (2010) Evaluating the Operation of the Crimes (Mental Impairment and Unfitness to be Tried) Act 1997 (Vic), unpublished Doctor of Psychology thesis, Clifton Hill: Monash University Centre for Forensic Behavioural Sciences.

Russakoff, D. (1998) Out of Grief Comes a Legislative Force, *The Washington Post*, 15 June, A01.

Russell, K. and Darjee, R. (in press) Sexual Violence, in L. Johnstone and C. Logan (eds) *Managing Clinical Risk: A Guide to Effective Practice*, Abingdon, England: Willan.

Sack, E.J. (2004) Battered Women and the State: The Struggle for the Future of Domestic Violence Policy, *Wisconsin Law Review*, 6: 1657–1740.

Sacks, S., Sacks, J., McKendrick, K., Banks, S. and Stommel, J. (2004) Modified TC for MICA Offenders: Crime Outcomes, *Behavioral Sciences and the Law*, 22(4): 477–501.

Sainsbury Centre for Mental Health, (2005) Back on Track? CPA Care Planning for Service Users Who are Repeatedly Detained under the Mental Health Act, London: Sainsbury Centre for Mental Health.

Sakry, T. (2009) St. Francis Failing to See Humor of Streaking Incidents, *ABC Newspapers*, 7 October.

Sales, B. and McKenzie, N. (2007) Time to Act on Behalf of Mentally Disordered Offenders, *British Medical Journal*, 334(7506): 1222.

Sanson, A. and Prior, M. (1999) Temperament and Behavioral Precursors to Oppositional Defiant Disorder, in H. Quay and A. Hogan (eds) *Handbook of Disruptive Behavior Disorders*, New York: Kluwer Academic/Plenum, pp. 397–418.

Scheikowski, M. (2007) Judge Blasts ASIO as Terror Case Dropped, *The Age*, 12 November. Available http://news.theage.com.au/national/judge-blasts-asio-as-terror-case-dropped-20071112-19jn.html (accessed 23 November 2010).

Scheingold, S., Olsen, T. and Pershing, J. (1992) The Politics of Sexual Psychopathy: Washington's Sexual Predator Legislation, University of Puget Sound Law Review, 15(3): 809–20.

Schoenmann, J. (2009) State Money Dries up for DNA Testing of Sex Offenders, *Las Vegas Sun*, 1 October. Available http://www.lasvegassun.com/news/2009/oct/01/state-money-dries-dna-testing-sex-offenders/ (accessed 23 November 2010).

Scott, E.S. and Steinberg, L. (2008) *Rethinking Juvenile Justice*, Cambridge: Harvard University Press.

Scott, P.D. (1977) Assessing Dangerousness in Criminals, *British Journal of Psychiatry*, 131: 127–42.

Scottish Executive (2000a) *Report of the Committee on Serious Violent and Sexual Offenders*, Edinburgh: Scottish Executive.

_____ (2000b) *Report of the Committee on Serious Violent and Sexual Offenders (Maclean Committee) Annex 3 Review of the Research Literature on Serious Violent and Sexual Offenders*, Edinburgh: Scottish Executive.

_____ (2001a) *Report on the Review of the Mental Health (Scotland) Act 1984*, Edinburgh: Scottish Executive.

_____ (2001b) *Reducing the Risk—Improving the Response to Sex Offending—Report of the Expert Panel on Sex Offending*, Edinburgh: Scottish Executive.

_____ (2001c) *The Right Place—the Right Time: Improving the Patient Journey for Those who Need Secure Mental Health Care: A Review of the Governance and Accountability of the State Hospital Board: Proposals for Consultation*, Edinburgh: Stationery Office.

_____ (2001d) *Criminal Justice: Serious Violent and Sexual Offenders: White Paper*, Edinburgh: Scottish Executive.

Scottish Government (2007) *Guidance for Forensic Services: CEL 13*, Edinburgh: Scottish Government. Available http://www.sehd.scot.nhs.uk/mels/CEL2007_13.pdf (accessed 23 November 2010).

_____ (2009) *Recorded Crime in Scotland 2008–09*, Edinburgh: Scottish Government. Available http://www.scotland.gov.uk/Publications/2009/09/28155153/4 (accessed 23 November 2010).

_____ (2010) *Multi-Agency Public Protection Arrangements (MAPPA) Guidance*, Edinburgh: Scottish Government.

Scottish Government Health Department (2010) *Memorandum of Procedure on Restricted Patients*, Edinburgh: Scottish Government Health Department. Available http://www.scotland.gov.uk/Publications/2010/06/04095331/37 (accessed 23 November 2010).

Scottish Home and Health Department (1969) *Forensic Psychiatry: Report of a Subcommittee of the Standing Medical Advisory Committee (Harper Report)*, Edinburgh: HMSO.

Scottish Human Rights Commission (2009) *Human Rights in a Health Care Setting: Making it Work for Everyone: An Evaluation of a Human Rights-Based Approach at the State Hospital*, Glasgow: Scottish Human Rights Commission.

Scottish Office (1996) *Circular No. SWSG 16/96 Community Care: Care Programme Approach for People with Severe and Enduring Mental Illness Including Dementia*, Edinburgh: Scottish Office.

_____ (1997) *The Framework for Mental Health Services in Scotland*, Edinburgh: Scottish Office.

_____ (1998) *Acute Services Review*, Edinburgh: Scottish Office.

_____ (1999) Health, Social Work and Related Services for Mentally Disordered Offenders in Scotland, Edinburgh: Scottish Office.

Scottish Personality Disorder Network (2010) Available http://www.scottishpersonalitydisorder.org (accessed 23 November 2010).

Scottish Prison Service (2002) *Positive Mental Health*, Edinburgh: Scottish Prison Service.

_____ (2010) *Prison Statistics*, Edinburgh: Scottish Prison Service.

Scottish Prisons Commission (2008) *Scotland's Choice: Report of the Scottish Prisons Commission*, Edinburgh: Scottish Prisons Commission.

Seagrave, D. and Grisso, T. (2002) Adolescent Development and the Measurement of Juvenile Psychopathy, *Law and Human Behavior*, 26(2): 219–39.

Shedler, J. and Block, J. (1990) *Adolescent Drug Use and Psychological Health: A Longitudinal Inquiry*, American Psychologist, 45(5): 612–30.

Silver, E. (2006) Understanding the Relationship Between Mental Disorder and Violence: The Need for a Criminological Perspective, *Law and Human Behavior*, 30(6): 685–706.

Simerman, J. (2010) Sex Offender Agency Faults Megan's Law Drawbacks, *Contra Costa Times*, 16 February.

Singleton, N., Meltzer, H. and Gatward, R. (1998) *Psychiatric Morbidity Among Prisoners in England and Wales*, London: Stationary Office.

Skeem, J. and Eno Louden, J. (2008) Mandated Treatment as a Condition of Probation: Coercion or Contract?, in A. Redlich (chair) *Understanding in Mandated Community Treatment*, Symposium conducted at the annual meeting of the American Psychology-Law Society, Jacksonville, FL, March 2008. Available https://webfiles.uci.edu/skeem/Downloads_files/coercion_contract_2.pdf (accessed 23 November 2010).

Skeem, J., Eno Louden, J., Manchak, S., Vidal, S. and Haddad, E. (2009) Social Networks and Social Control of Probationers with Co-Occurring Mental and Substance Abuse Problems, *Law and Human Behavior*, 33(2): 122–35.

Skeem, J., Eno Louden, J., Polaschek, D. and Camp, J. (2007) Assessing Relationship Quality in Mandated Treatment: Blending Care with Control, *Psychological Assessment*, 19(4): 397–410.

Skeem, J., Manchak, S., Johnson, T. and Gillig, B. (2008) Comparing Specialty and Traditional Supervision for Probationers with Mental Illness, in A. Redlich (chair) *Understanding in Mandated Community Treatment*, Symposium conducted at the annual meeting of the American Psychology-Law Society, Jacksonville, FL, March 2008. Available https://webfiles.uci.edu/skeem/Downloads.html (accessed 23 November 2010).

Skeem, J.L., Manchack, M. and Peterson, J.P. (in press) Correctional Policy for Offenders with Mental Illness: Creating a New Paradigm for Recidivism Reduction, *Law and Human Behavior*.

Skeem, J., Manchak, S., Vidal, S. and Hart, E. (2009) *Probationers with Mental Disorder: What (Really) Works?*, paper presented at American Psychology and Law Society Annual Conference, San Antonio, March 2009. Available https://webfiles.uci.edu:443/skeem/Downloads.html (accessed 23 November 2010).

Skeem, J., Polascheck, D.L. and Manchank, S. (2009) Appropriate Treatment Works, but How? Rehabilitating General, Psychopathic, and High-Risk Offenders, in J. Skeem, K. Douglas and S. Lilienfeld (eds) *Psychological Sciences in the Courtroom: Consensus and Controversy*, New York: Guilford Press, pp. 358–84.

Skilling, G. and Thomson, L.D.G. (2010) A Study of Appeals against Excessive Security, personal communication.

Skipworth, J., Brinded, P., Chaplow, D. and Frampton, C. (2006) Insanity Acquittee Outcomes in New Zealand, *Australian and New Zealand Journal of Psychiatry*, 40(11–12): 1003–9.

Slobogin, C. (2003) Jurisprudence of Dangerousness, *Northwestern University Law Review*, 98(1): 1–62.

_____ (2006) *Minding Justice: Laws that Deprive People with Mental Disability of Life and Liberty*, Cambridge: Harvard University Press.

_____ (2007) *Proving the Unprovable: The Role of Law, Science and Speculation in Adjudicating Culpability and Dangerousness*, New York: Oxford University Press.

_____ (2009) Capital Punishment and Dangerousness, in R.E. Schopp, R.L. Weiner, B.H. Borstein and S.L. Willborn (eds) *Mental Disorder and Criminal Law: Responsibility, Punishment and Competence*, New York: Springer, pp. 119–33.

Slobogin, C. and Fondacaro, M.R. (2009) Juvenile Justice: The Fourth Option, *Iowa Law Review*, 95: 1–62.

Smiles, S. and Marriner, C. (2007) PM Defiant: No Visa and No Apology, The Age, 31 July. Available http://www.theage.com.au/articles/2007/07/30/1185647828688.html (accessed 23 November 2010).

Smith, D. (2008) The Constitutionality of Civil Commitment and the Requirement of Adequate Treatment, *Boston College Law Review*, 49(5): 1383–1429.

Smith, R.K.M. (2007) *Texts and Materials on International Human Rights*, New York: Routledge-Cavendish.

Snowden, P. and Kane, E. (2003) Personality Disorder: No Longer a Diagnosis of Exclusion, *Psychiatric Bulletin*, 27: 401–3.

Snyder, H. (2000) *Sexual Assault of Young Children as Reported to Law Enforcement*, Washington: Department of Justice, Bureau of Justice Statistics. Available http://bjs.ojp.usdoj.gov/content/pub/pdf/saycrle.pdf (accessed 23 November 2010).

Snyder, H.N., Sickmund, M. and Poe-Yamagata, E. (1996) *Juvenile Offenders and Victims: 1996 Update on Violence*, Washington: Office of Juvenile Justice and Delinquency Prevention.

Sommers, C.H. (1994) *Who Stole Feminism?: How Women Have Betrayed Women*, New York: Simon & Schuster.

South East Coast Strategic Health Authority, Kent County Council and Kent Probation Area (2006) *Report of the Independent Inquiry into the Care and Treatment of Michael Stone*. Available http://www.southeastcoast.nhs.uk/Downloads/Independent%20investigation%20reports/Report%20of%20the%20independent%20inquiry%20into%20the%20care%20and%20treatment%20of%20Michael%20Stone.pdf (accessed 23 November 2010).

Spokes, J., Pare, M. and Royle, G. (1988) *Report of the Committee of Inquiry into the Case and After-Care of Sharon Campbell*, London: HMSO.

Sreenivasan, S., Frances, A. and Weinberger, L.E. (2010) Normative versus Consequential Ethics in Sexually Violent Predator Laws: An Ethics Conundrum for Psychiatry, *Journal of the American Academy of Psychiatry and the Law*, 38(3): 386–91.

Stanko, E. (2000) Naturalizing Danger: Women, Fear, and Personal Safety, in J. Pratt and M. Brown (eds) *Dangerous Offenders: Punishment and Social Order*, New York: Routledge, pp. 147–63.

Stankove, L., Higgins, D., Saucier, G. and Knežević, G. (2010) Contemporary Militant Extremism: A Linguistic Approach to Scale Development, *Psychological Assessment*, 22(2): 246–58.

Steadman, H.J. (2000) From Dangerousness to Risk Assessment of Community Violence: Taking Stock at the Turn of the Century, *Journal of the American Academy of Psychiatry and the Law*, 28(3): 265–71.

Steadman, H.J., Dupius, S. and Morris, L. (2009) *For Whom Does Jail Diversion Work? Results of a Multi-Site Longitudinal Study*, paper presented at American Psychology and Law Society Annual Conference, San Antonio, TX, March 2009.

Steadman, H.J., Osher, F.C., Robbins, P.C., Case, B. and Samuels, S. (2009) Prevalence of Serious Mental Illness Among Jail Inmates, *Psychiatric Services*, 60(6): 761–5.

Steel, R.G.D., Torrie, J.H., and Dickey, D.A. (1997) *Principles and Procedures of Statistics: A Biometrical Approach*, 3rd edn, New York: McGraw Hill.

Stein, L. and Test, M. (1980) Alternative to Mental Hospital Treatment 1: Conceptual Model, Treatment Program and Clinical Evaluation, *Archives of General Psychiatry*, 37(4): 392–97.

Steinberg, L. and Schwartz, R. (2000) Developmental Psychology Goes to Court, in T. Grisso and R.G. Schwartz (eds) *Youth on Trial: A Developmental Perspective on Juvenile Justice*, Chicago: University of Chicago Press, pp. 9–31.

Stern, J. and Wiener, J. (2006) Precaution Against Terrorism, Journal of Risk Research, 9(4): 393–447.

Stone, A. (1975) *Mental Health and the Law: A System in Transition*, New York, NY: Jason Aronson Inc.

Stout, C.E. (ed) (2004) *Psychology of Terrorism: Coping with the Continuing Threat*, Westport: Praeger.

Sunstein, C. (2005) *Laws of Fear: Beyond the Precautionary Principle*, Cambridge: Cambridge University Press.

Sutherland, E.H. (1950) The Diffusion of Sexual Psychopath Laws, *American Journal of Society*, 56: 142–8.

Swanson, J.W., van Dorn, R.A., Swartz, M.S., Smith, A., Elbogen, E. and Monahan, J. (2008) Alternative Pathways to Violence in Persons with Schizophrenia: The Role of Childhood Antisocial Behavior Problems, *Law and Human Behavior*, 32: 228–40.

Szasz, T. (1961) *The Myth of Mental Illness: Foundations of a Theory of Personal Conduct*, New York: Delta.

Tarrier, N. (2006) *Case Formulation in Cognitive Behaviour Therapy: The Treatment of Challenging and Complex Cases*, New York: Routledge.

Taylor, P., Hill, J., Bhagwagar, Z., Darjee, R. and Thomson, L. (2008) Presentations of Psychosis with Violence: Variation in Different Jurisdictions. A Comparison of Patients with Psychosis in the High Security Hospitals of Scotland and England, *Behavioral Sciences and the Law*, 26(1): 1–18.

Thomas, A. and Chess, S. (1977) *Temperament and Development*, New York: Brunner/Mazel.

Thomas, J. (2005) *Youth Court Statistics*, 2003/04, Ontario: Juristat.

Thomson, L.D.G. (2005a) Psychiatric Systems and Services for Mentally Disordered Offenders, in J.J. McManus and L.D.G. Thomson, *Mental Health and Scots Law in Practice*, Edinburgh: W. Green and Sons.

_____ (2005b) Report of the Working Group on Services for People with Personality Disorder, *Forensic Services Managed Care Network*. Available http://www.forensicnetwork.scot.nhs.uk/documents/reports/Personality%20disorder.pdf (accessed 23 November 2010).

_____ (2006) The Mental Health (Care and Treatment) (Scotland) Act 2003: Legislation for Mentally Disordered Offenders, *Psychiatric Bulletin*, 30(11): 423–9.

_____ (2008) The Forensic Mental Health System in the United Kingdom in K. Soothill, M. Dolan and P. Rogers (eds) *Handbook of Forensic Mental Health*, Cullompton, England: Willan, pp. 19–63.

Thomson, L.D.G., Bogue, J., Humphreys, M., Owens, D. and Johnstone, E. (1997) State Hospital Survey: A Description of Psychiatric Patients in Conditions of Special Security in Scotland, *Journal of Forensic Psychiatry*, 8(2): 263–84.

Thomson, L. and Cherry, J. (2010) *Mental Health and Scots Law in Practice,* 2nd rev edn, Edinburgh: W. Green.

Thomson, L., Davidson, M., Brett, C., Steele, J. and Darjee, R. (2008) Risk Assessment in Forensic Patients with Schizophrenia: The Predictive Validity of Actuarial Scales and Symptom Severity for Offending and Violence over 8-10 Years, *International Journal of Forensic Mental Health*, 7(2): 173–89.

Thornton, D.M. (2003) *Scoring Guide for the Risk Matrix 2000.4*, unpublished.

_____ (2007) *Scoring Guide for Risk Matrix 2009.9/SVC*. Available http://www.cfcp.bham.ac.uk/Extras/SCORING%20GUIDE%20FOR%20RISK%20MATRIX%202000.9-%20SVC%20-%20(ver.%20Feb%202007).pdf (accessed 23 November 2010).

Toch, H. and Adams, K. (2002) *Acting Out: Maladaptive Behavior in Confinement*, Washington: American Psychological Association.

Torrey, W.C., Drake, R.E., Cohen, M., Fox, L., Lynde, D., Gorman, P. and Wyzik, P. (2002) The Challenge of Implementing and Sustaining Integrated Dual Disorders Treatment Programs, *Community Mental Health Journal*, 38(6): 507–21.

Trivitis, L.C. and Reppucci, N.D. (2002) Application of Megan's Law to Juveniles, *American Psychologist*, 57(9): 690–704.

Tyrer, P., Duggan, C., Cooper, S., Crawford, M., Seivewright, H., Rutter, D., Maden, T., Byford, S., and Barrett, B. (2010) The Successes and Failures of the DSPD Experiment: The Assessment and Management of Severe Personality Disorder, *Medicine Science and the Law*, 50(2): 95–99.

United States Surgeon General (1999) *Mental Health: A Report of the Surgeon General*, Rockville, Maryland: Department of Health and Human Services, US Public Health Service. Available http://profiles.nlm.nih.gov/NN/B/B/H/S/_/nnbbhs.pdf (accessed 23 November 2010).

van Zyl Smit, D. (2006) Life Imprisonment: Recent Issues in National and International Law, *International Journal of Law and Psychiatry*, 29(5): 405–21.

Vardeman, S.B. (1992) What about Other Intervals?, *American Statistician*, 46(2): 193–7.

Victoroff, V. (2005) The Mind of the Terrorist: A Review and Critique of Psychological Approaches, *Journal of Conflict Resolution*, 49(1): 3–42.

Vielmetti, B. (2010) Elderly Sex Offender Dies in Civil Commitment, *Journal Sentinel*, 8 January. Available http://www.jsonline.com/blogs/news/80933787.html (accessed 23 November 2010).

Vieth, V.L. (2006) Unto the Third Generation: A Call to End Child Abuse in the United States Within 120 Years (Revised and Expanded), *Hamline Journal of Public Law and Policy*, 28: 1–74.

Vojt, G., Marshall, L.A. and Thomson, L.D.G., (2010) The Assessment of Imminent Inpatient Aggression: A Validation Study of the DASA-IV in Scotland, *Journal of Forensic Psychiatry and Psychology*, 21(5): 789–800.

Waggoner, J., Wollert, R., and Cramer, E. (2008). A Respecification of Hanson's Updated Static-99 Experience Table that Controls for the Effects of Age on Sexual Recidivism Among Young Offenders, *Law, Probability and Risk*, 7, 305–312.

Wald, N.J., Hackshaw, A.K. and Frost, C.D. (1999) When Can a Risk Factor Be Used as a Worthwhile Screening Test, *British Medical Journal*, 319(7224): 1562–5.

Walker, L. (1979) *The Battered Woman*, New York: Harper & Row.

Walker, N. (1978) Dangerous People, *International Journal of Law and Psychiatry*, 1(1): 37–49.

_____ (ed.) (1996) *Dangerous People*, London: Blackstone Press.

Walsh, N. and Velazquez, T. (2009) Registering Harm: The Adam Walsh Act and Juvenile Sex Offender Registration, Champion Magazine: The National Association of Criminal Defense Lawyers. Available http://www.jdaihelpdesk.org/Docs/Documents/http___www.nacdl.org_public.pdf (accessed 23 November 2010).

Ward, T., Polaschek, D.L.L. and Busch, A.R. (2006) *Theories of Sexual Offending*, Chichester: Wiley.

Warren, J., Burnette, M., South, S., Chaucan, C., Bate, R., Friend, R. and van Patten, I. (2003) Psychopathy in Women: Structural Modelling and Comorbidity, *International Journal of Law and Psychiatry*, 26(3): 223–42.

Washington State Strategic Plan for Victim Services (2005) Washington: State of Washington. Available http://www.commerce.wa.gov/DesktopModules/CTEDPublications/CTEDPublicationsView.aspx?tabID=0&ItemID=2283&MId=950&wversion=Staging (accessed 23 November 2010).

Watzke, S., Ullrich, S. and Marneros, A. (2006) Gender- and Violence-Related Prevalence of Mental Disorders in Prisoners, *European Archives of Psychiatry and Clinical Neuroscience*, 256(7): 414–21.

Websdale, N. (2003) Reviewing Domestic Violence Deaths, National Institute of Justice Journal. Available http://www.baylor.edu/content/services/document.php/28815.pdf (accessed 23 November 2010).

Webster, C.D., Douglas, K., Eaves, D. and Hart, S.D. (1997) *HCR-20 Assessing Risk for Violence*, 2nd edn, Burnaby, British Columbia: Simon Fraser University.

Welsh Assembly Government (2002) *Adult Mental Health Services: A National Service Framework for Wales*, Cardiff: Welsh Assembly Government.

Welsh, J.L., Schmidt, F., McKinnon, L., Chatta, H.K. and Meyers, J.R. (2008) A Comparative Study of Adolescent Risk Assessment Instruments: Predictive and Incremental Validity, *Assessment*, 15(1): 104 Cardiff 15.

Wettstein, R.W. (1992) A Psychiatric Perspective on Washington's Sexually Violent Predators Statute, *University of Puget Sound Law Review*, 15(3): 655–708.

Wexler, D.B. and Winick, B.J. (1991) *Essays in Therapeutic Jurisprudence*, Durham, NC: Carolina Academic Press.

White, J., Moffit, T., Earls, F., Robins, L.N. and Silva, P.A. (1990) How Early Can We Tell? Predictors of Childhood Conduct Disorder and Adolescent Delinquency, *Criminology*, 28(4): 507–33.

Whitticker, A. (2008) *Derek Percy: Australian Psycho*, Melbourne: New Holland Publishers.

WHO European Ministerial Conference (2005) *Mental Health: Facing the Challenges, Building Solutions*. Available http://www.euro.who.int/__data/assets/pdf_file/0008/96452/E87301.pdf (accessed 23 November 2010).

Wilson, E.B. (1927) Probable Inference, the Law of Succession and Statistical Inference, *Journal of the American Statistical Association*, 22(158): 209–12.

Wilson, P. (2008) Terrorism in Australia, in K. Fritzon and P. Wilson (eds) *Forensic Psychology and Criminology: An Australian Perspective*, North Ryde: McGraw-Hill Australia.

Wittes, B., Chesney, R. and Benhalim, R. (2010) The Emerging Law of Detention: The Guantanamo Habeas Cases as Law-Making, Governance Studies at Brookings. Available http://ssrn.com/abstract=1540601 (accessed 23 November 2010).

Wittgenstein, L. (1958) *Philosophical Investigations*, 4th ed., Oxford: Blackwell.

Wong, S. (2000) Psychopathic Offenders, in S. Hodgins and R. Müller-Isberner (eds) *Violence, Crime and Mentally Disordered Offenders: Concepts and Methods for Effective Treatment and Prevention*, Chichester: Wiley, pp. 87–112.

Wood, J. and Kemshall, H. (2010) Effective Multi-Agency Public Protection: Learning from the Research in K. Harrison (ed.) *Managing High-Risk Sex Offenders in the Community: Risk Management, Treatment and Social Responsibility*, Cullompton, England: Willan, pp. 39–60.

Wood, J., Kemshall, H., Maguire, M., Hudson, K. and Mackenzie, G. (2007) *The Operation and Experience of Multi-Agency Public Protection Arrangements (MAPPA)*. Available http://www.homeoffice.gov.uk/rds/pdfs07/rdsolr1207.pdf (accessed 23 November 2010).

Worling, J.R. and Curwen, T. (2001) The ERASOR: Estimate of Risk of Adolescent Sexual Offense Recidivism: Version 2.0. SAFE-T Program, Toronto: Thistletown Regional Centre.

Worrall, A. (2009) Background to the Dano Sonnex Case. Available http://socandcrimatkeele.blogspot.com/2009/06/background-to-dano-sonnex-case.html (accessed 23 November 2010).

Yin, R.K. (2003) *Case Study Research: Design and Methods*, 3rd edn, Thousand Oaks, CA: Sage.

———— (2009) *Case Study Research: Design and Methods*, 4th edn, Thousand Oaks, CA: Sage.

Young, K., Ashby, D., Boaz, A. and Grayson, L. (2002) Social Science and the Evidence-Based Policy Movement, *Social Policy and Society*, 1(3): 215–24.

Young, S., Chick, K. and Godjonsson, G. (2010) A Preliminary Evaluation of Reasoning and Rehabilitation 2 in Mentally Disordered Offenders (R&R2M) Across Two Secure Forensic Settings in the United Kingdom, *Journal of Forensic Psychiatry and Psychology*, 21(3): 336–49.

Young, S.J., and Ross, R.R. (2007) *R&R2 for Youths and Adults with Mental Health Problems: A Prosocial Competence Training Program*, Ottawa: Cognitive Centre of Canada.

Youth Justice Board for England and Wales (2000) *ASSET—Young Offender Assessment Profile: Introduction*, London: Youth Justice Board for England and Wales.

———— (2004) *A Summary of the Evaluation of the Assessment Intervention and Moving-On (AIM) Framework for the Assessment of Adolescents who Display Sexually Harmful Behaviour*, London: Youth Justice Board for England and Wales.

Zedner, L. (2007) Pre-Crime and Post-Criminology?, *Theoretical Criminology*, 11(2): 261–81.

———— (2009) *Security*, New York: Routledge.

Zevitz, R.G. (2006) Sex Offender Community Notification: Its Role in Recidivism and Offender Reintegration, *Criminal Justice Studies*, 19(2): 193–208.

Zgoba, K. and Witt, P. (2010) Summary of Findings From the Study on the Practical and Monetary Effectiveness of Megan's Law in New Jersey, *Sex Offender Law Report*, 11(3): 33–34, 43–48.

Zimring, F. (2004) *An American Travesty: Legal Responses to Adolescent Sexual Offending*, Chicago: University of Chicago Press.

Zuckerman, M., Eysenck, S. and Eysenck, H.J. (1978) Sensation Seeking in England and America: Cross-Cultural, Age and Sex Comparisons, *Journal of Consulting and Clinical Psychology*, 46(1): 139–49.

Index